Fundamentals of Risk Management

To a safe, secure and sustainable future

Fifth Edition

Fundamentals of Risk Management

Understanding, evaluating and implementing effective risk management

Paul Hopkin

First published in Great Britain and the United States in 2010 by Kogan Page Limited
Fifth edition 2018

2nd Floor, 45 Gee Street	c/o Martin P Hill Consulting	4737/23 Ansari Road
London	122 W 27th St, 10th Floor	Daryaganj
EC1V 3RS	New York, NY 10001	New Delhi 110002
United Kingdom	USA	India

www.koganpage.com

ISBN   978 0 7494 8307 4
E-ISBN   978 0 7494 8308 1

British Library Cataloguing-in-Publication Data

A CIP record for this book is available from the British Library.

Library of Congress Cataloging-in-Publication Control Number

Names: Hopkin, Paul, author.
Title: Fundamentals of risk management : understanding, evaluating and
   implementing effective risk management / Paul Hopkin.
Description: 5th Edition. | New York : Kogan Page, [2018] | Revised edition
   of the author's Fundamentals of risk management, [2017]
Identifiers: LCCN 2018000956 (print) | LCCN 2017060887 (ebook) | ISBN
   9780749483081 (ebook) | ISBN 9780749483074 (pbk.) | ISBN 9780749473081
   (eISBN)
Subjects: LCSH: Risk management.
Classification: LCC HD61 (print) | LCC HD61 .H567 2018 (ebook) | DDC
   658.15/5–dc23
LC record available at https://lccn.loc.gov/2018000956

Typeset by Integra Software Services, Pondicherry
Print production managed by Jellyfish
Printed and bound by CPI Group (UK) Ltd, Croydon, CR0 4YY

CONTENTS

PART FOUR Risk response 169

PART FIVE Risk strategy 215

19   Core business processes 219

20   Reputation and the business model 228

21   Risk management context 239

22   Risk management responsibilities 252

LIST OF FIGURES

LIST OF TABLES

FOREWORD
Importance of enterprise risk management

Organizations face an increasingly challenging and complex environment in which to undertake their activities. Since the fourth edition of this textbook, the consequences of the global financial crisis have continued to challenge public-, private- and third-sector organizations. To add further complexity, the second decade of the 21st century has been marked by political instability in many parts of the world and the recent decision of the United Kingdom to exit the European Union has added further global uncertainty.

It is within this increasingly uncertain environment that organizations are required to deliver higher stakeholder expectations, whilst fulfilling greater corporate governance requirements in relation to ethical and social responsibility. For example, legislation has been introduced in many countries to broaden the scope of requirements regarding management of bribery risk and the avoidance of modern slavery.

Given all these developments, the updating of this textbook to place greater emphasis on the importance of enterprise risk management (ERM) to organizational success is very timely. Successful ERM, including the protection of corporate reputation, continues to be a business imperative for all organizations. A successful ERM initiative enhances the ability of an organization to achieve objectives and ensure sustainability, based on transparent and ethical behaviours.

The Institute of Risk Management (IRM) has long supported the development of ERM, as a contribution to development and delivery of successful business models and strategy for all types of organizations. The training courses and qualifications offered by the IRM enable risk professionals and others to support their employer and/or clients in achieving maximum benefit from an ERM initiative.

Although this textbook has been designed specifically for the IRM International Certificate in Enterprise Risk Management, the contents outline approaches to achieving successful ERM that will support any type of organization in their efforts to deliver corporate objectives and satisfy stakeholder expectations. This textbook is a valuable resource for all organizations and anyone with an interest in risk management.

Ian Livsey PhD MBA

Ian Livsey is Chief Executive at the Institute of Risk Management, risk management's leading worldwide professional education, training and knowledge body. Further information about the Institute and the International Certificate is available from the IRM website, **www.theirm.org**.

ACKNOWLEDGEMENTS

The risk management profession and the expertise of risk professionals continues to develop in line with the ever-increasing expectations placed on risk managers and risk consultants. Many more organizations have appointed individuals with the job title chief risk officer (CRO) and this development has increased the need for robust professional qualifications and designations for risk management practitioners.

Given the ever-increasing complexity of the business environment, it is not surprising that production of the fifth edition of *Fundamentals of Risk Management* became necessary, just 18 months after production of the fourth edition. The importance and contribution of risk management continues to increase and centres of risk management expertise and excellence continue to thrive in all business sectors, whether private, public or third sector.

Lectures, seminars, special interest groups and other group meetings, as well as one-to-one conversations with risk specialists assisted with the updating of this book. It is clear that ideas and experiences related to enterprise risk management are continuing to expand. New guidance from COSO, together with an updated version of ISO 31000 have recently been published and the level of knowledge and expertise involved in the production of these risk management standards proved to be a very valuable source of information for the revision of the book.

The main challenge in producing the fifth edition of this textbook has been to align the material in the book more closely with the syllabus of the IRM qualifications in Enterprise Risk Management (ERM). When undertaking this task, I have received considerable help and support from colleagues at the Institute of Risk Management (IRM), as well as many insightful comments from risk professionals working as presenters and lecturers on IRM training and teaching courses.

I continue to be grateful to the large number of people who have helped with the development of the ideas presented and discussed in this book. I am sure that developments in risk management will continue apace and keeping abreast of developments and enhancements to risk management theory and practice will remain a challenge for risk management practitioners, all of whom are seeking to bring the benefits of enhanced risk management to their employer and/or client organizations.

Paul Hopkin

Boost your career with the IRM

IRM is the leading professional body for risk management. We drive excellence in managing risk to ensure organisations are ready for the opportunities and threats of the future.

We do this by providing internationally recognised qualifications and training, publishing research and guidance, and setting professional standards. We are a not-for-profit body, with members working in all industries, in all risk disciplines and in all sectors around the world.

What IRM offers Risk Professionals

Training courses
Our risk management training gives you the knowledge, tools and techniques you need to protect your organisation.

Free webinars
You can access free webinars that cover a wide range of presentations, helpful for professionals at every level.

Blended Learning
Increase your chances of exam success and learn directly from module coaches in our face-to-face Blended Learning workshops.

Qualifications
Our risk management qualifications give you the broad knowledge and the practical skills you need to manage risks.

Building a community
We help people connect with our sector-specific Special Interest Groups, Regional Groups and social media platforms.

IRM qualifications provide a practical framework and a structured way of thinking.
This is vital to success in a risk role. **"**

The Institute of
Risk Management

irm

Find out more at **www.theirm.org** »

Introduction

Risk management in context

This book is intended for all who want a comprehensive introduction to the theory and application of risk management. It sets out an integrated introduction to the management of risk in public and private organizations. Studying this book will provide insight into the world of risk management and may also help readers decide whether risk management is a suitable career option for them.

Many readers will wish to use this book in order to gain a better understanding of risk and risk management and thereby fulfil the primary responsibilities of their jobs with an enhanced understanding of risk. This book is designed to deliver the syllabus of the International Certificate in Risk Management qualification of the Institute of Risk Management. However, it also acts as an introduction to the discipline of risk management for those interested in the subject but not (yet) undertaking a course of study.

An introduction to risk and risk management is provided in Part One and Part Two of this book and administration of risk management is considered in Part Five (Risk strategy). Parts Three and Four describe the application of risk management in terms of risk assessment and risk response. Part Six considers risk culture, Part Seven describes risk governance and Part Eight considers risk assurance and risk reporting. Parts Seven and Eight concentrate on the application of risk management tools and techniques, as well as considering the outputs from the risk management process and the benefits that arise.

We all face risks in our everyday lives. Risks arise from personal activities and range from those associated with travel through to the ones associated with personal financial decisions. There are considerable risks present in the domestic component of our lives, and these include fire risks in our homes and financial risks associated with home ownership. Indeed, there are also a whole range of risks associated with domestic and relationship issues, but these are outside the scope of this book.

This book is primarily concerned with business and commercial risks and the roles that we fulfil in our job or occupation. However, the task of evaluating risks and deciding how to respond to them is a daily activity, not only at work but also at home and during leisure activities.

The importance of context is emphasized throughout the book and Chapter 7 specifically discusses the first stage of the risk management process, which is 'establish the context'. Further consideration of context is provided by Chapter 21 which describes the risk management context in more detail.

Nature of risk

Recent events in the world have brought risk into higher profile. Terrorism, extreme weather events and the global financial crisis represent the extreme risks that are facing society and commerce. These extreme risks exist in addition to the daily, somewhat more mundane, risks mentioned above.

Evaluating the range of risk responses available and deciding the most appropriate one in each case is at the heart of risk management. Responding to risks should produce benefits for us as individuals, as well as for the organizations where we work and/or are employed.

Within our personal and domestic lives, many of the responses to risk are automatic. Our ways of avoiding fire and road traffic accidents are based on well-established and automatic responses. Fire and accident are the types of risks that can only have negative outcomes, and they are often referred to as *hazard risks*. Compliance requirements are viewed by many organizations as hazard risks, whereby failure to comply can only be negative. However, other organizations have the view that achieving compliance can bring additional benefits or deliver the 'upside of risk'.

Some other risks have established or required responses that are imposed on us as individuals and/or on organizations as mandatory requirements. For example, in our personal lives, buying insurance for a car is usually a legal requirement, whereas buying insurance for a house is often not, but is good risk management and very sensible.

Keeping your car in good mechanical order will reduce the chances of a breakdown. However, even vehicles that are fully serviced and maintained do occasionally break down. Maintaining your car in good mechanical order will reduce the chances of breakdown, but will not eliminate them completely. These types of risks that have a large degree of uncertainty associated with them are often referred to as *control risks*. The risks associated with owning a car are explored in some detail in the book, because this represents a practical example within the experience of most people.

As well as hazard and control risks, there are risks that we take because we desire (and probably expect) a positive return. For example, you will invest money in anticipation that you will make a profit from the investment. Likewise, placing a bet or gambling on the outcome of a sporting event is undertaken in anticipation of receiving positive payback.

People participate out of choice in motor sports and other potentially dangerous leisure activities. In these circumstances, the return may not be financial, but can be measured in terms of pride, self-esteem or peer group respect. Undertaking activities involving risks of this type, where a positive return is expected, can be referred to as taking *opportunity risks*.

Risk management

Organizations face a very wide range of risks that can impact the outcome of their operations. The desired overall aim may be stated as a mission or a set of corporate objectives. The events that can impact an organization may inhibit what it is seeking to achieve (hazard risks), enhance that aim (opportunity risks), or create uncertainty about the outcomes (control risks). There is a fourth category of risk related to mandatory obligations placed on organizations and these risks are referred to as compliance risks.

Risk management needs to offer an integrated approach to the evaluation, control and monitoring of these three types of risk. This book examines the key components of risk management and how it can be applied. Examples are provided that demonstrate the benefits of risk management to organizations in both the public and private sectors. Risk management also has an important part to play in the success of not-for-profit organizations such as charities and (for example) clubs and other membership bodies.

The risk management process is well established, although it is presented in a number of different ways and often in differing terminologies. The different terminologies that are used by different risk management practitioners and in different business sectors are explored in this book. In addition to a description of the established risk management standards, a simplified description of risk management that sets out the key stages in the risk management process is also presented to help with understanding.

The risk management process cannot take place in isolation. It needs to be supported by a framework within the organization. Once again, the risk management framework is presented and described in different ways in the range of standards, guides and other publications that are available. In all cases, the key components of a successful risk management framework are the communications and reporting structure (architecture), the overall risk management strategy that is set by the organization (strategy) and the set of guidelines and procedures (protocols) that have been established. The importance of the risk architecture, strategy and protocols (RASP) is discussed in detail in this book.

The combination of risk management processes, together with a description of the framework in place for supporting the process, constitutes a risk management standard. There are several risk management standards in existence, including the IRM Standard and British Standard BS 31100:2011. There is also the American COSO ERM cube. The most high-profile addition to the available risk management standards is the international standard, ISO 31000, first published in 2009 and updated in 2018. The well-established and respected Australian Standard AS 4360 (2004) was withdrawn in 2009 in favour of ISO 31000. AS 4360 was first published in 1995 and ISO 31000 includes many of the features and offers a similar approach to that previously described in AS 4360.

Further information on existing standards and other published guides is set out in Chapter 6. Additionally, references are included in each part of this book to provide further material to enable the reader to gain a comprehensive introduction to the subject of risk management. Abbreviations and acronyms are used throughout the book as an aim to learning and understanding. A list of all abbreviations and acronyms is included in Appendix A.

Risk management terminology

Most risk management publications refer to the benefits of having a common language of risk within the organization. Many organizations manage to achieve this common language and common understanding of risk management processes and protocols at least internally. However, it is usually the case that within a business sector, and sometimes even within individual organizations, the development of a common language of risk can be very challenging.

Reference and supporting materials use a great range of terminologies. The different approaches to risk management, the different risk management standards that exist and the wide range of guidance material that is available often use different terms for the same feature or concept. This is regrettable and can be very confusing, but it is inescapable.

Attempts are being made to develop a standardized language of risk, and ISO Guide 73 has been developed as the common terminology that should be used in all ISO standards. The terminology set out in ISO Guide 73 is used throughout this book as the default set of definitions wherever possible. However, the use of a standard terminology is not always possible and alternative definitions may be required. Indeed, ISO itself also publish a terminology guide, ISO/IEC Guide 51:2014, entitled 'Safety aspects – guidelines for their inclusion in standards', and the definitions in Guide 51 are not fully aligned with those in Guide 73.

To assist with the difficult area of terminology, Appendix B sets out the basic terms and definitions that are used in risk management. It also provides cross reference between the different terms in use to describe the same concept. Where appropriate and necessary a table setting out a range of definitions for the same concept is included within the relevant chapter of the book, and these tables are cross-referenced in Appendix B.

Benefits of risk management

There are a range of reasons why organizations undertake risk management activities. These reasons are summarized in this book as mandatory, assurance, decision-making and effective and efficient core processes (MADE2). Mandatory refers to risk management activities designed to ensure that an organization complies with legal and regulatory obligations, as well as customer or client requirements.

The board of an organization will require assurance that significant risks have been identified and appropriate controls put in place. In order to ensure that correct business decisions are taken, the organization should undertake risk management activities that provide additional structured information to assist with business decision making.

Finally, a key benefit from risk management is to enhance the effectiveness and efficiency of operations within the organization. Additionally, it should help ensure that business processes (including process enhancements by way of tactics, projects and other change initiatives) are also effective and efficient. Finally, the selected strategy also needs to be effective and efficient, in that it is capable of delivering exactly what is required.

Risk management inputs are required in relation to strategic decision making, but also in relation to the effective delivery of projects and programmes of work, as well as in relation to the routine operations of the organization. The benefits of risk management can also be identified in relation to these three timescales of activities within the organization. The outputs from risk management activities can benefit organizations in three timescales and ensure that the organization achieves effective and efficient strategy, tactics and operations.

Strategy, tactics and operations are underpinned by the need to achieve compliance. Strategic, tactical, operational and compliance (STOC) core processes and activities encompass the whole range of processes of an organization. These processes are the core processes of the organization and analysis of the core processes provides a comprehensive approach to risk management that is used in several sections of the book.

In order to achieve a successful risk management contribution, the intended benefits of any risk management initiative have to be identified. If those benefits have not been identified, then there will be no means of evaluating whether the risk management initiative has been successful. Therefore, good risk management must have a clear set of desired outcomes/benefits. Appropriate attention should be paid to each stage of the risk management process, as well as to details of the design, implementation and monitoring of the framework that supports these risk management activities.

Features of risk management

Failure to adequately manage the risks faced by an organization can be caused by inadequate risk recognition, insufficient analysis of significant risks and failure to identify suitable risk response activities. Also, failure to set a risk management strategy and to communicate that strategy and the associated responsibilities may result in inadequate management of risks. It is also possible that the risk management procedures or protocols may be flawed, such that these protocols may actually be incapable of delivering the required outcomes.

The consequences of failure to adequately manage risk can be disastrous and may result in ineffective and/or inefficient operations, projects that are not completed on time and strategies that are not delivered, or were incorrect in the first place. The hallmarks of successful risk management are considered in this book. In order to be successful, the risk management initiative should be proportionate, aligned, comprehensive, embedded and dynamic (PACED).

Proportionate means that the effort put into risk management should be appropriate to the level of risk that the organization faces. Risk management activities should be aligned with other activities within the organization. Activities will also need to be comprehensive, so that any risk management initiative covers all the aspects of the organization and all the risks that it faces. The means of embedding risk management activities within the organization are discussed in this book. Finally, risk management activities should be dynamic and responsive to the changing business environment faced by the organization.

As with all management activities and processes in an organization, risk management needs to be adapted and modified to align with the core processes, and organizational culture. In relation to risk management, an organization will first need to specifically respond to statutory obligations and the requirements of regulators. Once they have been satisfied, most organizations can work on the basis that whatever works within the organization and delivers the required benefits, outputs and outcomes is the correct and appropriate approach to ERM for that organization.

Book structure

The book is presented in eight parts, together with three appendices. Part One provides the introduction to risk management and introduces all of the basic concepts. Part Two considers the alternative approaches to risk management and starts by considering established risk management standards. The importance of establishing the context is then considered in detail, followed by an analysis of the features and benefits of enterprise risk management.

Part Three considers the importance of risk assessment as a fundamental requirement of successful risk management. Risk classification and risk analysis tools and techniques are considered in detail in this part. Part Four sets out the options for risk response in detail. Analysis of the various risk control techniques is presented, together with examples of options for the control of selected hazard risks. This part also considers the importance of insurance and risk transfer, as well as business continuity planning.

Part Five explores the importance of risk management strategy and considers the vital importance of the risk management policy, as well as exploring the successful implementation of that policy. There is also a consideration of reputation and the business model and the importance of the risk management context. Part Six starts by considering the nature of a risk-aware culture and then goes on to consider the importance of risk appetite. Risk training and communication, together with risk practitioner competencies, are also included in Part Six. Part Six also reflects on the fact that the emergence of risk management as a profession has resulted in more attention being paid to risk management competency frameworks and the importance of people or soft skills.

Part Seven considers the importance of risk governance, and this extends to the evaluation of broader corporate governance requirements and the impact of risk on organizations. Also, the analysis of stakeholder expectations and the relationship between risk management and a simple business model are considered. Finally, Part Eight considers risk assurance and risk reporting. The role of the internal audit function, together with the importance of corporate social responsibility and the options for reporting on risk management are all considered. Throughout the book, information is presented in tables and figures to make the information more readily accessible. Extensive use is made of the increasingly common approach of using a bow-tie representation of the risk management process.

Appendix A is a full list of the main acronyms and abbreviations used in the book. Appendix B provides a glossary of terms and cross-references the different terminologies used by different risk management practitioners. Appendix C provides a step-by-step implementation guide to enterprise risk management (ERM), as described in Chapter 8. This is based on the plan, implement, measure and learn (PIML) approach which is similar to the plan–do–check–act (PDCA) approach described in several risk-related standards. Appendix C also includes reference to the acronyms used in the book and sets out the key concepts relevant to each step of the successful implementation of an ERM initiative.

Risk management in practice

In order to bring the subject of risk management to life, short illustrative examples are used throughout the text. These examples focus on a small number of organizations in order to give some context to the ideas described. Risk management activities cannot be undertaken out of context, and so these organizations provide context to the ideas and concepts that are described.

The most often used examples to illustrate a point are a haulage company, a sports club, a theatre, a publisher and the large stock-exchange-listed company that, for the sake of illustration, owns the sports club and the haulage company. Examples are also used of how risk management principles can be applied to the personal risks faced in private life.

In addition to these general examples, real-life situations and examples are also used, where a case study is helpful. Each part of the book commences with a brief extract from the report and accounts of three selected companies to illustrate the main risk management topics covered in the part. Although many of these examples are mainly from the UK, the principles are equally applicable to other parts of the world.

Because of the global financial crisis, and the continuing economic difficulties around the world, risk management continues to be a very high-profile topic. Therefore, there are many examples of the application of risk management tools and techniques to difficult business and commercial situations. The book takes advantage of the wealth of information that is available in order to present examples, opinions and commentary on the risk management issues affecting organizations.

Throughout the book, boxes are included within the text. These boxes either provide practical examples of the application of the theory being discussed, or they provide opinions and commentary on real situations that have arisen. The case studies included at the beginning of each part of the book have been taken from the websites of high-profile organizations or from the published annual reports and accounts that are available in the public domain.

Future for risk management

As the global financial crisis has unfolded, there is an increasing tendency for news reports to indicate that risk is bad and risk management has failed. In reality, neither of these two statements is correct. Organizations have to address the risks that they face because many of them have to undertake high-risk activities, either because these activities cannot be avoided, or because the activities are undertaken in order to produce a positive outcome for the organization and its stakeholders.

The global financial crisis does not demonstrate the failure of risk management, but rather the failure of the management of organizations to successfully address the risks that they faced. Achieving benefits from risk management requires carefully planned implementation of the risk management process in the organization, as well as the design and successful embedding of a suitable and sufficient risk management framework.

By setting out an integrated approach to risk management, this book provides a description of the fundamental components of successful management of business/ corporate risks. It describes a wealth of risk management tools and techniques and provides information on successful delivery of an integrated and enterprise-wide approach to risk management.

Risk management is changing rapidly, in terms both of the tools and techniques that are applied and the governance structures that are being introduced to ensure successful management of risk. Organizations need to be more cost conscious, and this has resulted in the emergence of approaches such as Governance Risk and Compliance (GRC). GRC represents an approach that is designed to be both effective and cost efficient in terms of the results that are achieved.

With many organizations having to introduce cost-cutting and finding the current trading conditions difficult, emerging risks have never been more important. For many organizations, it is a challenge to keep their risk exposure within the risk capacity of the organization. Events can occur that could be devastating for the organization. In these difficult circumstances, organizations need to pay more attention to an analysis of the triggers that could result in significant risks materializing, as well as developing detailed plans to manage any crisis that does arise.

The list below offers a summary of the actions that would help to avoid a repeat of the global financial crisis. Many organizations lack a common risk management framework across the enterprise. This has many elements, each of which is required to help avoid similar disasters in the future:

- First, there should be common processes, terminology and practices for managing risks of all kinds.
- Second, it is essential that risk tolerances be fully understood, communicated and monitored across the enterprise.
- Third, risk management practices should be incorporated into all key business processes and decisions.
- And, fourth, management should make risk-related decisions using dedicated high-quality risk information.

Changes for the fifth edition

Risk management continues to be a dynamic and developing discipline and the changes that were necessary in the production of the fifth edition of this book reflect that fact. Certain types of risk have increased dramatically and the need for a robust ERM initiative to be adopted by organizations has never been greater. Risks that have increased considerably since the fourth edition of this book include the global phenomenon of youth unemployment, the increasing level of political instability in the world, the increasing number of incidents associated with climate change, and the increasingly sophisticated levels of cyber-crime.

Changes made for the fourth edition remain valid, including amendments to ensure that the contents remain relevant in an increasingly uncertain world, and increasingly complex business environment. Several chapters required substantial updating to accommodate the developments in risk management over the previous two years. In particular, Part Two consolidates the chapters concerned with the different approaches to risk management and includes consideration of risk management standards, outlines the importance of establishing the context and considers ERM in detail in Chapter 8.

The opportunity was also taken to provide more information on establishing the context, by a more detailed analysis of the external and internal context of an organization in Chapter 7, together with discussion of the risk management context in Chapter 21. Also, there was greater use of case studies in the fourth edition with three different case studies included in each of the eight parts of the book. The case studies have been selected to provide examples of good practice in risk management by various companies around the world.

One of the most important considerations in producing the fourth edition was to more closely align the order of the chapters in the textbook with the structure of the Institute of Risk Management (IRM) International Certificate in Enterprise Risk Management (ERM). Accordingly, the first four parts of the textbook are concerned with the basic principles of risk and risk management. Parts Five through to Eight are concerned with the practice of risk management and include consideration of risk strategy, culture, governance and assurance. Aligning the structure of the textbook with the IRM international certificate has provided a better structured order in which to present the technical content.

The need to produce the fifth edition just 18 months after the fourth edition arose from the publication of updated risk management guidance from both COSO and ISO. In mid-2017, an additional version of the COSO ERM framework was published. This recent COSO guidance has not yet replaced the COSO ERM framework (2004) and both the existing 2004 framework and the new (2017) framework are considered in the textbook in Chapters 6 and 8 respectively. To avoid confusion, the 2004 framework is referred to as the COSO ERM cube throughout the book. The 2017 COSO ERM framework is a significant development, because it focuses on integrating the ERM initiative with strategy and performance. Early in 2018, the long-awaited update of ISO 31000 was published, and the 2018 version of ISO 31000 is considered in detail in Chapter 6.

PART ONE
Introduction to risk management

LEARNING OUTCOMES FOR PART ONE

- produce a range of established definitions of risk and risk management and describe the usefulness of the various definitions;
- list the range of characteristics of a risk that need to be identified in order to provide a full risk description and justify the inclusion of each item;
- summarize the options for the attachment of risks to various attributes of an organization and describe the advantages of each approach;
- identify the features of the four types of risk that enable them to be identified as compliance, hazard, control and opportunity risks;
- summarize the origins and development of the discipline of risk management, including the various specialist areas and approaches;
- explain the characteristics of enterprise risk management (ERM) and the benefits of the ERM approach over traditional risk management;
- summarize the principles (PACED) and aims of risk management and its importance to strategy, tactics, operations and compliance (STOC);
- describe the key outputs of risk management in terms of mandatory obligations, assurance, decision making and effective and efficient core processes (MADE2).

PART ONE FURTHER READING

Bernstein, P (1998) *Against the Gods: The Remarkable Story of Risk*, **www.wiley.com**

British Standard BS 31100:2011 *Risk Management: Code of Practice and Guidance for the Implementation of BS ISO 31000*, **www.standardsuk.com**

Institute of Risk Management (2002) *A Risk Management Standard*, **www.theirm.org**

Institute of Risk Management (2010) *A Structured Approach to Enterprise Risk Management (ERM) and the Requirements of ISO 31000*, **www.theirm.org**

International Standard ISO 31000:2018 *Risk Management – Guidelines*, **www.iso.org**

Pullan, P and Murray-Webster, R (2011) *A Short Guide to Facilitating Risk Management*, **www.gowerpublishing.com**

PART ONE CASE STUDIES

Rank Group: How we manage risk

Rank operates a comprehensive risk management methodology which is closely integrated to its management structure to provide clear oversight and governance of the risks which are considered to be material to its business, and to maintain continual surveillance of its operating environment for emerging risks. The approach endeavours to ensure that a clear risk appetite is set that balances risks and opportunities to contribute to the achievement of the group's strategic objectives.

The board has responsibility for the risk framework and establishing the group's risk appetite, as well as ensuring that risk controls are built into management's approach to operations. The audit committee holds the responsibility for assessing the effectiveness of the risk management systems which are in place and undertaking independent review of the risk mitigation plans which have been designed for material risks.

Rank's risk committee meets on a monthly basis with a remit to conduct a thorough review of the risk register and to ensure that management are working effectively to identify and manage risks as they arise and on a continual basis. Working sessions of the committee are held with departmental and divisional management to ensure that risks are being identified in a timely manner and effective action plans put into place. This approach ensures that risk is identified in both a 'top-down' and a 'bottom-up' manner from the various management levels of the organization to give assurance that risk registers are comprehensive.

Group internal audit works in support of the risk committee to help manage risk identification and conduct independent reviews of both the business's risks and its progress in performing the mitigating action plans agreed for any relevant risks, the status of which is reported to the risk committee monthly.

Edited extract from The Rank Group Plc
Annual Report and Financial Statements 2015

ABIL: Risk management overview

The ABIL risk management strategy is to embed a risk culture and support business units within the group. The key focus is to ensure that business units operate within risk parameters that will lead to sustainable business and enhanced risk management practices. The structure is supported by three pillars: competence, collaboration and independence.

In the 2013 financial year, the customer value proposition was enhanced by offering new products such as short-term insurance (funeral) and investments that introduced additional operational and compliance risk. These products are aimed at providing a diversified income stream, lowering the cost of funding and attracting a more diversified customer base. The group risk function has been broadened with regard to systems and people in order to focus on key areas, such as non-compliance with regulatory requirements. This function has been particularly critical in fraud mitigation this year, to assist with early detection and timely resolution.

The group risk management approach is an approved enterprise-wide risk management methodology and philosophy to ensure adequate and effective risk management. In addition, the methodology also provides regulatory principles and a risk management approach that ensures the following core principles are adhered to:

- clear assignment of responsibilities and accountabilities;
- common enterprise-wide risk management framework and process;
- identification of uncertain future events that may influence achievement of business plans and strategic objectives; and
- integration of risk management activities within the company and across its value chains.

ABIL's risk management objective is to ensure a proactive identification, understanding and assessment of risks, including activities undertaken that result in risks which could impact on business objectives. This is executed through various risk management and governance mechanisms and risk management oversight bodies.

Edited extract from African Bank Investments Limited
Risk report for the financial year ended 30 September 2013

BIS: Approach to risk

Our risk management approach is based on devolved accountability across the departmental groups and our partner organization network, so that risks are assigned to those best placed to manage them, whilst maintaining clear accountability. Risks that can and should be managed at group or partner organization level remain within those entities and are subject to their own risk assurance and scrutiny processes in line with the overall risk management process set by the department.

A corporate performance and risk team acts as a central point for advice and guidance on effective risk management. The team co-ordinates the top level risk register, which is the route by which our most significant risks are escalated. Risks for escalation to the top level risk register are proposed at all working levels, but only those risks that could have a significant, cross-cutting impact on the department are included.

Following a risk management review by internal audit, we have continued to focus on building skills and capacity within our approach to risk management. This has further enhanced consistency across the department and our partner organizations. A continued emphasis on sharing good practice in risk management, supported by training and development for our staff has improved our agreed processes to risk management.

The risk management process has continued to work well in BIS with risks escalated throughout the department and scrutiny provided by our boards, committees and non-executive board members. Work over the next 12 months will focus on further building skills and capacity to fully embed the BIS risk management processes, ensuring a comprehensive understanding amongst the department and our partner organizations.

Edited extract from Department for Business Innovation and Skills
Annual Report and Accounts 2013–14

Approaches to defining risk

Definitions of risk

The *Oxford English Dictionary* definition of risk is as follows: 'a chance or possibility of danger, loss, injury or other adverse consequences', and the definition of at risk is 'exposed to danger'. In this context, risk is used to signify negative consequences. However, taking a risk can also result in a positive outcome. A third possibility is that risk is related to uncertainty of outcome.

Take the example of owning a motor car. For most people, owning a car is an opportunity to become more mobile and gain the related benefits. However, there are uncertainties in owning a car that are related to maintenance and repair costs. Finally, motor cars can be involved in accidents, so there are obvious negative outcomes that can occur. It is also important to remember the legal obligations associated with car ownership and the rules that must be obeyed when the car is being driven on a road.

Definitions of risk can be found from many sources, and some key definitions are set out in Table 1.1. An alternative definition is also provided to illustrate the broad nature of risks that can affect organizations. The Institute of Risk Management (IRM) defines risk as the combination of the probability of an event and its consequence. Consequences can range from positive to negative. This is a widely applicable and practical definition that can be easily applied.

The international guide to risk-related definitions is ISO Guide 73, and it defines risk as the 'effect of uncertainty on objectives'. This definition appears to assume a certain level of knowledge about risk management and it is not easy to apply to everyday life. ISO Guide 73 is currently (April 2018) under review and the 2018 version of ISO 31000 has already modified some of the definitions. These modified definitions are considered in more detail in Chapter 6.

An earlier version of Guide 73 (2002) also notes that an effect may be positive, negative, or a deviation from the expected. These three types of events can be related to risks as opportunity, hazard or uncertainty, and this relates to the example of motor car ownership outlined above. The guide notes that risk is often described by an event, a change in circumstances, a consequence, or a combination of these and how they may affect the achievement of objectives.

The Institute of Internal Auditors (IIA) defines risk as the uncertainty of an event occurring that could have an impact on the achievement of objectives. The IIA adds that risk is measured in terms of consequences and likelihood. Different disciplines define the term risk in very different ways. The definition used by health and safety professionals is that risk is a combination of likelihood and magnitude, but this may not be sufficient for more general risk management purposes.

Given that there are many available definitions for the word risk, it is important that the organization chooses the definition that is most suitable for its own purposes. The definition can be as narrow or as comprehensive as the organization wishes. As a version of a comprehensive definition of the word risk, the author offers the following:

> An event with the ability to impact (inhibit, enhance or cause doubt about) the effectiveness and efficiency of the core processes of an organization.

Risk in an organizational context is usually defined as anything that can impact the fulfilment of corporate objectives. However, corporate objectives are usually not fully stated by most organizations. Where the objectives have been established, they tend to be stated as internal, annual, change objectives. This is particularly true of the personal objectives set for members of staff in the organization, where objectives usually refer to change or developments, rather than the continuing or routine operations of the organization.

It is generally accepted that risk is best defined by concentrating on risks as events, as stated in a note to the definition of risk provided in ISO 31000 and the definition provided by the Institute of Internal Auditors, set out in Table 1.1. In order for a risk to materialize, an event must occur. Therefore, perhaps a risk can simply be considered to be 'an unplanned event with unexpected consequences'. Greater clarity is likely to be brought to the risk management process if the focus is on events. For example, consider what could disrupt a theatre performance.

Table 1.1 Definitions of risk

Organization	Definition of risk
ISO Guide 73	Effect of uncertainty on objectives. Note that an effect may be positive, negative, or a deviation from the expected. Also, risk is often described by an event, a change in circumstances or a consequence.
Institute of Risk Management (IRM)	Risk is the combination of the probability of an event and its consequence. Consequences can range from positive to negative.
Orange Book from HM Treasury	Uncertainty of outcome, within a range of exposure, arising from a combination of the impact and the probability of potential events.
Institute of Internal Auditors	The uncertainty of an event occurring that could have an impact on the achievement of the objectives. Risk is measured in terms of consequences and likelihood.

The events that could cause disruption include a power cut, the absence of a key actor, or a substantial transport failure or road closures that delay the arrival of the audience, as well as the illness of a significant number of staff. Having identified the events that could disrupt the performance, the management of the theatre needs to decide what to do to reduce the chances of one of these events causing the cancellation of a performance. This analysis by the management of the theatre is an example of risk management in practice.

Types of risks

Risk may have positive or negative outcomes or may simply result in uncertainty. Therefore, risks may be considered to be related to an opportunity or a loss or the presence of uncertainty for an organization. Every risk has its own characteristics that require particular management or analysis. In this book, risks are divided into four categories:

- compliance (or mandatory) risks;
- hazard (or pure) risks;
- control (or uncertainty) risks;
- opportunity (or speculative) risks.

In general terms, organizations will seek to minimize compliance risks, mitigate hazard risks, manage control risks and embrace opportunity risks. However, it is important to note that there is no 'right' or 'wrong' subdivision of risks. Readers will encounter other subdivisions in other texts and these may be equally appropriate. It is, perhaps, more common to find risks described as two types, pure or speculative. Indeed, there are many debates about risk management terminology. Whatever the theoretical discussions, the most important issue is that an organization adopts the risk classification system that is most suitable for its own circumstances.

There are certain risk events that can only result in negative outcomes. These risks are hazard risks or pure risks, and these may be thought of as operational or insurable risks. In general, organizations will have a tolerance of hazard risks, and these need to be managed within the levels that the organization can tolerate. A good example of a hazard risk faced by many organizations is that of theft.

There are other risks that give rise to uncertainty about the outcome of a situation. These can be described as control risks and are frequently associated with project management. In general, organizations will have an aversion to control risks. Uncertainties can be associated with the benefits that the project produces, as well as uncertainty about the delivery of the project on time, within budget and to specification. The management of control risks will often be undertaken in order to ensure that the outcome from the business activities falls within the desired range. The purpose is to reduce the variance between anticipated outcomes and actual results.

At the same time, organizations deliberately take risks, especially marketplace or commercial risks, in order to achieve a positive return. These can be considered as opportunity or speculative risks, and an organization will have a specific appetite for investment in such risks. Opportunity risks relate to the relationship between risk and return. The purpose is to take action that involves risk to achieve positive gains. The focus of opportunity risks will be towards investment.

The application of risk management tools and techniques to the management of hazard risks is the best and longest-established branch of risk management, and much of this text will concentrate on hazard risks. There is a hierarchy of controls that apply to hazard risks, and this is discussed in Chapter 16. Hazard risks are associated with a source of potential harm or a situation with the potential to undermine objectives in a negative way and hazard risk management is concerned with mitigating the potential impact. Hazard risks are the most common risks associated with operational risk management, including occupational health and safety programmes.

Control risks are associated with unknown and unexpected events. They are sometimes referred to as uncertainty risks and they can be extremely difficult to quantify. Control risks are often associated with project management and the implementation of tactics. In these circumstances, it is known that the events will occur, but the precise consequences of those events are difficult to predict and control. Therefore, the approach is based on managing the uncertainty about the potential impacts and consequences of these events

There are two main aspects associated with opportunity risks. There are risks/dangers associated with taking an opportunity, but there are also risks associated with not taking the opportunity. Opportunity risks may not be visible or physically apparent, and they are often financial in nature. Although opportunity risks are taken with the intention of obtaining a positive outcome, this is not guaranteed. Nevertheless, the overall approach is to embrace the opportunity and the associated opportunity risks. Opportunity risks for small businesses include moving a business to a new location, acquiring new property, expanding a business and diversifying into new products.

Risk description

In order to fully understand a risk, a detailed description is necessary so that a common understanding of the risk can be identified and ownership/responsibilities may be clearly understood. Table 1.2 lists the range of information that must be recorded to fully understand a risk. The list of information set out in Table 1.2 is most applicable to hazard risks and the list will need to be modified to provide a full description of control or opportunity risks.

So that the correct range of information can be collected about each risk, the distinction between compliance, hazard, control and opportunity risks needs to be clearly understood. The example below is intended to distinguish between these four types of risk, so that the information required in order to describe each type of risk can be identified.

Table 1.2   Risk description

Name or title of risk

Statement of risk, including scope of risk and details of possible events and dependencies

Nature of risk, including details of the risk classification and timescale of potential impact

Stakeholders in the risk, both internal and external

Risk attitude, appetite, tolerance, limits for the risk and/or risk criteria

Likelihood and magnitude of event and consequences should the risk materialize at current/residual level

Control standard required, target level of risk or risk criteria

Incident and loss experience

Existing control mechanisms and activities

Responsibility for developing risk strategy and policy

Potential for risk improvement and level of confidence in existing controls

Risk improvement recommendations and deadlines for implementation

Responsibility for implementing improvements

Responsibility for auditing risk compliance

Range of computer risks

In order to understand the distinction between compliance, hazard, control and opportunity risks, the example of the use of computers is helpful. Operating a computer system involves fulfilling certain legal obligations; in particular, data protection requirements and these are the compliance risks. Virus infection is an operational or hazard risk and there will be no benefit to an organization suffering a virus attack on its software programs. When an organization installs or upgrades a software package, control risks will be associated with the upgrade project.

The selection of new software is also an opportunity risk, where the intention is to achieve better results by installing the new software, but it is possible that the new software will fail to deliver all of the functionality that was intended and the opportunity benefits will not be delivered. In fact, the failure of the functionality of the new software system may substantially undermine the operations of the organization.

Inherent level of risk

It is important to understand the uncontrolled level of all risks that have been identified. This is the level of the risk before any actions have been taken to change the likelihood or magnitude of the risk. Although there are advantages in identifying the inherent level of risk, there are practical difficulties in identifying this with some types of risks.

Identifying the inherent level of the risk makes it possible to identify the importance of the control measures in place. The IIA has previously held the view that the assessment of all risks should commence with the identification of the inherent level of the risk. The guidance from the IIA has previously stated that: 'in the risk assessment, we look at the inherent risks before considering any controls.' Although there is considerable debate about whether to undertake risk assessment at inherent or current level, the purpose of any risk assessment remains the same. It is to identify what is believed to be the current level of the risk and identify the key controls that are in place to ensure that the current level is actually achieved.

Often, a risk matrix is used to show the inherent level of the risk in terms of likelihood and magnitude. The residual or current level of the risk can then be identified, after the control or controls have been put in place. The effort that is required to reduce the risk from its inherent level to its current level can be clearly indicated on the risk matrix.

Terminology varies and the inherent level of risk is sometimes referred to as the absolute risk or gross risk. Also, the current level of risk is often referred to as the residual level, net level or the managed level of risk. The example in the box below provides an example of how inherently high-risk activities are reduced to a lower level of risk by the application of sensible and practical risk response options.

Crossing the road

Crossing a busy road would be inherently dangerous if there were no controls in place and many more accidents would occur. When a risk is inherently dangerous, greater attention is paid to the control measures in place, because the perception of risk is much higher. Pedestrians do not cross the road without looking and drivers are always aware that pedestrians may step into the road. Often, other traffic calming control measures are necessary to reduce the speed of the motorists or increase the risk awareness of both motorists and pedestrians.

Risk classification systems

Risks can be classified according to the nature of the attributes of the risk, such as timescale for impact, and the nature of the impact and/or likely magnitude of the risk. They can also be classified according to the timescale of impact after the event occurs. The source of the risk can also be used as the basis of classification. In this case, a risk may be classified according to its origin, such as counterparty or credit risk.

A further way of classifying risks is to consider the nature of the impact. Some risks can cause detriment to the finances of the organization, whereas others will have an impact on the activities or the infrastructure. Further, risks may have an impact on the reputation of the organization, or on its status and the way it is perceived in the marketplace.

Risks may also be classified according to the component or feature of the organization that will be impacted. For example, risks can be classified according to whether they will impact people, premises, processes or products. An important consideration for organizations when deciding their risk classification system is to determine whether the risks will be classified according to the source of the risk, the component impacted or of the consequences of the risk materializing.

Individual organizations will decide on the risk classification system that suits them best, depending on the nature of the organization and its activities. Also, many risk management standards and frameworks suggest a specific risk classification system. If the organization adopts one of these standards, then it will tend to follow the classification system recommended.

The risk classification system that is selected should be fully relevant to the organization concerned. There is no universal classification system that fulfils the requirements of all organizations. It is likely that each risk will need to be classified in several ways in order to clearly understand its potential impact. However, many classification systems offer common or similar structures, as described in Chapter 11.

Risk likelihood and magnitude

Risk likelihood and magnitude are best demonstrated using a risk matrix. Risk matrices can be produced in many formats. Whatever format is used for a risk matrix, it is a very valuable tool for the risk management practitioner. The basic style of risk matrix plots the likelihood of an event against the magnitude or impact should the event materialize.

Figure 1.1 is an illustration of a simple risk matrix, also referred to as a risk map or heat map. This is a commonly used method of illustrating risk likelihood and the magnitude (or severity) of the event should the risk materialize. The use of the risk matrix to illustrate risk likelihood and magnitude is a fundamentally important risk management tool. The risk matrix can be used to plot the nature of individual risks, so that the organization can decide whether the risk is acceptable and within the risk appetite and/or risk capacity of the organization.

Throughout this book, a standard format for presenting a risk matrix has been adopted. The horizontal axis is used to represent likelihood. The term likelihood is used rather than frequency, because the word frequency implies that events will definitely occur and the risk matrix is registering how often these events take place. Likelihood is a broader word that includes frequency, but also refers to the chances of an unlikely event happening. However, in risk management literature, the word 'probability' will often be used to describe the likelihood of a risk materializing.

The vertical axis is used to indicate magnitude in Figure 1.1. The word magnitude is used rather than severity, so that the same style of risk matrix can be used to illustrate compliance, hazard, control and opportunity risks. Severity implies that the event is undesirable and is, therefore, related to compliance and hazard risks. The magnitude of the risk may be considered to be its gross or inherent level before controls are applied.

Figure 1.1   Risk likelihood and magnitude

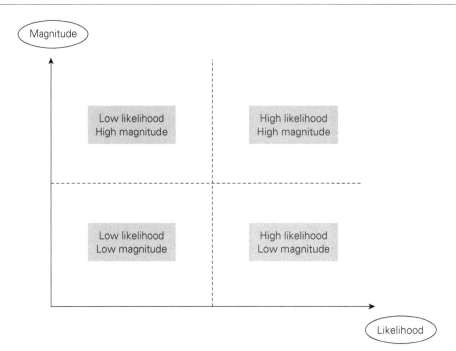

Figure 1.1 plots likelihood against the magnitude of an event. However, the more important consideration for risk managers is not the magnitude of the event, but the impact of the event and the consequences that follow. For example, a large fire could occur that completely destroys a warehouse of a distribution and logistics company. Although the magnitude of the event may be large, if sufficient insurance is in place, the impact in terms of financial costs for the company could be minimal, and if the company has produced plans to cope with such an event, the consequences for the overall business may be much less than would otherwise be anticipated.

The magnitude of an event may be considered to be the inherent level of the event and the impact can be considered to be the risk-managed level. Because the impact (and the associated consequences) of an event is usually more important than its magnitude (or severity), every risk matrix used in the remainder of this book will plot impact against likelihood, rather than magnitude against likelihood.

The risk matrix is used throughout this book to provide a visual representation of risks. It can also be used to indicate the likely risk control mechanisms that can be applied. The risk matrix can also be used to record the inherent, current (or residual) and target levels of the risk.

Shading or colour coding is often used on the risk matrix to provide a visual representation of the importance of each risk under consideration. As risks move towards the top right-hand corner of the risk matrix, they become more likely and have a greater impact. Therefore, the risk becomes more important and immediate and effective risk control measures need to be in place.

Impact of risk on organizations 02

Level of risk

Following the events in the world financial system during 2008, all organizations are taking a greater interest in risk and risk management. It is increasingly understood that the explicit and structured management of risks brings benefits. By taking a proactive approach to risk and risk management, organizations will be able to achieve the following four areas of improvement:

- Strategy, because the risks associated with different strategic options will be fully analysed and better strategic decisions will be reached.
- Tactics, because consideration will have been given to selection of the tactics and the risks involved in the alternatives that may be available.
- Operations, because events that can cause disruption will be identified in advance and actions taken to reduce the likelihood of these events occurring, limit the damage caused by these events and contain the cost of the events.
- Compliance will be enhanced because the risks associated with failure to achieve compliance with statutory and customer obligations will be recognized.

It is no longer acceptable for organizations to find themselves in a position whereby unexpected events cause financial loss, disruption to normal operations, damage to reputation and loss of market presence. Stakeholders now expect that organizations will take full account of the risks that may cause disruption within operations, late delivery of projects or failure to deliver strategy.

The exposure presented by an individual risk can be defined in terms of the likelihood of the risk materializing and the impact of the risk when it does materialize. As risk exposure increases, the likely impact will also increase. Guide 73 refers to this measurement of likelihood and impact as being the current or residual 'level of risk'. This level of risk should be compared with the risk attitude and risk appetite of the organization for risks of that type. The risk appetite will sometimes be described as a set of risk criteria.

Throughout this book, the term 'magnitude' is used to indicate the size of the event that has occurred or might occur. The term 'impact' is used to define how the event affects the finances, infrastructure, reputation and/or marketplace (FIRM) of the organization. This use of terminology is also consistent with the use of impact in business continuity planning evaluations. This is a measure of the risk at the current level. The term 'consequences' is used in this book to indicate the extent to which the event results in failure to achieve effective and efficient strategy, tactics, operations and compliance (STOC).

Injury to key player

A sports club will wish to reduce the chances of a key player being absent through injury. However, key players do get injured and the club will need to consider the impact of such an event in advance of it happening. If the injury is serious, the player may be absent for a significant length of time. There is likely to be a substantial impact, which will be most obvious on the pitch where the success of the team is likely to be reduced.

However, other consequences may also result and these could include the loss of revenue from the sale of shirts and other merchandise with that player's name and number. Arrangements to reduce the potential for loss of income should also be considered.

Impact of hazard risks

Hazard risks undermine objectives, and the level of impact of such risks is a measure of their significance. Risk management has its longest history and earliest origins in the management of hazard risks. Hazard risk management is closely related to the management of insurable risks. Remember that a hazard (or pure) risk can only have a negative outcome.

Hazard risk management is concerned with issues such as health and safety at work, fire prevention, avoiding damage to property and the consequences of defective products. Hazard risks can cause disruption to normal operations, as well as resulting in increased costs and poor publicity associated with disruptive events.

Hazard risks are related to business dependencies, including IT and other supporting services. There is increasing dependence on the IT infrastructure of most organizations and IT systems can be disrupted by computer breakdown or fire in server rooms, as well as virus infection and deliberate hacking or computer attacks.

Theft and fraud can also be significant hazard risks for many organizations. This is especially true for organizations handling cash or managing a significant number of financial transactions. Techniques relevant to the avoidance of theft and fraud include adequate security procedures, segregation of financial duties, and authorization and delegation procedures, as well as the vetting of staff prior to employment.

It is worth reflecting on terminology, because this is especially important in relation to hazard risks, if an event occurs. If a hazard risk materializes, it may have a very large magnitude, such as the destruction of the main distribution warehouse of an organization. This large magnitude event will have an impact on the organization related to potential financial costs, destruction of infrastructure, damage to reputation and the inability to function in the marketplace. Magnitude represents the gross or inherent level of the risk.

However, the impact of the event will be reduced because of the controls that are in place. Impact represents the net, residual or current level of the risk. These controls reduce the financial impact, the extent of destruction of infrastructure, as well as controls designed to protect reputation and marketplace activities. But, what is also important for the organization is the consequences of the major warehouse fire. These consequences relate to the effect that the fire might have on the strategy, tactics, operations and compliance activities within the organization.

It is possible that a major fire will cause significant financial loss that is covered by insurance, so that this large magnitude event has little impact on the finances of the organization. Effective crisis management and business continuity will ensure that the consequences of this major fire from the point of view of customers will be so well managed that customers need not be aware that a major fire has taken place.

Finally, the importance of compliance risks should not be underestimated. Compliance risks can be substantial for many organizations, especially those business sectors that are heavily regulated. In some cases, compliance with mandatory requirements, represents a 'licence to operate' and failure to achieve the level of compliance activities required by the relevant regulator can have a significant impact on the reputation of the organization and substantial consequences for routine business activities.

Attachment of risks

Although most standard definitions of risk refer to risks as being attached to corporate objectives, Figure 2.1 provides an illustration of the options for the attachment of risks. Risks are shown in the diagram as being capable of impacting the key dependencies that deliver the core processes of the organization. Corporate objectives and stakeholder expectations help define the core processes of the organization. These core processes are key components of the existing nature and future enhancement of the business model and can relate to operations, tactics and corporate strategy, as well as compliance activities, as considered further in Chapter 19.

The intention of Figure 2.1 is to demonstrate that significant risks can be attached to features of the organization other than corporate objectives. Significant risks can be identified by considering the key dependencies of the organization, the corporate objectives and/or the stakeholder expectations, as well as by analysis of the core processes of the organization. For example, the failure of Northern Rock occurred because the wholesale money markets, on which the bank depended, stopped functioning. Another way of viewing the concept of attachment of risks is to consider that the features shown in Figure 2.1 offer alternative starting points for undertaking a risk assessment. For example, a risk assessment can be undertaken by asking 'what do stakeholders expect of us?' and 'what risks could impact the delivery of those stakeholder expectations?'

In the build-up to the recent financial crisis, banks and other financial institutions established operational and strategic objectives. By analysing these objectives and identifying the risks that could prevent the achievement of them, risk management made a contribution to the achievement of the high-risk objectives that ultimately led to the failure of the organizations. This example illustrates that attaching risks to

Figure 2.1   Attachment of risks

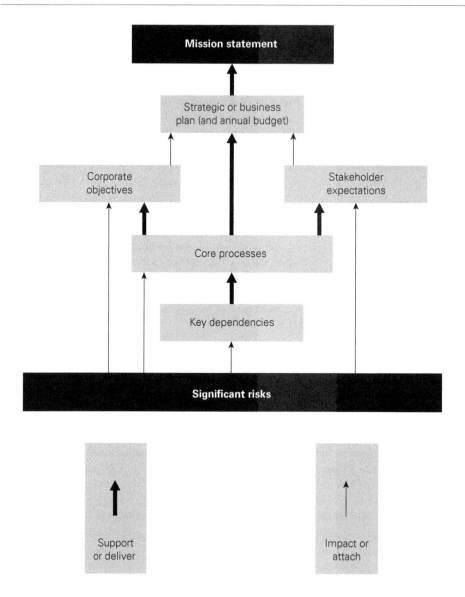

attributes other than objectives is not only possible but may well have been desirable in these circumstances.

It is clearly the case that risks are greater in circumstances of change. Therefore, linking risks to change objectives is not unreasonable, but the analysis of each objective in turn may not lead to robust risk recognition/identification. In any case, business objectives are usually stated at too high a level for the successful attachment of risks.

To be useful to the organization, the corporate objectives should be presented as a full statement of the short-, medium- and long-term aims of the organization. Internal, annual, change objectives are usually inadequate, because they may fail to fully identify the operational (or efficiency), change (or competition) and strategic (or leadership) requirements of the organization.

The most important disadvantage associated with the 'objectives-driven' approach to risk and risk management is the danger of considering risks out of the context that gave rise to them. Risks that are analysed in a way that is separated from the situation that led to them will not be capable of rigorous and informed evaluation. It can be argued that a more robust analysis can be achieved when a 'dependencies-driven' approach to risk management is adopted.

It remains the case that many organizations continue to use an analysis of corporate objectives as a means of identifying risks, because some benefits do arise from this approach. For example, using this 'objectives-driven' approach facilitates the analysis of risks in relation to the positive and uncertain aspects of the events that may occur, as well as facilitating the analysis of the negative and compliance aspects.

If the decision is taken to attach risks to the objectives of the organization, it is important that these objectives have been fully and completely developed. Not only do the objectives need to be challenged to ensure that they are full and complete, but the assumptions that underpin the objectives should also receive careful and critical attention.

Core processes are discussed in Chapter 19 and may be considered as the high-level processes that drive the organization. In the example of a sports club, one of the key processes is the operational process of 'delivering successful results on the pitch'. Risks may be attached to this core process, as well as being attached to objectives and/or key dependencies. Core processes can be classified as strategic, tactical, operational and compliance (STOC). In all cases, the core processes need to be effective and efficient. Mature (or sophisticated) risk management activities can then be designed to enhance the effectiveness and efficiency of core processes.

Although risks can be attached to other features of the organization, the standard approach is to attach risks to corporate objectives. One of the standard definitions of risk is that it is something that can impact (undermine, enhance or cause doubt about) the achievement of corporate objectives. This is a useful definition, but it does not provide the only starting point for identifying significant risks.

Attachment of risks to key dependencies and, especially, stakeholder expectations is becoming more common. The importance of stakeholders and their expectations is considered in more detail in Chapter 29. The use of key dependencies to identify risks can be a straightforward exercise. The organization will need to ask what are the features or components of the organization and its external context that are key to success. This will result in the identification of the strengths, weaknesses, opportunities and threats facing the organization. This is often referred to as a SWOT analysis. Having identified the key dependencies, as set out in Table 13.1, the organization can then consider the risks that will impact these dependencies. This approach is discussed in more detail with practical examples of risks provided in Table 13.1 and Table 15.2.

Risk and reward

Another feature of risk and risk management is that many risks are taken by organizations in order to achieve a reward. Figure 2.2 illustrates the relationship between the level of risk and the anticipated size of reward. A business will launch a new product because it believes that greater profit is available from the successful marketing of that product. In launching a new product, the organization will put resources at risk because it has decided that a certain amount of risk taking is appropriate. The value at risk represents the risk appetite of the organization with respect to the activity that it is undertaking.

When an organization puts value at risk in this way, it should do so with the full knowledge of the risk exposure and it should be satisfied that the risk exposure is within the appetite of the organization. Even more important, it should ensure that it has sufficient resources to cover the risk exposure. In other words, the risk exposure should be quantified, the appetite to take that level of risk should be confirmed, and the capacity of the organization to withstand any foreseeable adverse consequences should be clearly established.

Not all business activities will offer the same return for the same level of risk taken. Start-up operations are usually high risk and the initial expected return may be low. Figure 2.2 demonstrates the probable risk versus reward development for a new organization or a new product. The activity will commence in the bottom right-hand corner as a start-up operation, which is high risk and low return.

Figure 2.2   Risk and reward

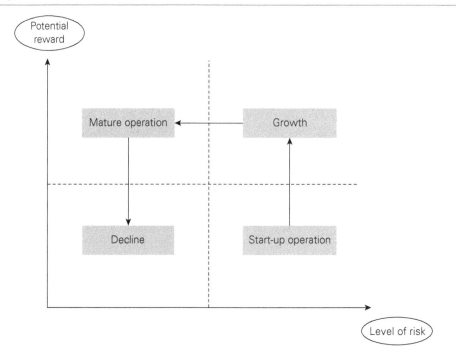

As the business develops, it is likely to move to a higher return for the same level of risk. This is the growth phase for the business or product. As the investment matures, the reward may remain high, but the risks should reduce. Eventually, an organization will become fully mature and move towards the low-risk and low-return quadrant. The normal expectation in very mature markets is that the organization or product will be in decline.

The particular risks that the organization faces will need to be identified by management or by the organization. Appropriate risk management techniques will then need to be applied to the risks that have been identified. The nature of these risk responses and the nature of their impact is considered in Part Four of this book.

The above discussion about risk and reward applies to opportunity risks. However, it must always be the case that risk management effort produces rewards. In the case of hazard risks, it is likely that the reward for increased risk management effort will be fewer disruptive events. In the case of project risks, the reward for increased risk management effort will be that the project is more likely to be delivered on time, within budget and to specification/quality.

For opportunity risks, the risk versus reward analysis should result in fewer unsuccessful new products and a higher level of profit or (at worst) a lower level of loss for all new activities or new products. In all cases, profit or enhanced level of service is the reward for taking risk. The concept of the risk versus reward analysis in relation to strategic risks is considered in more detail in Figure 15.2.

Risk versus reward

In a Formula 1 Grand Prix, the Ferrari team decided to send a driver out on wet-weather tyres, before the rain had actually started. Wet-weather tyres wear out very quickly in dry conditions and make the car much slower. If the rain had started immediately, this would have proved to be a very good decision.

In fact, the rain did not start for four or five laps, by which time the driver had been overtaken by most other drivers and his set of wet-weather tyres were ruined in the dry conditions. He had to return to the pits for a further set of new tyres more suited to the race conditions. In this case, a high-risk strategy was adopted in anticipation of significant rewards. However, the desired rewards were not achieved and significant disadvantage resulted.

Attitudes to risk

Different organizations will have different attitudes to risk. Some organizations may be considered to be risk averse, whilst others will be risk aggressive. To some extent, the attitude of the organization to risk will depend on the sector and the nature and maturity of the marketplace within which it operates, as well as the attitude of the individual board members.

Risks cannot be considered outside the context that gave rise to them. It may appear that an organization is being risk aggressive, when in fact, the board has decided that there is an opportunity that should not be missed. However, the fact that the opportunity entails high risk may not have been fully considered.

One of the major contributions from successful risk management is to ensure that strategic decisions that appear to be high risk are actually taken with all of the information available. Improvement in the robustness of decision-making activities is one of the key benefits of risk management. Attitude to risk is a complex subject and is closely related to the risk appetite of the organization, but they are not the same. Risk attitude indicates the long-term view of the organization to risk and risk appetite indicates the short-term willingness to take risk. This is similar to the difference between the long-term or established attitude of an individual towards the food they eat and their appetite for food at a particular moment in time.

Other key factors that will determine the attitude of the organization to risk include the stage in the maturity cycle, as shown in Figure 2.2. For an organization that is in the start-up phase, a more aggressive attitude to risk is required than for an organization that is enjoying growth or one that is a mature organization in a mature marketplace. Where an organization is operating in a mature marketplace and is suffering from decline, the attitude to risk will be much more risk averse.

It is because the attitude to risk has to be different when an organization is a start-up operation rather than a mature organization, that it is often said that certain high-profile businessmen are very good at entrepreneurial start-up but are not as successful in running mature businesses. Different attitudes to risk are required at different parts of the business maturity cycle shown in Figure 2.2.

The referendum in the UK on continued membership of the European Union (EU) in June 2016 resulted in a vote in favour of British exit (Brexit). The UK government has to activate the procedure for the UK to leave the EU. The text box below provides an outline of the most commonly discussed options available to the UK government. Overall, the challenge for the UK government is to ensure the continued success of the UK economy based on a Brexit strategy and tactics that will ensure the continued resilience of the UK.

Brexit: What departure options exist for the UK

Key benefits for businesses that arise from EU membership include:

- the existence of a single market: there are no tariffs or other barriers to trade;

- the freedom to provide services and freedom of establishment;

- 'passporting' that allows financial services to be traded across the EU;

- visa-free migration of people within the EU;

- access to EU free-trade agreements with 53 countries around the world.

After the Brexit vote, the UK government now has to decide which of these agreements to retain. Broadly, there are three models that the UK could target.

The Norwegian model

Norway is a member of the European Economic Area, but not the EU. It has full access to the single market, but must adopt EU standards and regulations and is unable to impose immigration restrictions. Also, Norway must contribute towards the EU budget.

The Swiss model

Switzerland has had some success in building a two-way deal with the EU, which essentially allows it to access certain selected parts of the European market in return for accepting EU legislation in relevant areas as well as making contributions to the EU budget.

The Canadian model

Canada has recently (May 2017) ratified the most far-reaching trade deal with Europe that has ever been created, and it is possible that the UK could aim to replicate this sort of relationship. Such an agreement might not allow the continued passporting of financial services.

All these models struggle to reconcile the central issue of regulatory control. Using these three models as a base, the UK now has to evaluate how Brexit will create risks and opportunities for business.

Risk and triggers

Risk is sometimes defined as uncertainty of outcomes. This is a somewhat technical, but nevertheless useful, definition and it is particularly applicable to the management of control risks. Control risks are the most difficult to identify and define, but are often associated with projects. The overall intention of a project is to deliver the desired outcomes on time, within budget and to specification, quality or performance.

For example, when a building is being constructed, the nature of the ground conditions may not always be known in detail. As the construction work proceeds, more information will be available about the nature of the conditions. This information may be positive news that the ground is stronger than expected and less foundation work is required. Alternatively, it may be discovered that the ground is contaminated or is weaker than expected or that there are other potentially adverse circumstances, such as archaeological remains being discovered.

Given this uncertainty, these risks should be considered to be control risks and the overall management of the project should take account of the uncertainty associated with these different types of risk. It would be unrealistic for the project manager to assume that only adverse aspects of the ground conditions will be discovered. Likewise, it would be unwise for the project manager to assume that conditions will be better than expected, just because s/he wants that to be the case.

Because control risks cause uncertainty, it may be considered that an organization will have an aversion to them. Perhaps, the real aversion is to the potential variability in outcomes that then need to be managed. A certain level of deviation from the project plan can be tolerated, but it must not be too great. Tolerance in relation to control risks can be considered to have the same meaning as in the manufacture of engineering components, where the components must be of a certain size, within acceptable tolerance limits.

A means of representing the risk management process so that it becomes more accessible to managers and other stakeholders concerned with risk management activities is constantly developing. One of the tools for representing risk management activities that has recently been developed is the bow-tie. The bow-tie as a representation of the risk management process is used several times throughout this book. Figure 2.3 shows a simple representation of the bow-tie applicable to events that can cause disruption to normal efficient operations.

The left-hand side of the bow-tie represents the source of a particular hazard and will indicate the classification system used by the organization for sources of risk. In Figure 2.3, these sources of risk used are the high-level sources of strategic, tactical, operational and compliance (STOC) risks. The right-hand side of the bow-tie sets out the impact should the risk events occur, and Figure 2.3 uses the high-level components of financial, infrastructure, reputational and marketplace (FIRM) impact of a risk materializing.

In the centre of the bow-tie is the risk event. Table 3.2 indicates the categories of disruption that can affect organizations, and the same categories of people, premises, processes and products are used here. The purpose of using the bow-tie illustration is to demonstrate the risk classification systems used by the organization and the potential range of impacts should a risk materialize. Controls can be put in place to prevent the event occurring and these can be represented by vertical lines on the left-hand side of the bow-tie. In a similar manner, recovery controls can be represented on the right-hand side of the bow-tie.

The bow-tie representation of the risk management process can be used in many ways, including the representation of opportunity risks. Additionally, the bow-tie

Figure 2.3 Disruptive events and the bow-tie

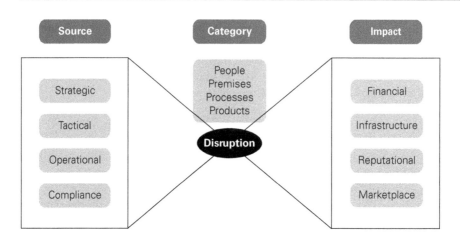

can be used to illustrate the various types of controls that are available to organizations and this is discussed in more detail in Chapter 13 on loss control.

Use of the bow-tie has become widespread, especially in the public sector. The box below provides a practical application of the bow-tie to the identification of preventive and response controls related to a fire in the kitchen of a residential home.

Risk management and the bow-tie

There are various risk analysis techniques available. The most popular method of analysing a risk is using a bow-tie.

A bow-tie is a simple way of analysing a risk to gain a greater understanding. The first stage is to put the risk description into the middle box. The causes of the risk then need to be recorded along with the preventive controls to stop the risk occurring. The impact of the risk is also considered. This enables the identification of response controls to lessen the impact of the risk should it occur.

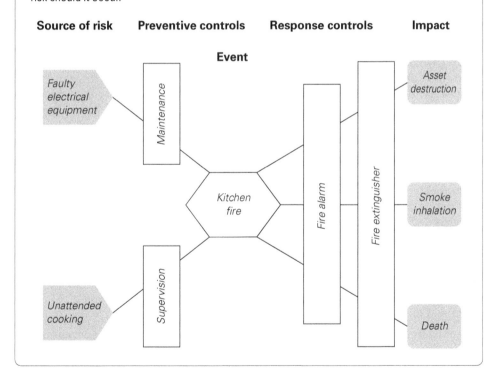

Types of risks 03

Timescale of risk impact

Risks can be classified in many ways. Hazard risks can be divided into many types of risks, including risks to property, risks to people and risks to the continuity of a business. There are a range of formal risk classification systems and these are considered in Chapter 11. Although it should not be considered to be a formal risk classification system, this part considers the value of classifying risks according to the timeframe for the impact of the risk.

The classification of risks as long-, medium- and short-term impact is a very useful means of analysing the risk exposure of an organization. These risks will be related to the strategy, tactics and operations of the organization, respectively. In this context, risks may be considered as related to events, changes in circumstances, actions or decisions.

In general terms, long-term risks will impact several years, perhaps up to five years, after the event occurs or the decision is taken. Long-term risks therefore relate to strategic decisions. When a decision is taken to launch a new product, the result of that decision (and the success of the product itself) may not be fully apparent for some time.

Medium-term risks have their impact some time after the event occurs or the decision is taken, and typically this will be about a year later. Medium-term risks are often associated with projects or programmes of work. For example, if a new computer software system is to be installed, then the choice of computer system is a long-term or strategic decision. However, decisions regarding the project to implement the new software will be medium-term decisions with medium-term risks attached.

Short-term risks have their impact immediately after the event occurs. Accidents at work, traffic accidents, fire and theft are all short-term risks that have an immediate impact and immediate consequences as soon as the event has occurred. These short-term risks cause immediate disruption to normal efficient operations and are probably the easiest types of risks to identify and manage or mitigate.

Insurable risks are quite often short-term risks, although the exact timing and magnitude/impact of the insured events is uncertain. In other words, insurance is designed to provide protection against risks that have immediate consequences. In the case of insurable risks, the nature and consequences of the event may be understood, but the timing of the event is unpredictable. In fact, whether the event will occur at all is not known at the time the insurance policy is taken out.

By way of example, consider the operation of a new computer software system in more detail. The organization will install the new software in anticipation of gaining efficiency and greater functionality. The decision to install new software and the choice of the software involves opportunity risks. The installation will require a project, and certain risks will be involved in that. The risks associated with the project are control risks. After the new software has been installed, it will be exposed to hazard risks. It may not deliver all of the functionality required and the software may be exposed to various risks and virus infection. These are the hazard risks associated with this new software system.

An increasingly important consideration for organizations is what will be the trigger mechanism that causes a risk to materialize. It may well be the case that the organization faces a number of serious risks and many of these might be catastrophic if they were to materialize. The challenge for management is then based on recognition of the circumstances in which one or more of the significant risk events may be triggered. The question of what would trigger such an event requires as much consideration as the source of the risk and the nature of the event if it was to happen. The box below considers the event that triggered the failure of Northern Rock.

Triggering major crises

In September 2007, Northern Rock – a bank formed by the conversion of the Northern Rock Building Society to banking status in 1997 – found that the liquidity crisis resulted in customers queuing to withdraw their savings. This was the first 'run' on a UK bank by its depositors for more than 150 years.

The immediate trigger for the crisis was the drying up of liquidity in the global institutional debt markets – known as the 'wholesale' markets – following a rise in mortgage defaults in the United States. These defaults were concentrated in 'sub-prime' mortgages – home loans to borrowers with a poor credit quality.

Northern Rock had been building up its mortgage portfolio very rapidly. Simultaneously it was becoming more and more reliant on the wholesale markets for finance, rather than personal savers. With the drying up of liquidity in the wholesale markets, Northern Rock's business model began to unravel. All this happened despite the fact that there was no evidence that the credit quality of the Northern Rock assets – its mortgages and loans – was in question.

Four types of risk

Chapter 1 states that risks can be divided into four categories and definitions of these four types of risk are also given in Appendix B. They are:

- compliance risks;
- hazard risks;
- control risks;
- opportunity risks.

A common language of risk is required throughout an organization if the contribution of risk management is to be maximized. The use of a common language will also enable the organization to develop an agreed perception of risk and attitude to risk. Part of developing this common language and perception of risk is to agree a risk classification system or series of such systems.

For example, consider people reviewing their financial position and the risks they currently face regarding finances. It may be that the key financial dependencies relate to achieving adequate income and managing expenditure. The review should include an analysis of the risks to job security and pension arrangements, as well as property ownership and other investments. This part of the analysis will provide information on the risks to income and the nature of those risks (opportunity risks).

As a practical example of the nature of compliance, hazard, control and opportunity risks, Table 3.1 considers the risks associated with owning a car. In this case, the compliance risks relate to the legal obligations associated with owning and driving a car. The hazard risks relate to events that the owner does not want to occur. Uncertainties are the costs that are known to be involved, but these may vary. Finally, the opportunities are the benefits that car ownership offers.

Regarding expenditure, the review will consider spending patterns to determine whether cost cutting is necessary (hazard risks). It will also consider leisure time activities, including holiday arrangements and hobbies, and there will be some uncertainties regarding expenditure and the costs of these activities (control risks).

Table 3.1 Risks associated with owning a car

	Opportunities of owning a car (events you hope will happen, but could fail to occur)
1	You can travel more easily than depending on others
2	Enhanced job opportunities because you will be more mobile
3	Save money on other forms of public transport
	Uncertainties of owning a car (events that you know will happen, but impacts are variable)
1	Cost of borrowing money to buy the car could change
2	Price of fuel (petrol or diesel) could go up or down
3	Maintenance, breakdown and repair costs will vary
	Hazards of owning a car (events that you do not want to happen and that can only be negative)
1	You pay too much for the car or it is in poor condition
2	You are involved in a collision or road accident
3	The car gets stolen or vindictively damaged
	Compliance requirements of owning a car (events that could result in regulatory enforcement)
1	Insufficient and/or inadequate third-party car insurance
2	Inattentive or aggressive driving results in traffic offence(s)
3	Tyres in poor condition and other maintenance obligations

Hazard risks are the risks that can only inhibit achievement of the corporate mission. Typically, these are insurable-type risks or perils, and will include fire, storm, flood, injury and so on. The discipline of risk management has strong origins in the control and mitigation of hazard risks. Normal efficient operations may be disrupted by loss, damage, breakdown, theft and other threats associated with a wide range of dependencies. Table 3.2 gives examples of disruption caused by people, premises, processes and products (4Ps). These dependencies can also be sources of risk and the 4Ps can be considered to be an example of a risk classification system.

Control risks are risks that cause doubt about the ability to achieve the organization's mission. Internal financial control protocols are a good example of a response to a control risk. If the control protocols are removed, there is no way of being certain about what will happen. Control risks are the most difficult type of risk to describe, but Chapter 31 on project risk management will assist with understanding.

Control risks are associated with uncertainty, and examples include the potential for failure to achieve legal compliance and losses caused by fraud. They are usually dependent on the successful management of people and effective implementation of control protocols. Although most organizations ensure that control risks are carefully managed, they may, nevertheless, remain potentially significant.

Opportunity risks are the risks that are (usually) deliberately sought or embraced by the organization. These risks arise because the organization is seeking to enhance the achievement of the mission, although they might inhibit the organization if the outcome is adverse. This is the most important type of risk for the future long-term success of any organization.

Many organizations are willing to invest in high-risk business strategies in anticipation of a high profit or return. These organizations may be considered to have a large appetite for opportunity investment. Often, the same organization will have the opposite approach to hazard risks and have a small hazard tolerance. This may be appropriate, because the attitude of the organization may be that it does not want hazard-related risks consuming the resources of the organization when it is putting so much value at risk investing in opportunities.

As well as hazard, control and opportunity risks, the further category of compliance risks may require separate consideration. For highly regulated industries, such as energy, finance, gambling and transportation, compliance issues are very important. Because of the particular nature of compliance risks, they are often considered a separate category of risk and they are often managed or minimized differently. Many organizations will wish to ensure full compliance with all rules and regulations and run zero risk in this category. This may be possible for compliance risks, but is almost certainly not going to be the case for hazard, control and opportunity risks. Further consideration of compliance risks is included in Chapter 19, as part of the discussion of strategic, tactical, operational and compliance (STOC) risks.

Embrace opportunity risks

Some risks are taken deliberately by organizations in order to achieve their mission. These risks are often marketplace or commercial risks that have been taken in the expectation of achieving a positive return. These opportunity risks can otherwise be referred to as commercial, speculative or business risks. Opportunity risks are the type of risk with potential to enhance (although they can also inhibit) the achievement of the mission of the organization. These risks are the ones associated with embracing business opportunities.

All organizations have some appetite for seizing opportunities and are willing to invest in them. There will always be a desire for the organization to have effective and efficient operations, tactics and strategy. Opportunity risks are normally associated with the development of new or amended strategies, although opportunities can also arise from enhancing the efficiency of operations and implementing change initiatives.

Every organization will need to decide what appetite it has for seizing new opportunities, and the level of investment that is appropriate. For example, an organization may realize that there is a requirement in the market for a new product that its expertise would allow it to develop and supply. However, if the organization does not have the resources to develop the new product, it may be unable to implement that strategy and it would be unwise for it to embark on such a potentially high-risk course of action.

It will be for the management of the company to decide whether they have an appetite for seizing the perceived opportunity. Just because the organization has that appetite, it does not mean that it is the correct thing to do. The board of the company should therefore be aware of the fact that, although they may have an appetite for seizing the opportunity, the organization might not have the risk capacity to support that course of action.

Opportunity management is the approach that seeks to maximize the benefits of taking entrepreneurial risks. Organizations will have an appetite for investing in opportunity risks. There is a clear link between opportunity management and strategic planning. The desire is to maximize the likelihood of a significant positive outcome from investments in business opportunities.

The example below, related to personal lifestyle decisions, considers risk factors by classifying them as controllable and uncontrollable. Although the example relates to personal health risk factors, consideration of whether business risks are within the control of the organization or not is an important component of successful business risk management.

Heart disease risk factors

Controllable risk factors for heart disease and stroke are those that can be changed through diet, physical activity and no tobacco use. These risk factors are in contrast to those that are uncontrolled, such as age, gender, race or genetic traits. Having one or more uncontrollable risk factors does not mean a person will have a heart attack or stroke; however, with proper attention to those risk factors that are controllable, one may reduce the impact of those risk factors that cannot be controlled or changed.

Controllable risk factors for heart disease or stroke include high blood pressure, high blood cholesterol, type-2 diabetes and obesity. Healthy lifestyle habits, such as developing good eating habits, increasing physical activity and abstaining from tobacco use, are effective steps in both preventing and improving the controllable risk factors.

Manage uncertainty risks

When undertaking projects and implementing change, an organization has to accept a level of uncertainty. Uncertainty or control risks are an inevitable part of undertaking a project. A contingency fund to allow for the unexpected will need to be part of a project budget, as well as contingent time built into project schedules. When looking to develop appropriate responses to control risks, the organization must make the necessary resources available to identify the controls, implement the controls and respond to the consequences of any control risk materializing.

The nature of control risks and the appropriate responses depend on the level of uncertainty and the nature of the risk. Uncertainty represents a deviation from the required or expected outcome. When an organization is undertaking a project, such as a process enhancement, the project has to be delivered on time, within budget and to specification. Also, the enhancement has to deliver the benefits that were required. Deviation from the anticipated benefits of a project represents uncertainties that can only be accepted within a certain range.

Control management is the basis of the approach to risk management adopted by internal auditors and accountants. The risk management requirements of the UK corporate governance code (April 2016) concentrate on internal control with little reference to risk assessment. Control management is concerned with reducing the uncertainty associated with significant risks and reducing the variability of outcomes.

There are dangers if the organization becomes too concerned with control management. The organization should not become obsessed with control risks, because it is sometimes suggested that over-focus on internal control and control management suppresses the entrepreneurial effort.

Mitigate hazard risks

As discussed in Chapters 1 and 2, organizations face exposure to a wide range of risks. These risks will be hazard risks, control risks and opportunity risks. Organizations need to tolerate a hazard risk exposure, accept exposure to control risks and invest in opportunity risks.

In the case of health and safety risks, it is generally accepted that organizations should be intolerant of these and should take all appropriate actions to eliminate them. In practice, this is not possible and organizations will minimize safety risks to the lowest level that is cost-effective and in compliance with the law.

For example, an automatic braking system fitted to trains to stop them passing through red lights is technically feasible. However, this may represent an unreasonable investment for the train operating company. The consequences of trains going through red lights may be regarded as the risk exposure or hazard tolerance of the organization but the cost of introducing the automatic braking system may be considered to be prohibitively high.

A less emotive example is related to theft. Most organizations will suffer a low level of petty theft and this may be tolerable. For example, businesses based in an office environment will suffer some theft of stationery, including paper, envelopes and pens.

The cost of eliminating this petty theft may be very large and so it becomes cost-effective for the organization to accept that these losses will occur. The approach to theft in shops may be very different in different retail sectors, as illustrated by the example below.

Shop security standards

An example can be seen in the operation of a security-conscious jewellery shop. Customers are allowed into the shop one at a time. They are recorded on CCTV as they wait to enter. Items are held securely, and customers are invited to ask to see specific items under the suspicious gaze of the shop assistants. Of course, some customers are put off, but equally the shops suffer negligible rates of shoplifting.

Contrast this with a supermarket, where there are no barriers on entry and customers are allowed to handle all of the items. There is CCTV monitoring the shops, and there are likely to be store detectives patrolling – but the object of the security is to deter rather than to prevent shoplifting. Shoplifting does occur, but at rates that are acceptable to the shop owners. Conversely, few potential customers are put off visiting the shop because of the measures.

The range of hazard risks that can affect an organization needs to be identified. Hazard risks can result in unplanned disruption for the organization. Disruptive events cause inefficiency and are to be avoided, unless they are part of, for example, planned maintenance or testing of emergency procedures. The desired state in relation to hazard risk management is that there should be no unplanned disruption or inefficiency from any of the reasons shown in Table 3.2.

Table 3.2 provides a list of the events that can cause unplanned disruption or inefficiency. These events are divided into several categories, such as people, premises, processes and products. For each category of hazard risks, the organization needs to evaluate the types of incidents that could occur, the sources of those incidents and their likely impact on normal efficient operations.

Management of hazard risks involves analysis and management of three aspects of the hazard risk. This is discussed in more detail in Chapters 16 and 23. In summary, the organization should look at the necessary actions to prevent the loss occurring, limit the damage that the event could cause and contain the cost of recovering from the event.

Hazard management is traditionally the approach adopted by the insurance world. Organizations will have a tolerance of hazard risks. The approach should be based on reducing the likelihood and magnitude/impact of hazard losses. Insurance represents the mechanism for limiting the financial cost of losses. Also, some hazard risks will be associated with regulatory requirements and may be considered to be compliance risks. Most organizations will seek to minimize compliance risks.

When an organization considers the level of insurance that it will purchase, the hazard tolerance of the organization needs to be fully analysed. Organizations may be willing to accept a certain number of motor accidents as a financial cost that will be funded from the day-to-day profit and loss of the organization. This will only be

Table 3.2 Categories of operational disruption

Category	Examples of disruption
People	Lack of people skills and/or resources Inappropriate behaviour by a senior manager Unexpected absence of key personnel Ill-health, accident or injury to people
Premises	Inadequate, insufficient or denial of access to premises Damage to or contamination of premises Damage to and breakdown of physical assets Theft or loss of physical assets
Processes	Failure of IT hardware or software systems Disruption by hacker or computer virus Inadequate management of information Failure of communication or transport systems
Products	Poor product or service quality Disruption caused by failure of supplier Delivery of defective goods or components Failure of outsourced services and facilities

tolerable up to a certain level and the organization will need to determine what level is acceptable. Insurance should then be purchased to cover losses that are likely to exceed that level.

Minimize compliance risks

All organizations will be aware of the wide range of compliance requirements that they have to fulfil. These compliance requirements vary considerably between business sectors, and many sectors are highly regulated with their own dedicated regulator for the industry or sector. For example, organizations operating in the gambling or gaming industry have significant regulatory requirements placed on them in most countries in the world. Failure to comply with regulatory requirements may result in the 'licence to operate' being withdrawn by the regulator. If a regulator were to take this extreme action, the organization could ultimately cease to exist.

All organizations that handle financial transactions are required to introduce procedures to reduce the chances of money-laundering activities being undertaken. Banks and other organizations that handle significant amounts of cash need to introduce money-laundering arrangements and, in many cases, a dedicated money-laundering senior executive.

In the insurance industry, compliance issues are significant and can be complex. If an insurance policy is issued in one country to protect the assets and/or cover the liabilities in other countries, compliance issues present particular difficulties. Failure to comply with all obligations may result in insurance claims not being paid or, in the extreme, being illegal in a particular country, if an unauthorized type of insurance or illegal insurance policies have been issued.

For organizations that do not have regulators dedicated to that industry or business sector, there are still a wide range of regulatory requirements that must be fulfilled. In particular, health and safety requirements exist in most countries in the world, and these place obligations on organizations to ensure the health, safety and welfare of employees and other persons who may be affected by their work activities. Typically, these safety requirements apply not only to the place of work under the direct control of the organization, but will extend to the health and safety of employees working in other countries. Also, detailed road safety obligations will apply to organizations that own vehicles, especially if they are engaged in the transportation of people or dangerous goods.

Generally speaking, organizations will work towards ensuring full compliance with all applicable rules and regulations and, thereby, minimize the compliance risks. In many cases, dedicated teams of specialist risk professionals will be employed and this is particularly the case in relation to health and safety, money-laundering and security arrangements. It is important for organizations to recognize their compliance risks and include consideration of these risks in their risk management activities. It is also important to ensure that the various areas of risk management expertise within the company co-operate with each other, so that an organized and/or co-ordinated approach to compliance is achieved.

Scope of risk management

04

Origins of risk management

Risk management has a variety of origins and is practised by a wide range of professionals. One of the early developments in risk management emerged in the United States out of the insurance management function. The practice of risk management became more widespread and better co-ordinated because the cost of insurance in the 1950s had become prohibitive and the extent of coverage limited. Organizations realized that purchasing insurance was insufficient if there was inadequate attention to the protection of property and people. Insurance buyers therefore became concerned with the quality of property protection, the standards of health and safety, product liability issues and other risk control concerns.

This combined approach to risk financing and risk control developed in Europe during the 1970s and the concept of total cost of risk became important. As this approach became established, it also became obvious that there were many risks facing organizations that were not insurable. The tools and techniques of risk management were then applied to other disciplines, as discussed later in this chapter.

Taking calculated risks

Risk management is not about controlling/mitigating risk out of existence. If business is to perform, management must learn to take more risk and to accept failure. To perform better than the rest, you must take greater risk, but it should be a calculated risk (the risk accepted is known, as is the likelihood and impact).

It is not acceptable to take risks unwittingly – the past practice of silo-based approaches for managing pockets of risk, leads to unclear responsibilities and a lack of visibility, thereby exposing the organization to unnecessary risk.

The maturity of the risk management discipline is now such that the links with insurance are much less strong. Insurance is now seen as one of the risk control techniques, but it is only applicable to a portion of hazard risks. Risks related to finance, commercial, marketplace and reputational issues are recognized as being hugely important, but outside the historical scope of insurance. The range of different approaches to risk management is illustrated by the definitions of risk management as set out in Table 4.1.

Table 4.1 Definitions of risk management

Organization	Definition of risk management
ISO Guide 73 BS 31100	Co-ordinated activities to direct and control an organization with regard to risk.
Institute of Risk Management (IRM)	Process which aims to help organizations understand, evaluate and take action on all their risks with a view to increasing the probability of success and reducing the likelihood of failure.
HM Treasury	All the processes involved in identifying, assessing and judging risks, assigning ownership, taking actions to mitigate or anticipate them, and monitoring and reviewing progress.
London School of Economics	Selection of those risks a business should take and those which should be avoided or mitigated, followed by action to avoid or reduce risk.

Providing a suitable definition of risk management is as difficult as providing a suitable and universally accepted definition of risk. Because it is commonly accepted that risk management should be concerned with the hazards, uncertainty and opportunities, a description and definition is required that reflects the broad scope of risk management activities. The following definition is offered by the author:

Risk management is the set of activities within an organization undertaken to deliver the most favourable outcome and reduce the volatility or variability of that outcome.

The increasing importance of risk management can be explained by the list of issues set out in Table 4.2. Many of these issues demonstrate that the application of risk management has moved a long way from its origins in the insurance world. Nevertheless, the insurance origins of risk management remain vitally important and are still part of the approach to hazard management.

This chapter considers the nature of risk management and the established stages that build into the risk management process. Historically, the term risk management has been used to describe an approach that was applied only to hazard risks. The discipline is now developing in a way that will enable risk management to make a contribution to the improved management of control risks and opportunity risks.

Development of risk management

Risk management as a formalized discipline has been around for at least 100 years. It has its early origins in the specialist activity of insurance, which can trace its history back for several centuries. As insurance became more formalized and structured, the need for risk control standards increased, especially in relation to the insurance of

Table 4.2   Importance of risk management

Managing the organization
Variable cost or availability of raw materials
Cost of retirement/pension/social benefits
Desire to deliver greater shareholder value
Greater transparency required from organizations
Pace of change in business ever increases
Impact of e-commerce on all aspects of business life
Increased reliance on information technology (IT) systems
Increasing importance of intellectual property (IP)
Greater supply chain complexity/dependency
Reputation becomes more and more important
Reputational damage – especially to worldwide brands
High-profile losses and failures ruin reputations
Regulatory pressures continue to increase
Changes/variation in national legislative requirements
Joint ventures becoming more common

Changes in the marketplace
Changing commercial and marketplace environment
Globalization of customers, suppliers and products
Increased competition in the marketplace
Greater customer expectations, often led by competitors
Need to respond more rapidly to stakeholder expectations
More volatile markets with less customer loyalty
Diversification leads to working in unfamiliar areas
Constant need to make bold strategic decisions
Short-term success required, without long-term detriment
Product innovation and continuous improvements
Rapid changes in (consumer) product technology
Threats to world/national economy
Threat of influenza or other pandemics
Potential for international organized crime
Increasing occurrences of civil unrest/political risks
Extreme weather events resulting in population shift

cargo being transported by ships around the world. Perhaps one of the earliest developments in this field was the introduction of the 'Plimsoll Line' to indicate the level of cargo that a ship could safely transport without being dangerously overloaded.

As risk management became more developed, education programmes emerged to support the development of risk management as a profession. It was at this time that risk management regulations associated with corporate governance began to develop and various regulators were given more authority in relation to specific hazards (such as health and safety), and also in relation to particular business sectors (such as financial institutions). The development of risk management qualifications became increasingly more formalized during the 1980s.

The development of education and qualifications in risk management, as well as the more structured approach of regulators, led to the emergence of risk management standards. Risk management standard AS/NZS 4360:1995 was one of the early examples of a comprehensive approach to the management of risk. As well as the generic risk management standards applicable to all industries, specific risk management approaches also emerged in particular sectors, including the finance sector. The emergence of regulated capital requirements for banks and insurance companies indicated the increased level of risk management maturity required of financial institutions.

The corporate risk management role in the United States during the 1950s became an extension of insurance purchasing decisions. During the 1960s, contingency planning became more important to organizations. There was also an emphasis beyond risk financing on loss prevention and safety management. During the 1970s, self-insurance and risk retention practices developed within organizations. Captive insurance companies also started to develop. Contingency plans then developed into business continuity planning and disaster recovery plans.

At the same time during the 1960s and 1970s, there were considerable developments in the risk management approach adopted by occupational health and safety practitioners. During the 1980s, the application of risk management techniques to project management developed substantially. Financial institutions continued to develop the application of risk management tools and techniques to market risk and credit risk during the 1980s. During the 1990s, the financial institutions further broadened their risk management initiatives to include structured consideration of operational risks.

Also, during the 1980s, treasury departments began to develop the financial approach to risk management. There was recognition by finance directors that insurance risk management and financial risk management policies should be better co-ordinated. During the 1990s, risk financing products emerged that combined insurance with derivatives. At the same time, corporate governance and listing requirements encouraged directors to place greater emphasis on enterprise risk management (ERM) and the first appointment of a chief risk officer (CRO) occurred at that time.

During the 2000s, financial services firms have been encouraged to develop internal risk management systems and capital models. There has been a rapid growth of CRO positions in energy companies, banks and insurance companies. Boards are now investing more time in ERM due to the Sarbanes–Oxley Act of 2002 in the United States. More detailed risk reporting and other corporate governance requirements have also been introduced.

However, the financial crisis of 2008 called into question the contribution that risk management can make to corporate success, especially in financial institutions. There is no doubt that the application of risk management tools and techniques failed to prevent the global financial crisis. This failure was a failure to correctly apply risk management processes and procedures, rather than inherent defects in the risk management approach.

Specialist areas of risk management

Risk management is a constantly developing and evolving discipline. As well as its origins in the insurance industry and in other branches of hazard management, risk management has strong connections with the credit and treasury functions. Many functions within large organizations will have a significant risk management component to their activities, such as tax, treasury, human resources, procurement and logistics. However, it is unlikely that specialists in those areas will consider their activities as simply a branch of the risk management discipline.

Perhaps one of the best known and specialist areas of risk management is that of health and safety at work. Another specialist area is that of disaster recovery planning and business continuity planning. Also, there is no doubt that quality management is a very well-developed branch of risk management, given the high profile attached to quality management systems, such as ISO 9000. Additionally, other specialist areas of risk management have developed over the past decades, including:

- project risk management;
- clinical/medical risk management;
- energy risk management;
- financial risk management;
- IT risk management.

All of the above specialist areas of risk management have contributed considerably to the development and application of risk management tools and techniques. Project risk management is an area where the application of risk management tools and techniques is particularly well developed. As discussed earlier, project risk management has its emphasis on the management of uncertainty or control risks.

Clinical risk management has been developing for some time. This area of risk management is primarily concerned with patient care, especially during surgical operations. The cost of medical malpractice claims and the inevitable delay in making insurance payments has resulted in risk management systems being introduced. Particular aspects of clinical risk management include greater attention to making patients aware of the risks that may be associated with the procedure they are about to undertake.

It is also important that surgeons report incidents that occur during the surgery. Considerable emphasis has been placed in clinical risk management on the need to report, in an accurate and timely manner, details of any incidents that occur in the operating theatre. There are many publications available on clinical risk management, and a great deal of work has been put into establishing the necessary systems and procedures to cover this specialist area of risk management.

As well as project and clinical risk management, risk management tools and techniques have also been applied in a range of specialist industries. In particular, risk management techniques have been applied in the finance and energy sectors. Risk management in the finance sector focuses on operational risks, as well as market, credit and other types of financial risks. It is in the finance sector that the title Chief Risk Officer was first developed.

The energy sector has also seen an increase in the attention paid to risk management tools and techniques. For some organizations in the energy sector, risk management is mainly concerned with the future price of energy and with exploration risk. Therefore, the risk management approach is similar to the activities of the treasury function, where hedging and other sophisticated financial techniques form the basis of the risk management effort.

Financial risk management has acquired a high profile in recent times, and Chapter 30 considers the importance of operational risk management within the finance sector. However, risk management within the finance sector is broader than just operational risk. Banks and other financial institutions will be concerned with the credit risk and market risk, as well as operational risk. Finance and insurance are highly regulated business sectors, governed by international standards such as Basel III and Solvency II.

IT risk management is another well-developed and specific branch of risk management. The increasing importance of information to organizations, in terms of the management of and security of data, has resulted in the development of specific standards applicable to IT risk management. Amongst the best established of these risk management standards is COBIT, which is similar in many regards to the COSO ERM cube discussed in Chapter 6.

Simple representation of risk management

Risk management has well-established stages that make up the risk management process, as described in Table 4.3. These stages build into valuable risk management activities, each of which makes an important contribution. There are many ways of representing the risk management process, and each of the standards mentioned in Chapter 6 provides a slightly different description.

Figure 4.1 provides a simple diagrammatic representation of the risk management process. This basic explanation of the risk management process is referred to as the 8Rs and 4Ts of hazard risk management. The activities associated with risk management are as follows:

- recognition of risks;
- rating of risks;
- ranking against risk criteria;
- responding to significant risks;
- resourcing controls;

Table 4.3   8Rs and 4Ts of (hazard) risk management

1 Recognition or identification of risks and identification of the nature of the risk and the circumstances in which it could materialize.

2 Rating or evaluation of risks in terms of magnitude and likelihood to produce the 'risk profile' that is recorded in a risk register.

3 Ranking or analysing the current or residual level of risk against the established risk criteria or risk appetite.

4 Responding to significant risks, including decisions on the appropriate action regarding the following options:
  - tolerate;
  - treat;
  - transfer;
  - terminate.

5 Resourcing controls to ensure that adequate arrangements are made to introduce and sustain necessary control activities.

6 Reaction planning and/or event management. For hazard risks, this will include disaster recovery or business continuity planning.

7 Reporting and monitoring of risk performance, actions and events and communicating on risk issues, via the risk architecture of the organization.

8 Reviewing the risk management system, including internal audit procedures and arrangements for the review and updating of the risk architecture, strategy and protocols.

- reaction (and event) planning;
- reporting of risk performance;
- reviewing the risk management system.

Risk management can improve the management of the core processes of an organization by ensuring that key dependencies are analysed, monitored and reviewed. Risk management tools and techniques will assist with the management of the hazard risks, control risks and opportunity risks that could impact these key dependencies. Organizations should ensure that the risk management process is repeated as often as necessary, to overcome the difficulty of a static snapshot of the status of the risks facing the organization. This will ensure that risk management remains a dynamic activity.

Enterprise risk management

Another area where the risk management discipline has developed in recent times is the approach that is referred to as enterprise or enterprise-wide risk management (ERM). This approach to risk management is discussed in more detail in Chapter 8.

Figure 4.1　8Rs and 4Ts of (hazard) risk management

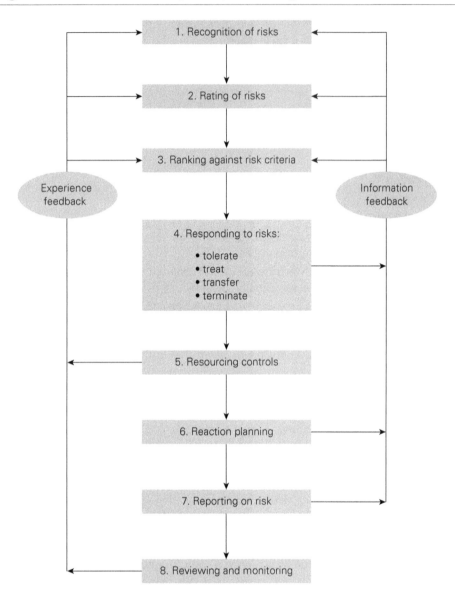

The main feature that distinguishes ERM from what might be considered more traditional risk management is the more integrated or holistic approach that is taken in ERM. In many ways, it can be considered to be a unifying philosophy that draws together management of all types of risks, rather than a new or different approach.

When an organization considers all of the risks that it faces and how these risks could impact its strategy, projects and operations, then the organization is embarking on an enterprise risk management approach. The US risk management association, the Risk and Insurance Managers Society (RIMS) defines enterprise risk management as follows:

> Enterprise Risk Management ('ERM') is a strategic business discipline that supports the achievement of an organization's objectives by addressing the full spectrum of its risks and managing the combined impact of those risks as an interrelated risk portfolio.

ERM in the pharmaceutical industry

A good example of the ERM approach is the pharmaceutical industry. If a person is reliant on a particular medication, then it is vitally important that the medication is constantly available. From the point of view of the pharmaceutical company, this means that a core process for the organization must be the 'constant availability of medication' process.

If the pharmaceutical company takes this approach, it will look at the risks that could affect this core process or stakeholder expectation on an enterprise-wide basis. This will involve analysis of the supply chain, evaluation of manufacturing activities and analysis of the delivery arrangements. The overall question that needs to be answered is what could prevent the continuous supply of medication. Risks to the continuous supply will include unavailability of ingredients, disruption to manufacturing activities, contamination of the product, breakdown in supply transportation arrangements and disruption to distribution.

An enterprise-wide approach has considerable advantages, because it analyses the potential for disruption to the overall stakeholder expectation. Health and safety, for example, is then viewed as a component in ensuring that staff are always available so that the overall operational core process will not be disrupted, rather than (or perhaps as well as) a separate hazard management issue.

Levels of risk management sophistication

This chapter describes the different styles of risk management that are currently practised. More professions and disciplines are now involved in risk management than in previous years. This adds diversity to the development of the risk management discipline. An organization needs not only to be sophisticated in its approach and expectations of risk management, but also mature in the way it conducts its risk management activities. The importance of risk maturity is considered in Chapter 24.

At first, an organization may be unaware of the legal and contractual obligations that it faces. In that case, it will be necessary to *inform* the organization of its obligations in relation to the risk. As the level of sophistication develops, the organization will become aware of the need to comply with obligations and the more general need for improved risk management. Once it is aware of obligations, there will be a need for the organization to *reform* in response to the hazard risks. As the organization responds to the risk, it will seek to *conform* to the appropriate risk control standards.

After this stage, the organization may realize that there are benefits to be obtained from the risk. The organization will then have the ability to *perform* and view the risk as an opportunity risk, as illustrated in Figure 4.2.

As a simple example, a publisher might realize that it was not fully complying with equal opportunities legislation, because there was no ethnic minority representation within the workforce. The company will identify the actions necessary in order to reform its procedures, so that it conforms to legal requirements.

Having achieved compliance, the publisher should become aware that a signifi-cant proportion of the workforce comes from ethnically diverse backgrounds. The company should see this diversity in its workforce as a benefit that will enable it to perform better in the marketplace by exploring opportunities to produce and publish new magazines that appeal to a more ethnically diverse readership.

The stages of reform to conform to perform represent levels of risk management sophistication. However, it is not necessary for a risk or the practice of risk manage-ment to progress from hazard to control to opportunity. In fact, risks can regress in certain circumstances. At any one time, a particular risk will be of a specific type in an organization. Benefits can be obtained from the successful management of that risk at whatever level of sophistication is appropriate at the time. In summary, risk management need only be as sophisticated as the organization requires in order to bring benefits.

Although the four levels of risk management sophistication illustrated in Figure 4.2 represent an improved approach to risk management, there is a danger that organizations will become obsessed with risk management to the point that important decisions are not taken. At this point, it may be said that too much atten-tion and concern about risk and risk management will cause the organization to deform its operations. In summary:

- unaware of obligations – INFORM;
- awareness of non-compliance – REFORM;
- actions to ensure compliance – CONFORM;
- achieve business opportunities – PERFORM;
- inactivity caused by obsession – DEFORM.

Most countries in the world have a wide range of voluntary organizations and char-ities. It is understandable and quite appropriate that the directors or trustees of these organizations should have a high level of concern and awareness in regard to risk management. However, it is often reported that trustees are more concerned with risk management and correct governance than with raising funds for the charity that they support. Allowing this concern with risk management to paralyse the activities of the organization would be to the detriment of the good causes that the charities are supporting.

As the level of sophistication increases and risk management professionals become aware of the alternative approaches to risk management, they should value the con-

Figure 4.2   Risk management sophistication

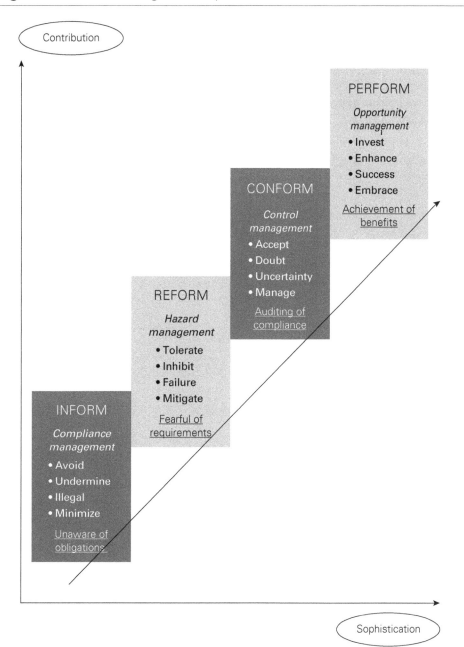

tribution that can be made by other approaches. The development in risk management approach can be summarized as follows:

- Compliance management must not be undertaken in a fragmented manner, even if excellent standards of compliance are achieved.
- Hazard management specialists may find that there has been a trend towards a desire to retain more insurable risks (and buy less insurance) as a result of a more holistic approach to risk management.
- Control management specialists must not squeeze entrepreneurial spirit and effort out of the organization.
- Strategic planners must recognize that risk management tools and techniques can contribute to better strategic decisions and the successful exploitation of business opportunities.

The approach to increasing risk management sophistication described in this section is also considered in Chapter 24 by the use of the 4Ns. An alternative approach to increasing levels of risk management sophistication or risk management maturity is the fragmented, organized, influential, leading (FOIL) approach that is also considered in more detail in Chapter 24.

Principles and aims 05
of risk management

Principles of risk management

The main principle of risk management is that it delivers value to the organization. In other words, risk management activities are designed to achieve the best possible outcome and reduce volatility or uncertainty of outcomes. However, risk management operates on a broader set of principles, and there have been several attempts to define these principles. ISO 31000 includes a detailed list of the suggested principles of risk management.

Many of the lists of principles set out a description of what risk management activity should be and what it should achieve. It is important to distinguish between what the risk management initiative has been set up to achieve and the nature of the risk management framework that will be put in place. It is suggested that a successful risk management initiative (and framework) will be:

- proportionate to the level of risk within the organization;
- aligned with other business activities;
- comprehensive, systematic and structured;
- embedded within business procedures and protocols;
- dynamic, iterative and responsive to change.

This provides the acronym PACED and provides a very good set of principles that are the foundations of a successful approach to risk management within any organization. A more detailed description of the PACED principles of risk management is set out in Table 5.1. The approach to risk management is based on the idea that risk is something that can be identified and controlled.

The above statement of principles relates to the essential features of risk management. These principles describe what risk management should be in practice. Some lists of principles also include information on what risk management should do or deliver. It is useful to separate the principles of risk management into two distinct lists: what should be the characteristics of risk management, as listed above; and what it should deliver, as listed below:

- mandatory obligations placed on the organization;
- assurance regarding the management of significant risks;
- decisions that pay full regard to risk considerations;
- effective and efficient core processes.

Table 5.1 Principles of risk management

Principle	Description
Proportionate	Risk management activities must be proportionate to the level of risk faced by the organization.
Aligned	ERM activities need to be aligned with the other activities in the organization.
Comprehensive	In order to be fully effective, the risk management approach must be comprehensive.
Embedded	Risk management activities need to be embedded within the organization.
Dynamic	Risk management activities must be dynamic and responsive to emerging and changing risks.

If organizations are to get maximum benefit out of their risk management activities, the above principles should be implemented when the risk management initiative is planned and the risk management framework is developed. In many ways, the starting point for all risk management activities is to decide what the organization is seeking to achieve. Table 5.2 sets out the possible purpose or motivation for a risk management initiative as mandatory, assurance, decision making and effective and efficient core processes (MADE2). Core processes represent the activities of the organization and can be strategic, tactical, operational or compliance (STOC) in nature.

The objectives for risk management provide the acronym MADE2 and this confirms that outputs from risk management will lead to less disruption to normal efficient operations, a reduction of uncertainty in relation to tactics and improved decisions in relation to evaluation and selection of alternative strategies. In other words, a key part of risk management is improved organizational decision making.

The resources available for managing risk are finite and so the aim is to achieve an optimum response to risk, prioritized in accordance with an evaluation of the risks. Risk is unavoidable and every organization needs to take action to manage it in a way that it can justify to a level that is acceptable. The appropriate range of responses will depend on the nature, size and complexity of the organization and the risks it faces.

Importance of risk management

Table 4.2 gives a number of examples that illustrate the importance of risk management. Risk management has taken on an increasingly high profile in recent times, because of the global financial crisis and the number of high-profile corporate

Table 5.2   Risk management objectives

Objective	Description
Mandatory	The basic objective for any risk management initiative is to ensure conformity with applicable rules, regulations and mandatory obligations.
Assurance	The board and audit committee of an organization will require assurance that risk management and internal control activities comply with PACED.
Decision making	Risk management activities should ensure that appropriate risk-based information is available to support decision making.
Effective and efficient core processes	Risk management considerations will assist with achieving effective and efficient strategy, tactics, operations and compliance to ensure the best outcome with reduced volatility of results.

failures across the world that preceded it. Also, risk management has become more important because of increasing stakeholder expectations and the ever-increasing ease of communication.

As well as assisting with better decision making and improved efficiency, risk management can also contribute to the provision of greater assurance to stakeholders. This assurance has two important components. The directors of any organization need to be confident that risks have been identified and that appropriate steps have been taken to manage risk to an appropriate level.

Also, there is greater emphasis on accurate reporting of information by organizations, including risk information. Stakeholders require detailed information on company performance, including risk awareness. The Sarbanes–Oxley Act of 2002 (SOX) in the United States has accuracy of financial reporting as its main requirement. It brings the issue of the accurate reporting of results to a higher priority (section 404), whilst also requiring full and accurate disclosure of all information about the organization (section 302).

Although SOX is a specific piece of legislation that only applies in certain circumstances, the principles that it contains are vitally important to all risk management practitioners. Accordingly, Chapters 35 and 36 consider risk assurance and accurate reporting as integral components of the overall risk management process.

When deciding the importance of risk management in the organization, the design of the risk management initiative and the risk management framework must reflect the reasons why risk management is being undertaken in the organization, in terms of MADE2. These decisions will need to be taken with due regard to the risk management drivers for the particular organization. The drivers may be related to a particular consideration within MADE2, such as the effectiveness and efficiency of operational core processes.

Some organizations have appointed a loss control manager with specific responsibility for reducing the frequency and cost of accidents to people and of damage to plant and equipment. Sometimes, the initiative will be based on the desire to improve the reputation of the organization by enhanced compliance with applicable rules and regulations, or the ability to demonstrate more ethical behaviour – including in the supply chain.

Risk management activities

Risk management is a process that can be divided into several stages. The IRM Risk Management Standard provides one representation of the stages involved in the risk management process. Alternative illustrations of the risk management process can be found in the International Standard ISO 31000 and in other publications. These standards are considered in more detail in Chapter 6.

Figure 4.1 illustrates the stages in the (hazard) risk management process. The terminology that is used to describe the stages in the risk management process has been deliberately selected, so that the process can be represented as the 8Rs and 4Ts of hazard risk management. Table 4.3 provides more information on each of the stages illustrated in Figure 4.1.

ISO Guide 73 and British Standard BS 31100 describe the risk management process as the systematic application of management policies, procedures and practices to the tasks of communicating, consulting, establishing the context, identifying, analysing, evaluating, treating, monitoring and reviewing risk. However, it could be argued that the setting of policies, procedures and practices, together with the tasks of communicating, consulting and establishing that context, is actually part of the risk management framework, rather than the risk management process itself.

Within this book, the risk management process is taken as a narrow set of activities, described above as identifying, analysing, evaluating, treating, monitoring and reviewing risk. This provides a clear distinction between the risk management process and the framework that implements and supports this process. Descriptions of the risk management process together with the risk management framework are required in order to produce a comprehensive risk management standard.

There has been much discussion about whether a single risk management process and/or diagram can be used to describe the management of compliance risks, hazard risks, control risks and opportunity risks. This book uses different terminology to describe the four types of risks and, therefore, Figure 4.1 and Table 4.3 are used to illustrate the stages in the hazard risk management process only.

There are a number of options when responding to hazard risks. These are often represented as the 4Ts of hazard risk management, and these risk response options are considered in more detail in Chapter 15. In summary, the options for responding to hazard risks are:

- tolerate;
- treat;
- transfer;
- terminate.

Effective and efficient core processes

Insurable or hazard risks can have an immediate impact on operations. Therefore, the initial application of risk management principles was to ensure continuation of normal efficient operations.

As risk management has developed, emphasis has been placed on project management and the delivery of programmes to provide enhancements to core business processes. Processes must be effective in that they deliver the results that are required, as well as being efficient. For example, there is limited value in having a software program that is efficient if it does not deliver the range of functions that are required.

Strategic decisions are the most important that an organization has to make. Risk management delivers improved information so that strategic decisions can be made with greater confidence. The strategy that is decided by an organization must be capable of delivering the results that are required. There are many examples of organizations that selected an incorrect strategy or failed to successfully implement the selected strategy. Many of these organizations suffered corporate failure.

Strategic decisions are often most difficult when changes in technology or in customer expectations emerge, as is often the case with grocery stores. The box below provides an example of a mature grocery business seeking to introduce a new strategy that failed; the company was taken over shortly afterwards.

Strategy should be designed to take advantage of opportunities. For example, a sports club may identify the possibility of selling more products to its existing customer base. Some clubs will establish a travel agency for fans of the club who travel overseas, together with the provision of associated travel insurance. Also, there is the possibility of creating a club credit card that will be managed by a new finance subsidiary.

Having identified these possibilities, the club will need to look at the risks associated with these potential opportunity investments and devise a suitable programme of projects to implement the selected strategies. Ensuring that adequate account is taken of risk during all of these activities will increase the chances of selecting the correct strategy, designing the appropriate tactics and, ultimately, ensuring efficient and profitable operations. It is worth noting that projects and programmes of work represent the tactics by which strategy is implemented.

Organizations that have effective and efficient tactics, operations and compliance, but an incorrect overall strategy will fail. This will be the case, however good the risk management activities are at operational and project level. Incorrect strategy has resulted in more corporate failures than ineffective or inefficient operations and tactics. Nevertheless, the importance of compliance activities cannot be over-emphasized, as demonstrated by the text box below from the Annual Report and Financial Statements of The Rank Group Plc.

Importance of compliance

The loss of licences could have an adverse effect on our business and profitability and prevent us from providing gambling services.

Rank's gaming licences are fundamental to its operation. In the British part of the business, there is a requirement to hold an operator's licence from the UK Gambling Commission (the body responsible for regulating commercial gambling in Great Britain) in respect of each of the licensed activities undertaken. Additionally, it is necessary to hold premises licences from the relevant local authority where each venue is situated, one for gambling activities and one for the sale of alcohol.

Rank has a dedicated compliance function that is independent of operations and a separate internal audit function that is independent of both operations and the compliance function. Rank maintains a strong and open relationship with the UK Gambling Commission and the other relevant regulatory bodies in all jurisdictions in which we operate.

The Rank Group Plc
Annual Report and Financial Statements 2015

Implementing risk management

In a rapidly developing discipline like risk management, there is scope for different practitioners to become intolerant towards the approach adopted by others. Internal control specialists who believe that risk management is all about the management of uncertainty and the achievement of corporate objectives should not become intolerant of the more traditional insurance risk management approach. There is no value in one group of specialists being dismissive of the approach adopted by others and being unwilling to utilize the expertise that is available in another group.

In any case, there is no single style of risk management or approach to risk management that offers all the answers. Clearly, the various styles that can be adopted should operate as complementary approaches within an organization. The integrative approach to risk management accepts that the organization must tolerate certain hazard risks and must have an appropriate appetite for investment in opportunity risks. Risk management tools and techniques should be used to achieve the following:

- compliance management provides risk governance;
- hazard management makes outcomes less negative;
- control management reduces the range of possible outcomes;
- opportunity management makes outcomes more positive.

Hazard management will make the outcome of any hazard event less negative. Within the context of hazard management, insurance represents the mechanism for restricting the financial cost of losses when a risk materializes. Risk control and loss management techniques will reduce the expected losses and should ensure that the overall cost is contained. The combination of insurance and risk control/loss management will reduce the actual cost of hazard losses and this will inevitably (and correctly) cause the hazard tolerance of the organization to decline. More of the risk capacity of the organization will then be available for opportunity investment.

Control management reduces the range of possible outcomes from any event. Control management is based on the established techniques of internal financial control, as practised by internal auditors. The main intention is to reduce losses associated with inadequate control management at the same time as reducing the range of possible outcomes. This is the contribution that internal control should make to the overall approach to risk management within an organization.

Opportunity management seeks to make positive outcomes more likely and more substantial. As part of the opportunity management approach, the organization should also look at possibilities for increasing the revenue from the product or service. In not-for-profit organizations, opportunity management should facilitate the delivery of better value for money.

Achieving benefits

These reward enhancement options can be discussed at strategy meetings and some options may be adopted, including the introduction of bonus and incentive schemes for staff and management. Clearly, in light of the lessons learnt from the global financial crisis, these incentive schemes should be balanced and should not reward excessive risk taking.

This chapter has considered the principles of risk management that describe what risk management should be and what it should deliver. Although organizations may realize that there are benefits from implementing risk management, the successful implementation has to be undertaken as an initiative or project. Appendix C sets out a detailed consideration of the stages involved in successful enterprise-wide risk management.

There is a more detailed consideration of the barriers to and enablers for implementation of risk management in Chapter 24. The most important point to make is that the support of senior management and (ideally) the sponsorship of a board member are essential. Also, an implementation plan to address the concerns of employees and other stakeholders is needed. Although risk management is vital to the success of an organization, many managers may need to be persuaded that the suggested implementation approach is correct.

It is important to note that not all activities and functions undertaken by managers should be claimed by the risk manager as being undertaken in the name of risk management. Not all activities in the organization will be driven by risk management, even if all decisions, processes, procedures and activities have risks embedded within them.

Risk management is not just the brakes

There is a popular question amongst risk managers: 'why do cars have brakes?' The answer offered is that they enable the car to go faster. This implies that risk management should be viewed as the brakes on the activities of the organization. This is a wholly negative view that presents risk management in an unfavourable light.

Risk management is also an enabler of operations, tactics and strategy. Therefore, it is worth revisiting the above question. To continue the metaphor, risk management should, in fact, be seen as all three pedals in a car. Risk management as the brakes mitigates operational hazards and helps the organization avoid disruption, thereby enhancing operational efficiency.

The clutch pedal is concerned with changing gear in a car in the same way as projects implement the tactics in an organization. Therefore, risk management is also the clutch pedal in that it helps assist with the successful management of tactical change and the reduction of the associated uncertainty, so that the organization can achieve successful change.

Finally, the accelerator helps the car go faster and risk management fulfils this function by helping the organization embrace strategic opportunities and seek rewards – thereby ensuring that the organization designs and successfully implements a strategy that delivers exactly what is required.

Much of this book is concerned with risk management input in operations. It is likely that operations will be impacted by hazard risks and so the focus of risk management in relation to operations is on hazard management. In order to achieve the maximum benefit from risk management input in operations, organizations need instead, however, to focus on loss control. Loss control is a combination of loss prevention, damage limitation and cost containment.

Projects should be completed on time, to budget and to specification, performance or quality. Inevitably, there will be a considerable amount of uncertainty associated with all projects. The contribution of risk management is to minimize these uncertainties. Management of the risks within projects is a style of control management.

Risk management input into strategy focuses on the risk assessment of the various strategic options available to an organization. The contribution of risk management to successful strategy is, therefore, focused on the decision-making activities. Figure 15.2 illustrates the 4Es of opportunity management and plots risk exposure against potential reward. Organizations undertaking strategic risk management will complete a careful review of viable new business prospects and undertake detailed risk assessment before making strategic decisions.

The overall benefits of risk management can be summarized in a number of ways. By undertaking a risk management initiative, less disruption to operations, successful delivery of projects and better strategic decisions are the expectations. Also underpinning risk management initiatives will be the desire for adequate risk assurance. These components – mandatory, assurance, decision making and effective and efficient core processes – provide the acronym MADE2.

Using the structure of the FIRM risk scorecard, an organization will be able to demonstrate the benefits that it has obtained from a risk management initiative. It is likely that the following benefits will have been delivered to a theatre that has been pursuing a structured proactive enterprise risk management approach for about three years:

- financial benefits arising from better allocation of funds, monitoring of expenditure and reduced exposure to fraud;
- infrastructure benefits that have included fewer failures of the IT systems and reduced staff absence rates;
- reputational benefits from ethical sourcing policies and use of organic food in the restaurant, as well as successful niche productions in the theatre;
- marketplace benefits resulting in 89 per cent occupancy rates, up from 83 per cent three years ago, as well as increased spend in the theatre by patrons.

The theatre will continue to develop the risk management initiative and continue to obtain benefits. Risk management activities are now embedded within the management culture of the organization.

PART TWO
Approaches to risk management

LEARNING OUTCOMES FOR PART TWO

- describe the key stages in the risk management process and the main components of a risk management framework;
- state the key features of the best-established standards, including ISO 31000, the COSO ERM cube and the IRM standard;
- describe the scope and importance of establishing the context as the first stage in the risk management process;
- explain the importance of the relationship between the external context, internal context and the risk management context;
- discuss the main considerations when designing a risk register and the benefits associated with using a well-designed risk register and provide examples;
- explain the features of an enterprise-wide approach to risk management and the various available definitions of ERM;
- outline the steps required in order to achieve successful implementation of an enterprise risk management initiative;
- consider the changing face of risk management and the increasing importance of managing emerging risks.

PART TWO FURTHER READING

Bernstein, P (1998) *Against the Gods: The Remarkable Story of Risk*, **www.wiley.com**

British Standard BS 31100:2011 *Risk Management: Code of Practice and Guidance for the Implementation of BS ISO 31000*, **www.standardsuk.com**

COSO *Enterprise Risk Management: Integrated Framework* (2004), **www.coso.org**

COSO *Enterprise Risk Management – Integrating with Strategy and Performance* (2017), **www.coso.org**

International Standard ISO 31000:2018 *Risk management – Guidelines*, **www.iso.org**

ISO Guide 73:2009 *Risk Management: Vocabulary*, **www.iso.org**

PART TWO CASE STUDIES

United Utilities: Our risk management framework

We have developed a sophisticated approach to the assessment, management and reporting of risks, with a process aligned to ISO 31000:2009 and a well-established governance structure for the group board to review the nature and extent of the risks that the group faces and for the audit committee to review process effectiveness.

Our risk profile currently illustrates around 200 event-based risks. All event types (strategic, financial, operational, compliance and hazard) are considered in the context of our strategic themes (best service to customers; lowest sustainable cost; and responsible manner). For internal or external drivers, each event is assessed for the likelihood of occurrence and the negative financial or reputational impact on the company and its objectives, should the event occur.

Responsibility for the assessment and management of the risk (including monitoring and updating) is assigned to the appropriate individual manager who is also responsible for reporting on assessment, management and control/mitigation at least twice a year, in line with the reporting to the group board at full- and half-year statutory accounting reporting periods.

By their nature, event-based risks in the context of our strategic themes will include all combinations of high to low likelihood and high to low impact. Heat maps are typically used in various managerial and group reports either as a method to collectively evaluate the extent of all risks within a certain profile or to illustrate the effectiveness of mitigation for a single risk by plotting the gross, current (net of existing controls) and the selected target position in an individual risk statement.

Edited extract from United Utilities Group PLC
Annual Report and Financial Statements for the year ended 31 March 2015

Birmingham City Council: Scrutiny, accountability and risk management

The Council has had a risk management strategy since July 2002, and this is regularly updated. Leadership is provided to the risk management process by the director of legal and democratic services, who is the corporate governance champion and the deputy leader who is designated as the member corporate governance champion.

The Council has approached embedding of risk management in accordance with best practice guidance as a 'top-down' process, with a corporate risk register supported by directorate and divisional risk registers. Birmingham Audit continues to give presentations, provide training, facilitate workshops and provide guidance through the publication of a risk management toolkit which has been produced to give managers at all levels a better understanding of how to implement risk management in their area of responsibility and to have some understanding of the process up and down the City Council.

The toolkit provides a step-by-step approach to implementing risk management using the Council's methodology. The high-level risk management methodology has been reviewed to provide more focus to member and senior officer management of risk. The Council's whistleblowing policy was introduced in the late 1990s and is well publicized throughout the workforce.

The City Council has a strong internal audit function (Birmingham Audit) and well-established protocols for working with external audit. The Council's external auditors have responsibilities under the Code of Audit Practice to review compliance with policies, procedures, laws and regulations within their remit.

Edited extract from Birmingham City Council
Statement of Accounts 2013/14

Tsogo Sun: Risk management process

The Tsogo Sun board recognizes that the management of business risk is crucial to our continued growth and success and this can only be achieved if all three elements of risk – threat, uncertainty and opportunity – are recognized and managed in an integrated fashion.

The audit and risk committee is mandated by the board to establish, co-ordinate and drive the risk process throughout the group. It has overseen the establishment of a comprehensive risk management system to identify and manage significant risks in the operational divisions, business units and subsidiaries.

The systems of internal control are designed to manage rather than eliminate risk, and provide reasonable but not absolute assurance as to the integrity and reliability of the financial statements, the compliance with statutory laws and regulations, and to safeguard and maintain accountability of the group's assets.

In addition to the risk management processes embedded within the group, the group executive committee identifies, quantifies and evaluates the group's risks twice a year utilizing a facilitated risk assessment workshop. The severity of risks is measured in qualitative as well as quantitative terms, guided by the board's risk tolerance and risk appetite measures.

The risk profiles, with the risk responses, are reviewed by the audit and risk committee at least once every six months. In addition to the group risk assessment, risk matrices are prepared and presented to the audit and risk committee for each operational division. This methodology ensures that risks and opportunities are prioritized and cost-effective responses are designed and implemented to counter the effects of risks and take advantage of opportunities.

Edited extract from Tsogo Sun
Integrated Annual Report 2013

Risk management standards

06

Scope of risk management standards

There are a number of established risk management standards and frameworks. The first was developed by the standards body in Australia in 1995, and has been followed by those being developed in Canada, Japan, the UK and the United States. Standards have also been developed by other national standards bodies, as well as by government departments across the world.

The overall approach of each of these standards is similar. The standard that had the widest recognition was the Australian Standard AS 4360 (2004), but this was withdrawn in 2009 in favour of ISO 31000. The ERM version of the COSO cube is also widely applied in many organizations. British Standard BS 31100:2011 'Risk Management: Code of Practice and Guidance for the Implementation of BS ISO 31000' was published in 2011. Further guidance to the ISO standard was published in 2013 as ISO/TR 31004:2013 'Risk Management – Guidance for the Implementation of ISO 31000'.

The international standard ISO 31000 (2009), 'Risk Management: Principles and Guidelines', was published in the latter part of 2009. This ISO standard was recently updated, and the revised version was published in early 2018 as ISO 31000 (2018), 'Risk Management – Guidelines'. The requirements of this updated standard are considered later in this chapter. ISO 31000 has international recognition and is a highly influential risk management standard. Although some standards are better recognized than others, organizations should select the approach that is most relevant to their particular circumstances.

It is important to distinguish between a risk management standard and a risk management framework. A risk management standard sets out the overall approach to the successful management of risk, including a description of the risk management process, together with the suggested framework that supports that process.

In simple terms, a risk management standard is the combination of a description of the risk management process, together with the recommended framework. The key features of a risk management framework are described later in this chapter. Table 6.1 provides a summary of the most widely used risk management standards and frameworks.

One of the best-established and most widely used risk management standards was produced by the IRM in 2002 in co-operation with Airmic and Alarm. The IRM Standard is a high-level approach aimed at non-risk-management specialists and it has been translated into many languages. The Australian Standard and the COSO ERM cube are designed for use primarily by specialist risk management practitioners.

Table 6.1   Risk management standards

Standard	Description	Reference
ISO 31000	Standard published by the International Standards Organization (2018)	Figure 6.4
Institute of Risk Management (IRM)	Standard produced jointly by Airmic, Alarm and the IRM (2002)	Figure 6.1
COSO ERM cube	Framework produced by the Committee of Sponsoring Organizations of the Treadway Committee (2004)	Figure 6.3
CoCo (Criteria of Control)	Framework produced by the Canadian Institute of Chartered Accountants (1995)	Figure 33.1

The IRM Standard is available as a free download from the IRM website, and the risk management process used in it is reproduced in Figure 6.1.

For organizations listed on the New York Stock Exchange, the approach outlined in the COSO Internal Control framework, referred to in this text as the COSO Internal Control cube, originally published in 1992 and updated in 2013 is recognized by the Sarbanes–Oxley Act of 2002 (SOX). The requirements of SOX also apply to subsidiaries of US-listed companies around the world. Therefore, the COSO approach is internationally recognized and, in many circumstances, mandated. It is worth noting that SOX requires the approach described in the COSO Internal Control cube (2013). (This is not the same as the COSO ERM cube (2004), although the COSO ERM cube does contain all of the elements of the recently revised Internal Control version.)

For many stock exchanges, the greater emphasis in the listing requirements and associated corporate governance code is on internal control, rather than risk management. This emphasis was maintained in the 2010 version of the Combined Code, which has now been renamed the UK Corporate Governance Code, although the 2010 version did include several enhanced specific risk management requirements. Sections of the 2010 version of the UK Corporate Governance Code have been updated and the current version of the UK Corporate Governance Code is dated April 2016.

The COSO Internal Control cube (2013) has become the most widely used internal control framework in the United States and it has been adopted and/or adapted by numerous countries and businesses around the world. An enterprise risk management (ERM) version of the COSO cube was produced in 2004 and this has both risk management and internal control within its scope. Although COSO published an updated ERM framework in mid-2017, the structure of the COSO ERM cube (2004) continues to be used as the basis for many ERM initiatives, and this is acknowledged by COSO in the text box below. The 2004 COSO ERM cube is considered later in this chapter and the revised COSO ERM framework (2017) is discussed in Chapter 8.

Figure 6.1   IRM risk management process

The Risk Management Process

The Organization's
Strategic Objectives

Risk Assessment

Risk Analysis
Risk Identification
Risk Description
Risk Estimation

Risk Evaluation

Risk Reporting
Threats and Opportunities

Decision

Risk Treatment

Residual Risk Reporting

Monitoring

Modification

Formal Audit

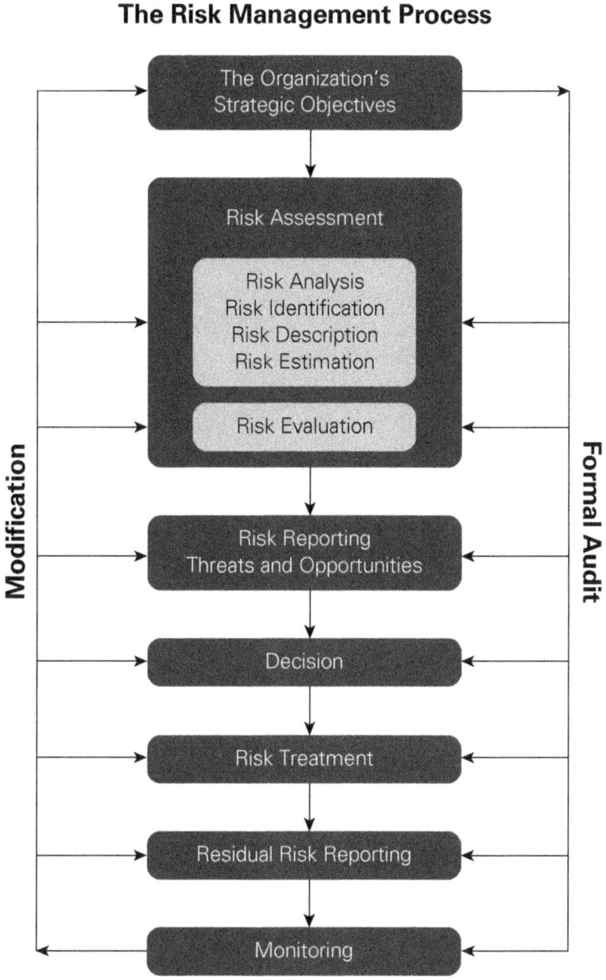

SOURCE IRM/Airmic/Alarm (2002).

COSO ERM cube (2004)

COSO acknowledges that there are many differing regulatory, stakeholder and industry requirements relating to ERM. As such, it is incumbent on management to determine if and how to adopt 'Enterprise Risk Management – Integrating with Strategy and Performance' to enhance the entity's ability to create, sustain and realize value.

The 'Internal Control – Integrated Framework' remains a viable and suitable framework for designing, implementing, conducting and assessing the effectiveness of internal control and for reporting.

> Since the adoption of the revised ERM framework is not mandatory, management may continue to utilize the 2004 'Enterprise Risk Management – Integrated Framework' (COSO ERM cube). However, COSO reserves the right to supersede or retire the 2004 ERM framework in the future.
>
> *Edited commentary from COSO, June 2017*

Apart from the British, ISO and COSO standards/frameworks, a number of others are also well regarded and in widespread use. The UK's risk guidance from the Financial Reporting Council (FRC) was updated in 2014 and is considered by the Securities and Exchange Commission (SEC) in the United States to be an acceptable alternative to the COSO Internal Control cube for Sarbanes–Oxley compliance. The updated risk guidance can be found as a free download from the website of the UK-based FRC.

As well as the established standards and frameworks, a considerable amount of guidance on risk management has been published by various government departments. HM Treasury in the UK has published the highly respected *Orange Book*, which contains a significant amount of useful information on risk management tools and techniques. Many of the ideas and concepts presented in the *Orange Book* are referenced throughout this volume.

Some of the available standards were developed by risk management professionals, whilst others were developed by accountants or auditors. There are three distinct approaches followed in the various standards:

- 'risk management' approach, followed by ISO 31000, British Standard BS 31100 and the IRM Standard;
- 'internal control' approach, developed by COSO Internal Control cube and by the FRC risk guidance;
- 'risk-aware culture' approach, developed by the Canadian Institute of Chartered Accountants, known as the CoCo framework.

Risk management process

A simple representation of the risk management process is provided by Figure 4.1 and a similar process is contained in all of the established risk management standards. Many of the standards distinguish between the risk management process and the framework that implements and supports the process. However, this distinction is not always clear in many of the established risk management standards/frameworks.

The best-established risk management approaches are the IRM Standard, ISO 31000, BS 31100, and the COSO ERM cube. All four provide a description of a risk management framework, but more emphasis is placed on the risk management process in the IRM Standard, ISO 31000 and BS 31100. The COSO approach does not provide the same clear distinction between the framework and the risk management process itself and is mainly concerned with framework considerations.

Several countries have developed their own internal control and risk management standards as part of their requirements for being listed on a stock exchange. Typically, these are frameworks similar to COSO Internal Control in approach, and this is certainly the case with the current FRC risk guidance requirements that exist in the UK.

Although there are many ways of representing the risk management process, the basic steps are all similar. There can be difficulties with the terminology that is used to describe the various steps, and Appendix B provides definitions of basic terms, as well as cross-referencing the different terminologies that can be used. Appendix C describes the stages involved in achieving successful risk management and this is structured in a plan–implement–measure–learn (PIML) format. This is very similar to the plan–do–check–act format followed in several international standards and often referred to as PDCA. PIML is intended to indicate a more structured and analytical approach.

Risk management context

There are many risk management standards and risk management frameworks that have been produced by various organizations. It is generally acknowledged that a standard is a document that produces information on both the risk management process and the risk management framework.

Within many risk management standards it is stated that risk management activities should take place within the context of the business environment, the organization and the risks faced by the organization. In order for the context to be described and defined, a framework is required to implement and support the risk management process. ISO 31000 places particular emphasis on context and states that consideration should be given to the internal context, external context and risk management context when undertaking risk management activities.

All of the established risk management standards refer to the risk management framework, although this is represented in different ways. In order to provide a simple explanation of the scope of the risk management framework, the acronym risk, architecture, strategy and protocols (RASP) has been developed. Figure 6.2 illustrates the key features of a risk management framework that is built around and supports the risk management process. The RASP approach is entirely consistent with the concept of the risk management context or risk management framework described in ISO 31000.

Part Five of this book describes the risk architecture, strategy and protocols (RASP) in more detail. It is these elements that define the framework within which the risk management process takes place. These three components of risk architecture, strategy and protocols are required for successful risk management activities. There needs to be a clear understanding of the risk management process, followed by a clear definition of the framework that supports the process. Because the framework is a supportive structure, it is shown in Figure 6.2 as a series of components built around and supporting the risk management process.

Figure 6.2   Components of the RM context

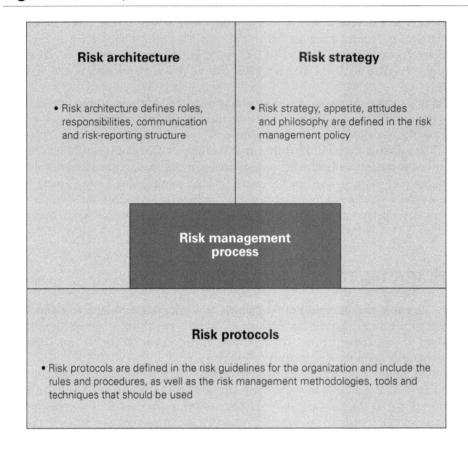

In implementing and supporting the risk management process, the risk management framework needs to facilitate communication and the flow of risk information. The risk management framework has two separate considerations. Firstly, it must be supportive of the risk management process and, secondly, it must ensure that the outputs from the process are communicated into the organization and achieve the anticipated benefits for the organization. If an organization decides to follow the structure of the IRM Risk Management Standard, it would then have to set up a framework that includes the structure, responsibilities, administration, reporting and communication components of risk management. All of these procedures will then be recorded in a risk management manual.

COSO ERM cube

An Enterprise Risk Management (ERM) version of the COSO cube was produced in 2004 and this has both risk management and internal control within its scope. Details of the COSO ERM cube are provided on the COSO website and there is a free download of the executive summary of COSO ERM cube. The approach adopted by the COSO ERM cube suggests that enterprise risk management is not strictly a serial set of activities, where one component affects only the next. It is considered to be a multidirectional, iterative process in which almost any component can and does influence all other components.

In the COSO ERM cube, there is a direct relationship between objectives, which are what an entity strives to achieve, and enterprise risk management components, which represent what is needed to achieve them. The relationship is depicted in a three-dimensional matrix, in the form of a cube, and this is reproduced as Figure 6.3.

The COSO ERM cube is a very influential risk management framework and it consists of eight interrelated components. These are derived from the way management runs an enterprise and are integrated with the management process. A brief description of the components of the COSO ERM cube is set out in Table 6.2.

The description of the COSO ERM cube includes the statement that: 'within the context of the established mission or vision of an organization, management establishes strategic objectives, selects strategy and sets aligned objectives cascading through the enterprise.' COSO has recently published additional guidance on ERM and how it can be integrated with strategy and performance and this guidance is reviewed in

Figure 6.3 COSO ERM cube

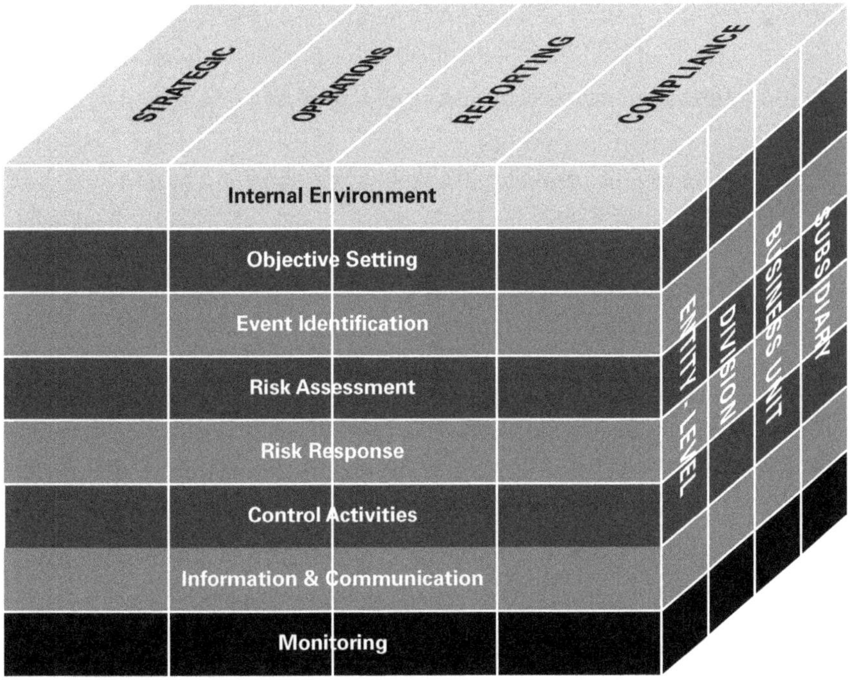

SOURCE COSO Enterprise Risk Management: Integrated Framework,

Table 6.2   COSO ERM cube

Internal environment – The internal environment encompasses the tone of
an organization and sets the basis for how risk is viewed and addressed.

Objective setting – Objectives must exist before management can identify potential
events affecting their achievement.

Event identification – Internal and external events affecting achievement of objectives
must be identified, distinguishing between risks and opportunities.

Risk assessment – Risks are analysed, considering likelihood and impact, as a basis for
determining how they should be managed.

Risk response – Management selects risk responses: avoiding, accepting, reducing, or
sharing risk.

Control activities – Policies and procedures are established and implemented to help
ensure the risk responses are effectively carried out.

Information and communication – Relevant information is identified, captured,
and communicated so that people can fulfil their responsibilities.

Monitoring – The entirety of enterprise risk management is monitored and
modifications made as necessary.

Chapter 8. This approach to enterprise risk management is geared to achieving corporate objectives, set out in four risk categories:

- strategic: high-level goals, aligned with and supporting its mission;
- operations: effective and efficient use of its resources;
- reporting: reliability of reporting;
- compliance: compliance with applicable laws and regulations.

Revised ISO 31000 (2018)

The main risk management standards that have been developed are the IRM
Standard, ISO 31000, British Standard BS 31100 and the COSO ERM cube. British
Standard BS 31100:2011, entitled 'Risk Management: Code of Practice and
Guidance for the Implementation of BS ISO 31000', was published in 2011. It
emphasizes the requirement for a risk management framework to support the separately described risk management process. In particular, British Standard BS
31100 states that the risk management process should provide a systematic, effective and efficient way by which risks can be managed at different levels throughout
the organization.

The risk management framework is described in the British Standard in some
detail. In fact, most of the standard is made up of a description of the risk management framework, together with a detailed part on how to develop risk management

activities. Part of the reason for updating the original BS 31100:2008 was to align it more closely with the 2009 version of ISO 31000. Therefore, the diagrams used in BS 31100:2011 are very similar, and in some cases identical, to those used in the 2009 version of ISO 31000.

ISO 31000:2018 is in the same format as the previous version of ISO 31000 dated 2009. The standard provides a statement of risk management principles, as well as a description of the risk management framework and process. A revised list of the principles of risk management is provided and these principles are centred around the central purpose of risk management, which is stated as the 'creation and protection of value'. A summary of these eight principles is set out below:

1 Risk management is an integral part of all organizational activities.

2 Structured and comprehensive approach is required.

3 Framework and processes should be customized and proportionate.

4 Appropriate and timely involvement of stakeholders is necessary.

5 Risk management anticipates, detects, acknowledges and responds to changes.

6 Risk management explicitly considers any limitations of available information.

7 Human and cultural factors influence all aspects of risk management.

8 Risk management is continually improved through learning and experience.

The revised standard also provides information on the development of a risk management framework. The framework is presented as a continuous improvement model similar to the plan, implement, measure and learn (PIML) model discussed throughout this book. The detailed information in the standard describes the necessary features of the risk management framework that are required in order to achieve continuous improvement. The text box below describes the overall approach taken by ISO in producing the revised standard.

Establishing the context remains the first stage of the risk management process, as described in ISO 31000. The requirements are described slightly differently in the 2018 version of ISO 31000, compared to the 2009 version. Establishing the context is presented in the diagram of the process as 'scope, context, criteria'. The components of establishing the context are described as defining the purpose and scope of risk management activities, followed by establishing the external, internal and risk management context, followed by defining the risk criteria. Defining the risk criteria involves specifying the amount and type of risk that the organization may or may not take, relative to objectives.

The diagram used to illustrate the risk management process in ISO 31000 is reproduced in Figure 6.4. It could be argued that Figure 6.4 contains elements of the risk management framework, as well as the key stages of the risk management process. An interesting point to note is that the risk management process is not shown as a series of activities or stages with connecting arrows. In this regard, the new representation of the process in ISO 31000 is similar to the approach taken by the COSO ERM cube in presenting the eight components of ERM. ISO 31000 acknowledges this similarity by stating the following: 'Although the risk management process is often presented as sequential, in practice it is iterative.'

ISO 31000:2018

A lot of the complicated language has been eliminated, so the text is leaner and more precise with the expectation that the reader will find it simpler to understand. The new draft is shorter, but it gains in clarity and precision and is much easier to read. It also includes some substantial improvements, such as the importance of human and cultural factors in achieving an organization's objectives and an emphasis on embedding risk management within the decision-making process. That said, the overall message of ISO 31000 remains the same – integrating the management of risk into a strategic and operational management system.

Edited extract from ISO website, www.iso.org

Figure 6.4 RM process from ISO 31000 (2018)

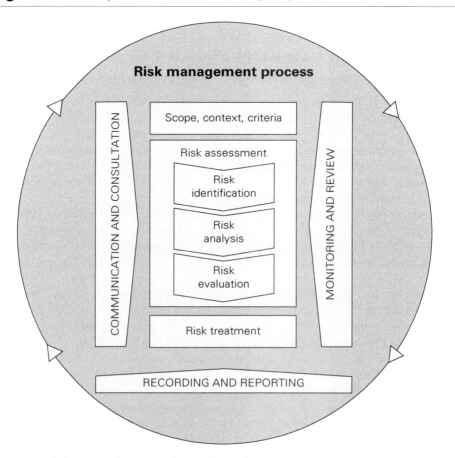

SOURCE Permission to reproduce extracts from British Standards is granted by BSI Standards Limited (BSI). No other use of this material is permitted. British Standards can be obtained in PDF or hard copy formats from the BSI online shop: www.bsigroup.com/Shop.

In addition to risk management standards, there are also a number of internal control standards in existence. These internal control frameworks have a different emphasis and are outside the scope of this book, with the exception of the Criteria of Control (CoCo) framework produced by the Canadian Institute of Chartered Accountants. The approach in CoCo is based on the evaluation of the culture or the internal control environment of the organization and is considered in more detail in Chapter 33.

In addition to developing ISO 31000 and the guide to risk management terminology, Guide 73, work has also been completed on a guide to risk assessment techniques. ISO/IEC 31010 'Risk Management: Risk Assessment Techniques' is a very comprehensive publication and it reflects current good practices in the selection and utilization of risk assessment techniques.

Standards institutions around the world have a requirement for routine review of standards, typically every four years. Therefore, the existing standards, as well as those additional standards that are being developed, will be subject to review on a regular basis. This will ensure that the advice and guidance given in the various standards will remain up-to-date and in line with current practice.

Updating of RM terminology

There is considerable benefit in adopting an established risk management standard, but it is undoubtedly the case that organizations will need to change and adapt the detailed requirements of any existing standard to their specific circumstances and/or external, internal and risk management contexts. Greater acceptance of a risk management approach within an organization will be achieved when the approach has been customized specifically for the organization by the organization itself.

An important part of customizing the approach to risk management is to establish the risk terminology to be used throughout the organization. There is considerable variation in the terminology used in different branches of the risk management profession and Appendix B includes alternative definitions for many terms. ISO itself has published two separate guides to risk-related vocabulary: ISO Guide 73:2009 'Risk Management – Vocabulary' and ISO/IEC Guide 51:2014 'Safety Aspects – Guidelines for their inclusion in standards'. It is interesting to note that Guide 73 is a for sale publication, whereas Guide 51 is a free download from the ISO website (www.iso.org).

Following the recent revision of ISO 31000, ISO is currently (April 2018) undertaking a review of Guide 73. In fact, the process of reviewing the terms and definitions has already commenced as several modified definitions are included in ISO 31000:2018. It is, perhaps, around the Guide 73 definition of risk as 'effect of uncertainty on objectives' that most discussion will occur. ISO 31000, in a note to the definition of risk, already acknowledges that 'risk is usually expressed in terms of risk sources, potential events, their consequences and their likelihood'.

As various organizations update their terms and definitions, there is a clear shift towards ensuring that any definition of risk includes a consideration of opportunities or the upside of risk. King IV (2016) states its position as follows:

King IV's understanding of risk thus balances the traditional, negative view of risk with one that recognizes the potential opportunities inherent in some risks. Thus, an opportunity may present itself as the potential upside of risk that could adversely affect the achievement of organizational objectives.

Significant difficulties could result from a definition that attaches risk to objectives. These difficulties arise from the fact that the objectives themselves may be incorrect. It could be argued that one of the causes of the global financial crisis in 2008 was that financial institutions had successfully achieved aggressive and ambitious objectives for many years and the successful achievement of these objectives led to financial instability. The definition of risk included in the new COSO ERM framework (2017) is set out in the text box below and it identifies the problem of incorrect objectives. The definition recognizes the dangers associated with seeking to implement strategy and objectives that are not aligned with the mission, vision and values of the organization.

Definitions underpin risk management standards; therefore, the challenge for standards organizations is to ensure that the risk management standards they publish are relevant to the future success of the organization. COSO has taken the approach, in publishing the new ERM framework (2017), that greater consideration should be paid to stakeholder expectations and the relationship between risk and strategy, as demonstrated in the text box below.

Definition and scope of 'risk'

Some of the most significant organizational failures in recent times have occurred when a strategy is selected that does not align with the mission, vision and core values of an entity. Further, even if that alignment is established, many organizations do not understand the implications of the selected strategy on their risk profile. Also, minor operational failures can escalate and threaten longer-term viability.

The revised framework elevates and expands the discussion of strategy and risk by focusing on the following three concepts:

- possibility of strategy and business objectives not aligning with mission, vision and values;
- implications from the strategy chosen; and
- risk of executing the strategy.

By distinguishing the three potential manifestations of risk impacting strategy, the framework provides a more detailed analysis and recognition of the role and importance of enterprise risk management.

Edited extract from the COSO website, www.coso.org

Establishing the context

07

Scope of the context

ISO 31000 states that the first stage in the risk management process is to establish the context, which is shown in Figure 6.4 as 'scope, context, criteria'. The former Australian Standard AS 4360 referred to context as having three components, in addition to the risk management process. These components are the risk management context, internal context and external context. The relationship between the three contexts is illustrated in Figure 7.1.

The three components of context may be considered as follows:

- *Risk management context* has already been described as the risk architecture, strategy and protocols or the risk management framework within the organization. This framework must fulfil two functions: 1) provide support for the risk management process within the organization; and 2) ensure that the outputs from the risk management process are communicated to internal and external stakeholders.

- *Internal context* refers to the organization itself, the activities it undertakes, the range of skills and capabilities available within the organization, and how it is structured. Internal stakeholders and their expectations are part of the internal context. This may be considered to be the strengths and weaknesses within the organization.

- *External context* is the environment within which the organization exists. This environment will include consideration of the business sector within which the organization operates, external stakeholders and their expectations and the external financial environment. This may be considered to be the opportunities and threats facing the organization.

The nature and extent of the risk management process is a major consideration when establishing the context for risk management. The key question is what the risk management process is expected to achieve or the answer to the question of why the organization has risk management activities in place. The risk management context also includes consideration of who will be responsible and identifies the resources that will be required in order to fulfil risk management activities.

Another important consideration within the risk management context is the establishment of risk appetite or risk criteria. This will help the organization decide what controls should be put in place and whether the residual or current level of risk

Figure 7.1   Three components of context

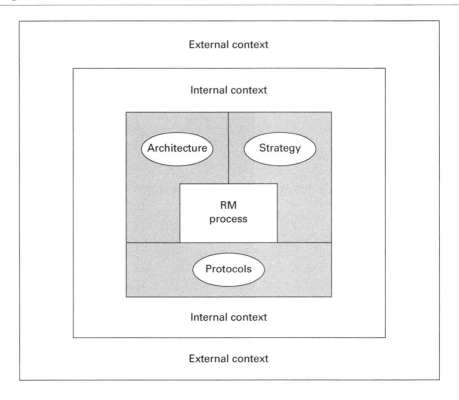

Shows the risk management context

is acceptable. The risk management context should also provide a means of establishing the overall total risk exposure so that this can be compared with the risk appetite of the organization and the capacity of the organization to withstand risk.

The internal context is about the culture of the organization, the resources that are available, receiving outputs from the risk management process and ensuring that these influence behaviours, and supporting and providing governance of risk and risk management. The internal context concerns objectives, the capacity and capabilities of the organization, as well as the business core processes that are in place. An important consideration regarding the internal context is how the organization makes decisions.

The external context is about stakeholder expectations, industry regulations and regulators, the behaviour of competitors and the general economic environment within which the organization operates. The external context also considers the drivers and trends that can affect the success of the organization and its ability to achieve objectives.

External context

Risk management standard ISO 31000 identifies 'establish the context' as the first stage in the risk management process. Establishing the context is represented in the ISO 31000 diagram, and reproduced as Figure 6.4, as 'scope, context, criteria.' Establishing the context is a fundamentally important aspect of successful risk management, and it is also identified by other international standards as an essential early stage in implementing a management system standard. For example, quality standard ISO 9001:2015 also identifies context as being part of the strategic planning that an organization must undertake.

There are three levels to establishing the context for risk management activity, and these are related to the external context, internal context and the risk management context. Establishing the external context must take account of the expectations of external stakeholders. The critical importance of stakeholder expectations is considered in more detail in Chapter 29.

For many organizations, the most important group of external stakeholders will be customers. The external context for an organization will be significantly influenced by the nature of the customers and the products or services that they are being offered. Consideration of customers and the customer offering form an important part of the business model for the organization and the relevance of the business model to risk management is considered in more detail in Chapter 20.

Having identified the expectations of external stakeholders, including consideration of customers and the services and products offered to customers, an organization can then view in more detail the factors that influence the external context for the organization. The FIRM risk scorecard provides a structure for carrying out a detailed evaluation of the context of the organization. The reputational and marketplace components of the FIRM risk scorecard are primarily related to the external context and the finances and infrastructure components are primarily related to the internal context.

Table 14.2 provides a detailed checklist of questions relating to the development of a riskiness index based on the structure of the FIRM risk scorecard. In summary, the reputational component of the external context for an organization defines the external perception of the organization and the desire of customers to trade with the organization and the level of customer retention. In particular, when evaluating the reputational component of the external context, the following issues should be addressed:

- public perception of the industry sector in which the organization operates;
- corporate social responsibility standards achieved by the organization;
- governance standards and whether the sector is highly regulated;
- quality of products or services and/or after-sales service standards.

The other component of the FIRM risk scorecard relevant to the external environment is the marketplace and the level of presence of the organization within the marketplace. This will impact the level of customer trade or expenditure. In particular, when evaluating the marketplace component of the external environment, the following issues should be addressed:

- level of revenue generation in the marketplace and return on investment;
- presence of aggressive competitors and/or high customer expectations;
- level of economic stability, including exposure to interest rates and foreign exchange rates;
- complexity of the supply chain and volatility of raw material costs;
- exposure to international disruption because of political risks, war and terrorism.

The FIRM risk scorecard offers one mechanism for evaluating the external context of the organization, but other structures may be employed, such as a strengths, weaknesses, opportunities and threats (SWOT) analysis or the use of one of the risk classification systems discussed in Chapter 11. The overall purpose of evaluating the external context is to determine the level of riskiness associated with the external environment within which the organization operates. This will enable the organization to validate the existing business model and develop strategy for the future, together with the tactics for implementing that strategy.

External stakeholders

Good stewardship by the board should not inhibit sensible risk taking that is critical to growth. However, the assessment of risks as part of the normal business planning process should support better decision taking, ensure that the board and management respond promptly to risks when they arise, and ensure that shareholders and other stakeholders are well informed about the principal risks and prospects of the company. The board's responsibility for the organization's culture is essential to the way in which risk is considered and addressed within the organization and with external stakeholders.

FRC risk guidance
September 2014

Internal context

Establishing the internal context of an organization must take account of the expectations of internal stakeholders. There will be a range of internal stakeholders, but the most important group will be the people on whom the organization directly depends. This will include members of staff and people providing services on an outsourced, contracted and/or supplier basis.

Having identified the expectations of internal stakeholders, including identification of the importance of these stakeholders to the operations and compliance activities of the organization, it will then be possible to view in more detail the factors that influence the internal context. The FIRM risk scorecard provides a structure for carrying out a detailed evaluation of the context of the organization. The financial and infrastructure components of the FIRM risk scorecard are primarily related to the internal context and the reputational and marketplace components are primarily related to the external context.

Table 14.2 provides a detailed checklist of questions related to the development of a riskiness index based on the structure of the FIRM risk scorecard. In summary, the financial component of the internal context of an organization defines the financial procedures and the means by which money is managed and profitability is achieved. In particular, when evaluating the financial component of the internal context, the following issues should be addressed:

- availability of adequate funds to fulfil strategic plans;
- existence of robust procedures for correct allocation of funds for investment;
- nature of internal financial control environment to prevent fraud;
- availability of funds to meet historical and anticipated future liabilities.

The other component of the FIRM risk scorecard relevant to the internal context is infrastructure, as this influences the nature of the processes undertaken within the organization. Infrastructure risks define the level of inefficiency and dysfunction that may arise during internal processes. In particular, when evaluating the infrastructure component of the internal context, the following issues should be addressed:

- senior management structure and the nature of the risk culture;
- availability of adequate people resources and people skills, including intellectual property;
- availability of adequate physical assets to support operational activities;
- information technology infrastructure sufficient to achieve resilience and protect data;
- business continuity plans in place to ensure continuity of activities following major disruption;
- arrangements for service delivery and/or transportation and reliable communication infrastructure.

The FIRM risk scorecard offers one mechanism for evaluating the internal context of an organization, but other approaches may be employed, including a SWOT analysis. Many organizations use the political, economic, social, technological, legal and environmental/ethical (PESTLE) risk classification system. The PESTLE risk classification system is considered in more detail in Chapter 11. Some components of the PESTLE risk classification system are related to the external context, some are related to the internal context and other components are relevant to both external and internal contexts.

There are many checklists available that will enable an organization to identify the nature of the external and internal context within which it operates. Which classification system or checklist of questions is used is less important than the need to identify the full range of risk issues faced by the organization. This will enable the organization to validate the existing business model, the resources required to deliver the business model, as well as the level of resilience within the existing business model.

Risk management context

Chapter 21 considers the risk management context in detail, in terms of the risk architecture, strategy and protocols (RASP) developed by the organization. The RASP of an organization defines the structure of the risk management context and how the components of that context are implemented to achieve the desired benefits from the enterprise risk management initiative.

It is important that the risk management context of an organization is capable of delivering the required risk management strategy and develop the necessary risk-aware culture. The components of a satisfactory risk-aware culture are leadership, involvement, learning, accountability and communication (LILAC), as considered in more detail in Chapter 24.

An important component of the risk management context is the mandate provided by senior management that provides the scope and level of authority for undertaking risk management activities in the organization. The mandate provided to the risk manager, head of internal audit and others involved in the risk management initiative should be defined in the risk management policy for the organization.

The risk attitude and risk appetite of the organization, as defined by the risk criteria for different types of risks, helps to define the risk management context of the organization and to provide the basis for undertaking risk assessments and recording the results in the risk register. The nature and extent of communication of the information contained in the risk register throughout the risk architecture of the organization also helps define the risk management context.

Perhaps the most important feature of the risk management context that will determine the success of the enterprise risk management initiative relates to how the initiative is implemented. Appendix C provides an outline of an implementation guide for an enterprise risk management initiative in terms of planning, implementing, measuring and learning (PIML).

The risk management context must contribute to the success of the organization and be supportive of the delivery of stakeholder expectations, both external and internal. A requirement of the risk management context is that it should identify emerging risks and support the response to changes in the external and internal context of the organization. The nature of emerging risks can be complex and, by definition, highly unpredictable.

In helping the organization identify the nature of emerging risks, the risk management context should provide the mechanism for providing early warning. This has been described as the 'risk radar' of the organization and it must include timely review and evaluation of information relating to emerging risks. In order to comprehensively determine the specific impact and consequences for the organization, the mechanism for identifying emerging risks should also include provision for identifying opportunities that may be exploited in the future.

In summary, the organization is required to identify each specific external, internal and risk management context issue that could impact the organization, acquire and evaluate timely knowledge and information about them, evaluate the risks and opportunities that these context factors present and take appropriate actions to mitigate the risks and embrace the opportunities. All of this must be documented within the scope of the risk architecture, strategy and protocols (RASP).

Designing a risk register

The use of risk registers has become established practice for many risk managers. There are disadvantages associated with the use of risk registers, including the danger that the information recorded in the risk register will not be used in a dynamic way. The risk register could become a static record of risk status, rather than the risk action plan for the organization.

A risk register is defined in the ISO Guide 73 as the 'document used for recording risk management process for identified risks'. The guide adds that the purpose of the risk register is to facilitate ownership and management of each risk. Typically, the risk register will cover the significant risks facing the organization or the project. It will record the results of the risk assessment related to the process, operation, location, business unit or project under consideration.

When a risk assessment is undertaken of strategic options, it is more usual for the risk assessment to be used as part of decision-making activities. Typically, this information will not be recorded in the format of a risk register, but will be presented to the decision maker as part of the full range of information available for making that strategic decision.

The purpose of the risk register is to form an agreed record of the significant risks that have been identified. Also, the risk register will serve as a record of the control activities that are currently undertaken. It will also be a record of the additional actions that are proposed to improve the control of the particular risk.

Other information about risks will also be included in the risk register. Although there is no fixed format for this document, Table 7.1 provides an outline of a basic format for a risk register. It may not be necessary to include all of the risk description information set out in the table in the risk register, as this could make it a complex and clumsy document.

Risk registers can be compiled in a number of formats, depending on the type of risk assessment that is being recorded. Table 7.2 provides an example of a partially completed risk register for a sports club and Table 7.3 provides an example of a risk register for a hospital.

At its most simple, the risk register can be stored as a document held on a computer. However, there are many more sophisticated forms of risk registers, including records of significant risks held on databases. Where quantification of exposure is required, then a simple risk register held as a document is unlikely to be sufficient. This is true of systems for recording operational risks, where quantification of risk exposure is required.

Table 7.1 Format for a basic risk register

| Risk index | Risk description | Current level of risk | | | Controls in place |
		Likelihood	Magnitude	Overall rating	
1	Serious traffic accident involving the transport of fuel/explosives. Anticipate fatalities and evacuation of 1 km radius, depending on substances involved. Potential for release of up to 30 tonnes of liquid fuel into local environment.	Low	High	Medium	Police emergency plans Highway Agency plans Local authority emergency plan Company emergency response Liaison with the families of staff Notification to customers
2	Storm-force winds affecting transport routes for up to six hours. Anticipate that most roads in the vicinity will be closed or restricted. Journey times will be extended and late deliveries probable.	Medium	Medium	Medium	Police emergency plans Highway Agency plans Investigate weather forecast Liaison with the families of staff Notification to customers

Table 7.2 Risk register for a sports club

Risk index	Risk description	Existing control measures	Current level	Further actions planned	Owner
Financial risks					
1.1	Insufficient funds for suitable new players.		High		
1.2	Pension fund inadequate to meet liabilities.		Medium		
Infrastructure risks					
2.1	Loss of highly respected young manager.		High		
2.2	Building of the new stadium is delayed.		Low		
Reputational risks					
3.1	Complaints that merchandise is too expensive.		Low		
3.2	Club supporters riot at an away game.		Medium		
Marketplace risks					
4.1	New range of merchandise is unattractive.		High		
4.2	Fans favour other activities rather than club attendance.		Low		

Using a risk register

A well-constructed and dynamic risk register is at the heart of a successful risk management initiative. However, there is a danger that the risk register may become a static document that records the status of risk management activities at a moment in time. The practical implications of this are that senior management may consider that attending a risk assessment workshop and producing a risk

Table 7.3 Risk register for a hospital

Risk index	Risk description	Current level of risk			Risk rating
		Likelihood	Magnitude	Overall rating	
1	The roofs on operating theatres 3 and 4 are leaking because of poor condition, resulting in disruption to the surgery lists and non-achievement of waiting times.	High	High	High	Ingress of water can lead to loss of theatre facility, with cancelled operations, loss of key activity and threat to waiting time targets. With high incidence of rain, it is likely that between one and seven days' surgery time will be lost. Problems in the last two years suggest that the failure will occur twice per year.
2	Progress towards achievement of standards in children's care will remain unsatisfactory due to failure to implement action plan for improved facilities, resulting in children receiving care below the national standards.	Medium	Medium	Medium	The perception of patients of the current environment is good and the level of care provided is good. Robust action needs to be taken to ensure that standards do not become unsatisfactory.

register fulfils their risk management obligations and no ongoing actions are required.

It is better to think of the risk register as a risk action plan that records the status of the organization with respect to risk management, but also provides a record of the critical controls that are in place, together with the details of any additional controls that need to be introduced. In producing such a risk action plan, the responsibility for undertaking the actions identified will be clearly established.

Chapter 26 considers the options for the use of a risk management information system (RMIS) to record the information held in the risk register. Also, the information held in the risk register may be available on the intranet of the organization, and this will help with risk understanding and communication. In some organizations, the risk register is given the status of a controlled document to be used by internal audit as one of the key reference documents for undertaking an audit of risk management activities.

Even if this is not the case, the information set out in the risk register should be very carefully considered and constructed. For example, the risks set out in the register need to be precisely defined so that the cause, source, event, magnitude and impact of any risk event can be clearly identified. Also, the existing control activities, together with any additional controls that are proposed, must be described in precise terms and accurately recorded.

Risk control activities should be described in sufficient detail for the controls to be auditable. This is especially important when the risk register relates to the routine operations undertaken by the organization. Risk registers should also be produced for projects and to support strategic decisions.

A project risk register has to be a very dynamic document. An example of a project risk register is provided in Table 7.4. Details of the risks faced by the project, as recorded in the risk register, should be discussed at every project review meeting. As well as risk registers being relevant to projects, they should also support business decisions. In this case, the precise format of a risk register may be less formal. When a strategic decision has to be taken at board level, the risk assessment of that strategy should be attached to the proposal. This risk assessment could include both the risks of undertaking the strategy and an analysis of the risks associated with not undertaking the proposed strategy.

Finally, a risk register should be attached to a business plan as a record of the risks that could impact the achievement of that plan. Table 7.5 shows a partially completed simple risk register in a format that could be attached to a business plan. Simple examples of the risks that could result in the business plan not being achieved are set out in this illustration.

For example, a sports club may wish to record risks to reputation in the risk register. There could be particular concerns regarding the reputation of the club, so that the board will require a detailed evaluation of the reputational risks related to:

- success on the pitch;
- legal compliance;
- supply of ethical goods at a fair price.

Table 7.4 Project risk register

| Risk index | Risk description | Current level of risk | | | Action to be taken |
		Likelihood	Magnitude	Overall rating	
1	Project management arrangements unable to deliver project.	High	High	High	Clear project management structure in place, with executive team established to oversee project. Smaller project team runs project on day-to-day basis with expert support, as required. Clear links between various management functions to ensure co-ordinated approach.
2	Project resources inadequate with insufficient staff to support project.	Medium	Medium	Medium	Project management team established with support from other staff departments, including HR and Finance.
3	Project resources has insufficient funds for the necessary external professional technical advice.	Low	High	Medium	Sufficient budget identified to fund external advice.
4	Project not co-ordinated with other developments in organization.	Low	Low	Low	Project management team also oversees related projects with cross-representation on other groups.

Table 7.5 Risk register attached to a business plan

Risk index	Circumstance	Assessment and controls	Current level of risk			Action and assurance
			Likelihood	Magnitude	Overall risk	
1.1	Loss of grant funding		High			Negotiations are in hand and final settlement figure should soon be notified.
1.2	Job upgrade costs		Medium			Provision has been made in reserves and any additional costs will be met from existing budgets.
1.3	Overtime claims		Medium			Heads of department should enforce the rules concerning overtime payments as a result of job upgrades.
1.4	Mileage claims		Low			Heads of department should ensure that only essential journeys are undertaken.

When considering reputational issues, the level of control that is required will be evaluated, together with responsibility for managing the brand. The club will also make sure that existing controls and any additional controls are described in a way that will ensure that implementation of the controls can be fully audited.

The board will probably wish to see the risk register on at least a quarterly basis, and more frequently if significant changes occur. This will ensure that the risk register remains a dynamic document and is kept fully up to date. It will also ensure the necessary actions are taken and reported to the board.

Enterprise risk management 08

Enterprise-wide approach

In the past few years, there have been important developments in the practice of risk management. Firstly, there has been the development of specialist branches of risk management, including project, energy, finance, operational risk and clinical risk management. Secondly, organizations have embraced the desire to take a broader approach to the practice of risk management.

Various terms have been used to describe this broader approach, including holistic, integrated, strategic and enterprise-wide risk management. It is the term enterprise or enterprise-wide risk management (ERM) that is now the most widely used and generally accepted terminology for this broader approach. The fundamental idea behind the ERM approach is to move away from the practice of risk management as the separate management of individual risks.

ERM takes a unifying, broader and more integrated approach. The ERM approach means that an organization looks at all the risks that it faces across all of the operations that it undertakes. ERM is concerned with the management of the risks that can impact the objectives, key dependencies or core processes of the organization. Also, ERM is concerned with the management of opportunities, as well as the management of control and hazard risks.

There has also been consideration of the fact that many risks are interrelated and that traditional risk management fails to address the relationship between risks. With the ERM approach, the relationship between risks is identified by the fact that two or more risks can have an impact on the same activity or objective. The ERM approach is based on looking at the objective, key dependency or core process and evaluating all of the risks that could impact the item being evaluated.

Organizations practise risk management in a number of different ways. However, there are many common features to most of these approaches. Table 8.1 gives an overview of the features of enterprise risk management as a comparison to the silo-based approach whereby risk management tools and techniques are applied to different types of risks independently. Enterprise risk management has become the established means of undertaking risk management activities within most organizations. This allows the organization to gain an overview of all the risks that it faces so that it can take co-ordinated actions to manage these risks. Nevertheless, the specialist risk management functions, such as health and safety and business continuity continue to make a valuable contribution.

Table 8.1   Features of an enterprise-wide approach

1	Encompasses all areas of organizational exposure to risk (financial, operational, reporting, compliance, governance, strategic, reputational, etc).
2	Prioritizes and manages those exposures as an interrelated risk portfolio rather than as individual 'silos' of risk.
3	Evaluates the risk portfolio in the context of all significant internal and external contexts, systems, circumstances and stakeholders.
4	Recognizes that individual risks across the organization are interrelated and can create a combined exposure that differs from the sum of the individual risks.
5	Provides a structured process for the management of all risks, whether those risks are primarily quantitative or qualitative in nature.
6	Seeks to embed risk management as a component in all critical decisions throughout the organization.
7	Provides a means for the organization to identify the risks that it is willing to take in order to achieve strategic objectives.
8	Constructs a means of communicating on risk issues, so that there is a common understanding of the risks faced by the organization, and their importance.
9	Supports the activities of internal audit by providing a structure for the provision of assurance to the board and audit committee.
10	Views the effective management of risk as a competitive advantage that contributes to the achievement of business and strategic objectives.

An example of the ERM approach is to consider a sports club where the core process is to maximize attendance at games. This process is made up of several activities, including marketing, advertising, allocation and sale of tickets as well as logistical arrangements to ensure that the experience at the game is as good as possible. Part of maximizing attendance at games will be to ensure there are adequate parking and transport arrangements, together with suitable catering and other welfare arrangements in the ground.

By identifying the key activities that deliver the selected core process, the club is able to identify the risks that could impact both these activities and the core process. Targets can then be set for increased attendance at future games, and responsibility for the success of this core process has been allocated to the commercial director of the club. A consideration of the opportunities for increasing attendance at games can also be included in this broader approach.

Definitions of ERM

Table 8.2 presents a number of suggested definitions of enterprise risk management. There are three components that are required in a comprehensive definition of the ERM process. These are: 1) the description of the process that underpins enterprise risk management; 2) identification of the outputs of that process; and 3) the impact (or benefit) that arises from those outputs.

Many of the definitions concentrate on the process by describing the activities that make up the ERM approach. This is a good starting point, but the outputs from that process are more important than the process itself. Some of the definitions do include reference to the outputs from the process, such as being able to manage risks within the risk appetite of the organization and provide reasonable assurance regarding the achievement of objectives.

To be comprehensive, however, the definition must also consider the intended impact of those outputs. In summary, the intended outputs from ERM are that better decisions will be taken, improved core processes will be identified and introduced, possibly by way of tactics that include projects or programmes of work, and operations will be effective, efficient and free from unplanned disruption. This list of outputs from enterprise risk management can be described as mandatory obligations fulfilled, assurance obtained, decision making enhanced and effective and efficient core processes introduced (MADE2).

Table 8.2   Definitions of enterprise risk management

Organization	Definition of enterprise risk management
RIMS	Enterprise risk management is a strategic business discipline that supports the achievement of an organization's objectives by addressing the full spectrum of its risks and managing the combined impact of those risks as an interrelated risk portfolio.
COSO	Enterprise risk management is a process, effected by an entity's board of directors, management and other personnel, applied in a strategy setting and across the enterprise, designed to identify potential events that may affect the entity, manage risk to be within its risk appetite and to provide reasonable assurance regarding the achievement of entity objectives.
IIA (Institute of Internal Auditors)	A rigorous and co-ordinated approach to assessing and responding to all risks that affect the achievement of an organization's strategic and financial objectives.
HM Treasury	All the processes involved in identifying, assessing and judging risks, assigning ownership, taking actions to mitigate or anticipate them and monitoring and reviewing progress.

The following is offered by the author as a comprehensive definition of ERM:

- ERM involves the identification and evaluation of significant risks, assignment of ownership, implementation and monitoring of actions to manage these risks within the risk appetite of the organization.
- The output is the provision of information to management to improve business decisions, reduce uncertainty and provide reasonable assurance regarding the achievement of the objectives of the organization.
- The impact of ERM is to improve efficiency and the delivery of services, improve allocation of resources (capital) to business improvement, create shareholder value and enhance risk reporting to stakeholders.

ERM in practice

The developing role of the risk manager is discussed in Chapter 22. It was mentioned that the seniority of the risk manager should be proportionate to the risks that the organization faces. For many organizations, including those in finance and energy, a board-level risk director is often appropriate.

Where it is appropriate and proportionate, the risk manager at board level is often referred to as a chief risk officer (CRO). To date, these appointments have been almost exclusively in the energy and finance sectors, although this may change as ERM becomes more clearly established in a wider range of organizations.

The seniority of the CRO is just one example of how ERM should be achieved in practice. The principles of risk management set out as PACED are fully applicable to the practice of enterprise risk management. The principles of risk management are that it should be proportionate, aligned, comprehensive, embedded and dynamic (PACED).

By taking a comprehensive approach to enterprise risk management, a wide range of benefits can be delivered and these are set out in Table 8.3. It is for each organization to decide how the enterprise risk management initiative will be structured and how these benefits will be achieved.

Table 8.3 Benefits of enterprise risk management

FIRM risk scorecard	Benefits
Financial	Reduced cost of funding and capital
	Better control of CapEx approvals
	Increased profitability for organization
	Accurate financial risk reporting
	Enhanced corporate governance

(continued)

Table 8.3   (*Continued*)

FIRM risk scorecard	Benefits
Infrastructure	Efficiency and competitive advantage
	Achievement of the state of no disruption
	Improved supplier and staff morale
	Targeted risk and cost reduction
	Reduced operating costs
Reputational	Regulators satisfied
	Improved utilization of company brand
	Enhanced shareholder value
	Good reputation and publicity
	Improved perception of organization
Marketplace	Commercial opportunities maximized
	Better marketplace presence
	Increased customer spend (and satisfaction)
	Higher ratio of business successes
	Lower ratio of business disasters

The key feature of ERM is that the full range of significant risks facing the organization is evaluated. The interrelationship between risks should be identified, so that the total risk exposure of the organization may be compiled. Having measured the total risk exposure of the organization, that level of risk exposure can then be compared with the risk appetite of the board and the risk capacity of the organization itself.

ERM and business continuity

There is an important relationship between enterprise risk management (ERM) and business continuity management (BCM). The risk assessment that is required as part of the risk management process and the business impact analysis that is the basis of business continuity planning (BCP) are closely related. This can be seen in Table 8.1, which describes the features of an enterprise-wide approach.

The normal approach to risk management is to evaluate objectives and identify the individual risks that could impact these objectives. The output from a business impact analysis is the identification of the critical activities that must be maintained for the organization to continue to function.

Based on the definition of ERM set out above and the fact that it should be applied to the evaluation of core processes, it can be seen that the ERM approach and the business impact analysis approach are very similar, because both approaches are based on the identification of the key dependencies and functions that must be in place for the continuity and success of the business.

The next activity differs between ERM and BCP, because the former is concerned with the management of the risks that could impact core processes, whereas business continuity is concerned with actions that should be taken to maintain the continuity of individual activities. The business continuity approach, therefore, has the very specific function of identifying actions that should be taken after the risk has materialized in order to minimize its impact. BCP relates to the damage-limitation and cost-containment components of loss control, as described in Chapter 13.

ERM in energy and finance

Risk management in the energy and finance sectors has become a well-developed specialist branch of the discipline. In the finance sector, the objective of an ERM initiative is to enhance shareholder value by:

- improving capital and efficiency by providing an objective basis for allocating resources and exploiting natural hedges and portfolio effects;
- supporting financial decision making by considering areas of high potential adverse impact and by exploiting areas of risk-based advantage;
- building investor confidence by stabilizing results and protecting them from disturbances and thus demonstrating proactive risk stewardship.

ERM in the energy sector is often dependent on the treasury function and the specialist expertise of hedging against the price of a barrel of oil. This area of financial risk management has become well established, with very large departments being set up in many energy companies. However, the practice of ERM in energy companies still remains very closely related to the management of treasury risks.

One of the drivers for risk management in the finance sector is the regulatory environment. Banks have been subjected to Basel II for some time, and are preparing for implementation of the Basel III requirements by 2019. The insurance sector in Europe is about to be subjected to similar requirements, set out in the Solvency II Directive. This gives rise to the obligation on financial institutions to measure their exposure to operational risk.

The output of operational risk management (ORM) activities in financial institutions is the ability to calculate the capital that should be held in reserve to cover the consequences of the identified risks materializing. The impact of these ORM activities is that risks will be better identified and managed, so that the capital required to meet the consequences of the risks materializing is lowered. ORM within financial institutions can be seen as a particular application of the ERM approach.

The failure of the world banking system called into question the effectiveness of risk management activities in banks and, in particular, the effectiveness of operational risk management. One of the consequences of the world financial crisis is that the news reports now routinely state that: 1) risk is bad; and 2) risk management has failed. In fact, taking risk is essential for the success of organizations.

The statement that risk management has failed in banks is more difficult to contradict. However, the reality is that it was not the failure of risk management principles that caused the banking crisis. It was the failure to correctly apply those principles. Many banks made two simultaneous mistakes:

- An accurate risk and reward analysis was not undertaken, so that banks made decisions on the basis of the rewards available, rather than taking a more balanced view of the risks involved in seeking those higher rewards.
- Quantification of the level of risk involved was not accurate, because the banks were taking such a risk-aggressive approach that certain events were considered to be so unlikely that they could be ignored.

Detailed analysis of the banking crisis in 2008 is outside the scope of this text. However, it appears that the crisis was caused by the failure of two different sets of risk analysis models. Firstly, the banks had assumed that re-packaged debts, including sub-prime mortgages, would continue to be tradable commodities in the market, but this proved not to be the case.

Secondly, the banks assumed that short-term borrowing on the wholesale money markets would continue to be available. This short-term money is used by banks so that they can continue to lend money on a long-term basis, at a more profitable rate. The collapse of the wholesale money markets was not anticipated by the credit models used by most banks.

Integrating strategy and performance

COSO published 'Enterprise Risk Management: Integrated Framework' (COSO ERM cube) in 2004. The purpose of that publication was to help organizations better protect and enhance stakeholder value. Since its publication, the COSO ERM cube has been implemented in organizations of all types and sizes to identify risks, manage those risks within risk appetite, and support the achievement of objectives. The COSO ERM cube is discussed in more detail in Chapter 6.

However, COSO has recognized that there needs to be stronger links between strategy, risk and performance. In response, an updated ERM framework was published by COSO in 2017 to more clearly connect ERM stakeholder expectations; position risk in the context of an organization's performance; and enable organizations to better anticipate risk.

'Enterprise Risk Management: Integrating with Strategy and Performance' was published in June 2017 and provides a framework to enhance management of risk for all types and sizes of organization. It puts forward the argument that integrating ERM practices throughout an entity will help to accelerate growth and enhance performance. The advice is to build on the current level of risk management that already exists in the normal course of business.

The updated COSO ERM framework (2017) adopts a components and principles structure. It clearly differentiates between ERM and internal control and enhances the references to risk appetite and risk tolerance. The intention of the revised framework is to elevate discussion of strategy, enhance the alignment between performance and ERM and more explicitly link ERM into decision-making. There is greater emphasis on the relationship between risk and value. Also, the benefits of integration of ERM are emphasized. Finally, the revised framework underlines the role of culture in the achievement of successful enterprise risk management.

The new framework outlines principles that can be applied from strategic decision making through to performance. It includes a set of principles organized into five interrelated components:

1 Governance and culture: Governance sets the tone for the organization and establishes oversight responsibilities for ERM. Culture relates to ethical values, desired behaviours and understanding of risk.

2 Strategy and objective setting: ERM, strategy and objective setting work together in the strategic planning process. Risk appetite should be aligned with strategy and business objectives to successfully implement strategy.

3 Performance: Risks that can impact achievement of strategy and business objectives need to be identified, assessed and prioritized by severity in the context of risk appetite, so that risk responses can be selected.

4 Review and revision: By reviewing entity performance, an organization can consider how well the ERM components are functioning over time and following substantial changes, and what revisions are necessary.

5 Information, communication and reporting: ERM requires a continual process of obtaining and sharing necessary information, from both internal and external sources, which flows up, down, and across the organization.

Over the longer term, ERM can also enhance enterprise resilience – the ability to anticipate and respond to change. It helps organizations identify factors that represent not just risk, but change, and how that change could impact performance and necessitate a shift in strategy. All organizations need to set strategy and periodically adjust it, always staying aware of both ever-changing opportunities for creating value and the challenges that will occur in pursuit of that value.

Organizations need to identify the best framework for optimizing strategy and performance in order to integrate ERM throughout the organization to achieve benefits, including:

- Increase the range of opportunities: Identify new opportunities and unique challenges associated with current opportunities.

- Identify and manage risk entity-wide: Identify and manage enterprise-wide risks to sustain and improve performance.

- Increase positive outcomes and reduce negative surprises: Identify responses, reduce surprises and related costs or losses, while profiting from advantageous developments.

- Reduce performance variability: Anticipate the risks that would affect performance and put in place the actions needed to minimize disruption and maximize opportunity.

- Improve resource deployment: Assess overall resource needs, prioritize resource deployment and enhance resource allocation.
- Enhance enterprise resilience: Anticipate and respond to change, not only to survive but also to evolve and thrive.

Successful implementation of ERM

Risk managers have the responsibility of selling the value added by risk management to the organization and its stakeholders, but this is not an easy task. How do risk managers sell the value they are generating when that value may only be realized when unforeseen events occur, or if the new control systems are successful, when the risk never occurs?

Risk managers need to remember that the actual implementation of an ERM programme generates value in itself. Often risk managers are so focused on successfully managing the programme that they do not have the time to clearly communicate this value to the organization. Risk managers can be their own worst enemies as one of the key elements of a successful practitioner is a passion to successfully tailor, implement and maintain an ERM programme. Correspondingly, this passion is a weakness as the practitioner needs to remember that others do not always share that passion.

One of the major challenges ERM programmes face is the development of an 'ivory tower' mentality. In this scenario, all risk knowledge and activities are based in one department. Risk managers need to devise a system that encourages the migration of risk management methodologies and tools out into the organization. There is also a balancing act required. Practitioners must not force the use of risk management processes on operational areas where there is little value. It is critical to the success of an ERM programme that it has a system that is flexible enough to work with the organization to capture and manage the critical risks successfully without adding unnecessary work on managing lower level risks.

Alternative approaches

09

Changing face of risk management

As with any management initiative that becomes embedded within the way the organization operates, a successful risk initiative is bound to develop and become more sophisticated. Developments in the discipline of risk management, especially during the past 10 years, have been dramatic. Also, the level to which risk management requirements have become embedded within corporate governance has been extensive.

Many new developments of risk management have appeared during that time. In the 1990s, risk management practitioners used to talk about integrated or holistic risk management, but now the universally accepted terminology for the broad application of risk management across the whole organization is enterprise risk management (ERM). Similarly, operational risk management (ORM) has been established and developed very substantially during a shorter time period of perhaps five years.

In many ways, the fact that the risk management discipline continues to develop and adapt itself to changing circumstances can be seen as beneficial. However, there is a danger that risk management practitioners will be seen to be delivering an ever-changing and therefore inconsistent message.

That is not to say that risk management should become a static discipline, but it is important to remember that changing the basis on which risk management analysis and advice is offered and appearing to be changing the very nature of the risk management process, will cause confusion and lack of interest amongst the senior board members.

Any review of the changing face of risk management has to acknowledge the global financial crisis and the role that risk management played in the development of this situation. As the global financial crisis developed, newspaper and television reports constantly repeated two messages: 'risk is bad' and 'risk management has failed'. Neither of these statements is true. It is essential that organizations take appropriate risks, and the failures that led to the global financial crisis were failures in the application of risk management, not failures of risk management itself.

It is undoubtedly the case that taking too much risk may be inappropriate and can result in failure of the whole organization. However, the experience of many organizations is that they almost always get away with it, or (at the very least) manage to survive. A detailed understanding of the level of risk embedded in the organization is not intended to put a stop to all bold strategic decisions. Risk awareness should not prevent an organization embarking on a high-risk strategy, but the decisions will be taken with full awareness of the risks that are involved.

Organizations should continue to look for opportunities and, from time to time, acknowledge that there is a good opportunity that looks very risky. The organization may still have an appetite for embarking on that risky strategy, but the next stage of discussion should be about how to manage the risks so that they remain within the risk capacity of the organization, and how to measure the risks so that the board remains aware of the actual risk exposure.

The global financial crisis does not represent a failure of risk management. It represents a failure to completely and correctly apply risk management procedures and protocols. Figure 25.3 illustrates the risk appetite of a risk-aggressive organization. When an organization is risk aggressive, it limits the range of risks that the board will consider, as there is limited scope for identifying risks as high likelihood/high impact. In other words, the universe of risk for that organization is severely restricted and will exclude risks that should receive the board's attention.

If the organization is risk aggressive and operates to a model in line with Figure 25.3 then very few priority significant risks will be identified. This will result in the organization creating a 'closed universe of risk' for the board that potentially restricts broader discussion and analysis. However, there is nothing inherently incorrect about an organization being risk aggressive. If an organization is risk aggressive, there is an increased need to revisit risk assessments, challenge the scope and results of risk analysis activities, and ensure that a highly dynamic approach to risk management is maintained at all times and at all levels in the organization.

In addition to the concerns about risk management raised by the global financial crisis, certain other challenging issues for risk management exist. The concepts of risk appetite and the upside of risk are useful ideas, but more development work is required before the definitions and successful application of these concepts can bring guaranteed benefits.

Managing emerging risks

All organizations are concerned about changes in the external and internal context that give rise to new challenges, uncertainties and opportunities. These changes can be considered to be the emerging risks facing the organization. However, consideration of emerging risks can be difficult unless the organization clearly understands the nature of the emerging risks that it faces. Emerging risks can be divided into three categories, as follows:

- new risks that have emerged in the external environment, but are associated with the existing strategy of the organization – new risks in known context;
- existing risks that were already known to the organization, but have developed or changed circumstances have triggered the risk – known risks in new context;
- risks that were not previously faced by the organization, because the risks are associated with changed core processes – new risks in new context.

Several business developments have increased the level of risk faced by organizations in recent times, including moving into new markets, embracing new technologies and developing increasingly complex supply chains. Generally, these increasing risks will be under the control of the organization itself. Additionally, there are many emerging or developing risks that are not within the control of an individual organization, including:

- climate change;
- sovereign debt;
- national security;
- changing demographics.

When seeking to manage these emerging risks, an organization should evaluate whether the risks are to be treated as hazard, control or opportunity risks. Depending on the activities of the organization, many of these emerging risks may simply be threats to the organization or represent opportunities for future development. In some cases, the emerging risks will simply represent additional uncertainties that need to be managed.

An important consideration when thinking about emerging risks is the speed at which they can become significant. Some risk management practitioners refer to the speed of development and change of risks as the risk velocity.

A good example of emerging risk is nanotechnology. Nanotechnology is used extensively in the medical and, to some extent, cosmetics industry to improve the effectiveness of cosmetic treatment of skin conditions. Whether any long-term risks will emerge from the use of nanotechnology has not yet been fully established.

Another good example is that associated with the use of mobile phones. Mobile phones have become commonplace, but the technology has developed rapidly over the past 25 years. Mobile phone signals were much more powerful 25 years ago. Therefore, if any health allegations begin to emerge against the use of mobile phones, these health effects are likely to be associated with the technology that is no longer used. This will represent significant challenges in deciding whether any health hazards no longer exist because the technology has changed, or whether the health hazards are just as significant and will prove to be equally associated with current technology.

Risks of nanotechnology

As nanotechnology is an emerging field, there is great debate regarding the extent that it will benefit or pose risks for human health. Nanotechnology's health impact can be split into two aspects: the potential for medical applications to cure disease, and the potential health hazards posed by exposure to nano-materials.

The extremely small size of nano-materials means that they are much more readily taken up by the human body than larger-sized particles. How these nano-particles behave inside the organism is one of the big issues that needs to be resolved. The behaviour of nano-particles is a function of their size, shape and surface reactivity with the surrounding tissue. Apart from what happens if non-degradable or slowly degradable nano-particles accumulate in organs, another concern is their potential interaction with biological processes inside the body: because of their large surface, nano-particles on exposure to tissue and fluids will immediately absorb onto their surface some of the macro-molecules they encounter.

The large number of variables influencing toxicity means that it is difficult to generalize about health risks associated with exposure to nano-materials; each new nano-material must be assessed individually and all material properties must be taken into account. Health and environmental issues combine in the workplace of companies engaged in producing or using nano-materials and in the laboratories engaged in nano-science and nanotechnology research. It is safe to say that current workplace exposure standards for dusts cannot be applied directly to nano-particle dusts.

Increasing importance of resilience

In recent years, there has been an increasing interest in the topic of resilience. Perhaps the trend started with government and local or municipal authorities. There was recognition during the 1990s and 2000s that society in general, and communities in particular, had to become more resilient. This developing awareness initially arose in relation to civil emergencies, as well as natural catastrophes such as earthquakes and extreme weather events. Although the initial concern with resilience may have started with the consideration of how to respond to wide area events, broader concerns have developed in recent times.

The increasing awareness and concern in relation to resilience is clearly demonstrated by the fact that the replacement for British Standard BS 25999:2006 Part 1 'Code of Practice – Business Continuity Management' was ISO 22301:2012 'Societal Security – Business Continuity Management Systems – Requirements'. A number of other standards in the ISO 22300 series are being developed and there are moves towards developing resilience standards in other countries. One of the best-established resilience standards is the Organizational Resilience Standard (ASIS SPC.1-2009) published by the American National Standards Institute.

This ASIS standard takes an enterprise-wide view of risk management, enabling an organization to develop a comprehensive strategy to prevent when possible, prepare for, mitigate, respond to, and recover from a disruptive incident. This allows integration with ISO 31000. It is also compatible with existing ISO management system standards (such as ISO 9001, ISO 14001, ISO 27001 and ISO 28000). The overall approach is that a resilient organization needs to 'prevent, protect and prepare' in relation to resources and assets and at the same time be able to 'respond, recover and review' when a crisis occurs.

When seeking to make an organization more resilient, it is essential to have a definition of the desired state of resilience that is being sought. ISO 22300:2012 'Societal Security – Terminology' defines resilience as the 'adaptive capacity of an organization in a complex and changing environment'. This is a useful definition, but resilience is often associated with crisis management, and this definition does not explicitly address the behaviour of an organization during a crisis. Perhaps a better definition would be the 'capacity of an organization to consistently achieve a desired state following a change in circumstances'. This definition is more inclusive of the management of a crisis, as well as the ability to successfully respond to less dramatic or disruptive events.

The emergence of resilience is an opportunity for risk management and business continuity specialists to work together to ensure a more co-ordinated approach to enterprise risk management, business continuity and crisis management. There are three behaviours that should be achieved by an organization if it is to achieve increased resilience:

- awareness of changes in the external, internal and risk management environments, so that constant attention to resilience is ensured;
- 'prevent, protect and prepare' in relation to all types of resources, including assets, networks, relationships and intellectual property;
- 'respond, recover and review' in relation to disruptive events, including the ability to respond rapidly, review lessons learnt and adapt.

Finally, it is worth noting that another trend in the structure of risk management and resilience standards appears to be emerging. Several standards are moving towards the 'plan–do–check–act' (PDCA) structure. This approach is entirely consistent with the plan, implement, measure, learn (PIML) approach to implementing a risk management initiative that is set out in Appendix C. The ASIS standard explicitly follows the PDCA format. PIML is preferred to PDCA because it is a more comprehensive and analytical approach. In fact, both the framework and the risk management process described in ISO 31000 are aligned with the PIML approach, once the 'leadership and commitment' for the framework and the 'establish the context' for the process stages (respectively) have been completed.

As the increasing importance of resilience is recognized, advice on achieving resilience is becoming more widespread. For example, the box below summarizes advice provided to organizations by the Cabinet Office of the UK government.

Increasing importance of resilience

Embedding organizational resilience into governance mechanisms should ensure that the management of the risks to critical infrastructure posed by natural hazards, major accidents and other malicious damage is considered by the board. The needs of organizational resilience would thereby inform strategic investment and procurement decisions, risk management and discussions with supply chain partners. It would enable infrastructure owners and operators to improve their understanding of the resilience of their infrastructure, measure the success of the strategy at regular intervals, and make necessary amendments to secure delivery or to match changing organizational priorities.

Different approaches

The approach adopted by the Canadian Criteria of Control (CoCo) framework (1995) produced by the Canadian Institute of Chartered Accountants is based on the idea that the risk culture of the organization is the most important consideration. If the risk culture is correct, then the successful management of risks should follow. The CoCo framework states that:

A person performs a task, guided by an understanding of its purpose (the objective to be achieved) and supported by capability (information, resources, supplies and skills). The person will need a sense of commitment to perform the task well over time. The person will monitor his or her performance and the external environment to learn about how to do the task better and about changes to be made. The same is true of any team or work group. In any organization of people, the essence of control is purpose, commitment, capability and monitoring and learning.

The COSO ERM cube refers to the control environment as the internal environment. This is equivalent to the control environment that is considered in the CoCo framework. CoCo provides a structured means of analysing the control environment that enables a quantitative assessment of the control environment, so that the features for improvements can be identified.

The CoCo framework is considered in more detail in Chapter 33. Although there are different versions of the CoCo questions, the following are the headings that are normally used in order to evaluate the risk-aware culture within an organization using the CoCo approach:

- purpose, vision and mission;
- commitment to integrity and ethical values;
- capability, authority and responsibilities;
- learning and development of competence.

In addition to the CoCo approach, there are many other risk management and internal control standards available throughout the world. The scope and intended purpose of the standards varies. For example, the *Orange Book* produced by HM Treasury in the UK is intended as guidance to central government departments on risk management.

An important development in standards is the emergence of the concept of Governance Risk and Compliance (GRC) and this is considered in more detail in Chapter 35. The approach underpinning the principle is related to the concept of the three lines of defence whereby different risk management and internal control responsibilities are allocated to senior management, specialist risk functions and internal audit. The overall approach to GRC is based on the separation of functions. Senior management is responsible for governance within the organization, specialist risk functions are responsible for risk management activities and assurance on adequate compliance is provided by internal audit.

In South Africa, the highly influential and detailed King corporate governance code was published in 2009, and updated as King IV in late 2016. Risk management remains important in the updated code and more detailed guidance is given on how it is to be accomplished. The board is responsible for the governance of risk and disclosure and management is responsible for the risk management design, implementation and monitoring of the risk management plan.

Detailed responsibilities for risk management are set out in King IV in relation to the responsibilities of the board or governing body of the company. The risk governance principle set out in King IV is that 'The governing body should govern risk in a way that supports the organization in setting and achieving its strategic objectives'. Selected examples of the recommended risk practices for the governing body of the company are set in Table 9.1.

In addition to risk management standards and corporate governance requirements, there are a number of specialist standards that apply to risk management.

In particular, the IT sector has produced a number of well-regarded and widely used standards. Perhaps the best-known of the standards is Control Objectives for Information and Related Technology (COBIT). COBIT provides good practices across a domain and process framework and presents activities in a manageable and logical structure. The COBIT approach is described in more detail in the box below.

Control Objectives for Information and Related Technology (COBIT)

The good practices described in COBIT represent the consensus of experts. They are strongly focused on control, less on execution. These practices will help optimise IT-enabled investments, ensure service delivery and provide a measure against which to judge when things do go wrong.

For IT to be successful in delivering against business requirements, management should put an internal control system or framework in place. The COBIT control framework contributes to these needs by:

- making a link to the business requirements;
- organizing IT activities into a generally accepted process model;
- identifying the major IT resources to be leveraged;
- defining the management control objectives to be considered.

The business orientation of COBIT consists of linking business goals to IT goals, providing metrics and maturity models to measure their achievement, and identifying the associated responsibilities of business and IT process owners.

Table 9.1   Selected risk practices from King IV

Risk management responsibility
1   Assume responsibility for the governance of risk by setting the direction of how risk should be approached and addressed, to encompass: • opportunities and associated risks when developing strategy; and • positive and negative effects on achievement of objectives.
2   Evaluate and agree the nature and extent of the risks that the organization should be willing to take and, in particular, approve: • risk appetite, namely the propensity to take appropriate levels of risk; and • limit on the potential loss the organization has the capacity to tolerate.

(continued)

Table 9.1   (*Continued*)

Risk management responsibility

3	Exercise ongoing oversight of risk management and, in particular, oversee that it results in the following:

- assessment of risks and opportunities related to context and capitals;
- assessment of the potential upside or opportunity presented by risk;
- assessment of the organization's dependence on resources;
- design and implementation of appropriate risk responses;
- implementation of business continuity arrangements; and
- embedding of risk management in business activities and culture.

Structure of management standards

ISO has produced guidance on the required structure of management system standards. This guidance is referred to as Annex SL and a number of existing standards have already been converted to this format, including ISO 14001:2004 'Environmental Management Systems – Requirements with Guidance for Use'. Also, ISO 22301:2012 'Societal Security – Business Continuity Management', which is discussed in more detail in Chapter 18, has been migrated to this new structure.

Major clause numbers and titles of all management system standards will become identical, once Annex SL has been adopted for standards. Following the introduction section, management system standards that comply with Annex SL will be structured with the following clauses:

1 Scope

2 Normative references

3 Terms and definitions

4 Context of the organization

5 Leadership

6 Planning

7 Support

8 Operation

9 Performance evaluation

10 Improvement

It is interesting to note that the structure does not explicitly describe framework and process as separate items, in the way that these are presented in ISO 31000. Perhaps this is part of the reason that there are currently (April 2018) no plans to convert ISO 31000 into the Annex SL format. Nevertheless, the Annex SL structure enables organizations developing their own approach to enterprise risk management to devise an approach that is compatible with any other ISO standards implemented in the organization, including the most popular of all ISO standards – ISO 9001 on quality management.

Many of the headings used in Annex SL will be familiar to risk professionals, including Clause 4: Context of the Organization. Clause 4 is intended to identify why the organization exists. As part of answering this question, the organization needs to identify external and internal issues that can impact on its intended outcomes, as well as all stakeholders and their requirements. Clause 5: Leadership and Clause 7: Support work together and can be considered to be equivalent to the risk architecture, strategy and protocols (RASP) in relation to Clause 5, and the components of embedded risk management as leadership, involvement, learning, accountability and communication (LILAC) in relation to Clause 7.

Clause 6: Planning, Clause 8: Operation, Clause 9: Performance evaluation and Clause 10: Improvement are exactly equivalent to the plan–implement–measure–learn (PIML) approach described in this book. The PIML approach is similar to the plan–do–check–act (PDCA) terminology used by several organizations. An important aspect of Annex SL is that the planning stage described in Clause 6 sets out two sub-clauses:

- actions to address risks and opportunities;
- management system, objectives and planning to achieve them.

This means that the requirement to plan and implement actions to address risks and opportunities is now embedded into ISO 9001 on quality management and will become embedded into other standards as the Annex SL format is progressively introduced.

The important lesson for risk professionals, as an increasing number of management system standards are migrated into the Annex SL format, is to seek to ensure that the enterprise risk management initiative is fully aligned with the Annex SL approach. This should ensure greater acceptance of an enterprise risk management initiative within the organization. One further important point to note is that Clause 8: Operation is described as having the bulk of the management system requirement, including the overall process and management that will include adequate criteria to control the processes.

It is under Clause 8 in the new format that the familiar steps of the risk management process would be included for organizations that decide to adopt the structure of Annex SL when implementing an enterprise risk management initiative.

Future of risk management

The emerging trends in risk management have been mentioned throughout the book. The development of international risk management standard ISO 31000 is undoubtedly an important step forward for risk management practitioners. The emergence of enhanced corporate governance codes has also added profile to the practice of risk management in many countries. The effects of the global financial crisis are still being felt and questions are still being asked of risk management and why it did not contribute more to the avoidance of this crisis.

Other important trends include the development of enhanced reporting require-ments that are being placed on organizations of all types. This is especially true of organizations that are listed on stock exchanges around the world. Risk manage-ment information systems are becoming more developed and sophisticated and can offer a significant benefit to organizations that use them. Despite all of these develop-ments and the undoubted increasing professionalism and competence of risk man-agement practitioners, there is still scope to ask questions about future developments in risk management.

The emergence of 'governance, risk and compliance' (GRC) has been mentioned and it represents a major step forward in the structure of risk management activities. The emergence of GRC, together with a better understanding of the benefits of the three lines of defence, has put organizations in a better position to practise risk man-agement. Risk management practitioners realize that their discipline makes a major contribution and they are also aware that risk management activity should be inte-grated with other management activities. In some cases, there is every danger that risk management activities will become integrated with audit activities, and these three lines of defence then become the two lines of defence.

There is a need for organizations to integrate risk activities throughout the whole of their organizations, rather than treating risk management activities as a separate management role that requires separate management information. Perhaps this is one of the major disadvantages of the use of the risk register in many or-ganizations. The risk register is a snapshot of risk management activities in the organization, but the risk is that it is not reviewed on a continuous basis. The risk register is often a static document that does little to add benefit to the management of the organization. Perhaps the time of the risk register has passed, and organiza-tions should now be integrating risk assessment, risk recording and risk action plans within the management information that is used for the day-to-day manage-ment of the organization.

Management initiatives often come and go. A particular approach becomes fash-ionable for a while and then fades away. It is unlikely that this will happen to risk management, because the requirement to have risk management procedures in place has become mandatory in many sectors. Also, the global financial crisis has resulted in a detailed analysis of the benefits that risk management can bring and how these can be achieved. The brief commentary below illustrates how risk management is valued around the world and why it is here to stay.

Risk management is here to stay

Every day, managers and employees practise risk management by making decisions on what to do, and how and when to do it. Decisions have to be based on factors like does the organization have the capacity, has the organization set aside the funds and will this impact other business units.

ERM is not just a passing trend. It is here to stay and is being driven by both governance issues and the demands of society. Companies, charities and public-sector organizations have successfully embraced ERM.

> Risk management does not have to be complex or a heavy resource user. It can be tailored to meet the needs of the organization in its early stages and modified as the level of sophistication and comfort with the process grows. It is a systematic and proactive approach to managing risk. This means that high-risk exposure areas are understood, managed and controlled to an acceptable level of exposure so that the organization is properly protected to minimize negative consequences. It allows the organization to focus on what is important to control versus what is easy to control.

Future developments in the practice of ERM are likely to be focused on two key areas: firstly, ensuring risk management activities are fully embedded in the core business processes of the organization; and secondly, demonstrating measurable financial benefits associated with the implementation of an enterprise risk management initiative. The embedding of ERM in the organization is achieved by leadership, involvement, learning, accountability and communication (LILAC). Developments in the practice of operational risk management are probably leading the way in the measurement of the total risk exposure of an organization.

Whilst considering the continued development of enterprise risk management, it is also worth commenting on the strong emergence of resilience as an organizational requirement for the 2010s. The ISO 22300 series of standards will cover business continuity, crisis management and broader requirements concerned with the resilience of society, in general, and organizations, in particular. ISO 22301 on business continuity is discussed in Chapter 18 and the importance of the other standards in the ISO 22300 series is considered in Chapter 9.

In summary, the discipline of enterprise risk management has become established and is here to stay, but it has to be able to demonstrate significant and measurable financial benefits. These financial benefits need to be demonstrated in the form of increased profit in private-sector organizations and in the form of the enhanced efficiency and/or value-for-money delivery of services in the public sector.

PART THREE
Risk assessment

LEARNING OUTCOMES FOR PART THREE

- describe the importance of risk assessment as a critically important stage in the risk management process;
- summarize the most common risk assessment techniques, plus the advantages and disadvantages of each technique, including SWOT;
- explain the importance of the long-term attitude of an organization to risk and how that affects the perception of risk;
- describe options for classifying risks according to the nature, source, timescale, impact and consequences of the risk;
- describe the importance of risk classification systems and describe the features of the established systems, including PESTLE, FIRM and the 4Ps;
- explain the attributes of each characteristic and illustrate by means of a risk matrix the nature and attributes of a risk in terms of likelihood and magnitude;
- illustrate, by using a risk matrix, the risk attitude of an organization and the importance of the concept of the 'universe of risk';
- provide examples of the use of a risk matrix, including using it to indicate the dominant risk response in each quadrant (4Ts);
- describe the main components of loss control as loss prevention, damage limitation and cost containment, and provide practical examples;
- summarize the alternative approaches to defining the upside of risk and the application of these approaches for core processes.

PART THREE FURTHER READING

Hillson, D (2016) *The Risk Management Handbook: A Practical Guide to Managing the Multiple Dimensions of Risk*, **www.koganpage.com**

HM Treasury (2004) *Orange Book: Management of Risk – Principles and Concepts*, **www.hm-treasury.gov.uk**

International Standard ISO/IEC 31010:2009 *Risk Management: Risk Assessment Techniques*, **www.iso.org**

Management Consultancies Association (2007) *The Upside of Risk*, **www.mca.org.uk**

Taylor, E (2014) *Practical Enterprise Risk Management*, **www.koganpage.com**

WA Government (2011) *Risk Management Guidelines*, **www.wa.gov.au**

PART THREE CASE STUDIES

AA: Risk governance

The group-wide risk assessment requires business units to formally review business risks each quarter. This approach to identification, analysis and assessment of risks ensures responsibility so that they are managed, controlled and monitored. A broad spectrum of risks is considered through this process including those relating to strategy, operational performance, finance, product engineering and technology, business reputation, human resources, health and safety and the environment. The causes and the consequences of each risk are considered and, where appropriate, linked to strategic and operational objectives.

Management controls designed to monitor and mitigate risks are documented. Risk owners are assigned to each risk. The risk response is based upon the assessment of potential risk exposure and the level of accepted tolerance. The response reflects whether we accept the risk on the basis of its assessed level of exposure and mitigating controls currently in place, where possible, or reduce the risk through additional mitigation to bring it in line with required levels of tolerance.

The duties of the risk committee include advising the board on the group's overall risk appetite, tolerance and strategy. The risk committee and the board have reviewed and approved a revised risk appetite since we became a listed public company.

As with any business, we face risks and uncertainties on a daily basis. It is the effective management of these that places us in a better position to be able to achieve our strategic objectives and to embrace opportunities as they arise. The board has considered carefully the nature and extent of the significant risks it is willing to take in achieving the group's strategic objectives and delivering a satisfactory return for shareholders.

Edited extract from AA plc
Annual Report and Accounts 2015

British Land: Our assessment of risk is a cornerstone

Internally we have undertaken some significant change projects to improve the operational effectiveness and efficiency of our business. While this inevitably presents a degree of operational risk, we believe we have the right people in place to manage change effectively. In the current year, we have been conscious of the increased risk of terrorist activities at our assets and have tested our crisis response plan to ensure it is robust.

At British Land, we take the view that our assessment of risk is a cornerstone of our strategy and our embedded risk management is fundamental to its delivery. Our integrated approach combines a top-down strategic view with a complementary bottom-up operational process.

The top-down approach involves a review of the external environment in which we operate. This guides assessment of the risks which we are comfortable taking in pursuit of our performance objectives – this is our risk appetite. This evaluation guides the actions we take in executing our strategy. Key risk indicators (KRIs) have been identified for each of our principal risks and are used to monitor our risk exposure. The KRIs are reviewed quarterly by the risk committee to ensure that the activities of the business remain within our risk appetite.

The bottom-up approach involves identifying, managing and monitoring risks in each area of our business. This way, risk management is embedded in our everyday operations. Control of this process is provided through maintenance of risk registers in each area. These risk registers are aggregated and reviewed by the risk committee, with significant and emerging risks escalated for board consideration as appropriate.

Edited extract from British Land PLC
Annual Report and Accounts 2015

Guide Dogs NSW/ACT: List of major residual risks

A (partial) list of major residual risks identified in the Guide Dogs NSW/ACT risk management plan and an update on the actions being taken to mitigate these risks follow:

1   Insufficient guide dogs to meet the demand. The breeding programme produced 140 puppies and 51 guide dogs graduated. We will continue to increase the number of dogs graduating each year, and further reduce the waiting time.

2   Insufficient instructors to meet growth in demand, as attrition has reduced our instructor numbers. Ten orientation and mobility instructor students will be recruited to commence studies in 2016.

3   Ongoing funding of the Centre for Eye Health. Guide Dogs NSW/ACT is investing significant effort to attract funding partners and donors and is working with an international fundraiser.

4   Potential for client injury while utilizing mobility skills taught by instructors. The review of the risk involved in delivering different types of client service programmes has been completed and programmes with unacceptably high risk have been eliminated from our offering.

5   Staff motor vehicle accidents. Driver training and increased vehicle choice with benchmark safety inclusions will continue.

6   Staff changes in the fundraising and planned giving departments potentially resulting in reduced income streams. Recruitment has yielded excellent staff who are settling into their roles extremely well and proving to be very effective in their responsibilities.

Edited extract from Guide Dogs NSW/ACT
Annual Report 2015

Risk assessment considerations   10

Importance of risk assessment

Risk recognition and risk rating together form the risk assessment component of the risk management process. Risk assessment involves the recognition of risks and the rating of them to determine the significant risks facing the organization, project or strategy. It is defined in British Standard BS 31100 as the overall process of risk identification, risk analysis and risk evaluation. Because the risk management input into strategy focuses on improved decision making, risk assessment is the main risk management input into strategy formulation.

Risks may be attached to corporate objectives, stakeholder expectations, core processes and key dependencies. Whichever of these features is selected as the starting point, risk assessment can be undertaken. The purpose of risk assessment is to identify the significant risks that could impact the selected feature.

Although risk assessment is vitally important, it is only useful if the conclusions of the assessment are used to inform decisions and/or to identify the appropriate risk responses for the type of risk under consideration. It should be considered as the starting point of the risk management process and it is certainly not an end in itself.

An important feature of undertaking a risk assessment is to decide whether the identified risk is going to be evaluated at the inherent level or at the current (or residual) level. Assessment of inherent risk is undertaken without taking account of the controls that are currently in place. This is the approach that has been recommended by internal auditors. An internal auditor will point out that two risks at the same current or net value may have significantly different inherent or gross values. It is important to know when this is the case.

The benefit of undertaking assessment of inherent risk is that the difference between the current level and the inherent level can be identified. This will give an indication of the importance of the existing control measures and the information is used by internal auditors to help identify critical controls and set audit priorities. Although this may be a useful approach, there can be considerable difficulties in identifying the value of the inherent level of risk.

Health and safety practitioners, for example, prefer to undertake risk assessment with the current controls in place. This can be a simpler approach, although it relies on the assumption that the current controls will always work to the assumed effectiveness. For example, if an assessment of an x-ray machine is being undertaken, the safety person will assume that the enclosure or cabinet is in good order and the risk should be assessed on that basis. The internal auditor will more easily recognize that the enclosure or cabinet is a vitally important control factor that has to be subject to a routine inspection.

Approaches to risk assessment

There are several approaches that can be taken when planning how to undertake risk assessment. One of the key decisions will be who to involve in the risk assessment exercise. Sometimes risk assessments are undertaken by the board of directors as a top-down exercise. Risk assessments can also be undertaken by involving individual members of staff and local departmental management. This bottom-up approach is also valuable.

The opinion of the chief executive officer (CEO) is critically important, especially as it helps to define the overall attitude of the organization to risk. There is no doubt that the CEO will be able to provide a well-structured view of the significant risks faced by the organization. The disadvantage in relying on the opinion of the CEO is that the focus is likely to be on external risks. Although CEOs will be concerned about the financial management and infrastructure risks, these internal risks may not be their major concern or area of interest.

In general, the overall approach by the organization to risk assessments will be heavily influenced by the risk assessment techniques that are selected. Certain techniques require the involvement of specific individuals and require a particular approach to undertaking risk assessments. It is important that the approach that is adopted is consistent with the culture of the organization.

For example, if an organization does not normally hold meetings and workshops, then a workshop may not be the most appropriate approach to risk assessments. Likewise, if the culture of the organization relies heavily on reports and written papers, this may be the best way of conducting the risk assessments.

The use of voting software has become popular in recent times. For organizations such as media companies familiar with this technology, this may be a very appropriate way of undertaking risk assessments. However, for organizations that are not keen on technology, the use of such tools may be seen as gimmicks that detract from the value of the workshop.

The use of the voting software can provide additional information in the risk assessment workshop. Not only is it possible to identify the majority position in relation to the likelihood and impact of a risk materializing, but it is also possible to identify the spread of opinions. If there is a broad spread of opinions, this needs to be explored, because it could represent a possible misunderstanding of the nature of the risk being discussed.

An important consideration for organizations is whether the risk assessment process should be undertaken on a top-down and bottom-up basis. In other words, will senior management lead the risk assessment process in the organization with the information being passed downwards for validation, or will a series of risk assessment exercises be undertaken starting at operational level? Table 10.1 provides examples of the advantages and disadvantages of undertaking a top-down risk assessment

Table 10.1 Top-down risk assessment

Advantages	Disadvantages
Likely to result in an enterprise-wide approach – the risks at the top will have impacts throughout the business.	Senior managers and directors tend to be more focused on risks external to the organization.
The most significant strategic risks for the organization can be captured quickly and there will be a manageable number.	Limited awareness of internal operational risks or interdependencies of risks within the business.
Shows risk management buy-in from the top, resulting in acceptance of risk management activities at all levels.	Danger that the approach becomes too superficial, because senior managers believe they can manage crises.
Since it originates from the top, there is likely to be consistent methodology throughout the organization.	New risks emerging from the operational activities of the organization might not be fully identified.

exercise. A top-down risk assessment exercise will tend to focus on risks related to strategy, tactics, operations and compliance (STOC) in that order.

Table 10.2 provides examples of advantages and disadvantages of undertaking a bottom-up risk assessment exercise. As with so many aspects of a successful enterprise risk management initiative, the organization should decide the risk assessment protocols and procedures that are most suitable. If it is a choice between top-down and bottom-up, the organization should decide whether visible senior management support

Table 10.2 Bottom-up risk assessment

Advantages	Disadvantages
Significant buy-in at all levels of the organization should be achieved.	There will be little focus on external risks or strategic risks.
Can be mirrored to an existing organization chart and risk impacts beyond immediate operational risks can be discussed.	Time-consuming and may demotivate, if it takes longer to develop the overall enterprise results.
Operational staff have great awareness of local risks and their causes, which might elude higher levels of management.	Danger that the approach becomes too detailed and blinkered, resulting in a silo approach to risk assessment.
Methodology can be varied according to local norms and culture and this is useful for a multinational organization.	New risks emerging from the operational activities of the business might not be reported by operational staff.

for the risk management initiative is more important than the greater involvement of operational people. A bottom-up risk assessment exercise will tend to focus on risks identified as compliance, hazard, control and opportunity in that order.

For most organizations, a combination of top-down and bottom-up risk assessments will be undertaken with the risk manager collecting information from as many stakeholders as possible. Often, the main constraint in undertaking a bottom-up exercise is the greater time commitment that is required from the risk management department to attend and/or facilitate a series of risk assessment exercises.

Risk assessment techniques

There is a wide range of risk assessment techniques available, and International Standard ISO/IEC 31010 'Risk Management: Risk Assessment Techniques', was published in 2009. This standard provides detailed information on the full range of risk assessments techniques that can be used. Table 10.3 lists the main risk assessment techniques that are in common use and also provides a brief description of each of these techniques. Probably the most common risk assessment approaches are the use of checklists/questionnaires and the use of brainstorming sessions, normally during risk assessment workshops.

Checklists and questionnaires have the advantage that they are usually simple to complete and are less time-consuming than other risk assessment techniques. However, this approach suffers from the disadvantage that any risk not referenced by appropriate questions may not be recognized as significant. A simple analysis of the advantages and disadvantages of each of the most common risk assessment techniques is set out in Table 10.4.

Table 10.3   Techniques for risk assessment

Technique	Brief description
Questionnaires and checklists	Use of structured questionnaires and checklists to collect information that will assist with the recognition of the significant risks.
Workshops and brainstorming	Collection and sharing of ideas at workshops to discuss the events that could impact the objectives, core processes or key dependencies.
Inspections and audits	Physical inspections of premises and activities and audits of compliance with established systems and procedures.
Flow charts and dependency analysis	Analysis of the processes and operations within the organization to identify critical components that are key to success.

Table 10.4   Advantages and disadvantages of RA techniques

Technique	Advantages	Disadvantages
Questionnaires and checklists	Consistent structure guarantees consistency Greater involvement than in a workshop	Rigid approach may result in some risks being missed Questions will be based on historical knowledge
Workshops and brainstorming	Consolidated opinions from all interested parties Greater interaction produces more ideas	Senior management tends to dominate Issues will be missed if incorrect people involved
Inspections and audits	Physical evidence forms the basis of opinion Audit approach results in good structure	Inspections are most suitable for hazard risks Audit approach tends to focus on historical experience
Flow charts and dependency analysis	Useful output that may be used elsewhere Analysis produces better understanding of processes	Difficult to use for strategic risks May be very detailed and time-consuming

Given that risks can be attached to other aspects of an organization as well as or instead of objectives, a convenient and simple way of analysing risks is to identify the key dependencies faced by the organization. Most people within an organization will be able to identify the aspects of the business that are fundamentally important to its future success. Identifying the factors that are required for success will give rise to a list of the key dependencies for the organization.

Key dependencies can then be further analysed by asking what could impact each of them. If a hazard analysis is being undertaken then the question is: 'What could undermine each of these key dependencies?' If control risks are being identified, then the question can be asked: 'What would cause uncertainty about these key dependencies?' For an opportunity risk analysis, the question would be: 'What events or circumstances would enhance the status of each of the key dependencies?'

For many organizations, quantification of risk exposure is essential and the risk assessment technique that is chosen must be capable of delivering the required quantification. Quantification is particularly important for financial institutions and the style of risk management employed in these organizations is frequently referred to as operational risk management (ORM).

Risk workshops are probably the most common of the risk assessment techniques. Brainstorming during workshops enables opinions regarding the significant risks faced by the organization to be shared. A common view and understanding of each risk is achieved. However, the disadvantage can be that the more senior people in the room may dominate the conversation, and contradicting their opinions may be difficult and unwelcome.

In order to have a structured discussion at a risk assessment workshop, several brainstorming structures are in common use. These may be qualitative or quantitative, depending on the level of analysis of the risk that is required. The most common of the qualitative brainstorming structures are the SWOT and PESTLE analysis. SWOT is an analysis of the strengths, weaknesses, opportunities and threats faced by the organization. The SWOT analysis has the benefit that it also considers the upside of risk by evaluating opportunities in the external environment. One of the strengths of the SWOT analysis is that it can be linked to strategic decisions. However, because it is not a structured risk classification system, there is a possibility that not all of the risks will be identified.

The other common qualitative approach is the PESTLE analysis that considers the political, economic, social, technological, legal and ethical (or environmental) risks faced by the organization. Table 11.3 considers the PESTLE risk classification system in more detail. PESTLE is a well-established structure with proven results for undertaking brainstorming sessions during risk assessment workshops.

Many organizations will wish to undertake a quantitative evaluation of the possibility of a risk event occurring. There are several techniques available for undertaking these quantitative evaluations. The most common are hazard and operability (HAZOP) studies and failure modes effects analysis (FMEA). Both of these techniques are structured approaches that ensure that no risks are omitted. However, the involvement of a wide range of experts is required in order to undertake an accurate quantitative analysis.

HAZOP and FMEA techniques are most easily applied to manufacturing operations. HAZOP studies are often undertaken of hazardous chemical installations and complex transport structures, such as railways. Also, HAZOP studies of complex installations, such as nuclear power stations, are often undertaken. They can also be applied to the analysis of the safety of products. In both cases, these are very analytical and time-consuming approaches, but such an approach will be necessary in a wide range of circumstances.

Nature of the risk matrix

When a risk has been recognized as significant, the organization needs to rate it so that the priority significant risks can be identified. Techniques for rating risks are well established, but there is also a need to decide what scope exists for further improving control. Consideration of the scope for further cost-effective improvement is an additional consideration that assists the clear identification of the priority significant risks.

An organization will need to establish the measures of risk likelihood and risk impact that will be used throughout the organization. Table 10.5 provides a typical list of definitions in relation to risk likelihood. Table 10.6 sets out definitions of impact that would be used in a typical organization. In both cases, four different definitions are provided and this will avoid any tendency for persons undertaking a

Table 10.5   Definitions of likelihood

Likelihood	Frequency
Unlikely	Can reasonably be expected to occur, but has only occurred 2 or 3 times over 10 years in this organization or similar organizations.
Possible	Has occurred in this organization more than 3 times in the past 10 years or occurs regularly in similar organizations, or is considered to have a reasonable likelihood of occurring in the next few years.
Likely	Occurred more than 7 times over 10 years in this organization or in other similar organizations, or circumstances are such that it is likely to happen in the next few years.
Almost certain	Has occurred 9 or 10 times in the past 10 years in this organization, or circumstances have arisen that will almost certainly cause it to happen.

Table 10.6   Definitions of impact

Descriptor	Definition
Small	No impact on patient health; minor reduction of reputation in the short run; no violation of law; negligible economic loss which can be restored.
Moderate	Minor temporary impact on patient health; small reduction of reputation that may influence trust for a short time; violation of law that results in a warning; small economic loss that can be restored.
Severe	Serious impact on health; serious loss of reputation that will influence trust and respect for a long time; violation of law that results; large economic loss that cannot be restored.
Catastrophic	Death or permanent reduction of health of patient; serious loss of reputation that is devastating for trust; serious violation of law; considerable economic loss that cannot be restored.

risk rating exercise to select the middle option. However, many organizations decide to have more than four options available both for likelihood and impact. The number of options available will depend on the nature, size and complexity of the organization.

There are many different styles of risk matrix. The most common form is one that demonstrates the relationship between the likelihood of the risk materializing and the impact of the event should the risk materialize. As well as likelihood and impact, other features of the risk can be represented on the risk matrix. For example, the scope for achieving further risk improvement is often represented using a risk matrix. In this case, the risk matrix will demonstrate the level of risk in relation to the additional measures that can be taken to improve the management of that risk, and thereby set a target level for it.

The risk matrix can be used to record the outcome of the risk rating exercise and this will provide a simple visual presentation of the significant risks that have been recognized or identified. In undertaking a risk assessment exercise, it is also necessary to rank the risks against the risk appetite of the organization or the risk criteria that have been established. The stage of risk rating is referred to in ISO 31000 as risk analysis and the stage of risk ranking is described as risk evaluation.

A risk is significant if it could have an impact in excess of the benchmark test for significance for that type of risk. Identification of potentially significant risks will be undertaken during a risk recognition exercise. It is necessary to decide the:

- magnitude of the event should the risk materialize;
- size of the impact that the event would have on the organization;
- likelihood of the risk materializing at or above the benchmark;
- scope for further improvement in control.

This will lead to the clear identification of the priority significant risks. Most organizations will find that the total number of risks identified in a workshop is between 100 and 200. After the risk rating has been completed, it is typical for the number of priority significant risks faced by the organization to be identified as between 10 and 20. The terminology used in Guide 73 is a combination of likelihood and impact of a risk, and is considered to be the level of risk, although this is referred to by many risk practitioners as the risk severity.

There are many alternative versions of tables that provide definitions for terms used to describe likelihood and impact. An organization will need to produce its own definitions, based on the size, nature and complexity of that organization. Table 10.5 provides generic definitions of likelihood in terms of the number of occasions when the event is likely to occur over a 10-year period. Table 10.6 provides definitions of impact that could be used in a hospital where patient safety is the primary consideration.

Risk perception

When undertaking risk assessment exercises, it is often the case that different attendees at the workshop will have different views of the risk. There are several ways of accommodating differing opinions. In some cases, voting software can be used in order to identify the majority view. This has the benefit that it is a simple means of identifying the average group position, at the same time as demonstrating the spread of opinions.

However, it is often beneficial to discuss why people have different views of a risk. By exploring why their views differ, it is often possible to reach an agreed common position. This will have the benefit that more appropriate control measures will then be identified and implemented. The perception of risk by individuals will be affected by a number of factors. The following are considered to increase concern amongst the general public in relation to a specific risk to health:

- involuntary (pollution) rather than voluntary (dangerous sports);
- inequitably distributed (some benefit while others suffer);
- inescapable by taking personal precautions;
- arising from an unfamiliar or novel source;
- resulting from human-made, rather than natural, sources;
- causing hidden and irreversible damage, perhaps years after exposure;
- posing particular danger to small children or pregnant women;
- threatening form of death (or illness/injury) arousing particular dread.

Different views on the importance of a risk can be present at different levels of seniority within the organization. It is useful for the risk assessment process to draw opinions from all levels of management, so that different perspectives of a risk can be identified. Again, the benefits of this approach are better risk communication, fuller risk understanding and the identification of appropriate and practical control measures.

In order to understand the risks facing an organization and be able to undertake an accurate risk assessment, extensive knowledge of the organization is required. To complete an accurate risk assessment that correctly identifies the significant risks and then goes on to identify the critical controls is a time-consuming and resource-intensive exercise.

In relation to the public perception of risk, members of the public often only have access to incomplete information and are subject to strong arguments from lobbying and other special interest groups. Therefore, the public understanding and perception of risk may not be sufficiently informed or entirely objective. Journalists and news reporters have a duty to present news stories in an objective and unbiased manner, which may not be easy when the people receiving the information do not have a full understanding of the risks involved.

Government risk assessments

Government will make available its assessments of risks that affect the public, how it has reached its decisions and how it will handle the risk. It will also do so where the development of new policies poses a potential risk to the public. When information has to be kept private, or where the approach departs from existing practice, it will explain why. Where facts are uncertain or unknown, government will seek to make clear what the gaps in its knowledge are. It will be open about where it has made mistakes and what it is doing to rectify them.

HM Treasury

Attitude to risk

Figure 10.1 provides an empirical illustration of risk attitude using a standard risk matrix. It represents the risk attitude of a risk-averse organization. It is becoming more common for a risk attitude matrix to contain four sections. These sections can be represented by the 4Cs of comfort, cautious, concerned and critical. Risk attitude represents the long-term approach of the organization to risk. These descriptors can also be attached to the four sections on a risk appetite matrix to describe the approach to short-term risk taking. The relationship between risk attitude and risk appetite is discussed further in Chapter 25.

The darkest area in Figure 10.1 represents the critical risks for the organization. For a risk-aggressive organization, there are fewer risks of concern, so that the 'universe of risk' considered by the board will be very restricted. The phrase 'universe of risk' is often used by internal auditors to identify audit priorities. Working with such a closed or restricted 'universe of risk' will increase the chances of an unidentified significant risk impacting the organization. Each different stakeholder will have a

Figure 10.1   Risk attitude matrix

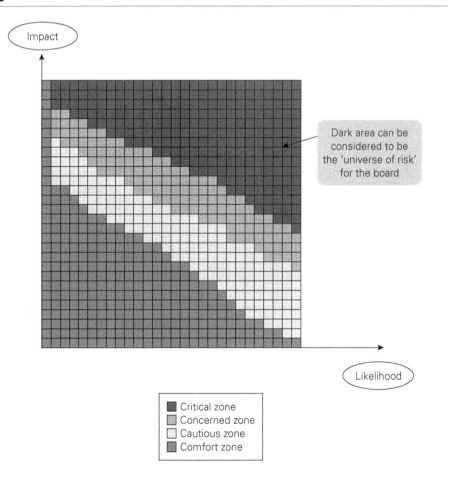

Impact

Dark area can be considered to be the 'universe of risk' for the board

Likelihood

■ Critical zone
▨ Concerned zone
☐ Cautious zone
■ Comfort zone

different 'universe of risk' and the risk manager is likely to have a 'universe of risk' that includes all of the risks that have already been identified, plus any emerging risks that are starting to appear.

Figure 10.1 illustrates that there will be a level of risk that the organization feels comfortable taking and embedding into core processes. This is because, regardless of the likelihood of the risk materializing, the impact is so small that it would not be significant if it did materialize. Likewise, there will be a likelihood of a risk materializing that is considered so remote that it is assumed that it will not occur, even though it would be very serious if it did. For example, most organizations do not consider the consequences of a jumbo jet crash-landing on their site.

The global financial crisis is an example of circumstances where certain risks were considered so unlikely that they could be ignored. Some banks were reliant on the wholesale money markets, but the possibility of these markets failing was considered to be too remote to require further analysis or to call for the development of contingency plans to respond to that situation.

Above these minimum levels of tolerable likelihood and impact, a range of risks can arise. Generally speaking, low-likelihood/low-impact risks will be tolerable, medium-likelihood/medium-impact risks will require some judgement before acceptance, and high-likelihood/high-impact risks will be intolerable. The overall attitude of an organization to risk can be described by a set of 'risk criteria' and this is the approach taken by ISO 31000. It is worth noting that there is no specific mention of risk appetite in ISO 31000 in favour of discussion of the risk criteria. The difference between risk attitude and risk appetite can be difficult to describe, but there is a similarity with attitude to food and the appetite for food at a particular time. Attitude to food is an established or medium-term to long-term set of criteria, but appetite for food represents an immediate need to eat. The same analysis can be applied to risk, so that the risk attitude is the established risk criteria and risk appetite is the more immediate need to take risk in order to achieve objectives.

Organizations will need to take a risk-by-risk approach when deciding whether a risk is acceptable. Different organizations will set tolerance levels differently and this will be an indication of risk attitude. Many organizations will take a cumulative review of risk where all risk exposures are added together, and this is a feature of the enterprise risk management approach. The organization will then be able to decide whether the overall exposure to risk is acceptable and consistent with the risk attitude of the organization.

When considering risk attitude, perception and appetite, it is worth reflecting on the fact that certain individuals may be more concerned about a low-impact risk with a high probability of occurrence (such as a car crash) than they will about a high-impact risk that is unlikely to happen (such as an earthquake). This difference in approach is often reflected in the risk assessment process and can affect the way in which significant risks are prioritized.

When all the potentially significant risks have been identified, one approach is to ask how likely it is that each of those risks will materialize above the threshold test for significance. The risks can then be prioritized as high likelihood, medium likelihood and low likelihood. The alternative approach is to prioritize the potentially significant risks in order of the impact at the same likelihood. The risks will then be presented as high impact, medium impact and low impact.

There is a difference in attitude and perception in these approaches. The first approach is based on how likely it is that the risk will be significant while the second is based on how much the risk will impact when it happens. Neither of these approaches is better than the other, and which approach an individual board member (or the collective board itself) may prefer is related to attitude to risk, as stated in the risk criteria for the organization. The impact associated with a risk is usually measured in terms of the effect on finances, infrastructure, reputation and/or marketplace (FIRM). One of the main requirements of risk management is that the consequences of high impact events for the strategy, tactics, operations and compliance (STOC) of the organization are successfully managed.

Risks involved in buying a car

As an example that brings together the ideas of risk appetite and hazard, control and opportunity risks, consider the decision to buy a car. When deciding which car to buy, there is a need to evaluate hazard tolerance and acceptance of uncertainty, as well as the sum of money that will be invested in the opportunity of owning a new vehicle. Together, these components represent the risk appetite to buy and run a car. In order to achieve an upside of taking the risk of buying a car, the benefits obtained must exceed the costs involved.

If undertaking a risk-based evaluation of buying a car is to help with the decision-making process, the intended benefits of car ownership should be established. This is equivalent to identifying the objectives associated with car ownership.

The actual financial capacity and ability to run a car also needs to be considered. When buying a new vehicle, the buyer needs to make sure that the vehicle selected will not lead to more risk and cost than anticipated. The risks that are associated with owning a vehicle include insurance, breakdown, repairs, accidents, servicing costs and insurance, as well as the purchase price and the anticipated annual depreciation.

Assume that the decision has been taken to buy a two-year-old prestigious car. The car will cost much less money than a new vehicle and the depreciation costs will be much less (opportunity risks). However, the repair and maintenance costs may be higher than for a new vehicle (control risks). The exposure to accidents, theft and repair costs will be similar for most vehicles (hazard risks).

Remember that the opportunity risks enhance the possible achievement of the benefits of owning a car. The control risks increase uncertainty or doubt about achieving these benefits and the hazard risks inhibit the achievement of the car ownership benefits.

Risk classification systems   11

Short-, medium- and long-term risks

Although it is not a formalized system, the classification of risks into short, medium and long term helps to identify risks as being related (primarily) to operations, tactics and strategy, respectively. This distinction is not clear-cut, but it can assist with further classification of risks. In fact, there will be some short-term risks to strategic core processes and there may be some medium-term and long-term risks that could impact operational core processes. Also, there is always the requirement to ensure compliance in operations, tactics and strategy. For most organizations, the attitude to compliance risks is based on the desire to minimize this type of risk.

A short-term risk has the ability to impact the objectives, key dependencies and core processes, with the impact being immediate. These risks can cause disruption to operations immediately when the event occurs. Short-term risks are predominantly hazard risks, although this is not always the case. These risks are normally associated with unplanned disruptive events, but may also be associated with cost control in the organization. Short-term risks usually impact the ability of the organization to maintain effective and efficient core processes that are concerned with the continuity and monitoring of routine operations. There is a need to mitigate short-term risks.

A medium-term risk has the ability to impact the organization following a (short) delay after the event occurs. Typically, the impact of a medium-term risk would not be apparent immediately, but would be apparent within months, or at most a year after the event. Medium-term risks usually impact the ability of the organization to maintain effective and efficient core processes that are concerned with the management of tactics, projects and other change programmes. These medium-term risks are often associated with projects, tactics, enhancements and other developments. There is a need to manage these medium-term risks.

A long-term risk has the ability to impact the organization some time after the event occurs. Typically, the impact could occur between one and five years (or more) after the event. Long-term risks usually impact the ability of the organization to maintain the core processes that are concerned with the development and delivery of effective and efficient strategy. These risks are related to strategy, but they should not be treated as being exclusively associated with opportunity management. Risks that

Figure 11.1 Bow-tie representation of risk management

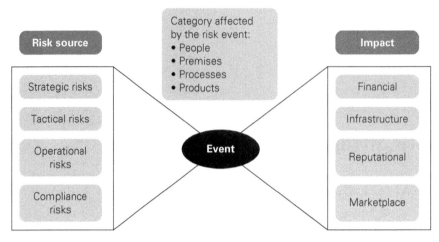

have the potential to undermine strategy and the successful implementation of strategy can destroy more value than risks to operations and tactics. Although long-term risks can undermine an organization, there is a need to embrace the appropriate level of risk embedded in the strategy.

Figure 11.1 illustrates short-term, medium-term and long-term risks in terms of the source of these risks. The risks arise from the operations, tactics and strategy adopted by the organization. For the sake of completeness, the category of compliance risks is also included, since this is an additional category to operations, tactics and strategy. The need to respond to risks according to whether they arise from strategy, tactics, operations or compliance (STOC) is summarized by embrace, manage, mitigate and minimize (EM3) respectively. The purpose of the bow-tie illustration of risk management is to demonstrate that sources of risk can lead to events that have consequences.

When a hazard event occurs, it will have an impact on the features of the organization that can cause disruption. For this reason, the event shown in the centre of the bow-tie would be listed in terms of the component of the organization that is impacted by the event. These components are people, premises, processes and products (4Ps), as listed in Table 3.2. It is worth noting that the 4Ps can also be considered to be a risk classification system.

The use of a bow-tie to represent risk management has become increasingly common. Figure 11.1 provides an example of the bow-tie being used to represent the three components of risk source, event and impact. In this high-level representation, risk sources are identified as strategic, tactical, operational or compliance. Impacts are represented using the FIRM risk scorecard, as described in Table 11.2. At the centre of the bow-tie is the event, as described by the component of the organization that will be impacted by the event. These components are represented in the same way as in Table 3.2 as people, premises, processes and products.

Nature of risk classification systems

In order to identify all of the risks facing an organization, a structure for risk identification is required. Formalized risk classification systems enable the organization to identify where similar risks exist within the organization. Classification of risks also enables the organization to identify who should be responsible for setting strategy for management of related or similar risks. Finally, appropriate classification of risks will enable the organization to better identify the risk appetite, risk capacity and total risk exposure in relation to each risk, group of similar risks or generic type of risk.

The FIRM risk scorecard provides such a structure, but there are many risk classification systems available. The FIRM scorecard builds on the different aspects of risk, including timescale of impact, nature of impact, whether the risk is hazard, control or opportunity, and the overall risk exposure and risk capacity of the organization. The headings of the FIRM scorecard provide for the classification of risks as being primarily financial, infrastructure, reputational or marketplace in nature.

The FIRM risk scorecard can also be used as a template for the identification of corporate objectives, stakeholder expectations and, most importantly, key dependencies. The scorecard is an important addition to the currently available risk management tools and techniques. It is compiled by analysing the way in which each risk could impact the key dependencies that support each core process. Use of the FIRM risk scorecard facilitates robust risk assessment by ensuring that the chances of failing to identify a significant risk are much reduced.

As with so many risk management decisions, it is for the organization to decide which risk classification system most fully satisfies its needs and requirements. As well as being classified according to the timescale of their impact, risks can also be grouped according to the nature of the risk, the source of the risk and/or the nature of the impact or size and nature of the consequences.

An organization will choose the risk classification system that is most suited to its size, nature and complexity. For example, banks and other financial institutions almost universally classify risks as market, credit and operational risks. Other commonly used risk classification systems that can also be employed to provide structure to risk assessment workshops are the SWOT and PESTLE analysis.

Figure 11.2 presents an operational version of the bow-tie representation of risk management, rather than the high-level overview presented in Figure 11.1. Figure 11.2 uses the bow-tie to represent the sources of potential damage to premises and retains the impacts as financial, infrastructure, reputational and marketplace. The sources of potential damage to premises are identified as flood, fire, earthquake and break-in.

Examples of risk classification systems

Table 11.1 provides a summary of the main risk classification systems. These are the COSO ERM cube, IRM standard, BS 31100 and the FIRM risk scorecard. There are similarities in most of these systems. It should be noted that identifying risks as: 1)

Figure 11.2   Bow-tie and risks to premises

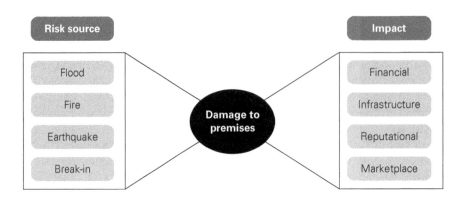

Table 11.1   Risk classification systems

Standard or framework	COSO ERM cube	IRM standard	FIRM risk scorecard
Classification headings	Strategic	Financial	Financial
	Operations	Strategic	Infrastructure
	Reporting	Operational	Reputational
	Compliance	Hazard	Marketplace

hazard, control or opportunity; 2) high, medium or low; and 3) short term, medium term and long term should not be considered to be formal risk classification systems.

Many organizations struggle to find a suitable risk classification system. Often, this is because there is insufficient attention paid to the nature of the risks that are being classified. The bow-tie representation of the risk management process illustrates that it is possible to classify risks according to their source, the component of the organization that the event impacts and the impact and/or consequences of the risk materializing.

Short-, medium- and long-term classification of risks represents the operational, tactical and strategic risks faced by the organization. The categories of disruption to organizations described in Table 3.2 uses a classification system according to the component of the organization that is impacted. This is the people, premises, processes and products (4Ps) risk classification system. The FIRM risk scorecard described in Table 11.2 classifies risks according to their impact.

There are similarities in the way that risks are classified by the different risk classification systems. However, there are also differences, including the fact that operational risk is referred to as infrastructure risk in the FIRM risk scorecard. COSO takes a narrow view of financial risk, with particular emphasis on report-

Table 11.2   Attributes of the FIRM risk scorecard

	Financial	**Infrastructure**	**Reputational**	**Marketplace**
Description	Risks that can impact the way in which money is managed and profitability is achieved	Risks that will impact the level of efficiency and dysfunction within the core processes	Risks that will impact desire of customers to deal or trade and level of customer retention	Risks that will impact the level of customer trade or expenditure
Internal or external risk	Internal	Internal	External	External
Quantifiable	Usually	Sometimes	Not always	Yes
Measurement (performance indicator)	Gains and losses from internal financial control	Level of efficiency in processes and operations	Nature of publicity and effectiveness of marketing profile	Income from commercial and market activities
Performance gap	**Procedures** Failure of procedures to control internal financial risks	**Process** Failure of processes to operate without disruption	**Perception** Failure to achieve the desired perception	**Presence** Failure to achieve required presence in the marketplace
Control mechanisms	CapEx standards Internal control Delegation of authority	Process control Loss control Insurance and risk financing	Marketing Advertising Reputation and brand protection	Strategic and business plans Opportunity assessment

ing. The different systems have been devised in different circumstances and by different organizations; therefore, the categories will be similar but not identical. In describing different risk classification systems, Table 11.1 illustrates that many classification systems offer a combination of source, event, impact and consequences categories.

British Standard BS 31100 sets out the advantages of having a risk classification system. These benefits include helping to define the scope of risk management in the organization, providing a structure and framework for risk identification, and giving the opportunity to aggregate similar kinds of risks across the whole organization. ISO 31000 does not suggest a risk classification system. In summary, examples of the advantages of having a risk classification system, include:

- Accumulations of risk that could undermine a key dependency or business objective and make it vulnerable can be more easily identified.
- Responsibility for improved management of each different type of risk can be more easily identified/allocated if risks are classified.
- Decisions and knowledge about the type of control(s) that will be implemented can be taken on a more structured and informed basis.
- Circumstances where the risk appetite of the organization is being exceeded (or the risk criteria not being implemented) can be more readily identified.

The British Standard states that the number and type of risk categories employed should be selected to suit the size, purpose, nature, complexity and context of the organization. The categories should also reflect the maturity of risk management within the organization. Perhaps the most commonly used risk classification systems are those offered by the COSO ERM cube and by the IRM risk management standard.

However, the COSO risk classification system is not always helpful and it contains several weaknesses. For example, strategic risks may also be present in operations and in reporting and compliance. Despite these weaknesses, the COSO ERM cube is in widespread use, because it is the recognized and recommended approach for compliance with the requirements of the Sarbanes–Oxley Act.

It is worth noting that the COSO ERM cube (2004) is the broader version of COSO, and it also includes the requirements of the recently updated COSO Internal Control cube (2013). The reporting component of the COSO Internal Control cube is specifically concerned with the accuracy of the reporting of financial data and is designed to fulfil the requirements of section 404 of the Sarbanes–Oxley Act.

FIRM risk scorecard

The four headings of the FIRM risk scorecard offer a classification system for the risks to the key dependencies in the organization. The classification system also reflects the idea that every organization should be concerned about its finances, infrastructure, reputation and marketplace success. In order to give a broader scope to commercial success, the headings of the FIRM risk scorecard are as follows:

F   Financial;

I   Infrastructure;

R   Reputational;

M   Marketplace.

The features of the FIRM risk scorecard are set out in Table 11.2. Financial and infrastructure risks are considered to be internal to the organization, while reputational and marketplace risks are external. Also, financial and marketplace risks can be easily quantified in financial terms, whereas infrastructure and reputational risks are more difficult to quantify.

The inclusion of reputational risks as a separate category of risk in the FIRM risk scorecard is not universally accepted. It is sometimes argued that damage to reputation is a consequence of other risks materializing and should not be considered as a separate risk category. However, if a broader view of risk is taken, it becomes obvious that reputation is vitally important. This is particularly important when organizations are seeking to use their brand name to enter additional markets, or achieve 'brand stretch' as it is sometimes called.

In any case, there is a wider argument that all risks are a consequence of broader business decisions. Adopting a particular strategy, undertaking a project and/or continuing with established operations all involve risks. If the organization did not undertake these strategic, tactical or operational activities, risks would not be present.

PESTLE risk classification system

Table 11.3 provides an outline of the PESTLE risk classification system. PESTLE is an acronym that stands for political, economic, sociological, technological, legal and ethical risks. In some versions of the approach, the final E is used to indicate narrower environmental considerations. This risk classification system is most applicable to the analysis of hazard risks and is less easy to apply to financial, infrastructure and reputational risks.

Table 11.3 PESTLE classification system

Category of risk	Description
Political	Tax policy, employment laws, environmental regulations, trade restrictions and reform, tariffs and political stability.
Economic	Economic growth/decline, interest rates, exchange rates and inflation rate, wage rates, minimum wage, working hours, unemployment (local and national), credit availability, cost of living, etc.
Sociological	Cultural norms and expectations, health consciousness, population growth rate, age distribution, career attitudes, emphasis on safety, global warming.
Technological	Technology changes that impact your products or services, new technologies, barriers to entry in given markets, financial decisions like outsourcing and supply chain.
Legal	Changes to legislation that may impact employment, access to materials, quotas, resources, imports/exports, taxation, etc.
Ethical or Environmental	Ethical and environmental aspects, although many of these factors will be economic or social in nature.

The PESTLE risk classification system is often seen as most relevant to the analysis of external risks. External risk in this context is intended to refer to the external context that is not wholly within the control of the organization but where action can be taken to mitigate the risks. It is often suggested that the PESTLE risk classification system should be used in conjunction with an analysis of the strengths, weaknesses, opportunities and threats (SWOT) facing the organization. A SWOT analysis of each of the six PESTLE categories is recommended by the *Orange Book*.

The advantage of the PESTLE risk classification system is that it provides a clear analysis of the issues that should be addressed within the external context. The PESTLE approach may be most applicable in the public sector, because the external factors analysed by the PESTLE approach are particularly relevant.

The PESTLE analysis is a commonly used structure for risk identification purposes within a risk assessment workshop. PESTLE may also be considered to be a risk classification system with the emphasis on hazard risks. There are several advantages and disadvantages to the PESTLE approach. The advantages are as follows:

- simple framework;
- facilitates an understanding of the wider business environment;
- encourages the development of external and strategic thinking;
- anticipates future business threats;
- helps identify actions to avoid or minimize impact of threats;
- facilitates identification of business opportunities.

However, there are certain disadvantages associated with the use of the PESTLE analysis as a means of identifying risks. These disadvantages are as follows:

- can over-simplify the amount of data used for decisions;
- needs to be undertaken on a regular basis to be effective;
- requires different people being involved with different perspectives;
- access to quality external data sources can be time-consuming and costly;
- difficult to anticipate developments that may affect an organization in the future;
- risk of capturing too much data that makes it difficult to see priorities;
- can be based on assumptions that subsequently prove to be unfounded.

Compliance, hazard, control and opportunity

Categorizing risks according to a single risk classification system is not always helpful. It may not be sufficient to simply understand the timescale of impact, especially when the nature of the impact is more important. It is for this reason that there will always be difficulties with a simple system for categorizing risks. It is for each organization to identify the risk classification system(s) that suits its particular needs and the nature of the risks facing the organization.

Risks need to be classified according to the source or impact as well as according to the timescale of the impact. Therefore, a combination of the FIRM risk scorecard and the classification of risks as hazard, control and opportunity risks can be used to provide a complete picture.

It is possible to design a personal risk matrix that classifies risks according to the FIRM risk scorecard and also classifies them according to whether they are short term, medium term or long term. This will provide an issues grid that will assist with the identification of all possible significant risks, using a format that can be easily understood. An example of a completed grid is set out in Table 11.4, which presents the issues that could face an individual so that the risks can be identified.

Table 11.4   Personal issues grid

Dependency	Long term	Medium term	Short term
Financial risks	Procedures gap: How well do your procedures manage your finances?		
1 Investments	Pension arrangements Property purchase	Share purchase Business opportunities	Betting habits Insurance arrangements
2 Expenditure	Accommodation Holiday pattern	Car purchase Rail season ticket Credit cards	Shopping behaviour Travel arrangements
Infrastructure risks	Process gap: How well does your body facilitate your processes?		
3 Health	Family history Personal lifestyle Vegetarianism	Medical treatment Dieting Weight gain	Exercise Alcohol and drugs Illness or accident
4 Emotional	Marriage and children Ethnic origins Sexuality	Friendships Cosmetic surgery	Hobbies Sex
Reputational risks	Perception gap: How are you perceived by your peer group?		
5 Personal	Personality Neighbourhood Criminal behaviour	Mood and temperament Charity work	Clothes Personal hygiene Charity donations
6 Professional	Intelligence Behaviour patterns	Qualifications Redundancy Changing jobs	Attending training Continuous learning

(*contiunued*)

Table 11.4 (*Continued*)

Dependency	Long term	Medium term	Short term
Marketplace risks	Presence gap: What is your presence in the marketplace?		
7 Occupation	Career selection Education	Society memberships Present training	Society activities
8 Income	Ambition Seniority	Extra part-time work Sale of shares	Selling possessions Casual work

Many risk classification systems do not pay due regard to compliance risks. Risks can be classified as hazard, control and opportunity or they can be classified as long term, medium term or short term. If either of these classification systems is used, then there is a possibility that compliance risks will not be identified, because they do not necessarily fit within a classification system based on timescales. A further difficulty associated with compliance risks is that there is often the requirement for a trigger event. In other words, an organization can be exposed to a number of compliance risks but it may be difficult to identify the particular compliance issue that will become a problem.

Table 11.4 illustrates the balance of operational, tactical and strategic issues for each of the four headings of the FIRM risk scorecard. It can be seen that hazard risks are closely related to infrastructure issues and strategic risks are more likely to arise in relation to issues concerned with the marketplace.

The risk classification systems discussed in this chapter are most easily applied to the analysis of hazard risks, except that the IRM standard and the COSO ERM cube offer strategic risk as a separate risk category. It will be for an organization to decide whether including a category of strategic risks is helpful and necessary. The FIRM risk scorecard offers a means of classifying strategic and project (or tactical) risks according to the main impact associated with the risk, should it materialize.

As with other core processes in an organization, classification of risks facing projects is essential, so that the appropriate response to each risk can be identified. Given that the requirements of any project are that it should be delivered on time, within budget and to specification, these components offer a means of classifying project risks. Separate lists could be devised of risks that threaten the timescale, risks that threaten the budget and risks that will affect the final specification, performance or quality of the project outcome.

Risk classification in the finance sector

There is no standard risk classification system that can be used by all types of organizations. Banks face a large number of risks and these are usually divided into three main categories of market risk, credit risk and operational risk. Often, the risk management framework and architecture will be different for the different types of risks.

Market risks are risks that occur due to fluctuations in the financial markets. The assets and liabilities of the bank are exposed to various kinds of market volatilities, such as changes in interest rates and foreign exchange rates. Market risk is primarily an opportunity risk that is embraced by the bank.

When the bank lends to a client there is an inherent risk of money not coming back, and this is the credit risk. Credit risk is simply the possibility of the adverse condition in which the client does not pay back the loan amount. It is primarily a control risk that has to be managed.

Operational risk relates to failure of internal systems, processes, technology and humans, and to external factors such as natural disasters, fires, etc. Basel II defines operational risk as 'the risk of direct or indirect loss resulting from inadequate or failed internal processes, people and systems or from external events'. Operational risk has gained profile because of the need to quantify operational risk exposure, the increased use of technology and recognition of the critical role played by people in finance sector processes. Operational risk is primarily a hazard risk that has to be mitigated.

Risk analysis and evaluation

12

Application of a risk matrix

The use of a risk matrix is a very simple way of demonstrating the level of risk that a particular event represents to an organization. A risk matrix is normally used to represent the residual or current level of risk. This can also be referred to as the net risk. When the risk matrix is used to illustrate the current level of risk, the vertical axis will normally be labelled as impact. However, the risk matrix can also be used to represent gross or inherent level of risk, which is the level of risk before controls are applied. When the risk matrix is used to illustrate the inherent level of risk, the vertical axis may sometimes be labelled magnitude.

The concept of consequences is a little different. Impact is used to represent the overall level of risk faced by the organization. This level of risk or impact will arise because of the potential consequences. Therefore, 'consequences' is used as a broader term that provides more detail and information on how successfully the risk is being managed. For example, a warehouse fire could represent a substantial loss that has a high magnitude. If the organization is fully insured, the impact on the finances should be minimal. However, the consequences of the fire could be significant, if (for example) other stakeholders in the vicinity are affected and the reputation of the organization is damaged.

Table 11.4 sets out the range of issues that could be faced by an individual. Using this 'issues grid', individuals would be able to identify the priority significant risks that they face. These risks are illustrated in the risk matrix shown in Figure 12.1. Having placed the various risks on a risk matrix, the relative importance of the risks can easily be identified. An overall view can then be taken as to whether the risk profile (or risk exposure) is within acceptable limits and within the risk appetite and risk capacity of the individual.

Large organizations frequently make use of a risk matrix as a means of summarizing their risk profile. The risk matrix is very useful and can be used for a range of applications. It can also be used to identify the type of risk response that is most likely to be employed.

Impact is not the same as magnitude, because a risk may have a high magnitude in terms of the size of the event, but the impact and consequences may be smaller. To take another example, a road transport company may suffer the complete loss of one of its vehicles but, depending on the exact circumstances, this may have a very small overall impact on the business. This will be especially true if the company did not have sufficient work to fully utilize the type of vehicle involved in the loss.

Figure 12.1   Personal risk matrix

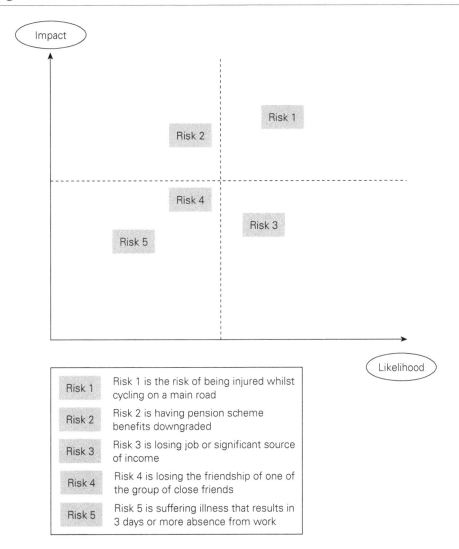

Inherent and current level of risk

Many risk management practitioners assess risk at its current (also referred to as residual) level. However, internal auditors prefer to undertake an assessment of the risk at its inherent level. As discussed in Chapter 10, there are advantages in considering the inherent level of a risk when undertaking a risk assessment. Considering the inherent level will enable the effect of individual control measures to be identified. Figure 12.2 illustrates the effect of controls on the level of risk. Control 1 is an existing control and it reduces the risk from the inherent level to the current (or re-sidual) level and it can be seen that this control has its main effect on the likelihood of the risk materializing.

Control 2 in Figure 12.2 is an additional control that will be introduced to reduce the risk from the current level to the target level. It is intended to have a significant effect on the impact of the risk, but little effect on the likelihood of it materializing. There are three levels of risk that are important on the risk matrix shown in Figure 12.2. The inherent or gross level is the level of risk that would be present if there were no controls in place. The current level is the level at which the risk exists at the time of the risk assessment, when only Control 1 is in place. This is often referred to as the residual level of risk.

The problem with describing the current level as the residual level is that there is an implication that the level of risk is static and that the organization cannot take any further risk mitigation action. Use of the phrase 'current level' gives a much more dynamic feel to the risk management process and so the phrase is used throughout this book. However, the level of risk that is of interest to risk managers is the target level. This is illustrated in Figure 12.2 by the introduction of Control 2, which is in-tended to reduce the impact of the risk, so that the target level of risk is within the bottom left-hand quadrant of the risk matrix, or the tolerate/comfort zone.

Figure 12.2   Inherent, current and target levels of risk

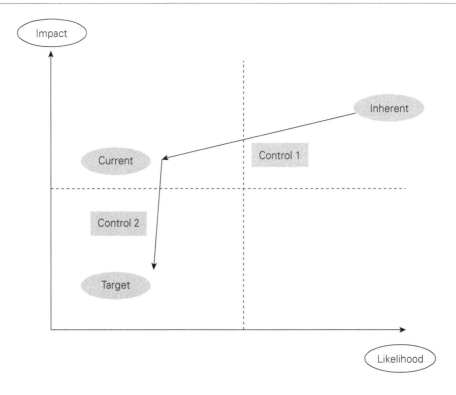

When seeking to establish the target level of risk, a concept that is often used by health and safety practitioners is seeking to reduce the risk to the level that is 'as low as reasonably practicable' (ALARP). ALARP is one of the fundamental principles of risk management for health and safety risks. It is not necessary to manage risk to the point where it is eliminated, but to the point where the cost of additional controls would exceed the benefits. The ALARP concept is illustrated in the text box below.

As low as reasonably practicable (ALARP)

The requirement for risks to be ALARP is fundamental and in simple terms it is a requirement to take all measures to reduce risk where doing so is reasonable. In most cases this is not done through an explicit comparison of costs and benefits, but rather by applying established relevant good practice and standards. The development of relevant good practice and standards includes ALARP considerations, so in many cases meeting those standards is sufficient. In other cases, either where standards and relevant good practice are less evident, or not fully applicable, measures must be implemented to the point where the costs of any additional measures (in terms of money, time or trouble) would be grossly disproportionate to the further risk reduction (or safety benefit) that would be achieved.

An organization will need to agree definitions for likelihood and impact. Both likelihood and impact can be described in terms of low, medium, high and very high. Many organizations will need to be more specific than these generic descriptions, depending on the type of risk and the size, nature and complexity of the organization. Because impact is used to describe the range of consequences, it is more important for an organization to describe low, medium, high and very high in terms of impact. There should be consistency between the definitions used for impact and the benchmark test of significance described in Table 12.1.

Table 12.1 Benchmark tests for risk significance

FIRM risk scorecard	Typical benchmark test for significance
Financial	Impact on balance sheet of 0.25%
	Profit and loss impact of 2.5% annual profit
Infrastructure	Disruption to normal operations of ½ day
	Increased cost of operation exceeds 10% budget
Reputational	Share price falls by 10%
	Event is on national TV, radio or newspapers
Marketplace	Impact on balance sheet of 0.5% turnover
	Profit and loss impact of 1% annual profit

Control confidence

The intended effect of an individual control measure is illustrated in Figure 12.2. It is not possible for an organization to be absolutely confident that controls will always be fully implemented and will be as effective as expected or required. Controls will need to be audited in order to allow confidence that the control selected has been properly designed and implemented and is producing the desired effect.

The level of control confidence can also be illustrated on a risk matrix. If the effectiveness of a control is uncertain, a greater variability of the outcome may be expected. This can be demonstrated on a risk matrix by using a circle or ellipse to represent a risk, instead of representing the risk as a single point on the risk matrix. By doing this, the level of uncertainty or variability in the outcome can be illustrated in relation to both the likelihood and impact of the event materializing.

An important consideration when undertaking a risk assessment and when evaluating the effectiveness of risk management in general, and risk control measures in particular, is the level of confidence that should be placed on a particular control. Two questions need to be asked: 'How confident are we that this is the correct control?' and 'How confident are we that it is fully implemented and effective in practice?' When there is limited confidence in the effectiveness of a control, it will be the role of internal audit to test the control and provide information on the likely level of variability of outcome, should the risk materialize.

It is the responsibility of internal auditors to check that the correct controls have been selected and that they are working correctly in practice. Internal auditors refer to effective and efficient controls respectively when reviewing these points. The use of effective and efficient is also included in this book in relation to core processes of the organization. Undertaking the testing of controls is a key function fulfilled by internal audit and the importance of the testing of controls should also be recognized by risk management practitioners.

Management needs to receive assurance of adequate control and this can come from internal audit activities, or measurement of the outputs of activities and projects, as well as from management reports. The responsibility for designing and implementing controls and auditing the effectiveness and efficiency of controls should be allocated within the risk management documentation.

4Ts of hazard risk response

Figure 4.1 provides a diagram of the risk management process. This diagram sets out the stages of the risk management process in relation to the management of hazard risks. The options presented for risk response can be described as the 4Ts of hazard management, which are: tolerate, treat, transfer and terminate.

It is possible to illustrate the 4Ts of risk response on a simple risk matrix and this is done in Figure 15.1. This figure suggests that in each of the four quadrants of the risk matrix, one of the 4Ts will be dominant, as follows:

- Tolerate will be the dominant response for the low-likelihood/low-impact risks.
- Treat will be the dominant response for high-likelihood/low-impact risks.
- Transfer will be the dominant response for high-impact/low-likelihood risks.
- Terminate will be the dominant response for high-impact/high-likelihood risks.

The corresponding responses for control and opportunity risks are considered in Chapter 15. Options for responding to opportunity risks are identified as the 4Es and decision making in respect of opportunities is described in terms of the 5Es. It is important to note that these responses are represented as the dominant or most likely response in each quadrant, but circumstances may dictate that another response may be required as well, or instead.

Different and/or additional responses may be appropriate, depending on the circumstances. For example, if high-impact/high-likelihood risks are embedded within mission-critical activities, they may be unavoidable. In this case, it will not be possible for the organization to terminate those risks.

A difficulty in presenting such a simple risk matrix showing the 4Ts of risk response is that they meet in the centre. Clearly, it cannot be as simple as suggested, because a small change in the likelihood and impact of a risk could take it from the terminate quadrant into the tolerate quadrant. A slightly modified approach that makes this analysis somewhat more realistic is considered in Chapter 16.

A practical difficulty for many organizations is that they may be forced to retain a risk that is recognized as being beyond the risk appetite, or even the risk capacity, of the organization. For example, a firefighting authority may have to accept circumstances where firefighters will be facing a critical level of risk that the organization has no choice but to tolerate, even though all possible controls have been implemented. Where organizations have to tolerate risks that are at the critical level, it is usual for enhanced monitoring of the risks to be put in place. This will enable the organization to ensure that it takes the earliest opportunity of introducing any enhanced controls as soon as they become available.

Risk significance

When undertaking a risk assessment, it is quite common to identify a hundred or more risks that could impact the objective, core process or key dependency that is being considered. This is an unmanageable number of risks and so a method is required to reduce the number that will be considered to be priority issues for management.

In order for an organization to concentrate on significant risks, a test for risk significance is required. Table 12.1 provides suggestions on the nature of the benchmark tests that could be used to decide whether a risk is significant. For risks that will have a financial or commercial impact, the benchmark test is likely to be based on monetary value. For risks that could disrupt the infrastructure or routine operations of the organization, a benchmark test based on the impact, cost and duration of disruption is appropriate. For reputational risks, the most likely benchmark will be based on the adverse publicity that would result if the risk materializes.

This may vary according to the nature of the risk and whether it is a financial or non-financial one. For large organizations, identifying a financial test for significance can be undertaken in a number of ways. Many organizations will have authorization procedures for spending money, and so the test for risk significance should be compatible with the authorization levels, which are often set out in a formal document referred to as a 'delegation of authority'.

For a large organization, it may be the case that full board approval is required for expenditure in excess of a particular financial threshold. This is an indication of the sum of money that is considered significant by the organization. Other tests include a percentage of the budgeted profit for the year or a percentage of the value of the balance sheet (or reserves) of the organization. Typically, 5 per cent of the annual profit or 0.25 per cent of balance sheet or 0.5 per cent of annual turnover are appropriate tests for significance. For an organization with a £2 billion balance sheet, £1 billion annual turnover and £100 million planned annual profit, the significant financial threshold would be £5 million.

Financial limits can be used to test whether a risk is significant in relation to financial and marketplace risk segments of the FIRM risk scorecard. For infrastructure and reputational segments, identifying a benchmark test for significance may be more difficult. One test of significance for infrastructure risks is to ask whether the risk would disrupt normal operations for more than (say) half a day. For reputational risks, the test for significance may be to determine how the event would be reported. A report on the front page of the local newspaper or in the national press may be an indication that a risk should be considered to be significant.

For an organization, it is possible that the external auditors might indicate that a sum of £1 million would be considered to be a material sum when compiling the accounts of the organization. This would offer guidance to the management of the company to use that amount as the benchmark test of significance, although it may be somewhat lower than the calculation above. Applying this test during a risk assessment workshop could reduce the number of risks for further consideration to about 20. The next stage would be to identify how likely each of the 20 potentially significant risks would be to materialize at or above the financial threshold level. A risk matrix could be used to record and display the results.

Risk capacity

There are several aspects that are important when an organization is deciding how much risk to take. Different approaches will be taken for different types of risks. Hazard risks will give rise to a hazard tolerance, control risks will give rise to a control acceptance and opportunity risks will give rise to an investment appetite. Overall, the organization will have a total risk exposure. This is the sum of the total risk that the organization has taken in these three categories. There will also be compliance risks, but most organizations seek to minimize compliance risks and have the necessary compliance controls embedded into core processes.

Risk exposure is the actual risk that the organization is taking and this may not be the same as the risk appetite that the board believes is appropriate for the organization. There is also another important measure of risk, and that is the risk capacity of the organization. This is a measure of how much risk the organization should take or can afford to take. All of these ways of analysing risk should be compatible with the attitude of the organization to risk.

In simple terms, the risk appetite of the board should be within the risk capacity of the organization and greater than or equal to the actual risk exposure that the organization faces. A contributing factor to the global financial crisis was that certain financial institutions were exposed to a level of risk beyond the risk-bearing capacity of those organizations.

It would be inappropriate for an organization to embark on a project that could exhaust all of its resources. The capacity of the organization to accept risk will depend on its financial strength, the robustness of its infrastructure, the strength of its reputation and brands and the competitive nature of the marketplace in which it operates.

The more rapidly the marketplace is changing, the greater capacity for risk the organization is required to have available. For example, if an organization is facing a significant change in technology, the strategic options may be limited. Consider an organization that is involved in the manufacture of DVD players when it becomes obvious that streaming technology is taking over. The organization will be faced with a significant risk related to the change in technology and will need to develop a new business model. It will have to acquire new production equipment, new skills and new distribution patterns. It may be that the transfer to the new technology and the risks that it involves are outside the resources and risk capacity of the organization. If that is the case, the organization may need to explore strategic options, including seeking a joint-venture partner, locating a buyer for the business or simply withdrawing from the marketplace.

The box below provides a real example of the consequences of the global financial crisis. The financial institution discussed here discovered that the risk exposure it faced was greater than its risk capacity. Having acknowledged that situation, the financial institution then released a statement to shareholders.

In this example, the bank is clearly stating that its risk exposure exceeded the risk appetite of the organization and even its risk capacity. Many circumstances will arise where organizations are faced with risks that could destroy them if those risks materialized. For some organizations, there may be several individual and even independent risks, each of which could destroy the organization.

In these circumstances, the challenge for the risk management function will be to focus on the circumstances that could trigger one or more of these risks. In the example in the box, the bank was lucky enough that circumstances did not arise that would trigger the event(s) that would have destroyed its balance sheet.

Risk capacity of a bank

Risk capacity is the level of risk the bank considers itself capable of absorbing, based on its earnings power, without damage to its dividend paying ability, its strategic plans and, ultimately, its reputation and ongoing business viability. It is based on a combination of budgeted, forecast and historical revenues and costs, adjusted for variable compensation, dividends and related taxes.

Risk exposure is an estimate of potential loss based on current and prospective risk positions across major risk categories – primary risks, operational risk and business risk. It builds as far as possible on the statistical loss measures used in the day-to-day operating controls. Correlations are taken into account when aggregating potential losses from risk positions in various risk categories to obtain an overall estimate of the risk exposure. The risk exposure is assessed against a severe but plausible constellation of events over a one-year time horizon to a 95 per cent confidence level or a 'once in 20 years' event.

Risk appetite is established by the board, which sets an upper boundary on aggregate risk exposure. A comparison of risk exposure with risk capacity serves as a basis for determining whether current or proposed risk limits are appropriate. It is one of the tools available to management to guide decisions on adjustments to the risk profile.

The risk exposure should not normally exceed risk capacity, but in the recent extremely difficult market conditions this relationship has not held. The bank recorded a large net loss, showing that the risk exposures remained greater than its risk capacity. Risk exposure remained high as a result of a lack of liquidity in the markets for securitized assets and due to significantly increased volatility levels in global markets. The reduction in risk exposure that was achieved through sales in addition to the significant write-downs incurred on risk positions was offset by a simultaneous decrease of risk capacity due to downward revisions of earnings expectations as a consequence of the deteriorating economic outlook.

Loss control 13

Risk likelihood

Risk likelihood indicates how often a risk is expected to materialize. It can also be described as risk frequency. However, using the phrase risk frequency assumes that the risk occurs on a regular basis. The more general term risk likelihood is used throughout this book. Risk likelihood can be determined on an inherent basis for any particular risk, or can be determined at the current level of risk, paying regard to the control measures that are in place.

For hazard risks, previous history may be a good indication of how likely the risk is to occur. For a fleet of motor vehicles, there is certain to be a history of vehicle accidents and breakdowns. Controls will be in place to reduce the likelihood of these events. A road haulage company should assess the likelihood of vehicle breakdowns on an inherent basis and also on the basis of current controls. There are, however, difficulties in assessing the inherent likelihood of vehicle accidents, because certain assumptions would have to be taken about what effect the removal of controls would have on the likelihood of accidents.

Even if an assessment of the breakdown likelihood at the inherent level cannot be undertaken, the company will still need to determine the importance of the vehicle maintenance programme in preventing vehicle breakdowns and whether the maintenance activities provide value for money. In relation to vehicle accidents, the company may have driver-training procedures in place and, again, the effectiveness of these procedures can be determined by evaluating inherent and current levels of risk. Whether levels of risk are evaluated at inherent or at current level, there is no doubt that benchmarking the performance of the fleet against the average performance of the industry will be a useful exercise.

An example of a control measure that has an effect on the magnitude of the risk but may have no effect on its likelihood is the use of seat belts in cars. In simple terms, the driver wears a seat belt to reduce the impact of an accident, because the seat belt has no effect on the likelihood of an accident occurring. The driver wears the seat belt as a control measure for when the accident happens.

A sports club will wish to reduce the chances of a key player being absent. The absence may be caused by inappropriate behaviour by a player, resulting in the need for sanctions against that person. Accordingly, the club may decide to introduce a 'code of behaviour' for senior players, and this would include a commitment by each player to follow an appropriate, healthy lifestyle. Failure to comply with the code of behaviour would result in financial and other punishments.

The club may also decide that additional controls are required to reduce player absence, including fitness monitoring and social support for overseas players who have recently moved to the country to join the team. It may also be agreed that an attempt should be made to place contractual limits on the ability of national teams to call on its overseas players. These actions will be taken in addition to other loss control activities, such as excellent medical facilities to provide immediate medical care and reduce the damage when an injury occurs. Also, the company may purchase insurance to protect itself against the financial losses associated with the absence of a player.

Risk magnitude

Reducing the magnitude of a hazard risk is very important. For hazard risks, magnitude is often referred to as the inherent severity of the risk should it materialize. Reduction in overall hazard risk severity will be achieved by reducing both the impact and consequences when the adverse event occurs. The seat belt in a car can reduce the impact of an accident, but has no effect on the likelihood of having an accident.

It is possible for a serious fire to occur that results in a considerable amount of property damage and is considered to be very severe and expensive. However, in reducing the severity of a serious fire, the requirement is to reduce the impact of the fire on the finances, infrastructure, reputation and marketplace (FIRM) of the organization. Actions to reduce impact will concentrate on damage limitation at the time of the fire and cost containment after the event. The consequences relate to the effect on the strategy, tactics, operations and compliance (STOC) of the organization. Loss control is concerned with mitigation of the magnitude, impact and consequences of an adverse event.

Damage limitation is also an important feature of reputational risk management. When a serious incident occurs that attracts public attention, an organization will need to be able to protect its reputation by reassuring stakeholders that the organization responded appropriately to the event. It is almost invariably the case that the CEO or chairman of the company will arrive at the scene when there has been a serious train or plane crash.

There have been examples where a serious incident has occurred and the management of the media by the organization has been very poor. In these cases, it is likely that inadequate attention was paid to pre-incident planning, so that the damage to the reputation of the organization was not effectively minimized at the time the incident occurred.

Organizations will also need to be concerned with cost containment. Cost containment following an event is usually based on the business continuity plan (BCP) or disaster recovery plan (DRP) that the organization put in place before the incident occurred. The development of effective BCP and DRP will put the organization in the best position to ensure that the overall cost of the incident is kept as low as possible.

Control of fires in hotels

Given the long emphasis on fire peril, perhaps it's not surprising that improvements in sprinkler systems have been a hallmark of the past 40 years. The single most impressive innovation as it relates to fire has been the advent of the suppression mode sprinkler. Standard sprinklers were control mode sprinklers, which controlled the fire until someone arrived to put it out. The fire could grow and produce a lot of smoke.

As hotel fittings became more susceptible to smoke and water damage, the desire was to suppress the fire, not just control it. The new sprinklers resulted in smaller areas being affected by fire with less smoke and less damage.

Sprinkler technology has evolved significantly. Where we had a single standard spray sprinkler head, we now have extra-large orifice heads and early-suppression, fast-response sprinkler heads. The use of sprinkler systems has also spread from more traditional manufacturing facilities into light-hazard exposures such as offices and nursing homes.

Corporations became more deeply involved in loss control efforts. For example, hotels carried out two initiatives in the early 1980s using controlled fires to prove the efficacy of plastic piping in hotel room sprinkler systems. Before the successful tests, sprinklers relied on iron piping, which was more difficult to install than plastic and which took rooms out of service for days during a re-fit.

Hazard risks

The range of hazard risks where reducing the magnitude of the adverse event is important will include fraud, health and safety, property protection and efficient operation of IT systems, as well as incidents with the potential to cause damage to reputation. Table 13.1 provides a list of the key dependencies that could give rise to hazard risks, using the structure of the FIRM risk scorecard. When hazard risks materialize, actions need to be taken to reduce the magnitude of the event, as well as mitigate the impact and consequences.

Although the main focus of managing hazard risks will be on loss prevention, successful management of hazard risks must also include consideration of damage limitation and cost containment. There is a developing trend in the insurance market towards settling claims in a more efficient and cost-effective manner. This trend is partly based on encouraging organizations to get back to normal operation as soon as possible. Indeed, some insurance companies refer to initiatives of this type as 'cost containment'.

As mentioned previously, reducing the severity of an incident should be seen as part of an overall attempt to implement loss control in an organization. An integrated approach to loss control is important because it will enable the organization to control both the likelihood and impact when a hazard risk materializes. In fact, loss control should be considered to be loss prevention plus damage limitation plus cost containment.

Table 13.1   Generic key dependencies

FIRM risk scorecard	Example dependencies
Financial	Availability of funds/finance
	Correct allocation of funds/finance
	Internal control (fraud)
	Liabilities under control (bad debts and pensions)
Infrastructure	People skills and experience
	Premises/plant and equipment
	IT hardware and software
	Communication and transport
Reputational	Brand and brand expansion
	Public opinion of sector
	Regulators' enforcement action
	Corporate social responsibility
Marketplace	Regulatory requirements
	Health of world or national economy
	Product development (technology)
	Competitor behaviour

Although the most important component of loss control is loss prevention, hazard risks can materialize despite the best efforts of organizations. Adequate assessment of hazard risks is vital, so that appropriate pre-planning of during-the-loss and post-loss actions can be undertaken. Plans should be in place to ensure that the damage caused by the incident is kept to a minimum and the cost consequences of the event are also tightly controlled and contained.

Figure 13.1 shows how a bow-tie can be used to illustrate the three components of loss control. Before the event occurs, the organization will have controls in place to seek to achieve loss prevention. As the event is developing, steps should be in place to limit the damage that the event is causing. After the event, cost containment controls by way of business continuity and arrangements to reduce the cost of repair should be activated. Disaster recovery plans will be relevant during both the damage limitation and the cost containment stages. The relationship between the three components of loss control and the type of control that will be selected is considered in more detail in Chapter 16. The types of hazard controls are described in Chapter 16 as preventive, corrective, directive and detective.

Figure 13.1 Loss control and the bow-tie

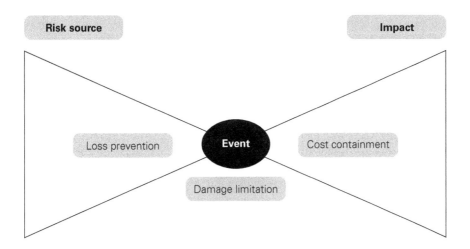

Loss prevention

Another way of looking at loss control activities is that loss prevention is about reducing the likelihood of an adverse event occurring, although it will also be concerned with reducing the magnitude of an event that does occur. Damage limitation is concerned with reducing the magnitude of the event when it does materialize. The contribution of damage limitation will be greatest if actions are planned that can be implemented as the event is actually taking place. Cost containment is concerned with reducing the impact and consequences of the event. Cost containment will be concerned with ensuring the lowest cost of repairs, as well as business continuity plans to ensure that the organization can continue operations following damage to the asset that has been affected.

Techniques for loss prevention will vary according to the type of hazard risk that is being considered. For health and safety risks, loss prevention is related to eliminating the activity completely or ensuring that, for example, hazardous chemicals are no longer used.

For risks to buildings, loss prevention techniques involve such controls as the elimination of sources of ignition and the control, containment and segregation of flammable or combustible materials. Loss prevention techniques will also include restrictions on smoking and other actions taken to reduce hazardous behaviours by persons using the buildings.

For fraud and theft risks, loss prevention techniques will include separation of responsibilities and security tagging of expensive items. Fraud prevention techniques may also involve pre-employment screening. A more detailed consideration of health and safety risks and fraud prevention is set out in Chapters 16 and 23.

Damage limitation

Damage limitation in relation to fire hazards is well established. Although sprinkler systems are often considered to be a loss prevention measure, they are in fact the major control measure for ensuring that only limited damage occurs when a fire breaks out. Other damage limitation factors related to fire include the use of fire segregation within buildings, the use of fire shutters, and having well-rehearsed arrangements in place to remove, segregate or otherwise protect valuable items. After the fire at Windsor Castle in 1992, arrangements were quickly put in place for valuable artwork to be removed from areas of the castle that had not (up to that time) been affected by the fire.

Accidents at work still occur, despite the considerable attention paid to health and safety standards and other loss prevention activities. Provision of adequate first aid arrangements is an obvious damage limitation activity and suitable first aid facilities are provided by most organizations. For some high-risk factory occupancies, emergency treatment arrangements and even medical facilities are provided on site.

In some cases, these medical facilities will include specialist treatment facilities related to the particular hazards on site. An example is the provision of cyanide antidotes in factories where chromium-plating activities take place using cyanide-plating solutions. A simpler example is the provision of emergency eye-wash bottles in locations where hazardous chemicals are handled.

The Deepwater Horizon oil spill in the Gulf of Mexico in 2010 provides many risk management lessons. One of the key issues was that the oil spill took some weeks to stop. Loss prevention measures were in place to prevent the oil spill starting and cost containment steps were taken to manage the cost of clean-up, recovery and business continuity. It is, perhaps, the case that the damage limitation measures were not as robust as may have been required. Because the oil leak lasted some weeks, there was opportunity for damage limitation measures to be introduced. However, it does not appear that these measures had been sufficiently planned in advance.

Cost containment

When a hazard risk materializes despite the efforts put into loss prevention and the efforts that have been put into damage limitation, there may well still be a need to contain the cost of the event. For example, among the activities for minimizing costs associated with serious fires are detailed arrangements for salvage and arrangements for decontamination of specialist items that have suffered water or smoke damage.

Cost containment in relation to a fire will also include arrangements for specialist recovery services. The actions that will be taken to ensure that post-incident costs are minimized should all be set out in business continuity, disaster recovery and crisis management plans, as appropriate. The topics of business continuity planning and disaster recovery planning are considered in more detail in Chapter 18.

A further consideration relevant to cost containment after an incident is what insurance companies refer to as 'increased cost of operation'. Most material damage/ business interruption insurance policies will allow for payment of increased cost of operation. This may arise when an organization has to sub-contract certain production activities, or has to undertake manufacturing work at another one of its factories, which may be located some distance away.

If a manufacturer discovers that faulty goods have been released into the market-place, a number of actions become necessary. The organization should have developed plans in advance of the event for notifying customers of the fact that faulty goods are in the marketplace and how to identify them. The box below considers the importance of product recall in these circumstances.

Product recall risk management

Any company or organization that manufactures, assembles, processes, wholesales or retails products could be financially impacted by the direct or indirect costs of a product recall. Direct costs can include wages for staff who have to implement the recall plan. Other direct costs include communications and this could entail purchasing air time on radio and television and notices in newspapers or industry publications.

Indirect costs can include lost production time for staff who must focus on the recall process, as well as the hiring of temporary employees to ensure continued production. However, the greatest indirect cost is the impact that adverse publicity could have on market share. A product recall should be designed to:

- protect the customer from bodily injury or property damage;
- remove the product from the market and from production;
- comply with specific regulatory requirements;
- protect the assets of the company.

Defining the upside of risk

14

Upside of risk

Defining the upside of risk is one of the greatest challenges for risk management. The overall contribution of risk management is to help deliver mandatory obligations, assurance, enhanced decision making, as well as effective and efficient core processes (MADE2). However, there is a desire amongst risk management practitioners to identify a more dynamic range of benefits that can be delivered by successful risk management. Often, these are the unexpected or greater than expected benefits of managing risk.

A range of interpretations of the phrase 'upside of risk' is possible, and some of these are offered in Table 14.1. There is a belief amongst risk management practitioners that risk management makes a significant contribution to the operation of the organization, and this contribution is often described as the upside of risk. In simple terms, the upside of risk is achieved when the benefits obtained from taking the risk are greater than any benefit that would have resulted from not taking it. In other words, the organization has received an overall benefit from undertaking the activities that resulted in exposure to the risk or set of risks involved.

For example, a manufacturing company that produces waste by-products that create a disposal problem may achieve the upside of risk by selling the unwanted by-product or by identifying a means of adding value to the waste product and selling it as another product stream. This is an example of identifying a difficulty for the business and, in solving that difficulty, acquiring additional benefits that had not been foreseen and were not otherwise available.

In simple terms, the upside of risk may just be the reward for taking the risk in the first place. Climbing a challenging mountain may be a significant risk, but the upside of taking that risk is when the climber has safely reached the summit and gains that reward. Another approach is to say that risk management is concerned with achieving the best possible outcomes and reducing uncertainty or volatility. If this is accepted as a definition of risk management, the upside of risk is simply achieving what the organization set out to achieve, by taking the risks that were embedded in the strategy, tactics and/or operations that were involved.

Another interpretation of the upside of risk is that the risk assessment workshop should also focus on identifying risks that have an upside outcome. The risk assessment workshop would therefore address questions like: 'What events would create a better outcome than expected?' A register of positive outcome risks can then be identified and actions can be taken to make those upside risks more likely

Table 14.1 Defining the upside of risk

Fewer disruptions to normal operations and greater operational efficiency resulting in less downside of risk.
Ability to seize an opportunity because competitors did not identify the cost-effective solution to a risky feature of a contract.
Specifically identifying positive events during the risk assessment and deciding how to encourage those events.
Opportunity management, by completing a detailed review of a business opportunity before deciding to embrace it.
Achieving a positive outcome in difficult circumstances as an unintended and/or automatic result of good risk management.

to occur and/or have more beneficial impact and consequences when they do materialize.

A more satisfactory explanation of the upside of risk is that the organization will be able to undertake activities that it would not otherwise have the appetite to undertake. In a commercial sense, this is enabling an organization to seize a business opportunity that a competitor does not have the appetite to take, or considers to be too risky. This may be because of the greater efficiency within the organization, or because a cost-effective means of changing the organization by a development project has been identified that the competitor failed to recognize. On a strategic level, this upside of risk may arise from the organization identifying a means of targeting the business opportunity, but only the profitable component of that business opportunity.

A further way of looking at the upside of risk is to reflect on a business venture that turned out successfully in circumstances where failure could have been foreseen. This is a somewhat retrospective approach based on the analysis: 'that could have gone wrong, but it did not and therefore we have enjoyed the upside of taking that risk.' This approach to the upside of risk depends on the organization being willing to pursue a risky venture, albeit with adequate controls in place, that leads to a positive outcome in circumstances where a competitor may not have been willing to take the risk.

Finally, there is the analysis of the upside of risk that reflects on the benefits of having a robust risk management process. Achieving the MADE2 benefits, especially benefits related to mandatory obligations, may be considered to be a sufficient reason for undertaking a risk management initiative. In these circumstances, certain organizations may consider that achieving compliance with mandatory obligations is an upside of risk.

At its most simplistic, and specifically in relation to hazard risks, the upside of risk is that there is less downside. However, that is not a very compelling reason for senior managers to support a risk management initiative. Perhaps the most easy to explain and the most compelling thought is that the upside of risk is the ability to pursue a business opportunity that competitors would be unwilling to embrace. It would also be part of the explanation to say that competitors would be too risk-averse to take such a high-risk opportunity.

With so much talk about the upside of risk, it has become a problem for risk management practitioners. The range of analyses from less downside to formalized opportunity management is wide and lacks focus. The board of an organization is not going to be persuaded by such a wide-ranging and ill-defined set of concepts and approaches. Clearly, the discipline of risk management needs to get a better understanding of the upside of risk and sell the message to the board.

Perhaps there is also scope for the risk management standards to take a more coherent approach to the upside of risk. An approach employed in some risk management standards is that the 4Ts should be extended to include the fifth T of 'take the risk' and become the 5Ts. Very often, the established standards fail to recognize that the organization will be taking the opportunity and the intended rewards, rather than deliberately taking the risk for its own sake.

The story in the box below is an example of an individual who saw an opportunity and embraced that opportunity. He did not seek, embrace or take the risk, except insofar as it was embedded in taking the opportunity. It is the case that individuals who are seen as risk takers are, in fact, individuals who are willing to pursue opportunities that others may consider too risky. Their behaviour is about embracing the opportunity, not necessarily enjoying taking the associated risks.

Honesty box and the upside of risk

Consider the case of the vendor in Wall Street, New York City, who set up a stand and sold donuts and coffee to passers-by as they went in and out of their office buildings. During the breakfast and lunch hours, he always had long lines of customers waiting. He noticed that the time wait discouraged many customers who left and went elsewhere. He also noticed that, as he was a one-man show, the biggest bottleneck preventing him from selling more donuts and coffee was the disproportionate amount of time it took to make change for his customers.

Finally, he put a small basket on the side of his stand filled with dollar bills and coins, trusting his customers to make their own change. You might think that customers would accidentally count wrong or intentionally take extra quarters from the basket, but what he found was the opposite – most customers responded by being completely honest, often leaving him with larger-than-normal tips. Also, he was able to move customers through at twice the pace because he didn't have to make change. In addition, he found that his customers liked being trusted and kept coming back. By extending trust in this way, he was able to double his revenues without adding any new cost.

Opportunity assessment

Successfully embracing business opportunities is more likely to be achieved if the organization undertakes opportunity assessments. Many consultancy firms undertake a detailed evaluation of each new business prospect. The organization will look at the new prospect and evaluate the scope for a profitable partnership, opportunities to earn extra income and the reputational benefits that might arise from having that potential client as a customer.

Opportunity assessment can be undertaken in relation to new business ventures, as well as new clients. This opportunity evaluation is designed to identify the additional business opportunities that could arise from winning that client business. The evaluation will also look at the potential disadvantages of successfully acquiring the client prospect. When undertaking such an opportunity assessment, there has to be the possibility that the organization will advise the client prospect that they do not wish to tender for the business.

Consider the options for a theatre that discovers that fewer people are coming to performances and decides to look at the opportunities to take more money from those who continue to attend. The options may include general improvement to the catering facilities within the theatre and the provision of organic produce in the theatre restaurant. Additionally, there is the possibility of selling merchandise themed to the particular performance.

As well as looking at increased revenue during performances, the theatre may also look at sponsorship arrangements and open dialogue with local businesses to discover what type of production would be most likely to gain local support and sponsorship. In future, part of the assessment of any proposed new production could include an evaluation of the level of sponsorship that might be available. As well as generating greater income, this approach could also enable the theatre to stage productions that otherwise would have been considered too risky.

Many organizations already practise opportunity management, although it may not be seen explicitly as a risk management approach. Ideally, opportunity management should be embedded into procedures for developing and implementing strategy and tactics and/or taking advantage of business opportunities. Some organizations do not have explicit opportunity management procedures for the evaluation of new business prospects, or for the evaluation of merger/acquisition opportunities.

When seeking to identify opportunities, many organizations facilitate a risk assessment workshop that seeks to identify and analyse hazards and opportunities at the same time. Figure 14.1 provides an example of a risk matrix that can be used to record the outcome of such a risk assessment workshop. The exact design of the risk matrix and the descriptors of likelihood and consequence will vary between organizations. Figure 14.1 should be treated as one example or illustration of how to record the output from the risk assessment workshop.

One of the challenges when undertaking a risk assessment workshop that covers both opportunities and hazards is that a wide range of people will need to attend the workshop. Hazards tend to be operational- and compliance-related, whereas opportunities tend to be associated with strategy and tactics. As with hazard risks, the identification and analysis of opportunities has to be followed by evaluation of the opportunities and the identification of actions or controls that will need to be in place to ensure that the anticipated benefits are more likely to be achieved. The opportunity assessment methodology described earlier in this section will need to be applied to the opportunities that have been identified, analysed and recorded on the risk matrix.

Figure 14.1   Risk matrix for opportunities and hazards

Upside Risk			Likelihood			Downside Risk
High	High	Medium	1:2 Probable	Medium	High	High
High	Medium	Low	1:10 Possible	Low	Medium	High
Medium	Low	Low	1:100 Unlikely	Low	Low	Medium
Major	Moderate	Minor		Minor	Moderate	Major
Consequence						
Multiple objectives exceeded beneficially	Objective delivered significantly early, better, or cheaper	Objective delivered slightly early, better or cheaper	Objective-driven (customer, people, society or key performance)	Slippage and minor deviation	Failure to meet an objective	Extinction of organization

Riskiness index

The risk profile of an organization can be represented in many ways. The most common method used is to prepare a risk register that contains details of the significant risks that it faces. However, a disadvantage of the risk register is that it is usually a qualitative evaluation of individual risks. Organizations need to develop a means of measuring, evaluating and quantifying the total risk exposure of the organization.

One of the features of the enterprise risk management approach is to develop a consolidated view of the risk exposure of the organization. The approach based on calculating the total risk exposure of an organization is similar to the approach taken to the measurement and quantification of risk in operational risk management.

This section introduces the idea of a 'riskiness index'. The idea is to present a semi-quantitative approach that takes a snapshot of the overall level of risk embedded in the organization. The overall level of risk will take account of the strategy currently being followed by the organization, the projects that are in progress, and the nature of the routine operations being undertaken. This approach can offer an opportunity to benchmark risk management performance and track changes over time.

Table 14.2 presents a set of questions that can be used to develop a riskiness index for an organization. The table uses the structure of the FIRM risk scorecard as a means of categorizing risks. By using the riskiness index, an organization should be able to identify the level of risk faced by its finances, infrastructure, reputation and the level of risk that it faces in the marketplace.

Table 14.2 Riskiness index

Allocate a score of between 0 and 5 to each component (in accordance with the key at the end of the table) of the generic example of the FIRM risk scorecard to determine the level of risk within the organization, project, operation or location being evaluated.

Financial component of the FIRM risk scorecard

Index	Description	Score
1.1	Lack of availability (or unacceptable cost) of adequate funds to fulfil the strategic plans	
1.2	Insufficiently robust procedures for correct allocation of funds for strategic investment	
1.3	Inadequate internal financial control environment to prevent fraud and control credit risks	
1.4	Inadequate funds to meet historical liabilities (including pensions) and meet future anticipated liabilities	
TOTAL for the financial component		

Infrastructure component of the FIRM risk scorecard

Index	Description	Score
2.1	Inadequate senior management structure to support organization and embed 'risk-aware culture'	
2.2	Insufficient people resources, skills and availability, including concerns about intellectual property	
2.3	Inadequate physical assets to support the operational and strategic aims of the organization	
2.4	Information technology (IT) infrastructure has insufficient resilience and/or data protection	
2.5	Business continuity plans are not sufficiently robust to ensure continuation of organization after major loss	
2.6	Product delivery, transport arrangements and/or communications infrastructure unreliable	
TOTAL for the infrastructure component		

(continued)

Table 14.2   (*Continued*)

Reputational component of the FIRM risk scorecard		
Index	**Description**	**Score**
3.1	Poor public perception of the industry sector and/or potential for damage to the brands of the organization	
3.2	Insufficient attention to ethics/corporate social responsibility/ social, environmental and ethical standards	
3.3	Poor governance standards and/or sector is highly regulated with high compliance expectations	
3.4	Concerns over quality of products or services and/or after-sales service standards	
TOTAL for the reputational component		

Marketplace component of the FIRM risk scorecard		
Index	**Description**	**Score**
4.1	Insufficient revenue generation in the marketplace or inadequate return on investment achieved	
4.2	Highly competitive marketplace with aggressive competitors and high customer expectations	
4.3	Lack of economic stability, including exposure to interest rate fluctuations and foreign exchange rates	
4.4	Marketplace requires constant innovation and/or product technology is rapidly developing	
4.5	Supply chain is complex and lacks competition and/or raw materials costs are volatile	
4.6	Organization is exposed to potential for international disruption because of political risks, war, terrorism, crime or pandemic	
TOTAL for the marketplace component		

Score	Description of the level of risk	Score	Description of the level of risk
0	No risk	3	Medium risk
1	Little risk	4	High risk
2	Some risk	5	Extreme risk

Having completed the riskiness index, the organization can then seek additional controls to reduce the level of risk. The main focus of risk management is then simply to reduce the level of riskiness within the organization without affecting its strategy, tactics, operations or compliance (STOC). The upside of risk then becomes that the organization can follow the desired STOC at the lowest level of risk that is reasonably and cost-effectively achievable.

The level of risk identified by the riskiness index represents the risk exposure of the organization. The board can then compare this level of risk exposure with the risk capacity of the organization and the attitude of the board towards risk.

Calculating the riskiness index of an organization requires identification of the hazard risks actually being taken by that organization. In other words, evaluating the riskiness index of an organization helps to identify the actual risk exposure of that organization. Having identified the actual level of risk embedded within an organization, the board of that organization can then ask whether the portfolio of risks is within the risk appetite and/or the risk capacity of the organization and compatible with the risk attitude of the board.

The 2016 version of the UK Corporate Governance Code contains the following requirement for companies listed on the London Stock Exchange:

> The board is responsible for determining the nature and extent of the principal risks it is willing to take in achieving its strategic objectives.

Organizations should be careful to ensure that, having identified the risks that they are taking by a mechanism similar to calculating the riskiness index, the board does not then simply decide that the risks it is currently taking must be the same as the risks it is willing to take.

Upside in strategy

Organizations will have a mission statement, together with a set of corporate objectives and an understanding of the expectations of the different stakeholders in the organization. The board of the organization then needs to develop an effective and efficient strategy that will deliver exactly what is expected in terms of the mission, objectives and expectations. In order to make correct strategic decisions, the board of the organization will need access to risk information. A risk assessment of the proposed strategy, together with a risk assessment of any viable alternative strategies, should be undertaken. The availability of this risk assessment information will ensure that the strategic decisions are more likely to be correct.

For opportunity risks, there is probably even less data available on which to predict risk likelihood. An organization may see an opportunity to acquire a new client or develop and market a new product. Accurate risk assessment of the likelihood of positive and negative events will be necessary in order to determine whether the new venture should go ahead. When a new product is launched, the requirement may well be to increase the likelihood of a positive event occurring. If a new product is being launched, advertising and press coverage will need to be maximized up to the point that this remains cost-effective. Actions should therefore be taken to increase the level of media interest in the launch.

Strategic core processes bring the disciplines of strategic planning and risk management together. Strategic planning is a systematic process for obtaining a consensus at board level on the small number of issues that could have a massive effect on the long-term performance of the organization. Strategic issues are vitally important, and failure to implement strategy or the selection of an inappropriate strategy can be amongst the most devastating risks to hit an organization. Implementation of strategy is usually achieved by developing tactics that are implemented by way of projects and then ultimately delivered by operational core processes. The operational core processes in place at a specific time represent the business model of the organization, as is discussed in more detail in Chapter 20.

Risk management activities are designed to ensure the best possible outcome and reduce uncertainty. Therefore, the upside of risk in strategy is that risk management efforts help with the design of an effective and efficient strategy. The implementation of that strategy will be achieved through the tactics employed. Those tactics will be designed to improve core processes in the organization, so that the organization is using the most effective and efficient core processes.

The boxed example describes an attitude to risk management that sees risk as opportunity. This approach to the management of the organization demonstrates the desire to embrace the upside of risk.

Upside in projects

It is essential that every organization adopts the correct core processes. A core process may be considered as the collection of activities that deliver a specific stakeholder expectation. This is the meaning of core process that is allocated by business process re-engineering (BPR) practitioners.

There is a difference between a process being efficient and effective. An efficient process means that there is no disruption and no excess cost. However, the process may be the incorrect one for cost-effectively delivering the requirements. Where processes need to be improved, a project will normally be undertaken and change achieved. In circumstances where a series of projects are required, this is often referred to as a programme of work. When a project, or programme of work, is implemented by an organization, the desire will normally be to improve the effectiveness and/or efficiency of core processes.

By undertaking adequate risk assessment of the intended change, the organization should be able to ensure that the project is more successfully delivered on time, within budget and to specification. Achieving the upside of risk in the project or programme management requires that projects are adequately managed and that the correct project or priorities have been selected by the organization.

Often, organizations will undertake a post-implementation review to ensure that the benefits expected from the project have been delivered in practice. This review is often undertaken by internal audit and is designed to ensure that the project was delivered successfully, delivered the benefits that were required and was overall worthwhile. During difficult financial times, it is important that the organization selects projects that are not only successful, but represent the best possible allocation of limited resources when compared with alternative projects that have not been selected.

Risk management in projects is associated with the implementation of tactics designed to achieve the strategy. In some organizations, projects that will implement tactics are only approved if the project reduces risk. For example, if a particular activity could fail because of poor IT systems, the project should be designed to make the activity more robust. In doing so, risks will be reduced and it should be possible to quantify the benefits that will result from activities that are more efficient because of better use of human resources and because of fewer failures of IT systems.

In summary, the benefits of good risk management within projects are that the project is more likely to be delivered on time, to budget and at the required quality. Risk management activities will assist the delivery of the project and, at the same time, help manage a situation when an outcome is different from what was expected as the project progresses. This different outcome will demonstrate whether the tactics have been successful and the correct project was selected. A negative difference will need to be mitigated and a positive difference will be embraced, as this is one example of the upside of risk.

Embracing opportunities

Consider two simple examples where the global financial crisis has resulted in benefit or upside of risk for organizations.

An international restaurant brand has discovered that landlords in city centre locations are looking for tenants. This has enabled the restaurant business to relocate into busier parts of a city centre at reduced rents, whilst also increasing trade and profits.

With the reduction in industrial activity resulting from the global financial crisis, an electricity generating company has been able to decommission old, costly generating facilities, and thereby reduce the overall cost per unit of producing electricity. This has increased profit per unit and enabled the company to revise strategic plans for future additional generating capacity to reduce generating costs over the long term.

Upside in operations

It is a fundamental requirement for organizations that they have effective and efficient operations. Efficient operations should make best use of the resources of the organization and should operate without unplanned disruption. Undertaking efficient operations that use minimum resources and produce maximum output will deliver the greatest benefit to the organization. Operations also need to be effective in that they represent the best way of conducting the operations. For example, it is possible to have an efficient journey by car or bus across a busy city. However, the effective way to travel in many large cities is by means of the metro or underground system.

Risk management evaluation of operations can enable the organization to deliver the most effective and efficient activities, operations and processes. By delivering the most effective and efficient operations, a commercial organization can achieve advantages over a competitor and undertake work for a lower cost and still make a profit.

For public services, the delivery of effective and efficient operations is equally important. Most public services have targets for delivery of those services that can be complex and challenging. Failure to anticipate and manage risks appropriately can undermine the delivery of public services. The contribution of risk management will also help achieve sustained improvements in service by bringing flexibility and resilience to the way in which services are delivered. This contribution by risk management may be considered to be part of delivering the upside of risk.

In a competitive marketplace, achieving the upside of risk will often be to the detriment of competitors, suppliers or other third parties. However, seeking the upside of risk taking requires awareness of a possible unexpected downside. Deciding not to do something because it appears to have become more hazardous may actually result in the risks increasing. Further aspects of risk appetite and personal perception of risk are discussed in Chapter 25. In terms of business decisions about operational risk, it is important that those risks are taken on an objective basis. Personal views and perceptions of risk can lead to incorrect business decisions. Ensuring the availability of accurate risk information in order to make business decisions is one of the key responsibilities of the risk manager.

Chapter 7 confirms that establishing the context is the first stage in the risk management process. The riskiness index set out in Table 14.2 provides a useful structure for establishing both the external context and the internal context of the organization. When establishing the context, it is important to consider the upside of risk and how opportunities will emerge for the organization and how these opportunities can be exploited, in relation to strategy, tactics and operations.

Finally, it is important to note that there is an upside that can be achieved in relation to compliance risks. For some organizations, there will be a regulator that grants licences and, without a licence, the organization cannot operate. In these circumstances, a good working relationship with the regulator can often provide an upside of risk. This will be especially true if the organization seeks to influence the regulator to require tighter control of regulated activities. In this way, the organization will set high standards that it is able to achieve, in the hope that competitors may suffer disadvantage, if they also have to achieve these high standards, but are not able to do so without additional expense.

PART FOUR
Risk response

LEARNING OUTCOMES FOR PART FOUR

- describe the risk response options in terms of tolerate, treat, transfer and terminate (4Ts), and explain how these can be shown on a risk matrix;
- explain the benefits of using a risk matrix to illustrate inherent, current and target levels of risk and the effect of controls;
- describe the types of controls that are available, in terms of preventive, corrective, directive and detective (PCDD) controls;
- explain the use of a risk matrix to identify the main type of control for different types of hazard risk and the concept of 'hazard risk zones';
- describe the importance and structure of insurance and the circumstances in which insurance is purchased and the purpose of a captive insurance company;
- explain the importance to the insurance purchasing activity of cost, coverage, capacity, capabilities, claims and compliance (6Cs);
- summarize the importance of business continuity planning (BCP) and disaster recovery planning (DRP) and provide practical examples;
- describe the approach taken during a business impact analysis (BIA) and the importance of established business continuity standards, such as ISO 22301.

PART FOUR FURTHER READING

HM Treasury (2004) *Orange Book: Management of Risk – Principles and Concepts*, **www.hm-treasury.gov.uk**

Institute of Risk Management (2011) *Risk Appetite & Tolerance*, **www.theirm.org**

International Standard ISO 22301:2012 *Societal Security. Business Continuity Management Systems – Requirements*, **www.iso.org**

Taleb, NN(2008) *The Black Swan: The Impact of the Highly Improbable*, **www.penguin.co.uk**

Taylor, E (2014) *Practical Enterprise Risk Management*, **www.koganpage.com**
United States Government (2004) *Every Business Should Have a Plan*, **www.ready.gov**

PART FOUR CASE STUDIES

Intu Properties: Insurance renewal

As part of the renewal processes for 2015, insurers were invited to visit Intu centres to see the business in action. As a result, significant interest was generated and a reduction in Intu's insurance renewal rates of more than £1 million on a like-for-like basis was achieved and passed on to tenants.

The site visits were accompanied by a detailed presentation highlighting how Intu's proactive approach reduces risk for both the insurers and the business, for example:

- National Counter Terrorism Security Office links for all centres;
- documented crisis management plan and procedures;
- documented emergency plans, for example threat-level response, business impact assessments;
- annual desktop testing of emergency plans for all centres;
- investing in ongoing training and development for employees to help them carry out responsibilities to a high standard;
- retailer duct-work inspection process to mitigate risk of fire;
- independent fire surveys carried out at all managed centres;
- direct relationships with loss mitigation company to minimize the impact of incidents;
- 24-hour CCTV in use at all centres;
- police presence at centres including a number of police offices within the centres.

Edited extract from Intu Properties plc
Annual report 2015

The Walt Disney Company: Disclosures about market risks

The company is exposed to the impact of interest rate changes primarily through its borrowing activities. The company's objective is to mitigate the impact of interest rate changes on earnings and cash flows and on the market value of its borrowings. In accordance with its policy, the company targets its fixed-rate debt as a percentage of its net debt between a minimum and maximum percentage.

The company transacts business globally and is subject to risks associated with changing foreign currency exchange rates. The company's objective is to reduce earnings and cash flow fluctuations associated with foreign currency exchange rate changes, enabling management to focus on core business issues and challenges.

The company enters into option and forward contracts that change in value as foreign currency exchange rates change, to protect the value of its existing foreign currency assets, liabilities, firm commitments and forecasted but not firmly committed foreign currency transactions. In accordance with policy, the company hedges its forecasted foreign currency transactions for periods generally not to exceed four years within an established minimum and maximum range of annual exposure.

The gains and losses on these contracts offset changes in the US dollar equivalent value of the related forecasted transaction, asset, liability or firm commitment. The principal currencies hedged are the euro, Japanese yen, Canadian dollar and British pound. Cross-currency swaps are used to effectively convert foreign currency-denominated borrowings into US dollar denominated borrowings.

Edited extract from The Walt Disney Company
Form 10-K 2013

Australian Mines Limited: Risk assessment and management

The board reviews the company's risk management systems and control frameworks, and the effectiveness of their implementation, annually. The board also considers the management of risk at its regular meetings. The company's risk profile is reviewed annually upon advice from management including, where appropriate, as a result of regular interaction with management and relevant staff from across the company's business.

The board or the company's senior management may consult with the company's external accountants on external risk matters as required. The company's risk management systems and control frameworks for identifying, assessing, monitoring and managing its material risks, as established by the board in conjunction with management, include:

- the board's ongoing monitoring of management and operational performance;

- a comprehensive system of budgeting, forecasting and reporting to the board;

- approval procedures for significant capital expenditure above threshold levels;

- regular board review of all areas of significant financial risk and all significant transactions not part of the company's normal business activities;

- regular presentations to the board by management on the management of risk;

- comprehensive written policies in relation to specific business activities;

- comprehensive written policies in relation to corporate governance issues;

- regular communication between directors on compliance and risk matters; and

- consultation and review processes between the board and external accountants.

The board requires that each major proposal submitted to the board for decision is accompanied by a comprehensive risk assessment and, where required, management's proposed mitigation strategies. The company has in place an insurance programme that is reviewed periodically by the board. The board receives regular reports on budgeting and financial performance. A system of delegated authority levels has been approved by the board to ensure business transactions are properly authorized and executed.

Edited extract from Australian Mines Limited
2013 Annual Report

Tolerate, treat, transfer and terminate

15

The 4Ts of hazard response

Priority significant risks facing an organization are those that have:

- high or very high impact in relation to the benchmark test for significance;
- high or very high likelihood of materializing at or above the benchmark level;
- high or very high scope for cost-effective improvement in control.

Generally speaking, it is only priority significant risks that require attention at the most senior level of the organization. However, it is appropriate that compliance risks also receive boardroom attention. In practice, the board will expect these compliance risks to be properly managed and the board will only receive routine/annual reports describing risk performance, or a special report if a specific issue has arisen. The organization will seek to introduce effective and efficient controls to minimize compliance risks.

The benchmark test for significance should be set at a level that represents a significant impact for the organization. Having identified the priority significant risks, the organization then needs to review the controls in place and decide whether further actions are required. For hazard risks, the range of responses available is often described as the 4Ts.

There is a broad range of terminology available to describe risk response options. In fact, both British Standard BS 31100 and ISO 31000 use the term 'risk treatment' as the more generic description. For example, the British Standard defines risk treatment as the 'process of developing, selecting and implementing controls'. Likewise, Guide 73 defines risk treatment as 'process to modify risk'.

The terminology used in the *Orange Book* has been adopted for this text for the risk response stage of the risk management process. The options for responding to risk can then be identified as the 4Ts. Appendix B contains information on the alternative definitions that are used by different publications.

More information and a brief description of each of the 4Ts is provided in Table 15.1. The 4Ts of hazard risk management can be summarized as:

- tolerate;
- treat;

- transfer;
- terminate.

Figure 15.1 suggests that there is a dominant response in relation to each of the 4Ts, according to the position of the risk on a risk matrix. For risks that are low likelihood/low impact, the main response is tolerate. For risks that are high likelihood/low impact, the main response is treat. For risks that are low likelihood/high impact, the main response is transfer, and for risks that are high likelihood/high impact, the main response is terminate.

In order to give some context to the range of risks that is being considered, Table 15.2 provides examples of the range of potentially significant risks associated with the headings of the FIRM risk scorecard. Assessment of each of the risks will enable the organization to place the risk on a risk matrix. The position of the risk on the risk matrix will then indicate the most likely response to that risk. If the risk assessment is undertaken at the current level of risk, the effect of the existing controls will already have been evaluated as part of the risk assessment exercise.

Consider the case of a theatre that needs to respond to the increasing use of agents who require payment at the time of the booking, rather than after the performance. Also, a recent failure of an actor to arrive on the night of the performance caused the theatre considerable financial loss. This has resulted in the theatre reviewing the booking and appearance arrangements for actors and deciding responses that are appropriate in relation to all 4Ts.

Table 15.1 Description of the 4Ts of hazard response

1	*Tolerate* Accept/retain	The exposure may be tolerable without any further action being taken. Even if it is not tolerable, the ability to do anything about some risks may be limited, or the cost of taking any action may be disproportionate to the potential benefit gained.
2	*Treat* Control/reduce	By far the greater number of risks will be addressed in this way. The purpose of treatment is that, whilst continuing within the organization with the activity giving rise to the risk, action (control) is taken to constrain the risk to an acceptable level.
3	*Transfer* Insurance/contract	For some risks the best response may be to transfer them. This might be done by conventional insurance, or it might be done by paying a third party to take the risk in another way. This option is particularly good for mitigating financial risks or risks to assets.
4	*Terminate* Avoid/eliminate	Some risks will only be treatable, or containable to acceptable levels, by terminating the activity. It should be noted that the option of termination of activities may be severely limited in government when compared to the private sector.

Figure 15.1 Risk matrix and the 4Ts of hazard management

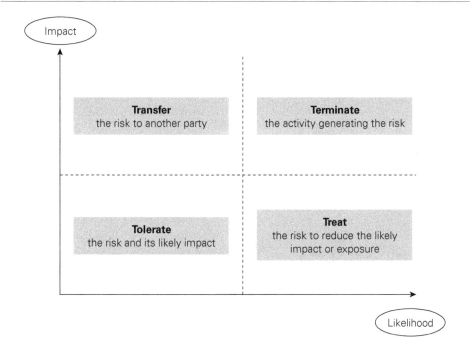

Table 15.2 Key dependencies and significant risks

FIRM risk scorecard	Example dependencies	Example of a significant risk
Financial	Availability of funds	Insufficient funds available from parent company
	Correct allocation of funds	Inadequate profit because of incorrect capital expenditure decisions
	Internal control	Fraud occurs because of inadequate internal controls
	Liabilities under control	Higher than expected liabilities arise in the pension fund
Infrastructure	People	Failure to achieve/maintain health and safety standards
	Premises	Damage to key location caused by insured peril
	Processes	IT control systems not available because of virus or hacker activity
	Products	Disruption because of failure of supplier

(*continued*)

Table 15.2   (*Continued*)

FIRM risk scorecard	Example dependencies	Example of a significant risk
Reputational	Brand	Product recall causes damage to product image and brand
	Public opinion	Lost sales or revenue because of change in public tastes
	Regulators	Regulator enforcement action causes loss of public confidence
	CSR	Allegations of unethical product-sourcing causes loss of sales
Marketplace	Regulatory environment	Change in tax regime results in unbudgeted tax demands
	Economic health	Decline in world or national economy reduces consumer spending
	Product development	Changes in technology reduce product appeal and sales
	Competitor behaviour	Competitor substantially reduces prices to win market share

The theatre might decide that it has to tolerate the new booking fee arrangements. It has also decided that in order to treat/reduce the risk, it will only deal with established agents in future and terminate existing arrangements with an agency that has proved unreliable in the past. The theatre might also investigate the possibility of buying insurance, so that the theatre can transfer the cost of a performance cancelled because the actor fails to arrive on the night.

Tolerate risk

Risk tolerance is defined in Guide 73 as the organization's or stakeholder's readiness to bear the risk after risk treatment in order to achieve its objectives. The guide then adds that risk tolerance can be influenced by legal or regulatory (compliance) requirements. The comment about legal or regulatory requirements is very relevant, in that organizations will often have to tolerate a risk because of legal or regulatory requirements, even in circumstances where the organization would otherwise not wish to tolerate that risk. It should be noted that tolerance relates to a specific or individual risk, rather than the more general approach represented by risk appetite. Risk appetite refers to the amount and type of risk that an organization is willing to pursue or retain.

There is a confusion of terminology between when an organization is willing to tolerate a risk and the concept of risk tolerance. The concept of tolerate is normally concerned with the organization being willing to retain or tolerate a risk, even if it is higher than the organization would choose to accept. The other concept is that of risk tolerance. Many organizations use risk tolerance in the engineering sense to represent the range of risk that is broadly acceptable. In Figure 25.1, the central sections of concerned zone and cautious zone draw the boundary around the risk tolerance. As with the engineering use of the word tolerance, these zones define the boundaries within which the organization desires the level of risk to be confined.

An organization may have to tolerate risks that have a current level beyond its comfort zone and its risk appetite. On occasions, an organization may even have to tolerate risks that are beyond its actual risk capacity. However, this situation would not be sustainable and the organization would be vulnerable during this period.

When the hazard risk is considered to be within the risk appetite of the organization, the organization will tolerate that risk. Risk tolerance is shown as the approach that will be adopted in relation to low-likelihood risks with low impact. However, an organization may decide to tolerate risk levels that are high because they are associated with a potentially profitable activity or relate to a core process that is fundamental to the nature of the organization.

It is unusual for a hazard risk to be accepted or tolerated before any risk control measures have been applied. Generally speaking, a risk only becomes tolerable when all cost-effective control measures have been put in place, so that the organization is accepting or tolerating the risk at its current level. Certain control measures may have been applied because the inherent level of the risk may have been unacceptable. Control effort seeks to move the risk to the low-likelihood/low-impact quadrant of the risk matrix, as illustrated in Figure 16.1.

Sometimes risks are only accepted as part of an arrangement whereby one risk is balanced against another. This is a simple description of neutralizing or hedging risks, but on a business level this may represent a fundamentally important strategic decision. For example, an electricity company operating independently in the northern states of the United States may have to accept the impact of variation in temperature on electricity sales. By merging (or setting up a joint venture) with an electricity company in the southern states, the north/south combined operation will be able to smooth the temperature-related variation in electricity sales. The combined operation will then sell more electricity in the northern states during cold weather, when demand in the southern states is low. Conversely, the combined operation will sell more electricity for air-conditioning units in the southern states in the summer, when demand for electricity in the northern states may be lower.

Treat risk

When the level of risk exposure (likelihood) associated with a particular hazard is high but the potential loss (impact) associated with it is low, the organization will wish to treat the risk. Risk treatment will often be undertaken with the risk at the inherent and/or current level, so that when the risk has been treated, the new current level or target level may become tolerable.

Actions to improve the standard of risk control will always be under constant review in an organization. On a personal level, wearing a seat belt when driving a car or fitting an intruder alarm in a house are examples of risk reduction actions. Improvements to standards of risk control in relation to physical (insurable) risks are well known. Fitting sprinklers to buildings, providing enhanced building security arrangements and employee security vetting are all examples of risk improvement actions designed to better manage hazard risks.

When identifying suitable risk treatment options, the organization will need to look at the effect of the treatment on the likelihood of the risk materializing as well as looking at the impact of the risk should it materialize. Cost-effective risk treatments will need to be selected and the effect of different control measures can be shown on a risk matrix, as in Figure 16.1.

There is an issue of terminology associated with treat risk. ISO 31000 considers that 'treat risk' is the main heading under which various options exist, such as:

- avoiding the risk by deciding not to start or continue with the activity;
- taking or increasing the risk in order to pursue an opportunity;
- removing the risk source;
- changing the likelihood or the consequences;
- sharing the risk with another party or parties;
- retaining the risk by informed decision.

Other risk management standards refer to 'risk response' as the main heading and this is the approach taken in this chapter. Using risk response as the main heading then gives rise to the options of tolerate, treat, transfer and terminate. As with all issues of terminology, it is for the organization to establish its own risk vocabulary, one that is consistent with the external, internal and risk management context.

In some cases, terminology will be dictated by the external context. For example, banks and other financial institutions will need to use the terminology of the regulator. On occasions, terminology is dictated by the internal context within the organization. If the terminology that has developed within the organization is inconsistent with the terminology in ISO 31000, it is probably the case that the risk manager would be better advised to use the terminology that already exists within the organization, rather than trying to introduce new terms or new meanings for existing terms.

Transfer risk

When the likelihood of a risk materializing is low but the potential is high, the organization will wish to transfer that risk. Insurance is a well-established mechanism for transferring the financial impact of losses arising from hazard risks and (to a lesser extent) control risks. The issues associated with the use of insurance as a risk transfer mechanism are considered in more detail in Chapter 17.

In some cases, risk transfer is closely related to the desire to eliminate or terminate the risk. However, many risks cannot be transferred to the insurance market, either because of prohibitively high insurance premiums or because the risks under consideration have (traditionally) not been insurable.

Risk transfer can be achieved by conventional insurance and also by contractual agreement. It may also be possible to find a joint-venture partner, or some other means of sharing the risk. Risk hedging or neutralization may therefore be considered to be a risk transfer option, as well as a risk treatment option.

The cost of risk transfer is a component of risk financing. Once again, there is variation in the definitions used. In relation to risk financing, BS 31100 states that risk financing involves the cost of contingent arrangements for the provision of funds to meet the financial impact of a risk materializing. Such arrangements are usually provided by insurance, and insurance is, therefore, finance that is contingent upon certain insured events taking place.

A difference in the definitions between the now both superseded BS 31100:2008 and ISO 31000:2009 is that ISO 31000 also considers that the cost of risk financing should include the provision of funds to meet the cost of risk treatment. In this text, resourcing of controls is considered to be a separate step in the risk management process. This is another example that illustrates that there is no universally agreed or common language of risk.

There is another issue of terminology with the use of the phrase 'risk transfer'. ISO 31000 recommends that risk sharing should be used in preference to risk transfer. The argument is that a risk can never be fully transferred and whatever the intention of the parties, the risk will always be, to some extent, shared. This is an accurate analysis, but the choice of terminology used within an organization will also be influenced by other factors. In relation to risk sharing, the insurance industry uses the terminology risk transfer. It may be difficult for the enterprise risk manager to insist on the use of the phrase risk sharing when the insurance manager in the organization prefers to use the terminology of risk transfer because that is the standard terminology used in part of the external context that is the insurance market.

Terminate risk

When a risk is both of high likelihood and high potential impact, the organization will wish to terminate or eliminate the risk. It may be that the risks of trading in a certain part of the world or the environmental risks associated with continuing to use certain chemicals are unacceptable to the organization and/or its stakeholders. In these circumstances, appropriate responses would be elimination of the risk by stopping the process or activity, substituting an alternative activity or outsourcing the activity that is associated with the risk.

An organization may wish to terminate a risk, but it could be the case that the activity that gives rise to it is fundamental to the ongoing operation of the organization. In such circumstances, the organization may not be able to terminate or eliminate the risk entirely and thus will need to implement alternative control measures.

This is a particular issue for public services. There may be certain risks that have high likelihood and high impact, but the organization is unable to terminate the activities giving rise to them. This may be because the activity is a statutory requirement placed on a government agency or public authority. The public service imperative may restrict the ability to cease the activity, so the organization will need to introduce control measures, to the greatest extent that is cost-effective.

It is likely that such control measures will be a combination of risk treatment and risk transfer. As these control measures are applied, the level of risk will move to a level where the organization will be able to tolerate the risk. Because of the variable nature of risks, it may not be possible to get all risks to a level that is within the risk appetite of the organization. The organization may find that it has to tolerate risks beyond its empirical risk appetite in order to continue to undertake a certain activity.

Strategic risk response

The overall approach to the management of control and opportunity risks is similar to the approach adopted for the management of hazard risks. However, there are sufficient differences in the range of options available for these to be presented separately. It is worth remembering that projects normally reflect and implement the tactics that are being employed to implement strategy.

Figure 16.1 illustrates the 4Ts of hazard risk management and the type of controls that are most likely to be associated with each type of hazard risk response. The types of controls are considered below. This chapter has been concerned almost exclusively with responding to hazard risks. The 4Ts represent the options for mitigating hazard risks.

Figure 15.2 suggests that there are a range of responses available for the management of opportunity risks. Developing and implementing effective and efficient strategy will require the evaluation of the level of risk associated with each available strategy and the level of reward that the strategy will deliver.

The 4Es of opportunity management are set out as exist, explore, exploit and exit. There is a close relationship between the 4Es and the status of the organization, as

Figure 15.2   Risk versus reward in strategy

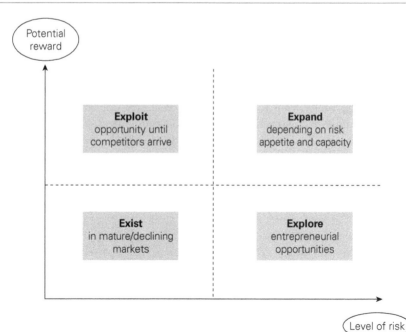

illustrated in Figure 15.2. A start-up operation will face a higher level of risk and low potential rewards.

Entrepreneurial opportunities will be explored at this time. As the organization grows, potential rewards will increase while the level of risk will remain high. The organization will seek to achieve growth, but may feel that growth is too slow or the level of risk remains too high, and if so it will exit from those operations.

After a period of growth, the organization should be achieving a high reward for a reduced risk. This represents the phase where the organization will exploit opportunities until competitors arrive. This is a mature operation. All mature operations are exposed to the possibility of decline, although many organizations choose to exist in a mature, declining market, where risk exposure is low and so are potential rewards.

The application of the 4Es to the management of strategic, opportunity or speculative risks is consistent with the description of risk and reward offered by Figure 2.2. However, pursuing opportunity risks and the development of strategic objectives are the most important issues for many organizations. Risk management input into strategic decision making may not always be as robust and well structured as the risk management input into operations and projects.

The allocation of the dominant types of responses and controls to each of the four quadrants shown in Figure 15.2 is similar to the allocation of the 4Ts using hazard risk management. Existing in a mature or declining market is similar to accepting uncertainty in tactics and tolerating hazard risks. Exploring opportunities is similar to looking at the options for treating hazard risks. It is in the area of exploiting opportunities and exiting opportunities where differences in approach between the management of hazards and uncertainties compared with the management of opportunities becomes most evident.

Figure 15.3 shows a refinement to Figure 15.2 in that the area of high risk and potentially high reward is evaluated in a little more detail by taking account of risk appetite. An organization may find that it has a viable business opportunity but does not have the resources to exploit it on its own. In these circumstances, the organization has three main choices. It may exit the opportunity because it does not have the risk appetite or risk capacity to pursue that opportunity. It may sell the opportunity on to an organization that does have the appetite, capacity and resources to exploit the opportunity or it may seek to share that opportunity.

Exiting the opportunity may be the appropriate option, because the organization does not have the risk appetite, capacity or resources to pursue the opportunity and has not been able or willing to find a partner to buy or share it. However, most organizations with a viable opportunity will wish to gain from the identification of that opportunity. Selling the opportunity may provide a profitable exit, but sharing it with, for example, a joint-venture partner may be a better long-term option.

Entering into a joint-venture partnership will reduce the level of risk faced by the organization, but will result in sharing of the benefits. This decision will depend on business strategy, risk appetite, risk capacity and the availability of suitable business partners. As well as a joint-venture partnership, exploiting business opportunities may be possible by sharing the risk, using means such as outsourcing to share the risk with others in the supply chain.

It should be noted that Figure 15.3 represents a flow chart from start-up (Explore opportunities) to growth (Expand), then to a mature organization (Exploit) before moving into decline (Exist). It is, therefore, similar to Figure 2.2. However, it has the added

Figure 15.3 Opportunity risks and risk appetite

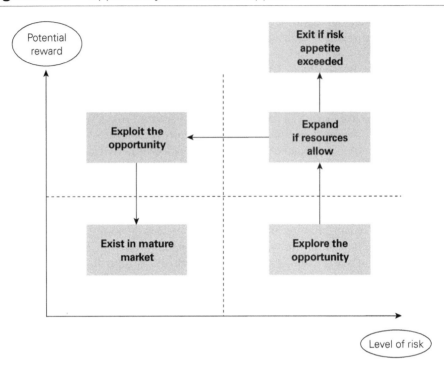

refinement that as the organization is looking to expand, it will have the option of exiting if the risk appetite and/or risk capacity of the organization would be exceeded. This extends the 4Es approach to become 5Es, depending on risk appetite. The text box below provides an example of this approach applied to opportunity management, although the terminology (as is often the case in risk management) is a little different.

Opportunity evaluation and response

The purpose of the evaluation and response is to decide which opportunities require a response and what the recommended response will be. The following are the key terms and concepts when deciding how to respond to an opportunity and they can be used in combination:

- Enhance: the opportunity equivalent of 'mitigating' a risk is to *enhance* the opportunity by increasing the probability and/or the impact.

- Exploit: equivalent to the 'avoid' response, but the 'exploit' strategy seeks to make the opportunity definitely happen.

- Ignore: the 'acceptance' strategy takes no measures to deal with a hazard risk, and opportunities can be *ignored*, with a reactive approach but no explicit actions.

- Sharing (transfer) opportunity: 'share' strategy for opportunities seeks a partner able to manage the opportunity who can maximize the chance of it happening.

Risk control techniques

16

Types of controls

There are a range of controls that can be applied to hazard risks. The most convenient classification system is to describe these controls as preventive, corrective, directive and detective. This is the risk classification system suggested in the *Orange Book*. Table 16.1 provides a more detailed description of each of these four types of hazard controls.

In relation to hazard risks, the control options of preventive, corrective, directive and detective (PCDD) represent a clear hierarchy of controls. The relationship between these four types of controls and the dominant risk of response for different levels of risks is illustrated on the risk matrix shown in Figure 16.1. Table 16.2 gives examples of these four types of controls in relation to health and safety risks.

Preventive controls are designed to limit the possibility of an undesirable hazard event occurring. The majority of controls implemented in organizations in response to hazard risks are preventive controls. For health and safety risks, preventive controls will include substituting a less hazardous material in the activity or enclosing the activity so that employee exposure to dust or fumes is eliminated. Examples of preventive controls for fraud risks are shown in Table 16.2.

Corrective controls are designed to correct undesirable circumstances and reduce unacceptable risk exposures. Such controls provide a key method whereby the risk is treated so that it becomes less likely to occur and/or the impact is much reduced. In general terms, corrective controls are designed to correct the situation. For example, machinery guards are corrective controls.

There has been debate about disaster recovery planning (DRP) and business continuity planning (BCP) and whether they fit into the PCDD classification of the different types of hazard risk controls. Some organizations consider DRP and BCP to be directive controls, whereas others argue that they are corrective controls. An alternative approach is to say that a DRP and BCP are concerned with crisis management and cannot be easily classified as a PCCD type of control and should be considered to be a fifth type of control.

In reality this argument, like so many other arguments about terminology, is not helpful. When an organization is faced with a crisis, it will be in a much better position to cope if plans have been considered and put in place before the crisis arises. Sometimes crisis management will involve the use of alternative facilities that have been put in place before the crisis arose. It could be argued that these are corrective controls.

Figure 16.1 Types of controls for hazard risks

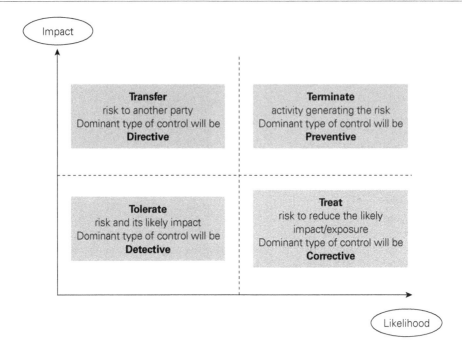

Table 16.1 Description of types of hazard controls

1	Preventive (terminate)	These controls are designed to limit the possibility of an undesirable outcome being realized. The more important it is to stop an undesirable outcome, then the more important it is to implement appropriate preventive controls.
2	Corrective (treat)	These controls are designed to limit the scope for loss and reduce any undesirable outcomes that have been realized. They may also provide a route of recourse to achieve some recovery against loss or damage.
3	Directive (transfer)	These controls are designed to ensure that a particular outcome is achieved. They are based on giving directions to people on how to ensure that losses do not occur. They are important, but depend on people following established safe systems of work.
4	Detective (tolerate)	These controls are designed to identify occasions when undesirable outcomes have been realized. Their effect is, by definition, 'after the event' so they are only appropriate when it is possible to accept that the loss or damage has occurred.

Table 16.2   Examples of the hierarchy of hazard controls

Generic control category	Hierarchy of controls for health and safety risks	Hierarchy of controls for fraud risks
Preventive	Elimination or removal of the source of the hazard Substitution of the hazard with something less risky	Limits of authorization and separation of duties Pre-employment screening of potential staff
Corrective	Engineering containment using barriers or guards Exposure reduction by job rotation or limitation on hours worked	Passwords or other access controls Staff rotation and regular change of supervisors
Directive	Training and supervision to enforce procedures Personal protective equipment and improved welfare facilities	Accessible, detailed, written systems and procedures Training to ensure understanding of procedures
Detective	Health monitoring to enquire about potential symptoms Health surveillance to find early symptoms	Reconciliation, audit and review by internal audit Whistleblowing policy to report (alleged) fraud

In all cases, crisis management will involve directions to the involved parties as to how they should behave if the crisis arises. It could be argued that these are directive controls. Normally, detective controls relate to identification of circumstances where a risk has materialized at a fairly low level with limited impact and consequences. Clearly, DRP and BCP relate to circumstances where risks have materialized at crisis level. Therefore, it is inappropriate to classify DRP and BCP as detective controls.

The bow-tie representation of the risk management process is a convenient way of illustrating the role of the four types of controls. Preventive controls are relevant to actions that are taken before the event occurs. The nature of detective controls means that they relate to circumstances after the event has occurred. Corrective and directive controls can be relevant to loss prevention, damage limitation and cost containment. These are the three phases of loss control. The relevance of the types of controls to the bow-tie presentation of the risk management process is shown in Figure 16.2. For the sake of illustration, this figure uses the same hazard of damage to premises as represented in Figure 11.2.

Directive controls are designed to ensure that a particular outcome is achieved. In health and safety terms, directive controls would include instructions/directions given to employees to follow, for example, in the use of personal protective equipment. Training in how to respond to a particular risk event and detailed instructions and

Figure 16.2 Bow-tie and types of controls

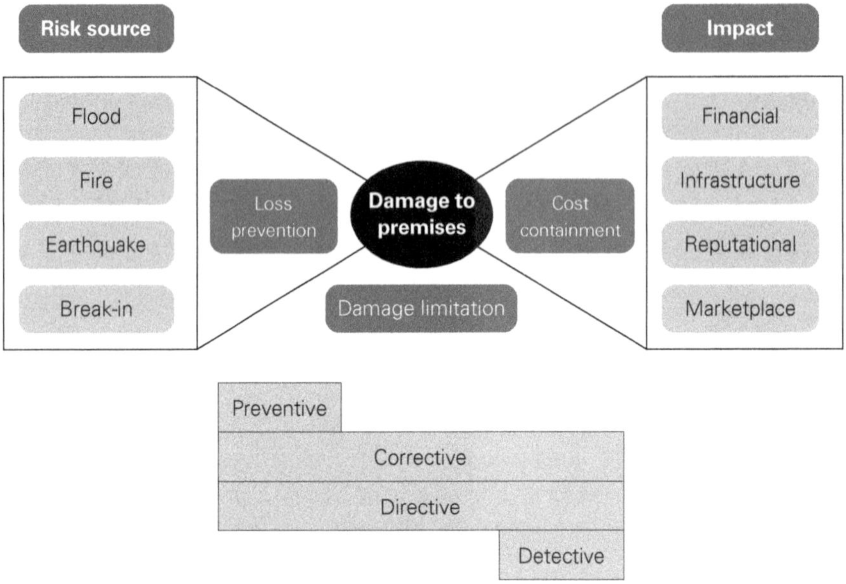

procedures are directive controls. Directive controls are also associated with actions that must be taken in the event of a loss to limit the damage and contain the costs.

Detective controls are designed to identify occasions when an undesirable outcome has occurred. The control is intended to detect when these undesirable events have happened, to ensure that the circumstances do not deteriorate further. An example of detective controls in a project is undertaking a post-incident review.

There is a clear hierarchy of effectiveness of controls that is represented by the order preventive, corrective, directive and finally detective. Preventive controls are clearly the most effective, followed by controls that correct adverse circumstances. Providing training and direction to staff is a weaker level of control, and detective controls only confirm that an adverse event has occurred.

The importance of DRP and BCP should not be underestimated. They are both methods of cost containment designed to ensure minimum disruption after a hazard risk has materialized, so they are aligned with detective controls. However, DRP and BCP do not conveniently fit into the PCDD classification system for controls, because they are post-loss procedures. Some control classification systems include BCP and DRP as a fifth category of control.

The example in the box below illustrates that an organization will use all four types of control in order to build a robust set of risk responses. The road transport company will make use of all four types of controls in order to reduce road traffic accidents.

Application of the 4Ts

Take the example of a road transport company and the desire to reduce the number of road traffic accidents per million miles driven, and the options for reducing this number. The company can look at the preventive, corrective, directive and detective control hierarchy and decide the following:

- The scope for introducing preventive controls includes review of vehicle routing and realistic estimates on delivery schedules so that drivers do not need to drive dangerously to arrive on time.

- The types of corrective controls that will be introduced include enhanced maintenance procedures and improved arrangements for drivers to report vehicle defects.

- Enhanced directive controls will be based on defensive driver training and the provision of a vehicle driver handbook with practical advice that is easy to understand and follow.

- Although some detective controls are already in place through the use of tachographs in the vehicles, the company may decide to also introduce a routine review of drivers' licences to check for penalty points.

Other controls that might be evaluated by the transport company include routine inspections of vehicles to discover and report damage, and a review of fuel consumption to identify drivers with an aggressive driving style. The company is then in a position to introduce structured and measurable loss-control programmes to reduce the overall cost of running the fleet of vehicles.

Hazard risk zones

Although the 4Ts of hazard response can be illustrated on a simple risk matrix, such as Figure 16.1, the options are not that clear cut. It can be seen that the tolerate and terminate options meet at the centre of the risk matrix. It is not sensible to suggest that a small increase in risk likelihood and potential impact would completely change the approach of the organization to that particular risk.

Figure 16.3 provides a slightly more realistic analysis by providing a diagram that builds on Figure 16.1. Figure 16.3 illustrates that there are three zones on the risk matrix, as the cautious and concerned areas combine into a central zone. The comfort zone is predominantly for low-likelihood/low-impact events. As can be seen, there is a level of potential impact that will always be within the comfort zone. Likewise, there is a level of risk likelihood that is always considered to be so low that it will not happen.

However, as risk likelihood and potential impact increase, a point is reached where judgement is required as to whether the risk is above the lower tolerance line and within the tolerance limits for the organization. Judgement is required within the cautious zone and actions will usually be taken to treat and/or transfer the risks within that zone. The line that divides the cautious zone and the concerned zone

Figure 16.3 Hazard risk zones

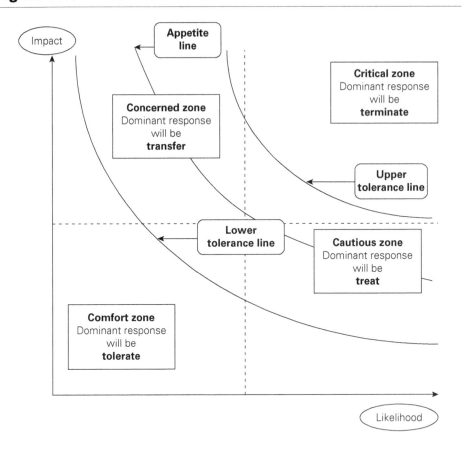

represents the risk appetite of the organization. The cautious zone and the concerned zone together illustrate the acceptable variability of the level of risk and can be considered to be the tolerance of the organization to acceptable variability or volatility in the level of that particular risk.

As the risk likelihood and potential impact further increases, the upper tolerance line is reached. When the risk gets above this line, the organization will consider those risks to be critical, as they are outside tolerance limits and will wish to terminate exposure to them. In certain circumstances, the organization will not be able to terminate these risks, either because they may represent a business imperative or because they are associated with a high-risk/high-reward strategy that the board has adopted.

Preventive controls

Table 16.1 provides a brief description of the nature of preventive controls. These are the most important type of risk controls, and all organizations will use preventive controls to treat certain types of risks. Prevention or elimination of all risks is not possible on a cost-effective basis, nor may it be desirable for the future of the organization and the continuation of certain activities.

Examples of preventive controls include the separation of duty, whereby no person has authority to act without the consent of another when paying an invoice. Also, expenditure systems should prevent the same person from ordering goods and then authorizing the payment for them. In health and safety terms, preventive controls include the elimination or removal of the hazard and providing a less risky substitute. For example, a hazardous chemical used in a cleaning operation may be substituted with a less harmful alternative.

The advantage of preventive controls is that they eliminate the hazard, so that no further consideration of it is required. In reality, this may not be a cost-effective option and may not be possible for operational reasons. The disadvantages of preventive controls are that beneficial activities may be eliminated and either outsourced or replaced with something less effective and efficient.

Health and safety practitioners refer to the elimination of hazardous activities 'so far as is reasonably practicable'. Achieving something so far as is reasonably practicable involves the balance between cost in terms of time, trouble and money against the benefit in terms of the reduction in the level of risk that is achieved. For example, reducing the risk of collapse can be achieved in underground mines by the provision of support beams and props. However, the extent to which this is reasonably practicable will need to take into account the cost of providing these props against the level of risk reduction that would be achieved in that particular mine.

Corrective controls

Table 16.1 provides a brief description of the nature of corrective controls. Corrective controls are the next option after it has been decided that preventive controls are not technically feasible, operationally desirable or cost-effective. Corrective controls are capable of producing an entirely satisfactory result, whereby the current level of risk is reduced to within the risk appetite of the organization.

Examples of corrective controls can be found in the management of health and safety at work. Engineering containment by way of barriers or guards is a very well-established type of corrective control. In relation to fraud exposures, use of passwords or other access controls can be considered to be corrective controls. Staff rotation and regular change of supervisors also fit into this category of controls.

The advantage of many corrective controls is that they can be simple and cost-effective. Also, they do not require that existing practices and procedures are eliminated or replaced with alternative methods of work. The controls can be implemented within the framework of existing activities. The disadvantage of some corrective controls is that the marginal benefits that are achieved may be difficult to quantify or confirm as cost-effective.

Sometimes, corrective controls are over-engineered and their cost is disproportionate to the benefit that is achieved. It is for risk management practitioners and internal auditors, as well as employees themselves, to identify where expensive and/or ineffective corrective controls have been implemented. Very often, corrective controls are put in place because of regulatory requirements. This may be unsatisfactory from the point of view of the organization and introduce additional costs and/or inefficiency. However, it is for the organization to ensure that the appropriate level of corrective control is achieved in order to comply with the minimum requirements of legislation.

The design and implementation of corrective controls is often the cause of considerable discussion and even disagreement. For example, there is sometimes discussion with building occupiers about fitting sprinklers as a corrective control that will activate in case of fire and reduce the damage caused by the fire. Occupiers of premises with computer installations will often say that sprinklers in computer rooms are inappropriate. Whilst understanding that water does damage computer installations, fire engineers will usually counteract the objections by pointing out that 'water causes damage, but fire destroys'. Although this analysis is correct and sprinklers do prevent total destruction, the disadvantages and unintended consequences of installing additional controls always need to be carefully considered.

Directive controls

Table 16.1 provides a brief description of the nature of directive controls. Organizations will be familiar with the directive controls, because staff will need to be advised of the correct way of undertaking specific tasks. Where tasks involve a level of risk, documented procedures, together with information, training and instruction, can be seen as directive controls. Therefore, directive controls are likely to be in place for most risks, regardless of whether other types of controls also exist.

An example of directive controls is the requirement to wear personal protective equipment when undertaking potentially dangerous activities. Staff will need to be trained in the correct use of the equipment and a level of supervision will be required in order to ensure that it is used correctly.

The advantage of directive controls is that the risk control requirements can be explained during a normal training and instruction session provided for staff. However, directive controls, especially in relation to health and safety risks, represent a low level of control that may require constant supervision in order to ensure that the correct procedures are being followed.

Although directive controls on their own represent an insecure and unreliable method of risk control, they will always be a component in the overall approach to risk control adopted by any organization. Developing systems, procedures and protocols are important for any organization. However, there is a danger that if the developed procedures are not implemented in practice, the organization will be more exposed to allegations of poor risk control. Developing detailed risk control procedures is an indication by the organization that risks exist and need to be managed. However, failing to implement the identified procedures will leave the organization unable to defend itself by claiming that it was not aware of the risks.

The value and relevance of directive controls is obvious. Chapter 18 discusses business continuity planning and the importance of providing clear directions to people in relation to managing the crisis as the immediate priority, followed by recovering from the disaster and finally, ensuring business continuity. Contracts, including insurance policies, are also a form of directive control, as discussed in Chapter 17 on insurance and risk transfer. All contracts provide written directions to people on how they should respond when a defined set of circumstances, such as an insurance claim, arises.

An important aspect of directive controls that is often overlooked is that when an unexpected event occurs, it is usually directive controls that are introduced as an immediate response to that unexpected event. The hierarchy of controls described in Table 16.2 represents the desired situation in established and stable circumstances. However, when the unexpected has been detected, the order in which new controls will be introduced may be somewhat different. The initial response is likely to involve introducing directive controls and/or preventive controls, if the event represents an immediate risk, especially if it is a safety risk. This immediate response will then allow corrective controls to be designed and implemented as the new set of circumstances becomes clear and/or stabilizes.

Detective controls

Table 16.1 provides a brief description of the nature of detective controls. As suggested in the title, detective controls are those procedures that identify when the hazard has materialized. Detecting that a hazard has materialized some time after the event is not entirely satisfactory, but can be justified in certain circumstances. Sometimes, other controls may be unable to completely eliminate the chances of a risk materializing.

Examples of detective controls include stock or asset checks to ensure that stock or assets have not been removed without authorization. Bank reconciliation exercises can detect unauthorized transactions. Also, post-implementation reviews can detect the lessons learnt from projects that can be applied in future. Detective controls are closely related to review and monitoring exercises undertaken as part of the risk management process.

The advantage of detective controls is that they are often simple to administer. In any case, they are essential in many circumstances where the organization will require early warning that other risk control measures have broken down. The disadvantage of the detective controls is that the risk will already have materialized before it is detected. It could be argued, of course, that the fact that detective controls are in place will deter certain individuals from attempting to circumvent other risk controls.

Detection of fraud is often only possible after the fraud has taken place. However, there are considerable advantages in detecting fraud early, so that the nature and scale of the fraud may be reduced and the scope for future similar fraudulent activities eliminated. The text box discusses introducing new financial controls in a charity.

Even in health and safety arrangements, there is scope for the use of detective controls. Certain work activities have hazards associated with them that can lead to permanent and serious health issues. By having detective controls to identify the early symptoms of these occupational ill health conditions, employees will be diagnosed early and further exposure can be eliminated. Examples of these types of controls in health and safety include early detection of lung disease from dust exposure, skin conditions such as dermatitis and finally deafness caused by exposure to occupational noise.

Financial controls for charities

The main reason for having financial controls is to reduce the risk of error and fraud. Errors are likely to result in a loss of money, because donors are more likely to give money to charities that they can trust.

Once you have established your financial controls, they should be discussed and approved by the trustees. You need to ensure that you have the support of all trustees before implementing any new controls. Then, implement the financial controls noting who is responsible for each control. By making someone accountable for a financial control, it is more likely to be effective.

Controls are only good if they are relevant; therefore, you need to ensure that you routinely review your controls to see if they are still effective. As things change, you need to think about making changes to your controls as your organization evolves. It can be hard to make changes to existing controls, but assessing why the controls are no longer valid and how new controls can help the organization will help you in putting the changes into place.

Insurance and risk transfer 17

Importance of insurance

Risk transfer is one of the main risk responses available in relation to hazard risks. This transfer normally takes place by way of insurance and it is often described as risk financing. The fundamental principle of insurance is that the insurance company is contracted to pay a certain sum of money in the event of defined circumstances arising or defined events occurring.

Insurance contracts can require the insurance company to pay for losses suffered directly by the insured. This is first-party insurance and includes property damage insurance. Other types of insurance contract the insurance company to pay compensation to other parties if they have been injured or suffer loss because of the activities of the insured. This is third-party insurance and includes motor third-party and public/general liability.

Insurance contracts are contracts of utmost good faith. This means that the insured party is required to disclose all information relevant to the insurance contract. If this information has not been disclosed, the insurance company or underwriter has the right to refuse to continue to provide insurance cover and may refuse to pay any claims that have arisen.

There are advantages and disadvantages associated with the use of insurance as a risk transfer mechanism. The advantages are that it provides indemnity against an expected loss. Insurance can reduce uncertainty regarding hazard events that may occur. It can provide economic benefits to the insured, because the loss may be greater than the insurance premium. Finally, insurance can provide access to specialist services as part of the insurance premium. These services may include advice on loss control.

The disadvantages include the delays often experienced in obtaining settlement of an insurance claim and the difficulties that can arise in quantifying the financial costs associated with the loss. There may be disputes regarding the extent of the cover that has been purchased and the exact terms and conditions of the insurance contract. Finally, the insured may have difficulty in deciding the limit of indemnity that is appropriate for liability exposures. This may result in under-insurance and the subsequent failure to have claims paid in full.

There are alternatives to insurance when an organization wishes to transfer the financial impact of a hazard event. Alternatives to insurance are sometimes referred to as alternative risk transfer or alternative risk financing techniques. The risk financing options available to an organization include:

- conventional insurance;
- contractual transfer of risk;
- captive insurance companies;
- pooling of risks in mutual insurance companies;
- derivatives and other financial instruments;
- alternative risk finance mechanisms; and
- single premium insurance bonds.

Organizations may decide to retain a certain amount of the financial impact associated with the losses. Risk retention may be achieved by accepting a large excess or deductible on an insurance policy, deciding not to insure a certain risk exposure (self-insurance) or setting up a captive insurance company. A number of organizations with similar risk exposures may decide to set up a joint captive insurance company. This is often referred to as risk pooling or the establishment of a mutual insurance company.

Insurance is a risk transfer or risk sharing response. It represents an after-the-event cost containment response to a risk. Insurance is most important for low-probability/high-impact risks, such as destruction of assets or the payment of liability costs in circumstances where liability insurance is legally required or catastrophic losses are possible. As well as repairing assets, insurance is available for the cost of implementing disaster recovery plans and the business continuity plans. Insurance can also be purchased to cover the increased cost of operation, as illustrated in Figure 18.1.

History of insurance

Insurance has a very long history that can be traced back to Chinese and Babylonian traders. There is evidence that marine insurance had become universal among the maritime nations of Europe by the mid-1300s. In more recent times, the Great Fire of London in 1666 gave rise to the modern insurance industry. In the 1680s, a coffee shop (Lloyd's) opened in London, which became the meeting place for parties wishing to insure cargoes and ships and those willing to underwrite such ventures.

Insurance developed rapidly during the 18th and 19th centuries. Prior to the formation of incorporated organizations, insurance policies were signed by individuals whose names and the amount of risk they were prepared to assume were written underneath the insurance proposal. This gave rise to the term 'underwriter'.

Modern insurance companies in the United States developed between the mid-1730s and mid-1750s. The development was frequently in response to major disasters, typically large fires. There was a significant fire in New York in 1835, and the Chicago Fire of 1871 illustrated the costly nature of fires in urban areas and the need for insurance. The Chicago Fire of 1871 is considered in more detail in the box on the next page.

Some insurance arrangements were also associated with protection for dependants following the death of the money-earning member of the household. These arrangements became more formalized with the establishment of friendly or benefit societies during the 19th century.

The development of liability insurance has a more recent history, spreading back perhaps only 100 years. Compulsory liability insurance is a requirement in many countries and it has an even more recent history of perhaps only 50 years. Compulsory liability insurance is normally restricted in most countries to employers' liability (or workers' compensation) and motor third party.

Chicago Fire of 1871

At about 9 o'clock on the night of 8 October 1871, a fire started in a cowshed behind a Chicago home. It had been an unusually dry summer and the flames jumped quickly from house to house, then from street to street. The blaze raced along from the south-west to the north-east, enveloping the business district. Then the lumber capital of the world, Chicago was a city built primarily of wood.

Chicago's business district was indeed impressive. With the development of the railroad and the economic boom that followed the American Civil War (1861–65), the city thrived. But the fire raged through four square miles of the metropolis; it demolished factories, stores, railroad depots, hotels, theatres and banks. Flames burned ships in the Chicago River and consumed nearly all the city's publishing and printing. In the end, property damage totalled $192 million. Nearly 300 people died in the blaze and 100,000 were made homeless.

The rebuilding of Chicago was a tremendous endeavour. Insurance companies in the United States and Europe rose to the occasion, producing the sums they were obliged to pay for the damages. Cities in the United States and abroad sent $5 million in relief funds, and thousands of donated books replenished Chicago's libraries. Before long Chicago began to attract entrepreneurs, businessmen and well-known architects, who found ways to profit from the reconstruction efforts.

Types of insurance cover

The different types of insurance cover that may be required by an organization are set out in Table 17.1. Generally speaking, there are three reasons why an organization will wish to purchase insurance cover. In summary, the reasons for buying insurance are as follows:

- mandatory legal and contractual obligations;
- balance sheet/profit and loss protection;
- employee benefit/protection of employee assets.

Table 17.1 provides more information on the different types of insurance that are available and the circumstances in which insurance should be purchased. In most

Table 17.1 Different types of insurance

Mandatory, legal and contractual obligations

Employers' liability – compensation to employees injured at work

Public liability – compensation to public or customers

Motor third party – compensation following motor accident

Product liability – compensation for damage or injury

Professional indemnity – compensation to client for negligent advice

Balance sheet / profit and loss protection

Business premises – damage to premises by adverse events

Business interruption – loss of profit and increased cost of working

Asset protection – losses, such as loss of cash, goods in transit, credit risk and fidelity guarantee (staff dishonesty)

Motor accidental damage – repair of own vehicles

Terrorism – compensation for damage caused by terrorism

Loss of a key person – compensation on loss of key staff member

Employee benefit / protection of employee assets

Life and health – benefits to employees that can include: life cover, critical illness cover, income protection, private medical costs, permanent health cover, personal accident and travel injury/losses

Directors' and officers' liability – legal and compensation costs

---

cases, the purchase of insurance is not compulsory. However, most countries make the purchase of insurance compulsory in certain circumstances. Typically, these are the liability classes, including insurance cover to compensate injured employees and for the parties involved in road accidents.

Apart from the compulsory classes, organizations can decide whether to purchase insurance. This decision will be based on the assessment of the risk and whether the nature and level of risk is within the hazard tolerance of the organization. The cost of insurance (premium) and the extent of insurance coverage are also important considerations when deciding whether to buy insurance. Typically, insurance is purchased for low-likelihood/high-magnitude risks, such as flooding, hurricane damage and major fires.

Consider the example of the insurance needs of a publisher. In relation to legal obligations, the company realizes that it has to buy employers' liability insurance and motor third-party insurance. Also, it is a requirement placed on magazine distributors by the wholesalers that the company purchases libel and slander insurance. In order to protect the balance sheet and profit and loss account, the company needs to purchase property damage and business interruption insurance, together with credit risk insurance and goods in transit insurance.

The publisher may also decide to provide benefits to staff by way of life, critical illness and private medical insurance, as well as personal accident and travel insurance. For the benefit of directors of the company, directors' and officers' liability (D&O) insurance will be purchased. By undertaking this evaluation, in consultation with insurance brokers, the company has ensured that it has put in place an insurance programme that provides cover only where it is necessary, appropriate and cost-effective.

Evaluation of insurance needs

Table 17.2 provides a checklist for organizations to decide which types of insurance are required. There is a wide range of different types of insurance available and the specific activities and features of the organization will assist in deciding the scope of insurance that needs to be purchased. Sometimes, there is a shortage of insurance capacity and although the organization has decided that it wishes to purchase that type of insurance, it may not be available at an affordable cost.

There has been a tendency in recent times for organizations to look at the whole portfolio of risks they face. This enterprise risk management approach to risk has resulted in a careful review of how much insurance an organization wishes to purchase. For example, if there are significant risks within a project, but insurance is only available for limited risk exposures, purchase of insurance for only those limited risks may not be appropriate. The enterprise approach to risk management has reduced the use of insurance as a risk control mechanism for some organizations.

One of the features of the insurance market is that the cost of insurance varies significantly during different cycles of the insurance market. The market will cycle between soft market conditions (low premium) and hard market conditions (high premium) over perhaps a 6–10 year period. When the premium rates are high, organizations will tend to buy less insurance and make greater use of a captive insurance company (as described below). When premium rates are low, organizations will purchase more insurance because the insurance becomes a more cost-effective control measure.

Purchase of insurance

When looking at the purchase of insurance cover, the organization will need to consider the 6Cs of insurance buying, as follows:

- cost;
- coverage;
- capacity;
- capabilities;
- claims;
- compliance.

Table 17.2   Identifying the necessary insurance

Feature of the business insurance requirement		
1	Business has employees	Employers' liability
2	Employees travel outside the country	Business travel
3	Members of the public could be affected	Public liability
4	Business supplies products or components	Product liability/recall
5	Business provides professional advice	Professional indemnity
6	Theft or dishonesty by employees could occur	Fidelity guarantee
7	Business occupies business premises	Premises insurance
8	Premises has machinery or other stock	Contents cover
9	Business depends on machinery or computers	Engineering insurance
10	Business could be disrupted by fire, flood etc	Business interruption
11	Business is involved in transporting goods	Goods in transit
12	Business has motor vehicles on public roads	Motor
13	Business provides life benefits to employees	Life and health
14	Certain staff are key to operation of business	Key person
15	Business would suffer in event of a bad debt	Trade credit
16	Business has directors and/or officers (D&O)	D&O liability

The cost of insurance is defined by the insurance premium that is required from the organization. A second component of the cost is the level of self-insurance (including excess or deductible) that is imposed by the policy. This means that if a claim occurs, the organization will have to pay the first part of the claim before receiving any money from the insurance company.

Insurance policies usually have limitations, warranties and exclusions. These will state that claims will be refused in certain circumstances. These coverage issues need to be explored in detail by the organization purchasing the insurance to ensure that adequate coverage is available. The only reason for buying insurance is that claims will be paid when one of the identified events occurs. The history of the particular insurance company in relation to the payment of claims and the reputation of that insurance company will be important factors when deciding which insurance company to appoint.

For very large organizations with considerable assets, one insurance company on its own may not be willing to offer coverage up to the full value of those assets. When buying insurance, the organization will need to think about the capacity that the insurance company is willing to offer in relation to the value of the assets/exposure that need to be insured.

Many insurance companies offer services in addition to insurance. These may include loss control services and assistance with business continuity planning. The capabilities of the insurance company in these areas may be an important factor in deciding which insurance company to choose.

An increasingly important issue for buyers of insurance is the financial security, status and capabilities of the insurance company. The nature of the business model operated by insurance companies means that they receive premiums at the beginning of the policy, but do not have to pay claims until some, often considerable, time after the event or loss. This results in a positive cash-flow position for insurance companies and the associated opportunity to earn investment income.

However, diversification of insurance companies into higher-risk financial activities has resulted in significant losses for some of them and a downgrading of their financial status. Also, low interest rates and the poor performance of stock markets has resulted in a reduction in investment income. Accordingly, buyers of insurance need to pay greater attention to the financial status or credit rating awarded to individual insurance companies when making decisions about which company to use.

Reference has already been made to insurance claims and the vital importance of insurance claims in relation to insurance. Apart from statutory and client requirements, the only reasons an organization buys insurance are to cover the increased cost of operation, recover the cost of repairing the damage and restoring the business following a loss. In respect of third-party insurance, it is the third-party injured person who will make the insurance claim.

The handling of insurance claims can be a detailed and forensic exercise. Sometimes claims handling involves complex legal procedures involving specialist engineers and accountants. Property damage claims may be easier to quantify, but claims associated with the business interruption element of the loss can be very difficult to measure and agree.

If an organization has devised adequate business continuity plans, the disruption to the business and the size of the insurance claim will be much reduced. In risk management terms, depending fully on insurance to make good all losses is not sufficient. Every organization should look to its business continuity plans to ensure that arrangements are in place to guarantee minimum disruption should an adverse event materialize.

There is increasing concern about compliance issues in relation to insurance policies. Most countries have introduced insurance premium taxes and these must be paid on a national basis where an organization has assets in several countries. Sometimes, the requirement to pay taxes may be on a city or regional basis, with the payment going to the local fire brigade. Compliance issues have also extended to the production of the insurance contract before the policy period commences. Timely issuance of insurance policies is often referred to as 'contract certainty'.

There are also compliance concerns related to whether a policy is admitted/approved/accepted within every country where the organization has operations. This can sometimes form a restriction on the operations of captive insurance companies. Certain countries may not accept the validity of an insurance policy written by a non-admitted insurer, including a captive insurance company.

Captive insurance companies

A captive insurance company is an insurance company owned by an organization that is not otherwise involved in insurance. The purpose of a captive insurance company is to provide insurance capacity for the organization by using its internal financial resources to fund certain types of anticipated losses or insurance claims. The organization that owns a captive insurance company is often referred to as the parent of the captive, or simply the parent organization.

In general, captive insurance companies are domiciled in a location that has a favourable regulatory and accounting regime that encourages the establishment of captive insurance companies. Domiciles for captive insurance companies include Guernsey, the Isle of Man, Gibraltar, Malta, Luxembourg, Bermuda and Ireland. The nature of captive insurance companies can vary quite widely. In theory, such a company may write insurance business directly into other countries, although compliance issues surrounding non-admitted policies may need to be carefully considered.

It is more common for a captive insurance company to operate as a re-insurer, providing insurance cover to the main insurance company appointed by the organization. This arrangement provides the insurance company of the organization, often referred to as the fronting insurer, with the means of receiving reimbursement for certain types of claims up to the financial limits or risk retention levels agreed with the captive insurance company.

A typical financial structure for a complex insurance programme is illustrated in Figure 17.1. The organization will accept deductibles or excesses on its different classes of insurance, and these may vary by class of insurance. The captive insurance company then accepts the next level of loss up to an agreed limit for any individual loss and also up to an agreed limit for total or cumulative losses during the policy year.

The primary or fronting insurer will then be responsible for payment of that part of larger losses that exceeds the captive insurance company limit. The fronting insurer will be responsible for payment of all losses once the cumulative totals for the captive have been breached. For statutory classes of insurance, the primary or fronting insurer will be responsible for the payment of the total claim.

The fronting insurer will then reclaim the money from the captive insurance company to the extent that the captive insurance company is liable. This can present a credit risk for the fronting insurance company, although this is usually overcome by the fronting insurance company not making any payment until it has received funds from the captive insurance company.

Some captive insurance companies accept business from third parties as well as providing insurance for the parent company. A typical example of a captive insurance company providing third-party insurance is extended warranty insurance policies offered by the retailers of electrical goods. Another example is that travel agents may set up a captive to provide travel cancellation insurance to customers. The customer will purchase a policy issued by a well-known insurance company, but the funding of the insurance will be provided by the captive by way of reinsurance of the fronting insurer. By setting up this arrangement, the travel agent should earn extra income and profit from its customers.

Figure 17.1   Role of captive insurance companies

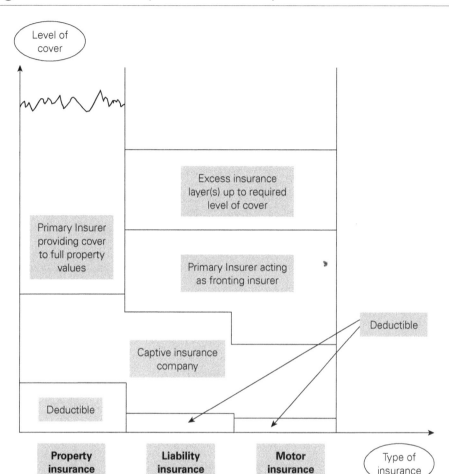

The advantages of captive insurance companies are as follows:

- Savings may be achieved in overall insurance costs because lower premiums are often set by captive insurance companies.
- The captive insurance company can gain access to reinsurance markets, where premium rates and risk capacity can be favourable.
- By being exposed to the cost of insurance claims, a greater risk awareness and greater concern about loss control can be achieved.
- Greater insurance cover can be offered by the captive insurance company than is available in the commercial market.
- Certain tax benefits may be available from having a captive insurance company, although these have reduced in recent times.

The disadvantages of captive insurance companies are as follows:

- The captive will be exposed to insurance claims that would otherwise have been paid by the commercial insurance market.
- The parent organization has to allocate capital to ensure adequate solvency of the captive insurance company.
- When large losses are paid by the captive, these are consolidated to the parent balance sheet and the organization ultimately pays these losses.
- Captives writing business in other territories will probably do so on a non-admitted basis and this may create compliance difficulties.
- Significant administrative cost, time and effort can be involved in the management of the captive by parent head office personnel.

An example of how the advantages of captive insurance companies are viewed is provided by the text box below. There is a wide range of suitable domiciles for captive insurance companies, including Guernsey, Ireland and Malta.

Benefits of captive insurance companies

For many years, large corporations have enjoyed many benefits from operating their own captive insurance companies. Most were established to provide coverage where insurance was unavailable or unreasonably priced. These insurance subsidiaries were often domiciled offshore, especially in Bermuda or the Cayman Islands.

The risk management benefits of these captives were primary, but their tax advantages were also important. A properly structured and managed captive insurance company can provide the following benefits:

- tax deduction for parent company for premium paid to captive;
- opportunity to accumulate funds in a tax-favoured domicile;
- distributions to captive owners at favourable income tax rates;
- asset protection from the claims of business and personal creditors;
- reduction in insurance premiums paid by the operating company;
- access to the lower-cost reinsurance market; and
- insuring risks that would otherwise be uninsurable.

Business continuity 18

Business continuity management

There has been considerable interest in the subjects of business continuity planning (BCP) and disaster recovery planning (DRP) in recent times. Several standards have been published around the world. This illustrates the importance of BCP as an integral part of risk management. This increased concern has been reinforced by the potential for major disruption posed by extreme weather events, terrorist attacks, civil emergencies and the fear of a flu pandemic.

In simple terms, BCP is how an organization prepares for future incidents that could jeopardize its existence. The range of incidents that should be covered will include everything from local events like fires through to regional disruption such as earthquakes or national security incidents and extend to international events like terrorism and pandemics.

British Standard BS 31100:2011 defines BCP as:

> [An] holistic management process that identifies potential threats to an organization and the impacts to business operations that those threats, if realised, might cause, and which provides a framework for building organizational resilience with the capability for an effective response to safeguard the interests of its key stakeholders, reputation, brand and value-creating activities.

In case of a serious incident such as loss of access to premises or the failure of a major part of an organization, it is important to have in place a well-defined, documented and tested disaster recovery plan. Such plans inevitably focus on recovery of access to IT systems and data, but also commonly cover the provision of alternative premises (if needed) and other facilities, as well as setting out plans for communications with employees and with other stakeholders such as suppliers, customers and the media at a time of crisis.

Business continuity plans build upon this by setting out longer-term plans for restoration of 'business as usual' in the immediate aftermath of a disaster. A business continuity plan is an important part of reducing the impact of a hazard incident. The plan should include arrangements for reducing the damage caused during the incident and containing the cost of recovery from it.

Disaster recovery plans are a particular component of BCP. If a computer system fails to operate correctly or data has become corrupted, the organization will need emergency procedures to ensure that the data can be recovered and/or ensure that the organization continues in existence. There may also be a wider need for a specific plan to manage any crisis that may result from an operational disaster. The main difference between the disaster recovery and crisis management plans is that the disaster recovery plan will be mainly concerned with actions to restore the infrastructure of the organization and a crisis plan will also be concerned with external stakeholders and actions to manage the associated stakeholder reaction and expectations.

For a printing firm IT systems are fundamental to the operation of the company, because the computer systems process orders, schedule printing and manage invoicing. For such a company, it may be appropriate to arrange for a mobile emergency computer facility to be available in case of major IT failure. If this decision is taken, a contract should be set up with an outside company for a duplicate computer to be delivered in a trailer to the premises of the company. The duplicate computer would then be connected and the operations would be controlled from the duplicate computer in the trailer. The success of this arrangement will depend on the availability of information from back-up disks that should be produced at least once per day and possibly several times per day.

There has been considerable discussion about the nature of business continuity and disaster recovery in terms of the types of control that they represent. HM Treasury in the UK considers these controls to be corrective, whereas the Scottish Government considers them to be directive. In terms of loss control, disaster recovery plans can be seen as primarily damage limitation controls, whereas business continuity controls are more concerned with cost containment.

The discussion of whether disaster recovery and BCP should be considered as types of control is, perhaps, not fundamentally important. The important issue is that disaster recovery and business continuity plans are concerned with circumstances where the event is taking place or has occurred. To that extent, DRP and BCP can be considered to be responses for when the event occurs and they do not take into account how likely it is that the event will occur.

An example in personal life is the use of seat belts in cars. Passengers in cars wear seat belts for when a road accident occurs. In many countries, the use of seat belts is compulsory and passengers are not required to undertake an evaluation of how likely they are to be involved in a road accident when deciding whether to wear their seat belts for that particular journey.

Many organizations are now taking the view that BCP should be viewed as having three components. The first response to any major event is to activate the crisis management plan to ensure appropriate response to the crisis and, in particular ensure that stakeholders are aware of the situation. This will require effective communication with all stakeholders, so that the damage to reputation resulting from the incident is kept to a minimum.

Secondly, the organization will then seek to recover from the event by implementation of a disaster recovery plan. However, as the disaster recovery plan is being implemented, the organization will still need to consider the ongoing management of the crisis. The organization should ensure that implementation of the disaster recovery plan is viewed as the second, but sometimes overlapping, stage of responding to the incident. In fact, in certain circumstances, it will only be possible to implement the disaster recovery plan once the immediate crisis has been contained.

When implementation of the crisis management arrangements is well advanced, and the disaster recovery plan has been activated, the organization will then be able to turn its attention to the third and broader operational issue of business continuity.

An example of this three-stage approach is when a serious road traffic accident occurs that obstructs a major road or highway. The initial response of the emergency services will be to deal with the crisis that may involve injuries to people and, in certain circumstances, a vehicle fire and/or other traffic travelling too fast towards the incident. When the immediate crisis has been contained, the disaster recovery phase can be implemented and this will include clearing the damaged vehicles and/ or repairing the road surface and crash barriers. It is only when these two stages have been completed that bringing the road back into use, or the business continuity aspect, can be addressed.

If the road traffic accident involved commercial vehicles or there was an allegation that a driver from the identified company caused the incident, the need for crisis management responses will extend to the road haulage or transportation company involved in the incident. The company should activate their crisis management plan to demonstrate social responsibility and to ensure minimum damage to their reputation. The road haulage company may also wish to take action during the crisis to support other stakeholders, including the families of drivers who may have been injured in the incident.

Figure 18.1 provides an illustration of a disaster recovery timeline and costs and this is discussed later in this chapter. The need to ensure adequate crisis management and effective communication with stakeholders covers the whole period of disruption (from point A to point D) and possibly beyond.

Business continuity standards

The British Standards Institute published a standard on business continuity management (BCM). This is BS 25999 Part 1 (2006) 'Code of Practice – Business continuity management' and was followed by BS 25999 Part 2 (2007) 'Business continuity management. Specification'. It has now been replaced by an internationally accepted standard ISO 22301 (2012) 'Societal Security – Business Continuity Management System – Requirements'. ISO 22301 is similar to BS25999 and is written in what is becoming the standard structure for management standards. It describes a plan–do–check–act (PDCA) approach that is similar to the plan–implement–measure–learn (PIML) approach used throughout this book and described in detail in Appendix C.

ISO 22301 identifies a BCP lifecycle that has the following five components related to the Business Continuity Management System (BCMS):

- identify crucial risk factors already affecting the organization;
- understand the needs and obligations of the organization;
- establish, implement and maintain your BCMS;
- measure the overall capability to manage disruptive incidents;
- guarantee conformity with stated business continuity policy.

Figure 18.2 provides a model for BCP that is consistent with ISO 22301. Table 18.1 provides a checklist of the key activities involved in BCP. Having business continuity plans is recognized as essential by most large organizations. Indeed, many governments take an active role in encouraging businesses (especially small businesses) to develop and implement adequate business continuity plans.

The main change introduced by ISO 22301 in comparison to BS 25999 is that ISO 22301 is the first standard to be written using the new high-level structure, which is

Figure 18.1   Disaster recovery timeline and costs

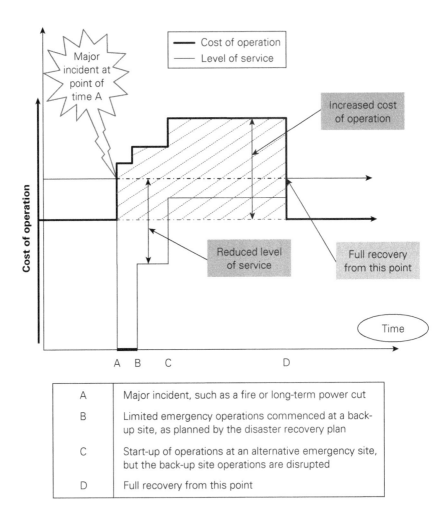

A	Major incident, such as a fire or long-term power cut
B	Limited emergency operations commenced at a back-up site, as planned by the disaster recovery plan
C	Start-up of operations at an alternative emergency site, but the back-up site operations are disrupted
D	Full recovery from this point

common to all new management systems standards. This will make integration straight-forward when implementing more than one management system. The phrase 'preventive action' has been replaced with 'actions to address risks and opportunities'. ISO 22301 puts a much greater emphasis on setting objectives, monitoring performance and metrics – aligning business continuity to executive management strategic thinking.

The overriding principles appropriate to successful BCP are that the plan should be:

- comprehensive;
- cost-effective;

Figure 18.2   Model for business continuity planning

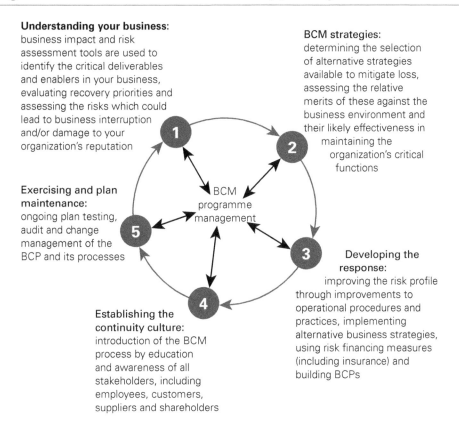

Understanding your business: business impact and risk assessment tools are used to identify the critical deliverables and enablers in your business, evaluating recovery priorities and assessing the risks which could lead to business interruption and/or damage to your organization's reputation

BCM strategies: determining the selection of alternative strategies available to mitigate loss, assessing the relative merits of these against the business environment and their likely effectiveness in maintaining the organization's critical functions

Exercising and plan maintenance: ongoing plan testing, audit and change management of the BCP and its processes

BCM programme management

Developing the response: improving the risk profile through improvements to operational procedures and practices, implementing alternative business strategies, using risk financing measures (including insurance) and building BCPs

Establishing the continuity culture: introduction of the BCM process by education and awareness of all stakeholders, including employees, customers, suppliers and shareholders

- practical;
- effective;
- maintained;
- practised.

It is important that the BCP should cover all the operations and premises of the organization to ensure that the plan can facilitate a complete resumption of normal business operations. It is also important that the plan is cost-effective and proportionate to the risk exposures.

The BCP must be practical and easily understood by staff and others who are involved in the execution of the plan. Overall, the BCP must be effective in that it will recognize the urgency of certain business components or functions and identify responsibilities for ensuring timely resumption of normal work.

In order to guarantee that the BCP will be effective, it needs to be tested, maintained and practised. All members of staff need to be familiar with the intended operation of the plan and training will need to be provided. The lessons learnt during testing and practice of the business continuity plan should be incorporated into the

Table 18.1   Key activities in business continuity planning

1 Assess company activities to identify critical staff, materials, procedures and equipment required to keep the business operating.

2 Identify suppliers, shippers, resources and other businesses that are contacted on a daily basis.

3 Plan what to do if any important buildings, plant or store were to become inaccessible.

4 Identify necessary actions to ensure continuity of critical business functions, especially payroll.

5 Decide who should participate in compiling and subsequently testing the emergency plans.

6 Define crisis management procedures and individual responsibilities for disaster recovery activities.

7 Co-ordinate with others, including neighbours, utility suppliers, suppliers, shippers and key customers.

8 Review the emergency plans annually and when the business changes and/or new members of staff are recruited.

plan so that it becomes more effective. The need for rehearsals is emphasized in Figure 18.2 and Table 18.1.

Testing of business continuity plans is an essential component of ensuring that they will be appropriate and effective. However, testing of plans can be time-consuming and, in some circumstances, disruptive and costly. Even the simple example of a fire evacuation drill from a building illustrates that the testing of procedures is inevitably going to disrupt normal routine operations.

Successful business continuity

The first stage in successful BCP, DRP and crisis management is to gain a thorough understanding of the organization and its interactions, both internal and external. Part of gaining this understanding will be to identify the objectives of the organization and its key dependencies. It is important to understand the critical functions within the organization and identify key resources.

Determining BCP strategy will require the identification of risks to the business and decisions about how likely it is that the risks will materialize. It is also necessary to understand the impact of risks on the business. These assessments should then be used to prioritize treatment of the risks and to agree the likelihood and impact of the risks materializing.

Developing and implementing a BCP and appropriate controls for each of the identified risks will require decisions on the appropriate risk responses. The range of risk responses available have already been discussed as the 4Ts of hazard risk management. In respect of each of the major risks, the decision will have to be taken whether to tolerate, treat, transfer or terminate the risk.

Building and embedding a business continuity management (BCM) culture will require good communication throughout the organization. All stakeholders will need to be engaged and involved in the business continuity activities and will need to understand the reasons for the development of the BCP and DRP. The important role of all employees in the avoidance of incidents that could result in major disruption should be emphasized.

When developing the BCP, the mission-critical activities should be identified, together with key roles and responsibilities. These may be produced in the form of clear instructions and checklists. It is important to exercise, maintain and review the BCP by creating a programme to test the plans, review and amend them as necessary, and rehearse staff to improve understanding of the plans. BCP and DRP should be reviewed at least annually, as well as after a test of the plans. Also, if an incident occurs, the lessons learnt should be incorporated into the plans.

The flu pandemic of 2009 provides an example of the importance of BCP. Advice and guidance was produced for companies and individuals in many countries around the world. The box below sets out a summary of the key points provided in that guidance and the practical implications of the flu pandemic for business continuity. It is accepted by many governments that a pandemic is one of the most disruptive circumstances that could affect a country.

Flu pandemic

Pandemic contingency plans for an organization should aim to ensure continuity of essential operations during an extended period of high illness rates in the workforce, suppliers and customers. It should ensure that employees are not exposed to a high risk of infection in their workplace and aim to resume operations rapidly and competitively as soon as the pandemic cycle is over.

Critical business processes can be protected by allocating additional back-up personnel, diversifying activities across multiple locations and maximizing home-based working. Additional investments in spare workplace capacity might be needed, training more personnel to take over essential roles, and improving IT capability. Plans should anticipate that suppliers, equipment providers and support companies will be unable to function for some time, and stockpiles of essential supplies should be established. Telecommunications infrastructure may be unable to cope with the greatly increased demand.

During a pandemic, employees are likely to become infected from their families, their children or contacts outside the workplace. Social contacts in the workplace then spread infection through the workforce. Lower-contact work environment practices that minimize the risk of infection spread include a well-informed workforce, fewer face-to-face meetings, rigorous hygiene and frequent biological cleaning of common area surfaces. Ultimately it may be necessary to close offices to prevent the spread of a virulent virus.

Staff who recover from a case of pandemic influenza are unlikely to catch it again and are no longer infectious to others. Recovered and vaccinated staff can return to work. As the pandemic subsides, resuming operations rapidly and efficiently could become a competitive issue.

Figure 18.1 on page 206 provides a practical example of DRP and BCP. This example is based on a broadcasting organization that suffers a major disruption at its main broadcasting facility at point A on the timeline. The disaster recovery plan will ensure that broadcasting resumes within a short space of time, but this may only be an emergency broadcast. The emergency broadcast starts from point B on the timeline. Note Figure 18.1 does not include the cost of repairing or restoring the facility that has been damaged.

After a short period of emergency broadcasts, the organization will be able to commence full broadcasting of its normal service from an alternative location. For example, the broadcaster may move the London broadcast facilities to studios in Manchester. In order to do this, however, the Manchester capability will be lost. Therefore, Figure 18.1 shows that the level of service is much improved at point C, which is the move to Manchester, but because the Manchester broadcast facility has been lost, the level of service is not up to the previous level.

There will be an increased cost of operation from the time of the incident. There will be a cost associated with implementing the disaster recovery plan and further costs associated with emergency broadcasting and then the move to Manchester. During the period of broadcasting from Manchester, increased costs will be involved by way of temporary accommodation for staff and increased technical facilities. Eventually, from point D on the timeline, the facilities in London have been repaired and full recovery has been achieved.

Figure 18.1 represents a typical set of circumstances for an organization that suffers a major incident. The impaired level of service will continue for some time and increased cost of operation will be involved. Insurance may be available for the increased cost of operation, provided that it does not exceed the indemnity period (duration of the disruption) quoted in the insurance policy. It is unlikely that insurance cover will be available to cover any losses associated with a reduced level of service from the time the incident occurs until the point of full recovery, unless specific types of costs or losses are identified and insured.

Business impact analysis (BIA)

A critical part of ensuring that adequate business continuity plans and disaster recovery plans are in place is completion of a business impact analysis (BIA). The BIA will identify the critical nature of each business function by assessment of the impact of interruption to that activity. This information will be required in order to identify appropriate continuity strategies for each function.

The BIA is similar to the risk assessment that is undertaken as part of the overall risk management process. However, the critical difference from BCP is that the emphasis of a BIA is the identification of the relative importance and criticality of each function, rather than identifying the events that could undermine that particular function.

Therefore, the risk assessment and the BIA are related and could well be undertaken together. The risk assessment will help in identifying the risks that might threaten the achievement of the business continuity objectives. For a television company, broadcasting continuity in excess of 99.9 per cent is likely to be the target and may even be a requirement imposed by the licensing authority. Both risk assessment and BIA require a structured and systematic approach.

The business impact analysis has three clear purposes, as follows:

1 Identify mission-critical activities and the required recovery time in the event of disruption. This identification activity will establish the timeframe within which the critical functions must be resumed after the disruptive event.

2 Establish the impact potential and the resource requirements for recovery within the agreed timescale. The business requirements for recovery of the critical function must be established.

3 Determine whether the likely impact is within the risk appetite of the organization as the basis for business continuity strategy. The technical requirements for recovery of the critical function also need to be established.

The business impact analysis could be based on the sources of disruption that are described as the 4Ps in Table 3.2. Once the sources of disruption that face the operations of an organization are identified, undertaking a BIA will become simpler. The focus of a business impact analysis, however, is likely to be based on processes within the organization and how these may be disrupted. This seems especially relevant as continuity of business processes safeguards the interests of key stakeholders, reputation, brand and value-creating activities.

Business continuity and ERM

There is an obvious link between BCP and enterprise risk management (ERM). ERM is concerned with the risks facing the whole organization and BCP takes an approach that business continuity arrangements should be in place. The BCP approach is to look at the continuity of operations across the whole organization. Ensuring continuity is obviously part of an ERM approach. It should therefore be considered that BCP is part of ERM, but it is not the whole of ERM activity. Nevertheless, there is a strong similarity in approach and the business continuity and disaster recovery activities should take place within the context of a broader ERM initiative, as appropriate. Both approaches seek to achieve continuity of effective and efficient core business processes.

Enterprise risk management is explored in more detail in Chapter 8. The basis of ERM is that the stakeholder expectations and the core processes of the organization that deliver those expectations are the focus of the risk assessment process. The intention of ERM is to ensure that the core processes are maintained.

Continuation of core business processes is also the basis of BCP. The difference in emphasis is that ERM seeks to identify the risks that could impact the effectiveness and efficiency of core processes. BCP seeks to identify the critical business functions that need to be maintained in order to achieve continuation of the business. The approaches are complementary and there is a good deal of similarity between BCP and this style of ERM.

Page 51 identifies the constant availability of prescription drugs as a core process for a pharmaceutical company. It is possible to take an ERM approach to this core process and identify the risks that could disrupt the process. In taking this approach to risk management, the pharmaceutical company will have combined the ERM and BCP approaches in a way that clearly focuses on the delivery of stakeholder expectations.

Scenario planning is an important component of business continuity and has broader implications for the successful implementation of enterprise risk management. For financial institutions, scenario planning extends to evaluation of the balance sheet capital that would be required by the financial institution in the event of difficulties similar to the global financial crisis of 2007/08. This type of scenario planning for financial institutions is usually referred to as 'stress testing' and is often a specific requirement of banking regulators.

Scenario planning needs to take account of the external and internal context of the organization, as well as the business impact analysis. Also, there is a strong relationship between scenario planning and crisis management. Disaster recovery planning and business continuity planning can take account of foreseeable incidents, but it is more difficult to foresee every crisis that might arise. Therefore, a useful aspect of scenario planning is that it anticipates highly unlikely circumstances and then challenges senior management to develop successful responses.

The lessons from scenario planning can then be used to take actions that will increase the resilience of the organization. The text box overleaf describes an approach to scenario planning supported by the Cabinet Office of the UK Government, in relation to disruption of national infrastructure, such as the electricity supply network.

Reasonable worst-case scenarios

Event standards can be established to set a level of resilience against an extreme event that the network or system should be able to continue to operate without widespread loss or disruption to the essential services. Describing reasonable worst-case scenarios for hazards will enable infrastructure owners and operators to identify and assess their resilience, and consider any gaps in resilience of an asset or network between the event and the actual or current design and service standards.

The ability and capability to manage and respond to events greater than these reasonable worst-case scenarios is dependent upon their generic organizational resilience. Alongside this, infrastructure owners should consider, in their business continuity plans, the speed with which they expect to be able to restore services in the event of supply being disrupted for whatever reason, including events that are not specifically itemized or which are more serious or extreme than those covered in the reasonable worst-case scenarios.

Civil emergencies

In many countries, there is an obligation placed on local government to ensure the continuity of local businesses in the event of a major civil emergency. The emergency may be triggered by a natural disaster such as flooding or an earthquake. Alternatively, it could be caused by terrorism, civil unrest or by an epidemic/pandemic. The ISO 22300 series of standards relate to societal resilience and the increasing importance of this series of standards is also considered in Chapter 9.

Many civil authorities publish guidance for businesses to assist them with their BCP. For example, the US government provides valuable information on its website. Also, several trade associations and small business associations offer practical guidance on BCP, including appropriate actions in the case of civil emergency.

Most local authorities have statutory responsibility for responding to civil emergencies. Factories and warehouses may have equipment and facilities that could be useful in the event of a civil emergency. Likewise, retail shops will have food and other goods that may be required for distribution as emergency supplies. The products that may be useful in a civil emergency will include food, bottled water, clothing and blankets. Also, schools and other civic buildings may be required as accommodation in the event of a civil emergency, such as the wide area floods that have become more frequent in several European countries.

Encouraging organizations to make arrangements to ensure business continuity will benefit local authorities in charge of civil emergencies, because there will be fewer problems and issues for them to take into account at the time of the emergency. The box below provides a summary of typical advice provided by a municipal authority to small businesses in the local area.

Secure your business

Thoroughly assessing the disasters that could threaten your firm will give you a clear idea of the business areas that are most important to secure. Usually, these will be the areas on which your business relies the most, and which are exposed to the greatest degree of risk. This is the most important part of your plan.

Clearly, your premises are fundamental to your business – so much so that you probably take them for granted. But you should consider the long-term impact that damage to or destruction of your premises would have on your business. The same applies to business-critical machinery, plant and equipment.

PART FIVE
Risk strategy

LEARNING OUTCOMES FOR PART FIVE

- explain the importance of dynamic business models and the relationship with strategy, tactics, operations and compliance (STOC) activities;
- outline the components and the importance of the business model and how this is supported by the resilience of the organization;
- explain the importance of corporate social responsibility, including supply chain, ethical trading risks and the importance of reputation;
- explain the key components of the risk architecture, strategy and protocols (RASP) for an organization and how these fit together;
- list the main sections of a typical risk management manual, describe the importance of each section and summarize the range of risk documentation and records;
- explain the importance of the allocation of risk management responsibilities, including the governance responsibilities of non-executive directors;
- produce practical examples of the control of selected hazard risks, including risks to finances, infrastructure, reputation and marketplace;
- describe the process of learning from controls in order to ensure that controls are cost-effective and risk/reward decisions are appropriate.

PART FIVE FURTHER READING

ASIS SPC.1-2009 *Organizational Resilience: Security, Preparedness and Continuity Management Systems*, **www.asisonline.org**

Financial Reporting Council (2014) *Guidance on Risk Management, Internal Control and Related Financial and Business Reporting*, **www.frc.org.uk**

Hopkin, P (2013) *Risk Management (Strategic Success)*, **www.koganpage.com**

Institute of *Risk* Management (2010) *A Structured Approach to Enterprise Risk Management (ERM) and the Requirements of ISO 31000*, **www.theirm.org**

Pullan, P and Murray-Webster, R (2011) *A Short Guide to Facilitating Risk Management*, **www.gowerpublishing.com**

Woods, M (2011) *Risk Management in Organizations: An Integrated Case Study Approach*, **www.routledge.com**

PART FIVE CASE STUDIES

AMEC Foster Wheeler: Principal risks and uncertainties

The board has overall responsibility for risk management, for determining the risk appetite in relation to the principal risks, for implementation of the risk management policy and for reviewing the effectiveness of the risk management systems.

A global mandatory procedure detailing the risk management process is used at project, operating unit, business unit and group levels to identify the key risks that could have a significant impact on the ability to achieve objectives.

These are recorded in risk registers and evaluated to determine the likely impact and probability of occurring. Control actions are developed to mitigate or eliminate risks that are considered unacceptable. Risk owners are identified and given responsibility for ensuring actions are implemented with appropriate review dates. The risk registers are reviewed and updated at least quarterly with the relevant risk owners.

The risk committee is chaired by the chief executive and meets at least twice each year to:

- review and advise the board on Amec Foster Wheeler's risk appetite in relation to the principal strategic risks, taking account of the current and prospective macro-economic, financial, political, business and sector environments;
- review and approve the risk management strategy, policies, procedures and processes;
- review and report to the board on the effectiveness of the risk management systems;
- review the Amec Foster Wheeler plc risk register and make recommendations as appropriate;
- review any new or emerging risks and any potential impact they may have on risk appetite and the ability of Amec Foster Wheeler to manage such risks;
- review any issues raised by other committees of the board that impact on the risk profile of Amec Foster Wheeler;
- review and consider reports on key risk issues such as new business and geographical locations for operations or projects;
- consider any internal or external risk trends and concentrations.

Edited extract from Amec Foster Wheeler plc
Annual Report and Accounts 2015

BBC: Internal controls assurance

We reviewed the effectiveness of the system of internal controls, taking account of the findings from internal and external audit reports. Our work in this area was influenced by the reports from the Director of Risk and Assurance on the effectiveness of internal control, identified frauds, and losses and assurance mapping.

We sought assurance from management that control issues identified by internal audit are being addressed. We considered the audit assurance over implementation of actions from a number of recent high-profile independent reviews in areas such as severance pay, freelancer tax treatment, child protection and whistleblowing arrangements. We considered the audit assurance over a number of high-profile implementation and change programmes concerning the upgrade of underlying IT systems and introduction of improved financial control processes.

We considered the processes for managing significant risks within the BBC and the BBC's risk appetite in the context of its key strategic and operating risks and how the BBC is managing its key strategic projects.

We continue to have an ongoing interest in project assurance so that we can ensure that the lessons learnt from previous projects are taken forward. Our review of the internal audit plan considered how audit work on project assurance was integrated with management's own project assurance activities. We satisfied ourselves that ongoing project assurance activity covers both governance and technical assurances.

Edited extract from BBC
Annual Report and Accounts 2014/15

Emperor Watch & Jewellery: Risk management

The risk management process includes risk identification, risk evaluation, risk management measures, and risk control and review. The management is delegated to identify, analyse, evaluate, respond, monitor and communicate risks associated with any activity, function or process within its scope of responsibility and authority. It is endeavoured to evaluate and compare the level of risk against predetermined acceptable levels of risk.

For risk control and monitoring, it involves making decisions regarding which risks are acceptable and how to address those that are not. The management will develop contingency plans for possible loss scenarios. Accidents and other situations involving loss or near-loss will be investigated and properly documented as part of the effort to manage risks.

The group is subject to certain risks that affect its ability to operate and protect assets. The key risks identified and their respective strategies are set out below:

1 Reliance on tourism of HK/Macau/Singapore:
  - change business model;
  - expand business to domestic consumer market by adjusting shop locations;
  - adjust stock portfolio to more affordable products to suit domestic consumers.
2 Economic, political and social conditions in HK/Macau/Singapore (eg strong HKD against other currencies, continued austerity initiatives in the PRC):
  - explore opportunities to develop networks in other countries;
  - be cautious in purchasing and stock replenishment;
  - relocate shops in the PRC;
  - develop and maintain multi-tier targeted customer segments.
3 Reliance on major watch suppliers and watch brands:
  - continuously expand jewellery business;
  - maintain strong and close relationship with watch suppliers;
  - keep a wider portfolio on brands.
4 Rental increment on retail shops:
  - bargain for rental negotiation or rental concession;
  - take advantage of coming trend in rental drop in prime shopping areas to maintain a balanced presence in strategically favourable geographical areas.

Edited extract from Emperor Watch & Jewellery Limited
Annual Report 2015

Core business processes

Dynamic business models

Organizations will often establish business objectives and strategic objectives as separate documents. When seeking to ensure that risk management makes a full contribution to the organization, it is important to view both of these sets of objectives and explore the relationship between them. Business objectives will often relate to the annual budget that has been produced by the organization. This budget will contain details of the anticipated sales as income and the cost of sales as expenditure.

Underpinning the business objectives of the organization will be the business delivery model (or business model for short) that the organization has developed. For example, a membership organization will seek sponsorship from organizations that deliver services to the membership. This source of sponsorship income will be a fundamental part of the business model and the annual business objectives. The membership body will need to estimate income from membership subscriptions and from sponsorship, and determine what services will be delivered to the members in return for their membership fee and what benefits will be delivered to the sponsors in return for their sponsorship money.

The risks that are attached to business objectives are associated with the robustness of the business model and the efficiency of the business model. When undertaking a risk assessment of the annual budget, the events that could undermine sponsorship and membership income, together with the events that could disrupt the delivery of services and benefits, should be considered. The essence of the business objectives normally relate to the organization as it currently exists.

The box below identifies the essential features of a business development model. It is worth remembering that an organization will have a current version of their business model, as discussed in Chapter 20. The business model is underpinned by the business objectives and the annual business plan. The organization will also have plans to develop and enhance the business model in line with long-term strategy. Figure 19.1 describes how the existing business model is developed by implementing the tactics that achieve that long-term strategy. The existing business model is defined by the existing operations or 'where the organization is now'.

Business delivery and development models

Whenever a business is established, it either explicitly or implicitly employs a particular business delivery model that describes the architecture of the value creation, delivery, and capture mechanisms employed by the business enterprise. The essence of a business delivery model is that it defines the manner by which the business delivers value to customers, entices customers to pay for value, and converts those payments to profit: it thus reflects the belief of the organization about what customers want, how they want it, and how the enterprise can organize to best meet those needs, get paid for doing so, and make a profit.

The business delivery model is used to describe and classify businesses, but is also used by management inside companies to explore possibilities for future development. Future enhancement of the business delivery model is achieved by implementation of a business development plan. In fact, a well-established business delivery model will act as the basis for creative organizations to develop future strategy.

Most organizations recognize that the existing business model will not continue to be successful on an open-ended basis. If business objectives are to be delivered year after year, then the business will need to develop. These developments could include exploring greater sponsorship opportunities, delivering new services and products that will generate new income, and increasing efficiency in the delivery of the existing business model. Development of the business model to fulfil strategic objectives can be considered to be the business development model and it is the main topic of this chapter.

In order to place risk management within the context of business operations, it is necessary to consider a simplified business development model. Figure 19.1 sets out the basic elements of a business development model in simple terms. The first stage for an organization is to decide the strategy that it is seeking to deliver. The strategic aims will be determined by considering the mission statement of the organization, the corporate objectives and the stakeholder expectations. The organization should establish a strategy that is capable of delivering the mission statement of the organization. In other words, the strategy of the organization needs to be effective and efficient.

Once the overall strategy is established, the tactics that will deliver it need to be identified. If the strategy requires changes to core processes or the introduction of new core processes, then projects or programmes of work will be required. The tactics introduced by the organization should ensure that effective and efficient core processes to deliver the desired outcomes in the most cost-effective manner are in place. In relation to operations, the desired state of the organization is the continuity of normal efficient operations with no unplanned disruption.

Figure 19.1 sets out the stages that are described above. The strategy can be seen as 'where the organization wants to be'. Review of the operations of the organization will collect information on 'where the organization is now' and the tactics define 'how the organization will get there'. This is a three-stage approach to development of the business model that has events at its centre. In many circumstances, these

Figure 19.1 Business development model

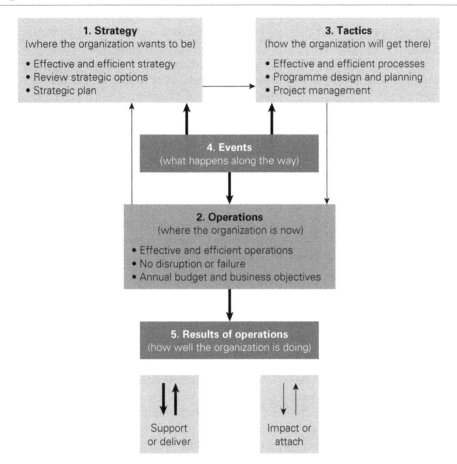

events will represent risks that could materialize. The other component of this business development model is the reporting of the results of operations.

Actions and events can be good, bad or routine, and enable the organization to monitor what progress is being made against the business strategy, tactics, operations and compliance. These actions and events impact the organization and its ability to sustain effective, efficient and compliant business operations and core processes. Although compliance core processes are not specifically mentioned, they represent the means by which the organization will ensure that it fulfills its legal and contractual obligations. Compliance core processes should underpin all the activities of the organization and will be similar in nature to operational core processes.

Identification of strategy will require an approach based on opportunity management. Delivery of tactics, often by way of projects, will require attention to uncertainties and management of control risks will be important. Delivery of effective and efficient operations will require particular attention to the successful management of hazard risks.

Types of business processes

An organization will have existing business processes and these may be satisfactory for generating the required income and controlling costs so that the business objectives are delivered. To ensure that risk management has an adequate input into the delivery of business objectives, the objectives must relate to routine operations within the organization. However, it is not unusual for organizations to fail to establish business-as-usual objectives. Most objectives tend to be annualized change objectives that relate to the delivery of the strategic plan for the organization. In summary, for risk management to make a full contribution to the success of an organization, objectives need to be fully established that cover strategy, tactics and operations.

A core process is one that is fundamental to the continued success (or even existence) of the organization. Core processes ensure that the organization is able to achieve the mission and corporate objectives and fulfil stakeholder expectations. Each core process creates value and is designed to deliver one or more of the stakeholder expectations.

There are four basic types of core process. These are processes designed, implemented and managed to ensure the following:

- development and delivery of strategy;
- management of tactics, projects and enhancements;
- continuity and monitoring of routine operations;
- activities that are designed to ensure compliance.

An activity is an individual job or task that builds into the processes that deliver stakeholder expectations. The processes themselves are designed and intended to add value to the organization, but the addition of extra activities will add cost. Therefore, the challenge is to develop effective core processes that are also efficient.

Having identified stakeholder expectations, core processes can then be put in place to ensure that these expectations are delivered to the level that the organization has decided is appropriate. No organization will be in a position to fully deliver all expectations to the level desired by all stakeholders. Often, this is because different stakeholder expectations are contradictory.

Weaknesses or gaps in the core processes of the organization are likely to be present, as follows:

- There may be weaknesses related to the development and delivery of strategy. These weaknesses will result in the organization failing to retain its position as a market leader. They give rise to a leadership gap.
- There may be weaknesses related to the management of tactics, including projects and product or service enhancements. These weaknesses will result in failure to keep up with competitors. They give rise to a competition gap.
- There may be weaknesses related to failure to ensure efficiency, continuity and monitoring of routine operations. These weaknesses will result in failure to maintain efficient operations. They give rise to an efficiency gap.
- There may be weaknesses related to the activities designed to fulfil mandatory requirements placed on the organization. These weaknesses will result in failure to maintain reputation. They give rise to a compliance gap.

Strategy and tactics

Business strategy is the statement of what the organization intends to achieve and how it plans to achieve it, and is based on the strategic decisions about the future of the organization. Establishing a detailed business strategy enables the organization to deliver its mission, objectives, strategy and plans. The overall objective of risk management input into strategy is to ensure effective and efficient strategy and strategic decisions that will deliver the desired outcomes.

The main risk management input into business strategy is likely to be risk assessment. This is a critical component for the formation of strategy. Risk assessment of the existing strategy and any proposed new strategy should be undertaken. If clear strategic options are present, then a risk assessment of each of the viable options should be undertaken individually.

Some organizations exist in a very competitive marketplace that is undergoing significant technological changes. In these circumstances, there are significant risks associated with the business and huge strategic decisions have to be taken. Often, these decisions are related to developments in technology that challenge the way in which the organization delivers customer solutions. Changes in technology can require huge and speculative investment decisions and these decisions establish the tactics that will be implemented. The investment decisions may be speculative because of untested new technology or because there are alternative technologies available.

A risk assessment of strategic options needs to be undertaken, including an analysis of stakeholder expectations, existing customer requirements and existing staff skills, as well as a strengths, weaknesses, opportunities and threats (SWOT) analysis. The strategic options available to the company might include joint ventures, outsourcing the work, sub-contracting or investing in new technologies.

Detailed risk assessment of strategic options will ensure that the board has the best available information in order to make correct strategic decisions. Events and other circumstances that could reduce the successful delivery of strategy should be identified during the risk assessment. The organization will then be able to decide the controls that should be put in place to optimize the likely impact if any of these risks materialize.

Often, strategic objectives will relate to the development of a business sector and the reputation of the organization within that sector. In this way, the enhancement of reputation and the development of individual brands become opportunity risks for the organization. The fundamental importance of brand and reputation is considered in more detail in Chapter 20.

Tactics are the means by which the organization will deliver the business strategy. Tactics need to be correctly selected, implemented and controlled to ensure the effectiveness and efficiency of operations and they should also deliver reliability of financial reporting and compliance with applicable laws and regulations. The intended outcome is effective, efficient and compliant core business processes.

Changes to core processes are delivered by projects, and the importance of risk management in projects is discussed in Chapter 31 of this book. When undertaking a project, the organization needs to be concerned about the risks within the project that could stop it being delivered on time, within budget and to specification.

However, there is a further consideration related to projects and that is the effectiveness of enhancements to core processes that the project is designed to deliver. There is little benefit in having a project delivered on time, within budget and to specification if the required increase in core process effectiveness and/or efficiency is not achieved. For example, the installation of a new business software system may be undertaken by a successful project, but if the new software system is inadequate, or does not deliver all of the additional benefits anticipated, then the improvement in business core processes may not have been achieved.

The main risk management inputs into tactics and projects will be risk assessment, risk response enhancement and the review and monitoring activities. The purpose in undertaking a risk assessment of a project is to identify necessary controls. When these controls have been implemented, the effectiveness and efficiency of the controls will need to be reviewed. Overall, the intention is to ensure that tactics and projects are themselves effective and efficient.

Effective tactics mean that the core processes are the correct ones for delivering what is required. Established core processes may be fully efficient, but that does not mean that they are the correct or most effective core processes that the organization could employ. In order to ensure that core processes are fully effective, change will be required by way of projects that will be designed to ensure that strategy is delivered.

Developing more effective core processes will be the way by which the organization ensures that it continues to satisfy customers, financiers and other stakeholders. In order to ensure that effective core processes are in place, the business model and business objectives may need to change.

Effective and efficient operations

The overall objective of risk management input into operations is to achieve operational efficiency that is protected from unplanned disruption. Disruption of operations is likely to be caused by a hazard risk materializing. The design of efficient operational core processes that are free from disruption will provide the organization with significant competitive advantage or place the organization in a better position to deliver value for money.

Risk management can have a major impact on the operations of an organization. All stages of the risk management process are relevant to the continuity of uninterrupted efficient core business processes. Risk recognition and rating (risk assessment), responding to significant risks, resourcing controls, reaction planning, reporting on risk and review and monitoring are all critical inputs. In summary, risk management input into operations needs to be comprehensive if operations are to be efficient and uninterrupted.

Internal audit also has an important role to play in the delivery of efficient operations. Internal auditors frequently refer to the added value that internal audit activities bring. This added value relates to the evaluation of control activities, especially in relation to operations. Not only should the operations be effective and efficient, but the controls that are in place should also be effective and efficient. Internal audit activities have a significant role to play in providing the appropriate risk assurance and providing confirmation of compliance, where relevant.

All organizations need effective and efficient operations. In difficult financial and economic circumstances, it is important that existing operations continue to be delivered as efficiently as possible. The efficiency of operations will determine whether the annual budget, which includes the annual business objectives, is delivered. Part of ensuring the success of the organization will be to improve the efficiency of operations. Delivering more efficient operations can be undertaken by developing activities so that they require less resources, and this may involve cost-cutting.

There is no point in operations being efficient if those operations are based on the incorrect activities or core processes for the organization. For example, it may be possible to arrange a very efficient means of travelling to your destination by car, so that the activity of travelling by car is as efficient as possible. However, it may be that the journey would be more effective if it was undertaken by train. In most busy cities in the world it is possible to hire a taxi and travel to your destination quite efficiently. However, the more effective way of travelling may be to use the underground or metro system, which is likely to prove to be quicker and less costly.

The business model is described in more detail in Chapter 20. It defines the customer offering delivered by the resources of the organization and underpinned by the resilience of the finances and the reputation of that organization (CORR). The business model (as represented by the acronym CORR) is considered in more detail in Chapter 20. The business model, therefore, represents the current (or existing) activities and operational core processes of an organization. Strategy and tactics will be designed to enhance and improve the business model by improving the effectiveness and efficiency of operational core processes. It is important to note that the business model represents the current status of the operational core processes in an organization.

Ensuring compliance

The reasons for undertaking risk management activities are described as mandatory, assurance, decision making, and effective and efficient core processes (MADE2). Core processes are identified as strategic, tactical, operational and compliance (STOC). There is a clear link between the reasons for undertaking risk management and the effectiveness and efficiency of core processes.

Mandatory requirements are fulfilled by organizations, because they are required by stakeholders. Stakeholders who can impose mandatory requirements include regulators, customers/clients and financiers. Mandatory requirements have to be fulfilled and this will be undertaken by the organization by ensuring that effective and efficient compliance core processes exist within the organization. Failure to comply with stakeholder requirements can have significant implications for most organizations. In the extreme, failure to comply with the mandatory requirements of a licence may result in that licence being withdrawn by the regulator and that could jeopardize the existence of the organization.

In almost all cases, there will be a number of ways in which the mandatory requirements imposed by stakeholders can be fulfilled. Although compliance core processes need to be effective and efficient, there will be risks involved, and risk management input will have a significant role to play in designing the compliance processes, protocols and procedures. This is an example of how risk management expertise and support can enable an organization to achieve compliance in a way that is not only effective, but also can be efficient to the extent that it becomes a competitive advantage.

The culture within many organizations will be highly compliant with a strong desire to comply with the mandatory obligations placed on the organization. This is a positive attribute and underpins the ethos of the organization, but if compliance is not achieved in an effective and efficient manner, wasted resources and competitive disadvantage will result. Part of the role of risk management professionals is to facilitate the development of effective and efficient compliance core processes that achieve compliance in the most cost-effective manner.

For example, most organizations will have mandatory health and safety requirements placed on them by legislation and enforced by a regulator. Some organizations may complain about the statutory obligations that are placed on them, and seek to avoid compliance if they believe there will be no consequences, or they think that they can 'get away with it'. An organization with a more sophisticated approach to risk management, as illustrated in Figure 4.2, will adopt the approach that achieving compliance with health and safety requirements will not only improve operational efficiency, but a good safety record could be a factor in securing new contracts and new clients.

Reporting performance

Operational reports indicate how well the strategy is being delivered. Data needs to be available on an ongoing basis, so that management can respond and modify the business core processes as necessary.

Operational reports also provide information that can be used to prepare reports to stakeholders on the performance of the organization. However, the organization needs to decide what will be reported and disclosed to stakeholders and the format that will be used for those reports. To ensure accurate reporting and disclosure, appropriate control activities need to be applied. In the United States, the Sarbanes–Oxley Act (SOX) sets out duties that are primarily concerned with the accuracy of financial reports to shareholders.

The main risk management input into reporting of performance is the risk assessment of the reporting lines and the data-handling procedures. The SOX duties have increased the attention paid to the control of reporting procedures. Section 404 of SOX requires that financial reports and the financial reporting procedures are attested by external auditors to confirm that they are accurate.

Aspects of the business development model can also be applied to personal strategic objectives and the achievement of personal success. Many books have been published on the actions to ensure career success and the personal traits of highly successful people. The box below provides a simple checklist of actions to ensure career progression. Although it is not set out in the format of Figure 19.1, the advice given is entirely compatible with an analysis based on: 1) where do I want to be? 2) where am I now? and 3) how am I going to get where I want to be?

Career success

Career planning can have multiple benefits, from goal setting to career change, to a more successful life. Here are 10 steps to success:

1	Make career planning an annual event	You will be better prepared for the many uncertainties and difficulties that lie ahead in all jobs and careers.
2	Map your path since last career planning	Take the time to reflect on your course and note why it looks the way it does.
3	Reflect on your likes and dislikes, needs and wants	Use this list to examine your current job and career path.
4	Examine your pastimes and hobbies	Decide if you can make a hobby into a career because people do it all the time.
5	Make note of your past accomplishments	One of these may trigger researching and planning a career shift.
6	Look beyond your current job for transferable skills	Every job requires a certain set of skills and it is better to define yourself in terms of skill sets.
7	Review career and job trends	Having information about career trends is vital to long-term career planning success.
8	Set career and job goals	Develop a roadmap for your job and career success through goal setting.
9	Explore new education and training opportunities	What types of educational experiences will help you achieve your career goals.
10	Research further career/ job advancement opportunities	Picture yourself in the future and develop multiple scenarios of that future.

Reputation and   20
the business model

Components of the business model

All organizations will have a business model that represents how they deliver the customer offering. Organizations that are public sector, third sector or would otherwise consider themselves to be a non-commercial organization will still have a means of delivering their vision and/or mission statement. The means of delivering the defined customer offering is the business model of the organization. In summary, customers receive the offering from the organization because it utilizes the resources that it has available. The customer offering is underpinned by the resilience of the organization and by arrangements to ensure that the organization remains sustainable.

Figure 20.1 illustrates the components of the business model as customer, offering, resources and resilience (CORR). Each of these components is described in more detail in Figure 20.1, and they can be summarized as follows:

- Customer includes analysis of customer segments, recruitment and retention, as well as how products or services will be delivered.
- Offering refers to the customer value proposition and the related benefits that are delivered to those customers.
- Resources include the data, capabilities and assets of the organization, as well as partnerships and networks.
- Resilience of the organization is reputational (based on ethos and culture) and financial resilience (based on expenditure and revenue).

The importance of the business model is that it represents how the operational and compliance core processes work together to deliver the customer experience. It is important for organizations to understand the business model, so that they can undertake a strengths, weaknesses, opportunities and threats (SWOT) analysis of the existing business model. A risk assessment of the existing business model will enable the organization to evaluate the efficiency of the existing arrangements and identify the events that could disrupt the efficient delivery of the offering, as well as identifying opportunities for improving operational and compliance efficiency.

It is important to note that the business model represents the existing mechanisms for the delivery of the customer offering and provides a description of operational and compliance activities. Risk assessment of the existing business model will enable the organization to identify options for improvements to customer offering and/or the business model. The identification of an updated business model will represent the

Figure 20.1   Components of the business model

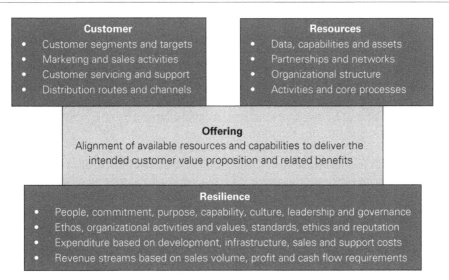

strategic position that the organization wishes to achieve. Tactics for implementing that strategy will need to be devised, as identified in Figure 19.1.

Business models can be quite complex and have a large number of dependencies, including suppliers and outsourced facilities. The weaknesses and inefficiencies in the existing business model need to be identified and analysis of the business model represents an additional way of undertaking a risk assessment. The importance of resilience within the business model is considered in the next section. Other factors that are important in the business model are related to reputation and ethical trading. A particular consideration for many organizations is corporate social responsibility within the supply chain. Analysis of the business model will enable an organization to assess the supply chain and identify embedded risks, including ethical risks that could damage the reputation of the organization.

Risk management and the business model

Each component of the business model can be subjected to a risk assessment. The business model represents how the organization fulfils its vision and mission statement, as well as its aims and objectives. Although the offering is at the heart of the business model, the starting point is often an assessment of the customer segment at which the offering will be targeted. Risks are associated with identifying and securing customers and providing customer service and support. Distribution routes and channels are very important in the provision of the customer offering.

The offering itself is important and is at the heart of the business model. It is important that the offering draws on available resources and capabilities to deliver the intended customer with a value position and related benefits. The nature and use of the resources and how they are structured represents a number of risks and these should be evaluated during the risk assessment of the business model. An important part of the business model is the resilience of the organization, together with its reputation. There are many alternative versions of the business model, but some fail to give sufficient profile to the reputation of the organization.

Culture and ethics, as well as the reputation of the organization are considered later in this chapter. Reputation is often a feature of the sector within which the organization operates. Reputation is often considered to be the most important aspect of any organization. Reputation also has a sustainability component in that an organization will wish to sustain and/or enhance its reputation.

All business models have to be sustainable and this is normally represented by financial sustainability of resources and the need to balance expenditure against revenue streams. Sustainability often has a wider context and may also include environmental considerations. The scope of the sustainability requirements of the organization and its business model will need to be included in the risk assessment. Assessment of the business model will focus on the hazards or operational risks, together with compliance risks. In order to achieve an effective and efficient business model, operational risks will need to be mitigated and compliance risks will need to be minimized.

Having identified the business model and undertaken a risk assessment, an organization will then need to decide whether the existing business model is sustainable. If it is considered that there is scope to improve the business model, a new or modified business model will need to be identified. Achieving this enhanced business model becomes the strategy of the organization. The means by which the business model is modified to achieve the strategy can be considered to be the tactics of the organization and these tactics will be implemented by way of projects and/or programmes of work that achieve the required changes.

Strategic risks associated with improving the business model will need to be embraced and the risks associated with implementing tactics will need to be managed. The overall approach of embracing strategic risks, managing tactical risks, mitigating operational risks and minimizing compliance risks, is referred to in this book as EM3. A component of a successful business model is that it is successful in recruiting new customers and draws the customer into a deeper relationship with the organization, so that the relationship is sustained and becomes more secure. Enhancements to the business model, therefore, need to not only recruit additional customers, but also retain existing customers at a constantly increasing level of customer satisfaction.

Reputation and corporate governance

Figure 28.1 illustrates corporate social responsibility (CSR) as a part of the overall corporate governance requirements of an organization. All types of organizations should be aware that good corporate social responsibility standards can enhance reputation and build stakeholder value. Conversely, incidents, events and losses associated with poor standards of social responsibility can create bad publicity and destroy stakeholder value.

The importance of good standards of corporate social responsibility is widely recognized and achieving good standards can enhance the organization by:

- protecting and enhancing reputation, brand and trust;
- attracting, motivating and retaining talent;
- managing and mitigating risk;
- improving operational and cost efficiency;
- giving the business a licence to operate;
- developing new business opportunities;
- creating a more secure and prosperous operating environment.

There are a variety of definitions available for corporate social responsibility. It is generally accepted that CSR is a wide-ranging agenda that involves organizations looking at how to improve their social, environmental and local economic impact and their influence on society and human rights. The CSR agenda also extends to consideration of fair trade issues and the elimination of corruption. Before corporate social responsibility became a widely used term, several organizations used to refer to social, ethical and environmental (SEE) concerns. The CSR agenda includes all of the issues previously included in the SEE agenda.

There is no doubt that CSR is an issue for large multinational companies as well as for small, locally based businesses and the public sector. Indeed, it is relevant to all types of organizations, including charities. The European Commission definition of corporate social responsibility is as follows:

> Corporate Social Responsibility is the concept that an enterprise is accountable for its impact on all relevant stakeholders. It is the continuing commitment by business to behave fairly and responsibly and contribute to economic development, while improving the quality of life of the workforce and their families, as well as of the local community and society at large.

CSR and risk management

The scope of issues covered by CSR is set out in Table 20.1. The range of topics extends from health and safety concerns to broader considerations related to employees, customers, suppliers, the community, the environment and products/services provided by the organization. Both the CSR and risk management agendas are very broad and they have a significant overlap.

Many of the issues listed in the table are risk-based subjects, including health and safety at work and environmental impact. However, management of these issues simply as risks will fail to fully address the CSR agenda. Nevertheless, this is a good starting point. Many risk assessment workshops consider corporate social responsibility and social, ethical and environmental considerations within the topics that are evaluated.

Table 20.1 Scope of issues covered by CSR

Health and safety
Commitment to a programme of activities to achieve continuous improvement in health and safety performance

Employees
Aim to deliver a competitive and fair employment environment and the opportunity to develop and advance – subject to personal performance

Customers
Strive to provide high-quality service and products and good value for money in all dealings with customers

Environment
Reduce impact on the environment, including factors contributing to climate change, through a commitment of continual improvement

Suppliers
Working with suppliers to ensure that worker welfare/labour conditions and environmental practices meet recognized standards

Community
Aim to be a responsible corporate citizen through support for appropriate non-political and non-sectarian projects, organizations and charities

Products/services
Designed not to unintentionally or by design cause death, injury, ill-health or social disruption, hardship or detriment

---

When assessing the CSR agenda, risk managers should take the opportunity to bring risk management tools and techniques to a broader agenda. The risk management approach of risk assessment, identification of control measures and auditing of compliance is an approach that can be transferred to corporate social responsibility and, indeed, to the broader corporate governance agenda.

Most organizations consider CSR to be a reputational issue and see the component parts of CSR as hazard risks. Such organizations will consider that they need to reform their core processes and procedures in order to comply with these requirements. This may well be an accurate starting point for many organizations. However, as Figure 4.2 illustrates, what starts off as a hazard risk can develop into a control risk and eventually into an opportunity.

As with other areas of risk management, organizations should seek to develop their level of sophistication in relation to CSR. Having got to the stage of complying with the CSR obligations, organizations should then look at the opportunities that are available. For example, it is now commonplace for supermarkets to offer goods that have been procured on a 'fair trade' basis and gain additional sales from offering this range of products.

Corporate social responsibility is an area of concern where it is likely that public opinion will be ahead of the thinking within many organizations. CSR issues therefore represent a great opportunity for an organization to develop corporate social responsibility plans and actions that respond to public opinion. Treating the CSR agenda as a dynamic, proactive set of issues will enable the organization to gain reputational advantage.

Many organizations have stakeholders that they do not necessarily want. This is certainly the case for several energy companies. Exploration for oil, coal and minerals is carefully scrutinized by environmental pressure groups. Even if they are 'unwanted stakeholders', environmental pressure groups are valid stakeholders in these organizations and can bring a considerable influence to bear on their activities. Environmental pressure groups have demands that are firmly within the CSR agenda.

The list of issues in Table 20.1 provides an indication of the stakeholders who are likely to have an interest in the CSR agenda. Employees, customers, suppliers and the general community are the key groups that are stakeholders in the CSR agenda of an organization. For CSR issues associated with the environment, it is fair to say that everybody is a stakeholder in the behaviour of organizations when that behaviour impacts the environment.

An example of the impact that a pressure group can exert is demonstrated by the following report on the website of the environment action group Greenpeace. This report relates to the proposed disposal by Shell of the Brent Spar oil storage facility in the mid-1990s.

Shell Brent Spar

In 1995, Greenpeace activists occupied the Brent Spar oil storage facility in the North Sea. Their purpose was to stop plans to scuttle the 14,500-tonne installation. The action was part of an ongoing campaign to stop ocean dumping and pitted Greenpeace against the combined forces of the UK government and the world's then-largest oil company.

Spontaneous protests in support of Greenpeace and against Shell broke out across Europe. Some Shell stations in Germany reported a 50 per cent loss of sales. Chancellor Kohl raised the issue with the UK government at a G7 meeting. But despite the UK government's refusal to back down on plans to allow the Spar to simply be dumped into the ocean, public pressure proved too much to bear for Shell and in a dramatic win for Greenpeace and the ocean environment, the company reversed its decision and agreed to dismantle and recycle the Spar on land.

The decision led to a ban on the ocean disposal of such rigs by the international body which regulates ocean dumping. Before the Brent Spar campaign, a number of oil companies had been planning sea-dumping of obsolete installations, such as oil storage buoys (like Shell's Brent Spar) and oil rigs. Greenpeace's action and the support of people throughout Europe ensured that no such structures have been dumped to this day.

Supply chain and ethical trading

Failure to ensure appropriate ethical behaviour is increasingly recognized as a major business risk. Newspaper reports describing bribery and other forms of dishonesty have serious consequences for corporate reputation and future profits. Easy access to information on the internet can result in organizations being investigated and exposed for unethical trading and/or unfair treatment of suppliers.

If the unethical behaviour extends into illegal activity, this can undermine the organization itself. Illegal behaviour and condoning actions that are outside the governance rules of the organization can have serious consequences. The perceived need to bribe officials in certain territories is both unethical and illegal.

There are several areas where unethical trading can result in damage to reputation, the loss of future profitability and a refusal on the part of the customers and suppliers to deal with the organization. These issues include:

- failure to comply with rules and regulations;
- trading with undesirable overseas governments;
- excessive payments to political parties;
- tax evasion or dubious tax arrangements;
- inappropriate criticism of competitors;
- false allegations against competitors;
- unethical alliances with competitors.

Another feature of the supply chain that may result in allegations of unethical trading relates to the sourcing of products produced in socially unacceptable working conditions. Also, the quality of products and failure to provide value for money can result in damage to reputation and may be associated with unethical trading. Goods that fall short of current safety standards can result in serious adverse publicity and damage to reputation.

When a sports club decides that it wants all merchandise for sale to fans to be ethically sourced, it needs to look at the controls that can be placed on the importer to ensure that it only obtains merchandise from ethically produced sources. The club could require the importer to produce a routine CSR report as part of the contract terms and conditions. This report will include the following information:

- details of the policy that the importer has on ethical behaviour of suppliers;
- confirmation of the contractual terms and conditions of manufacture;
- statement that manufacturers do not sub-contract work, unless authorized;
- details of staff training, accident/absence rates and pay/conditions;
- results of audits/physical inspection of manufacturing premises.

The club can then advertise to fans that all goods are ethically sourced and encourage other teams in the league to do the same. This will gain good publicity and promote the club as having high corporate social responsibility awareness.

Positive reporting on corporate social responsibility issues can be a significant benefit for an organization. This will be especially true when the organization operates in an area where the public is suspicious. The public may not be sympathetic towards an organization, because of perception of the business sector and/or the organization itself. When an organization operates in a sector that does not have universal public support, there may be benefit in producing an ethics policy. The importance of the ethics policy will be reinforced if the organization also undertakes an ethics audit.

For example, a sector that does not have full public support is gaming and gambling. Therefore, organizations operating in this area should seek to enhance the reputation of the sector by working with competitors on social responsibility standards for problem gambling. An individual organization can then gain further benefit by being able to demonstrate that it exceeds the minimum standards established for the sector.

Many organizations now include comment on corporate social responsibility in their annual report and accounts, and some produce a separate CSR supplement. The production of a report on corporate social responsibility activities enables the organization to gain advantage from the CSR agenda.

Where an organization has a positive story to tell about CSR achievement, it will have taken a CSR agenda from the need to reform to the position where the organization can demonstrate that it does conform. The next stage in this developing sophistication is for the organization to demonstrate that adherence to a CSR agenda enables it to perform better and more successfully fulfil stakeholder expectations.

Reporting on corporate social responsibility

The annual report should:

- include information on social-, ethical- and environmental-related risks and opportunities that may significantly affect the company's short- and long-term value and how they might impact on the business;

- describe the company's policies and procedures for managing risks to short- and long-term value arising from social, ethical and environmental matters;

- include information about the extent to which the company has complied with its policies and procedures for managing social, ethical and environmental risks;

- describe the procedures for verification of social, ethical and environmental disclosures, which should be such as to achieve a reasonable level of credibility.

Importance of reputation

Reputation is fundamentally important to organizations. In fact, it is often said that the reputation of an organization is the most valuable asset that it possesses. Because reputation is so vitally important and can so easily be lost, organizations should make sure that they understand the basis of their reputation. Reputation is based on the size, nature and complexity of an organization, but it is useful to put more structure into what makes a good reputation.

There have been many attempts to identify the components of reputation. Table 20.2 shows the components of reputation and these are also illustrated as a spidergram in Figure 20.2. The four main components of reputation (CASE) are as listed below:

- Capabilities, including purpose and resources;
- Activities, including processes and finances;

- Standards, including services/products and support;
- Ethics, including values and integrity.

Reputation is a component of the FIRM risk scorecard and is generally considered to be a consequence of other events that occur. The importance of a good reputation is that customers or clients will have a desire to trade with that organization. Therefore, organizations should look carefully at the reputation of the sector within which they work, as well as their own reputation within that sector. Many organizations deliberately plan actions that will enhance their reputation and thereby achieve greater success.

An organization should have the necessary capabilities to plan strategy, implement tactics, continue operations and ensure compliance. The capability should be reflected in a clear statement of purpose, intent or commitment. The activities that an organization undertakes will be dependent on the sector in which it operates. Also, the organization will require the necessary finances and financial stability to support its activities. Together, the capabilities and activities of the organization define that organization from an internal perspective.

The organization will offer a range of services and products and the standards of service and service delivery will be a critical component of reputation. Finally, the organization will have business ethics that demonstrate its integrity. Integrity will be demonstrated, to some extent, by the monitoring of performance in order to learn and achieve continuous improvement in performance.

The use of a chart, such as that shown in Figure 20.2 will enable the organization to map its overall reputation, within the context of the sector in which it operates. For each of the four segments, or eight attributes, an organization should be able to plot its current status in a ranking of 1 to 4, representing poor, adequate, good and excellent. It will then be possible for the organization to identify the sectors that represent the greatest threats to the reputation of the organization. Table 20.3 provides examples of how the threats can arise.

Table 20.2   Components of reputation

Component	Comments
Capabilities	Does the organization have a clear purpose or resolve, together with the commitment, vision, capabilities and resources to deliver that purpose?
Activities	Which sector and what activities does the organization undertake and does it have the financial resources and stability to support those activities?
Standards	What range of services or products does the organization offer and what are the standards of quality, delivery, support, execution, innovation and investment?
Ethics	Does the organization adhere to appropriate CSR, integrity, values and governance, and continuously monitor performance to learn and achieve improvements?

Figure 20.2 Mapping the components of reputation

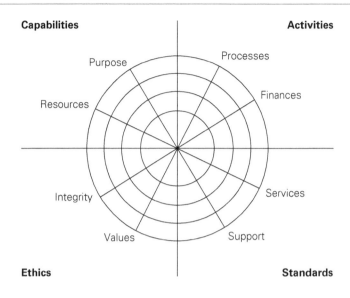

Table 20.3 Threats to reputation

Component	Comments
Capabilities	• Failure to provide a clear indication to stakeholders that the organization recognizes its purpose. • Failure to have adequate resources within the organization to ensure satisfactory governance and/or deliver quality services and products.
Activities	• Business sector in which the organization operates suffers adverse publicity. • Finances are weakened, reducing the desire of customers to trade with the organization.
Standards	• Insufficient innovation in services and products so that customers go elsewhere. • Reduction in quality of products and/or services or failure to deliver customer support.
Ethics	• Unethical behaviour by the organization (CSR) indicating unacceptable values. • Failure to deal with customer complaints appropriately and with integrity.

This chapter has considered the importance of reputation in general and used corporate social responsibility as an example of one of the main pillars of reputation. However, reputation is a broader issue than just business ethics. Indeed, customers will often trade with an organization even though they do not believe it to have a particularly ethical business model. Although only a cursory insight and discussion of reputation has been included in this book, the overriding importance of reputation is fully acknowledged, especially in relation to risk management.

The importance of brand and reputation is recognized by all organizations. Several companies that deal directly with the public have sought to build a reputation based on trust and ethical behaviour. For many organizations, this is not a recent innovation, but is the ethos that underpins their customer offering. The importance of reputation is demonstrated by the extract from the 2015 Annual Report and Accounts from Unilever PLC in the text box below.

Monitoring reputation

A global business working in many countries comes across numerous issues in its everyday operations. It is crucial therefore that the corporate responsibility committee seeks regular briefings on the systems and processes in place for managing issues. The committee requests an annual summary of the most material issues Unilever is dealing with, which in 2015 included issues such as climate change, food and beverage taxes, the responsible use of technology and human and labour rights.

Given the committee's role in ensuring Unilever's reputation is well managed, it can also seek independent views on how Unilever is perceived in society. One of the major annual surveys of reputation in sustainability is conducted by a research agency and the methodology draws on the views of over 800 sustainability experts across more than 80 countries. It reveals that an increasing number of them see that corporate leadership in sustainable development is mainly driven by making sustainability part of the company's core business model. Some 38 per cent of respondents said that Unilever is 'integrating sustainability into its business strategy', putting it well ahead of others in this respect.

Unilever PLC
Annual Report and Accounts 2015: Strategic Report

Risk management context 21

Architecture, strategy and protocols

This part provides information on the risk architecture, strategy and protocols (RASP) for an organization. The RASP provides details of the risk management framework for the organization and this helps to define the risk management context. Table 21.1 sets out key features of the risk architecture, strategy and protocols in more detail. The most important component of the RASP is the risk management policy statement. The RM policy will set out the overall strategy of the organization towards risk management. Other sections of the overall risk management manual define risk management roles and responsibilities and set out the protocols that should be followed.

The risk architecture, strategy and protocols create the risk framework that supports the risk management process. British Standard BS 31100 provides notes on the risk management framework that state that it should include the objectives, mandate and commitment to manage risk (strategy), and the organizational arrangements that include plans, relationships, accountabilities, resources, processes and activities (architecture), and that the framework should be embedded within the organization's overall strategic and operational policies and practices (protocols).

The risk architecture, strategy and protocols are equivalent to the risk framework, as described in ISO 31000. In effect, the risk architecture, strategy and protocols represent the context for risk management within the organization. The risk strategy component will normally be set out as a one-page statement of what the organization is seeking to achieve with respect to risk management. Guide 73 refers to this one-page statement as the risk management policy.

The risk management policy will form part of a larger risk management manual in many organizations. Most large organizations will document their risk protocols as a set of risk management guidelines. The range of guidelines that are required will vary according to the size, nature and complexity of the organization. The types of documentation that will need to be kept are as follows:

- risk management administration records;
- risk response and improvement plans;
- event reports and recommendations;
- risk performance and monitoring reports.

One of the standard documents produced by organizations as part of their risk management initiatives is the risk register. Risk registers can be produced for a variety of operational, project and strategic purposes. The likely format of the risk register is discussed in Chapter 7 and the basic format is illustrated in Table 7.1.

The working relationship between risk management and internal audit is critically important. Risk management expertise rests in the assessment of risk and the identification of existing and additional controls. Internal audit has its expertise in the evaluation of controls and the testing of their efficiency and effectiveness. Successful implementation of a risk management initiative will require close co-operation and understanding between risk management and internal audit. The RASP should set out the details of how this close co-operation will be achieved in practice.

Table 21.1　Risk management framework

Risk management architecture
- Committee structure and terms of reference
- Roles and responsibilities
- Internal reporting requirements
- External reporting controls
- Risk management assurance arrangements

Risk management strategy
- Risk management philosophy
- Arrangements for embedding risk management
- Risk appetite and attitude to risk
- Benchmark tests for significance
- Specific risk statements/policies
- Risk assessment techniques
- Risk priorities for the present year

Risk management protocols
- Tools and techniques
- Risk classification system
- Risk assessment procedures
- Risk control rules and procedures
- Responding to incidents, issues and events
- Documentation and record keeping
- Training and communications
- Audit procedures and protocols
- Reporting/disclosures/certification

The risk architecture defines how information on risk is communicated throughout the organization. The risk strategy defines the overall objectives that the organization is trying to achieve with respect to risk management. The risk protocols are the systems, standards and procedures that are put in place in order to fulfil the defined risk strategy. The risk architecture forms part of the risk management framework. The risk management framework, in turn, is part of the overall risk governance arrangements within the organization.

Risk management policy for a council

Introduction

Risk management is an integral part of good management practice and a key part of corporate governance. This strategy statement outlines the arrangements put in place to ensure the council identifies and deals with the key risks it faces.

The council has adopted proactive risk management arrangements to enable decisions to be based on comprehensively assessed risks, ensuring the right actions are taken at the right time.

How successful the council is in dealing with the risks it faces can have a major impact on the achievement of its key strategies, priorities and service delivery to the community. The risk management strategy helps to support the aim of the council to be a world-class organization.

Objectives

The objectives of this strategy are to:

- fully integrate risk management into the culture of the council and its strategic and service planning processes;
- ensure that the risk management framework is understood and implemented by staff with an operational responsibility for risk;
- communicate the risk management approach of the council to stakeholders;
- ensure the benefits of risk management are realized through maximizing opportunities and minimizing threats;
- ensure consistency throughout the council in the management of risk.

Risk management

The focus of good risk management is the identification and treatment of risks. It increases the probability of success and reduces the likelihood of failure and the uncertainty of achieving objectives. Risk management should be a continuous and evolving process that runs throughout the strategies and service delivery of the council.

Learning lessons from past activities helps inform current and future decisions by reducing threats and optimizing the uptake of opportunities. Celebrating and communicating successful risk management in turn encourages a more daring but calculated approach.

Risk architecture

The risk management organization and arrangements of an organization can be described as the risk architecture. The risk architecture sets out lines of communication for reporting on risk management issues and events. It is vital that the risk architecture reinforces the fact that the responsibility for managing risks remains with the owner of that risk.

In order that risk management can be fully embedded into the core processes and operations of an organization, a clear statement of risk management responsibilities is required. Also, as part of the analysis of each significant risk, risk management responsibilities need to be clearly allocated to the following aspects of managing that risk:

- development of risk strategy and standards;
- implementation of the agreed standards and procedures;
- auditing compliance with the agreed standards.

The risk architecture can be represented diagrammatically as a means of identifying the committees with risk management responsibilities and the relationships between those committees. The importance of the risk architecture of an organization is discussed in Chapter 22 and examples of typical risk architectures are provided. The risk architecture will include details of the terms of reference of the various committees. This will include details of the membership and responsibilities of the various committees. The risk architecture should also provide information on how risk information is communicated between the various committees.

The risk architecture shows the relationship between various committees that have been established within the organization. The membership and responsibilities of the committee will need to be established in suitable terms of reference. The risk architecture will also include details of reports that are received by individual committees and the reports that are required from those committees. An important aspect of the risk architecture is to ensure that risk escalation procedures are embedded within the organization, including appropriate whistleblowing arrangements.

When considering the range of documentation that needs to be produced, organizations should distinguish between the risk protocols that are recorded in the risk management manual and those documents or reports that are intended to track and monitor changes and improvements. The risk management manual may be considered to be a static record of processes and procedures, whereas the other documentation, for example the risk register, should be a dynamic record of actions that are planned or are in progress. In effect, the risk register should be considered to be the risk management action plan.

Risk management strategy

It is important for an organization to have a clearly established strategy in relation to risk management. The risk management strategy for the organization will be set out in the risk management policy statement. The strategy needs to be based on the overall approach of the organization to risk and risk management. An important component of that risk strategy will be the requirement that there is risk management input into strategy, tactics, operations and compliance (STOC).

In order to establish the risk management strategy, important decisions will need to be made about the risk appetite of the organization. Risk appetite is discussed in more detail in Chapter 25. The risk appetite will be based on the opportunity investment, control acceptance and the hazard tolerance of the organization.

It is important that the risk appetite is within the total risk capacity of the organization. Decisions will need to be taken on how the risk capacity will be calculated. Also, thought will need to be given on how the total risk exposure of the organization will be recorded and used in decision-making processes. Measurement of the total risk exposure of an organization is an important feature of operational risk management, as discussed in Chapter 30.

There are important decisions to be made in relation to the risk processes that will be adopted by the organization, as well as decisions about the design and implementation of the risk management initiative that will be planned and implemented in order to fulfil the requirements of the risk strategy.

The risk management strategy will include details of what the organization is seeking to achieve with respect to risk management. The strategy may set out the details of the level of risk maturity that is desired, together with the information on the level of contribution that is expected from risk management. In effect, risk management strategy will establish the way in which risk management activities are aligned with the other activities in the organization and the contribution that is expected from risk management activities.

Risk management protocols

The risk management manual will set out responsibilities for risk as well as the arrangements for implementing the policy. Risk management protocols will be set out in a series of risk procedures and guidelines and these are described later in this chapter.

Procedures and protocols for undertaking the assessment of risks to strategy, projects and operations will need to be established in writing. The organization will also need to produce guidance on the frequency and nature of risk reports and who is responsible for compiling the information.

Typically, the risk management protocols will need to be reviewed on an annual basis, so that they are kept up-to-date. The risk protocols should also describe the extent of record keeping that is required. The range of risk management documentation that may be necessary is extensive and Table 21.2 provides an overview of the types of documents that may be appropriate.

Risk management protocols describe the range of activities that are undertaken in the name of risk management. The protocols define the activities that must be undertaken and how they will be undertaken. Risk management guidelines normally refer to the standards that should be achieved. In some cases, they include details of the

Table 21.2   Types of RM documentation

Risk governance
Risk management policy (and priorities)
Specific risk statements (health and safety policy)
Terms of reference of the risk/audit committees
Risk protocols and procedures
Risk awareness training records
Risk response
Results of risk assessments (risk register)
Risk control standards
Risk improvement recommendations
Risk assurance reports
Business continuity plans/disaster recovery plans
Event reports
Loss/claim reports and recommendations
Legal and litigation reports
Enforcement action/customer complaints
Incident and near-miss investigations
Business performance reports/key performance indicators
Risk performance
Control risk self-assessment (CRSA) returns
Audit procedures and protocols
Internal audit reports
Unit risk management reports
External disclosure reports

controls that are in place. This will be especially true for guidelines that identify procedures that must be undertaken. These procedures will provide direction for directors, managers and staff within the organization.

Risk management manual

The extent of the documentation produced by an organization in respect of risk management will vary significantly. The documentation that is produced should be proportionate to the level of risk faced by the organization, in accordance with the principles that apply to risk management, as set out in Table 5.1. Whatever is produced will need to be structured in a way that suits the organization and is aligned with the other activities that take place within the organization.

The first section of the risk management manual is the risk management policy. An example of a risk management policy statement for a council is set out in the box on page 241. The policy sets out the risk strategy for the organization. It is a statement of intent and establishes the risk management context for the organization. The risk management policy should facilitate successful implementation of risk management in the organization.

The risk management manual contains details of all of the responsibilities, procedures, protocols and guidelines regarding the risk management process and risk management framework for the organization. An illustration of suitable contents for a risk management manual is set out in Table 21.3. The manual should confirm the protocols for undertaking the activities, as set out in the risk guidelines for the organization. The risk guidelines may be produced as a separate set of documents, so that they can be more easily updated.

The risk management manual will include the strategy that the organization is seeking to achieve with respect to risk management, as the risk management policy. The risk management manual will also set out details of the systems and procedures that will be put in place to monitor performance, as well as the means for reporting and communicating on risk management. It will, in effect, define the context within which risk management activities take place.

A range of risk management protocols or guidelines will need to be produced, and a typical set of protocols is listed in Table 21.4. The risk protocols provide more information on how the risk protocols should be interpreted and how they should be

Table 21.3   Risk management manual

A risk management manual should include the following sections:

Risk management and internal control objectives

Statement of the attitude of the organization to risk (risk strategy)

Description of the control environment

Level and nature of risk that is acceptable

Risk management organization and arrangements (risk architecture)

Arrangements for communicating risk information

Standard procedures for risk recognition and rating (risk assessment)

List of documentation for analysing and reporting risk (risk protocols)

Risk mitigation requirements and control mechanisms

Allocation of risk management roles and responsibilities

Criteria for monitoring and benchmarking risks

Allocation of appropriate resources

Risk priorities and performance targets

Risk management calendar for the coming year

---

delivered. The risk management protocols can be seen as the standing instructions relating to risk management. They will often require the keeping of records, for example the risk register. The detailed risk management protocols or guidelines will set out:

- risk assessment procedures;
- risk control objectives;
- risk resourcing arrangements;
- reaction planning requirements;
- risk assurance systems.

The framework or risk architecture that has been set up to achieve adequate management of risks should also be presented in the risk management manual. It will

Table 21.4   Risk management protocols

1 Risk assessment procedures
Governance procedures
Response to significant risks
Projects and CapEx approvals
Procedures for strategy and budgets
2 Risk control objectives
Brand management guidelines
Health and safety at work
Environmental protection
Contract risk management
3 Risk resourcing arrangements
Opportunity management
Project resource allocation
Insurance programme
Captive insurance company
4 Reaction planning requirements
Loss and claims management
Disaster and recovery planning
Cost containment procedures
Risk management record keeping
5 Risk assurance systems
Maintenance of risk register
Corporate RM committee
Terms of reference for audit committee
Control self-certification arrangements

then be for the individual companies within the group to operate within the established framework and arrange their own additional procedures and protocols as necessary. Specifically, the risk management manual should include details of at least the following:

- the board member responsible for risk management;
- language and perception of risk in the organization;
- framework for identifying significant risks;
- role of the risk manager and internal auditors;
- terms of reference for the risk management committees;
- risk management structure or risk architecture.

Many organizations find that it is necessary to update the risk management manual each year, even if the overall risk management strategy remains unchanged. This is undertaken for a number of reasons, including the desire to ensure that risk management activities and the overall risk management approach is in line with current best practice. Updating the risk management manual, including the risk management policy, every year also gives the organization the opportunity to identify the risk priorities for the coming year and ensure that appropriate attention is paid to the significant risks.

Issuing an updated risk management policy every year also ensures that the board pays appropriate attention to risk management and that the organization understands that it is a dynamic activity that requires constant management attention.

Risk management documentation

Table 21.4 indicates the extent of risk management guidelines or protocols that may need to be produced by an organization. This should not be seen as an exhaustive list and other types of protocols, guidelines or procedures may be necessary, depending on the exact nature of the organization and the risk strategy that it is following.

Preparation of a risk management manual, including the policy statement, is a good opportunity for an organization to establish detailed procedures on a range of risk management topics, as well as setting out the risk management priorities for the following year. For example, many organizations produce an annual health and safety and/or environmental policy and procedures, and this should be an integral part of the risk management documentation.

Many organizations face significant risks that need routine or even constant management attention. This is particularly true in the case of hazard risks, where the health and safety policy and procedures, business continuity plans and disaster recovery plans (for example) need to be routinely updated.

For many organizations, the risk guidelines will be established in writing. Other organizations will operate a more informal means of embedding risk management into management activities. The risk guidelines will often include details of the risk management structure in place in the organization. Also, details of the risk strategy and risk protocols will need to be included in the risk guidelines. They should also include details of the (internal) control responsibilities of managers.

The structure described in Table 21.4 reinforces the importance of the activities involved in the risk management process. Each of these activities produces several outputs, and the required outputs can be discussed in the risk guidelines.

The guidelines need not include a set of risk control or loss control standards, but should describe how risk control decisions will be taken, implemented and audited. In fact, the risk guidelines for a diverse group of companies cannot include physical control requirements and standards. Each unit, division or department should set its own standards for risk control, including health and safety, fire safety, physical security, information security and environmental protection. This may be appropriate because of the diverse nature of the different units within the organization.

The risk guidelines should define the means by which embedded risk management is to be achieved in the organization. The setting of strategy, standards and procedures needs to be undertaken within the framework of the risk guidelines. The format for the risk guidelines will depend on the organization and the nature of the risks that it faces. Typically, these guidelines will contain information on at least the following:

- financial and authorization procedures;
- insurance arrangements;
- managers' control responsibilities;
- project risk management;
- incident reporting and investigation;
- event and reaction planning;
- physical risk control objectives and responsibilities.

Table 21.2 sets out the range of risk management documentation that may need to be kept by an organization. In order to successfully embed risk management, it is necessary to maintain a range of risk management records. These records will include details of various risk management activities, including:

- risk management administration;
- risk response and improvement plans;
- event reports and recommendations;
- risk performance and certification reports.

Embedded risk management will be achieved when the cycle of risk management activities is fully aligned with the planning cycle of the organization. A primary purpose of risk guidelines is to help managers understand the risk management framework of the organization. This understanding will ensure that managers pay appropriate attention to risk implications when making decisions.

The risk guidelines for the organization also provide practical guidance to managers on how to fulfil their risk management responsibilities. Keeping necessary records will allow the organization to demonstrate the successful implementation of the risk guidelines. The risk management administration documentation should extend to (at least) the items listed in Table 21.2.

It is not the intention that the keeping of risk management records should become overly bureaucratic or burdensome. However, adequate records need to be kept so that the information is available for decision making, necessary advice for managers is accessible and confirmation can be provided to auditors that necessary controls have been correctly implemented. The importance of record keeping is highlighted below.

Importance of records

There are many benefits to be gained from implementing records management. Records management is a key driver in increasing organizational efficiency and offers significant business benefits. Records management:

- reduces the time spent by staff looking for information;
- facilitates the effective sharing of information;
- reduces the unnecessary duplication of information;
- identifies how long records need to be kept;
- optimizes the legal admissibility of records to defend malicious litigation;
- supports risk management and business continuity planning.

In short, records management improves control over information assets, frees up staff time and other resources, and helps protect individuals and the organization from various risks. Records management means that too much reliance is not placed on the memories of a few individuals.

The only reason for undertaking a risk assessment is so that current controls can be validated and the need for any further actions to improve control of risk can be identified. The risk register is the means of recording information on current controls and details of intended additional controls. It is important that the risk register should not become a static document. It should be treated as a dynamic element and considered to be the risk action plan for a unit or the organization as a whole.

As well as risk response plans, information will also need to be recorded about the responsibility for individual controls. If additional controls are required, then the deadline, as well as the responsibility, for the implementation of those improved controls should be recorded.

Part Four of this book considers risk response options in more detail. For hazard risks and control risks, the risk register is the location for recording details of the significant threats. Detailed analysis of risk improvement plans will be required. Often, risk improvement plans will require capital expenditure, and this may need to be approved via the expenditure authorization procedures in the organization.

It has become standard practice to produce a risk register for projects, especially for construction and software projects. Risks to construction and software projects can create a lot of uncertainty and the risks will usually be control risks. Again, the record of the actions taken to minimize the uncertainty should be a dynamic one, and further actions should be planned.

It is a common criticism of risk registers that they are undertaken once or twice a year and represent a static snapshot of the risks facing the organization. In order to be effective and make a significant contribution, risk management needs to be a dynamic activity that produces outputs that have an impact on the organization. If this is going to happen, then the risk register needs to become a document that drives changes and improvements. Perhaps, it would be better if the risk register was referred to as the 'risk management action plan' for the organization.

Event reports, analyses and recommendations are related to recording details of the events that occur and managing the impacts and consequences of those events. Details of incident investigations and analysis of the performance of business operations, together with risk improvement recommendations, are all covered by this type of risk management documentation. Risk improvement recommendations address significant control weaknesses and aim to eliminate the potential for future material or significant failures.

Recording of events is an important activity, especially in relation to hazard risks. Also, recording and analysing events during a project will be vitally important. Event reports are most relevant to hazard and control risks. Annual evaluation of risk performance will also give rise to reports that require detailed analysis. Evaluation of risk performance is an important role for internal audit.

Clinical risk management is a well-developed branch of the risk management discipline. Accurate record keeping is vital in order to identify that appropriate risk mitigation actions have been put in place, as well as to provide records of any clinical mishaps that occur. The box below provides an overview of the importance of record keeping in relation to managing clinical risk.

Managing clinical risk

Even if all adverse clinical events could be avoided, the legal cost of malpractice litigation cannot be eliminated. While very few negligent injuries lead to claims, there are many negligence claims in cases where there was no injury and no negligence. This means that, if the right risk management processes and systems are in place, hospitals and doctors should be able to rebut allegations of negligence in these circumstances and successfully argue that no compensation payment should be made.

The implementation of risk management activities in hospitals is the immediate responsibility of hospital management. Nevertheless, doctors have a vital role to play by developing an understanding of the importance of risk management and helping to devise a practical approach to recording that procedures have been followed and any incidents have been recorded.

Risk performance and certification reports include consideration and analysis of preliminary reports of the results of operations, as well as more formal declarations and certified reports to stakeholders. In some cases, certification of the results of operations of the organization will be undertaken as a formal attestation of the results of operations. This approach is required by the Sarbanes–Oxley Act in relation to financial reporting.

This attestation will often be undertaken by a third party, such as an external auditor. Such an attestation could also relate to an evaluation of the effectiveness of the control activities.

Management will be interested in receiving details of risk performance. This will be especially important when the organization is exposed to a portfolio of risks that bring the total risk exposure close to the limit of the risk appetite and/or risk capacity of the organization. For example, an organization may have budgeted for a certain level of loss in relation to hazard risks. If this budget is challenging, then careful monitoring of losses will be required in order to ensure that the exposure to the specific type of hazard risk is not being exceeded.

The hazard tolerance may be limited and so the organization will need to monitor hazard losses very carefully. For example, a transport company will need to monitor the number of motor vehicle accidents and the breakdown frequencies related to the vehicles run by the company.

Risk management responsibilities 22

Allocation of responsibilities

Everybody working for an organization will need to be made aware of their risk management responsibilities, as will contractors and suppliers. There are many professional people in large organizations who have an understanding of risk and a substantial contribution to make to the successful management of the priority significant risks. Unfortunately, there is not always a common view of risk management or the issues that are important to the organization.

Ownership of core processes, key dependencies and risks is important, because it enables the risk management and audit committees (see Part Eight) to monitor actions and responsibilities. This ownership is important for all risks, although the audit committee will only monitor the priority significant risks.

Any confusion of responsibilities and reporting structure must be eliminated. There should be clear statements of responsibilities for the following aspects of the management of each priority significant risk:

- setting required risk standards;
- implementing risk standards;
- monitoring risk performance.

A detailed set of responsibilities will ensure that the roles of risk owners, process owners, internal audit, risk management functions, members of staff, contractors and outsourced operations as well as all others are clearly defined and understood. The allocation of responsibilities to committees, as part of the risk architecture is also an important consideration. The membership, responsibilities and reporting structure will normally be described in the terms of reference of each committee.

Information on ownership of each priority significant risk should be included in the risk register. It is important that the activities of the risk manager, risk management committee, audit committee, internal auditors and others do not reduce local ownership of significant risks. Managers must see ownership of risks as integral to the management of core processes and business activities, not as a separate issue that is the responsibility of specialist professional risk management and/or internal audit practitioners.

Range of responsibilities

Table 22.1 sets out examples of the range of risk management responsibilities of line management, the main functional departments and individual employees involved in risk management. The risk management professionals involved will include the following individuals (at least), depending on the size of the organization:

- insurance risk manager;
- corporate treasurer;
- finance director;
- internal auditor;
- compliance manager;
- health, safety and environment manager;
- business continuity manager.

The structure of Table 22.1 is also important. Items 1, 2 and 3 allocate responsibilities to the management of the organization. Item 1 is concerned with the allocation of responsibilities to top management, being the board and executive. Item 2 is concerned with the allocation of responsibilities to heads of department or middle management. Item 3 is concerned with the allocation of risk management responsibilities to staff. Together, these three layers of management represent the first line of defence in ensuring that adequate attention is paid to risk management and internal control.

Item 4 of Table 22.1 describes the responsibilities of the risk manager for the organization. Item 5 sets out the responsibilities of specialist risk management func-

Table 22.1   Risk management responsibilities

---

1   Main risk management responsibilities for the CEO:

Determine strategic approach to risk

Establish the structure for risk management

Understand the most significant risks

Consider the risk implications of poor decisions

Manage the organization in a crisis

2   Main RM responsibilities for the location manager:

Build risk-aware culture within the location

Agree risk management performance targets for the location

Evaluate reports from employees on risk management matters

Ensure implementation of risk improvement recommendations

Identify and report changed circumstances/risks

(continued)

Table 22.1   *(Continued)*

---

3   **Main RM responsibilities for individual employees:**

Understand, accept and implement RM processes

Report inefficient, unnecessary or unworkable controls

Report loss events and near-miss incidents

Cooperate with management on incident investigations

Ensure that visitors and contractors comply with procedures

4   **Main risk management responsibilities for the risk manager:**

Develop the risk management policy and keep it up-to-date

Facilitate a risk-aware culture within the organization

Establish internal risk policies and structures

Coordinate the risk management activities

Compile risk information and prepare reports for the board

5   **Main RM responsibilities for specialist risk management functions:**

Assist the company in establishing specialist risk policies

Develop specialist contingency and recovery plans

Keep up-to-date with developments in the specialist area

Support investigations of incidents and near misses

Prepare detailed reports on specialist risks

6   **Main risk management responsibilities for internal audit manager:**

Develop a risk-based internal audit programme

Audit the risk processes across the organization

Provide assurance on the management of risk

Support and help develop the risk management processes

Report on the efficiency and effectiveness of internal controls

---

tions, such as health and safety or business continuity. In providing specialist support to management, these functions may be considered to be the second line of defence in achieving satisfactory risk management and internal control. Item 6 of Table 22.1 sets out the responsibilities of the internal audit manager. Internal audit activities may be considered to be the third line of defence in ensuring adequate standards of risk management and internal control.

Externally, insurance brokers, insurance companies, accountancy firms and external auditors also have a contribution to make to the improved management of risk in their client organizations. It is important that risk management professionals work together. However, it is also important that the benefits of risk management are embedded into the core processes of the organization.

Three lines of defence

An objective of operational risk management is not to remove operational risk altogether, but to manage the risk to an acceptable level, taking into account the cost of minimizing the risk as against the resultant reduction in exposure. Strategies to manage operational risk include avoidance, transfer, acceptance and mitigation by controls.

To ensure appropriate responsibility is allocated for the management, reporting and escalation of operational risk, the group operates a 'three lines of defence' model that outlines principles for the roles, responsibilities and accountabilities for operational risk management.

The three lines of defence model and the policy standards apply throughout the group and are implemented taking into account the nature and scale of the underlying business. The standards provide the direction for delivering effective operational risk management. They comprise principles and processes that enable the consistent identification, assessment, management, monitoring and reporting of operational risk across the group. The objectives of the standards are to protect the group from financial loss or damage to its reputation, its customers or staff and to ensure that it meets all necessary regulatory and legal requirements.

There is a need to ensure that management of risks receives a sufficiently high profile. It will normally be a board member who sponsors risk management awareness at the board and presents risk management reports to the board. Typically, the risk manager will report to that board member, and have responsibility for the risk architecture, strategy and protocols (RASP).

One of the most important responsibilities to be allocated is that of 'risk owner'. ISO Guide 73 defines a risk owner as a 'person with authority and accountability to make the decision to treat, or not to treat a risk'. The guide also states that anyone who has accountability for an objective also has accountability for the risks associated with the objective and the implementation of the controls to manage those risks.

Statutory responsibilities of management

There has been a developing trend in many countries towards ensuring greater clarity in regard to the obligations of company directors. The general duties of directors have developed in the common law over many years in most countries. The Companies Act 2006 in the UK has consolidated the common law duties of directors and codified the general duties, as follows:

- act in accordance with allocated responsibilities;
- act in accordance with the constitution of the company;
- promote the success of the company;
- exercise independent judgement;

- exercise reasonable care, skill and diligence;
- avoid/declare conflicts of interest;
- not accept benefits from third parties.

The responsibilities of directors are important in relation to risk management, and adequate management of risk will assist in the successful fulfilment of these obligations. Risk management is particularly important in promoting the success of the organization and exercising reasonable care, skill and diligence. Directors of organizations need a good understanding of risk management so that they will be in a better position to fulfil their statutory and other duties.

Usually, board directors will be either executive or non-executive directors of the organization. In certain organizations, such as charities and most government departments, executive directors will meet separately as an 'executive committee' and the non-executive directors will form a 'board of governors'. Typically, executive directors will be full-time employees of the organization with a specific area of responsibility.

Non-executive directors have an important role to play in risk management within the organization. However, this role will normally be restricted to audit, assurance and compliance activities. It may be inappropriate for non-executive directors to become involved in the management of the individual risks, because of the conflict with non-executive audit responsibilities and because executive directors are in a better position to understand and deal with the risks that the organization faces.

The box below provides an example of the role and expectations of non-executive directors. In general, non-executive directors should not become directly involved in the day-to-day management of the organization. In most cases, their role is to assist with the formation of strategy and the monitoring of performance. Implementation of strategy is the responsibility of executive directors.

Role of non-executive directors

The role of the non-executive director has the following specific key elements:

Strategy	constructively challenge and help develop proposals on strategy
Performance	scrutinize the performance of management
Risk	challenge the integrity of the financial information
Controls	seek assurance that financial controls and systems of risk management are robust and defensible
People	determine the appropriate level of remuneration for the executive directors and have a prime role in succession planning
Confidence	seek to establish and maintain confidence in the conduct of the company
Independence	be independent in judgement and promote openness and trust
Knowledge	be well informed about the company and the external environment in which it operates, with a strong command of relevant issues

Role of the risk manager

The typical historical role of the insurance risk manager is set out in Table 22.2. Traditionally, the risk manager has been involved in assessing overall risk policy and procedures with endorsement from the board. Decisions on insurance risk management issues and the provision of statistical analysis of insurance losses have been part of these historical responsibilities.

The insurance risk manager needs to evaluate the current status of risk management and reflect on the current state of the insurance market. Increases in insurance rates and a more sophisticated approach to risk financing have affected the amount of insurance purchased by large organizations. In many cases, there has been less insurance purchased and this has led to a reduced premium spend and a lower budget for the insurance risk management department.

There is no single established reporting position in the structure of an organization for the risk manager. At present, risk managers may report to human resources, the finance director or the company secretary. Sometimes, the risk manager reports to the corporate treasurer and, occasionally, the chief executive officer (CEO).

There is still a need for a risk management facilitator and coordinator in most large organizations. This will enable the organization to apply risk management tools and techniques to a wider range of issues. Risks have historically been divided into insurable (pure) and non-insurable (speculative) risks. From a business success perspective, these are artificial divisions between types of risks.

The risk manager should be responsible for the corporate learning that has to take place so that the organization can understand the benefits of risk management. As the person having responsibility for the risk architecture, strategy and protocols, (RASP), the risk manager will be responsible for developing the strategy, systems and

Table 22.2 Historical role of the insurance risk manager

---

1 To establish the risk management strategy for protecting company property and people.
2 To coordinate the company insurance programme through the captive insurance company.
3 To work with the manager of the captive to maximize the contribution made by the captive insurance company.
4 To maintain key insurer relationships, monitor service providers and ensure cost-effective placement of insurance contracts.
5 To measure and monitor cost of risk performance of the group and individual group companies.
6 To ensure safekeeping and adequate retention of all insurance contracts and agreements.
7 To supervise the coordination of service provider activities and place the group and global insurances.
8 To coordinate the property survey programme, risk management procedures and incentive schemes.

---

procedures by which the required risk management outcomes for the organization are achieved.

Historically, the insurance risk manager has probably not been involved in the strategic management and development of the organization. The broader role now required of a risk manager should lead to a greater involvement in project management and strategy formulation and delivery. The risk manager who enjoys a broad range of responsibilities will have a very challenging role within the organization. It will be a role that enables the risk manager to obtain a better level of understanding and involvement than most other roles or functions achieve.

Perhaps, the title 'risk manager' has too many historical connections for it to be used as an appropriate description of what is now required. There is a need to find a new title and re-define the role of risk management at the same time. The developing importance of organizational resilience may offer an opportunity for the risk manager to develop into the 'risk and resilience manager' and fulfil a much broader role that is designed to be more aligned with the success of the organization.

Many organizations in the finance and energy sectors have identified the benefits of bringing the management of credit, market and operational risks together. It has been the case for some time in the finance sector that risk management has been separate from the purchase of insurance. The development of the role of chief risk officer (CRO) reporting directly to the CEO reflects this fact.

Given that one of the key principles of risk management is that the approach to risk should be proportionate to the level of risk faced by the organization, it is unlikely that the majority of organizations will need to appoint someone of the seniority of a CRO. Nevertheless, organizations should, when reviewing their risk architecture, decide the appropriate range of responsibilities and level of seniority of the risk manager.

The introduction of the job title 'chief risk officer' is not universal, but it is becoming common in the specialist finance and energy sectors. The box below provides an overview of the developing role of the chief risk officer. For organizations where it is proportionate for a CRO to be appointed, the contribution that can be made by that individual will be substantial.

Role of the chief risk officer

As champion of the ERM process, the CRO plays a key part in bringing together disparate risk management processes to ensure that limited company resources are applied effectively. The COSO ERM cube defines the role of the CRO as working with other managers to establish effective risk management, monitoring progress, and assisting other managers in reporting relevant risk information up, down and across the organization.

Internal auditors should work with the CRO as part of their risk management duties. In this role, internal auditors are responsible for evaluating the accuracy of ERM reporting and providing independent and value-added recommendations to management about its ERM approach. The IIA International Standards specify that the scope of internal auditing should include evaluating the reliability of reporting effectiveness, efficiency of operations and compliance with laws and regulations.

Risk architecture in practice

Figure 22.1 shows the risk architecture for a typical large corporate entity that is subject to the requirements of the Sarbanes–Oxley Act. This risk architecture should be set out in the risk management manual for the organization. Terms of reference of the various committees and a schedule of the activities should also be established, either in the risk management manual or in a calendar of risk management activities. This schedule of activities should be aligned with the other corporate activities in the organization.

Figure 22.1   Risk architecture for a large corporation

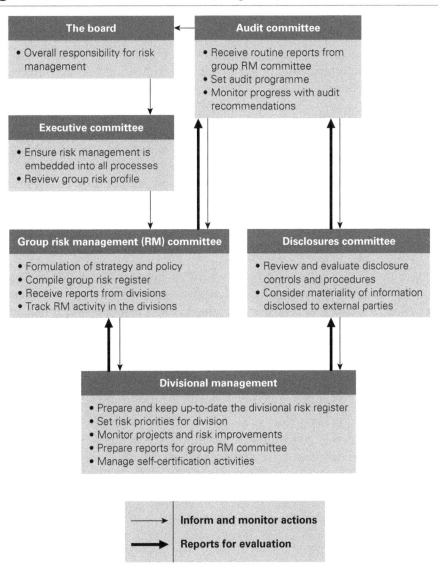

For a large organization with non-executive directors, the audit committee should also be shown in the risk architecture. The role of the audit committee and the role of the head of internal audit are important in fulfilling the risk management strategy of the organization.

For organizations subject to the requirements of the Sarbanes–Oxley Act, there will also be a requirement to ensure that all information disclosed by the company is accurate. In many large organizations, this requirement has resulted in the establishment of a disclosures committee. The role of the disclosures committee is to check the source and correctness of all information that is disclosed by the organization. Sarbanes–Oxley requires that financial information is evaluated to a higher level of scrutiny.

The risk architecture of an organization sets out the hierarchy of committees and responsibilities related to risk management and internal control. In the structure shown in Figure 22.1, the corporate risk management committee focuses on executive risk management activities.

Risk management responsibilities for activities at divisional or unit level should be allocated to divisional management. Divisional management is responsible for coordinating the identification of significant risks at divisional level, compiling the risk register for the division and ensuring that adequate controls are identified and implemented.

Divisional management should be provided with guidance from the group risk management committee. If there is a divisional committee, it should be required to send reports to the group risk management committee, so that the corporate or group overview of risk management priorities can be established.

For a public-sector or charity organization, the risk architecture will be somewhat different. Figure 22.2 sets out a typical risk architecture for a charity. In this case, risk management activities are focused on the governance and risk committee. The flow of information and the control of risk management activities are illustrated by the arrows in Figure 22.2.

It is clear from Figure 22.2 that risk governance for charities is a much higher-profile issue than in many other organizations. There have been reports that trustees of charities consider governance issues to be their primary concern. This implies that many trustees of charities consider that governance is more important than raising money for the charity that they support. This could be an example of concerns about risk management becoming so great that they deform the nature of the organization.

There are many ways for risk management reporting lines to be established. The reporting structure should be proportionate to the level of risk and the complexity of the organization. For high-risk organizations, such as those in the finance sector, the risk committee is likely to be a direct sub-committee of the board. In these circumstances, it is likely that the risk committee will be chaired by the group finance director and it will have other senior representation from the board.

In general, the risk management committee should be an executive committee made up entirely of executive directors with no non-executive director membership. This is because the management of risk is an executive function and non-executive directors are primarily responsible for audit and risk assurance. Typically, the risk management committee will send reports to the audit committee, and that will be the opportunity for non-executive directors to evaluate risk performance and obtain risk assurance.

Figure 22.2   Risk architecture for a charity

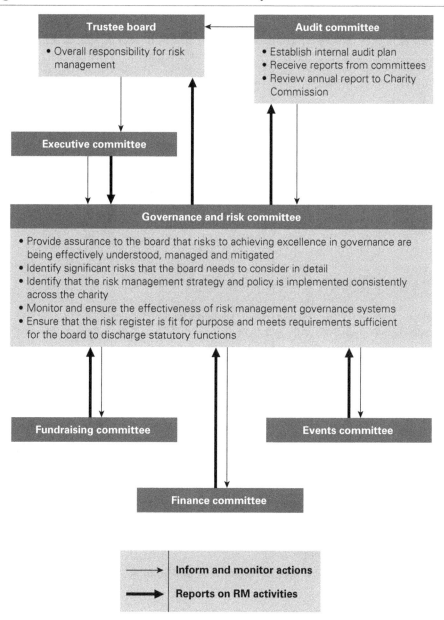

For organizations that are not operating in such a high-risk environment, it may not be necessary for the risk committee to be a direct report to the main board. In these circumstances, the risk committee may be a sub-committee of the executive committee or the operations committee. In all cases, the corporate structure for the management of risk should be proportionate to the level of risk within the organization and the size, complexity, nature and risk exposure of the organization.

However, there are no specified correct structures for the risk architecture of an organization. Provided that the risk committee delivers the required outputs, the membership and terms of reference will be for the organization to decide. Nevertheless, the general point remains that management of risk is an executive function, whereas audit activities should be led by non-executive directors.

Risk committees

Table 22.3 sets out typical responsibilities for a risk management committee (RMC). Most large organizations will already have an audit committee, chaired by a senior non-executive director. An option considered by many organizations is to extend the role of the audit committee to include all aspects of risk management or to establish a separate risk management group chaired by an executive director.

Table 22.3 Responsibilities of the RM committee

To advise the board on risk management and to foster a culture that emphasizes and demonstrates the benefits of a risk-based approach to risk management.

To make appropriate recommendations to the board on all significant matters relating to the risk strategy and policies of the company.

To monitor the performance of the risk management systems and review reports prepared by relevant parties.

To keep under review the effectiveness of the risk management infrastructure of the company, including:

- assessment of risk management procedures in accordance with changes in the operating environment;
- consideration of risk audit reports on the key business areas to assess the level of business risk exposure;
- consideration of any major findings of any risk management reviews and the response of management;
- assessment of the risks of new ventures and other strategic, project and operational initiatives.

To review the risk exposure of the company in relation to the risk appetite of the board and the risk capacity of the company.

To consider the development of risk management and make appropriate recommendations to the board.

To consider whether disclosure of information regarding risk management policies and key risk exposures is in accordance with financial reporting standards.

There is a strong argument for the RMC to be an executive group, rather than part of any existing non-executive audit committee. This is necessary because risks need to be managed in a proactive manner as an executive responsibility. The existing audit committee is likely to treat the management of risk as a non-executive (reactive) auditing of compliance. Separation of executive responsibility for the management of risk from non-executive responsibility for auditing and review of compliance will also be consistent with good corporate governance principles.

Some organizations have established the RMC as a sub-committee of the audit committee. If this is the case, actions need to be taken to ensure that risk is managed as an executive responsibility, rather than audited as a compliance/assurance issue. In fact, establishing the RMC as a sub-committee of the audit committee could impair the work of the RMC because of increased bureaucracy and an unhelpful emphasis on auditing and compliance, rather than proactive management of risks.

Membership of the RMC is another question that needs to be addressed. The fundamental decision to be taken in large organizations is whether the risk management committee should be a small senior executive group setting strategy and policy or whether it should be a knowledge-sharing group with representation from each of the units or departments within the organization. The answer will depend on the structure of the organization and the intended role of the committee.

The terms of reference and the position of the risk committee within the risk architecture of the organization have been the subject of much discussion. There is an argument that the risk committee should be an executive-only function, because the management of risk is the responsibility of top executive management within the organization. However, for some business sectors, the level of risk that the organization should take is a fundamental business strategy decision. This is certainly true in banks and other financial institutions.

In these circumstances, deciding on a risk appetite and the monitoring of actual risk exposure becomes a high-profile board responsibility. Therefore, the risk committee will need to be a committee of the board with executive and non-executive membership. Even in these circumstances, however, the risk committee will probably not be a non-executive committee, as will be the case with the audit committee. If a risk committee is established as a sub-committee of the board, then it will be important for the organization to maintain the integrity of the three lines of defence model.

The terms of reference of the risk committee and its position within the risk architecture are fundamentally important decisions for any organization. In all circumstances, the arrangements should be appropriate for the organization and aligned with business activities. Also, the nature of the risk committee will need to be appropriate and proportionate within the external, internal and risk management contexts of the organization.

In simple terms, there is no single answer that is appropriate for all organizations. In many cases, a separate risk management committee may not be proportionate to the level of risk faced by the organization. In these cases, the responsibilities that would have been undertaken by a risk committee will still need to be allocated to a committee of appropriate seniority. Some organizations allocate risk management responsibilities to the executive committee or the finance committee of the board.

The overall aim is to achieve a prioritized, validated and audited improvement in risk management standards in the organization. The risk management committee and the audit committee should, therefore, operate in a way that provides mutual support. However, combining the two committees into a single group, or placing one committee as superior to the other will not be the best way forward for most organizations. The major concern when combining risk and audit committees is that the organization will then be operating a two lines of defence model, rather than the three lines of defence model that will provide greater protection.

Control of selected 23
hazard risks

Cost of risk controls

The inherent level of a risk is the level of the risk with no control measures in place. This is sometimes referred to as the gross level of the risk. The current level of risk is the level that takes account of the control measures currently in place. This is sometimes referred to as the net level of risk or the residual risk. Throughout this book, 'current level' has been used instead of 'residual level', because this implies a much more dynamic approach to risk management.

Figure 23.1 provides an illustration of the control effect or control vector when controls are put in place. When considering the inherent, intermediate (when more than one control is in place) and target risk levels, the organization should be aware of the cost involved in implementing controls. The cost of the control measures should be considered to be part of the total cost of risk for the organization. The organization can then evaluate whether the controls in place are cost-effective.

As can be seen in Figure 23.1, a series of lines can be drawn for Risk A to represent the effect of each individual risk control measure. It is obvious that the longer the line, the greater the effect of the control. It is also the case that the longer the line, the greater the control effort, in terms of management time, effort and money. For Risk A, three controls (Control A1, Control A2 and Control A3) are required to get to the target level of risk. For Risk B, only one control is required (Control B1) and this demonstrates that much more effort is needed to maintain Risk A at the target level of risk. Management and internal audit need to be aware of this, so that they can ensure that all of the controls (especially for Risk A) are operating in an effective and efficient manner.

A simple diagram like Figure 23.1 provides an illustration of the distance between the inherent and current level of the risk. If a lower target level of risk is established, additional control effort will be required in moving the level of risk from the current to a new target level (not shown in the figure). This simple illustration of control effort is important, and demonstrates that there is value in undertaking a risk assessment at the inherent level of risk (if this is possible), so that the required control effort can be clearly identified and illustrated.

If a calculation is undertaken of the risk exposure at the original level and a further calculation is undertaken of the risk exposure at the new level, the overall benefit of each control can be measured. Consideration of the cost of each control can then be undertaken, so that a cost–benefit analysis of individual controls may be

Figure 23.1   Illustration of control effect

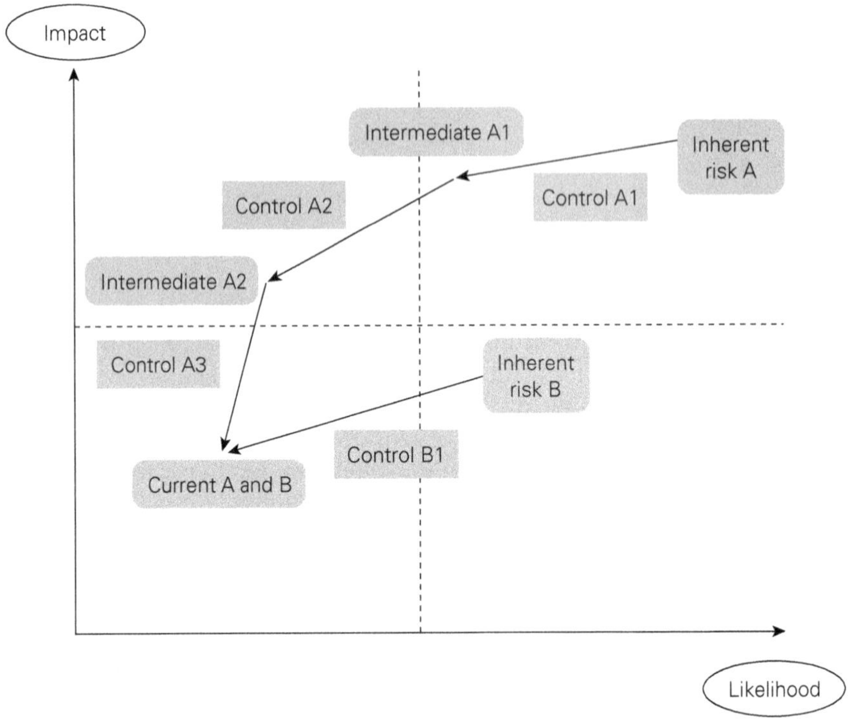

completed. This will be an important exercise for the organization to undertake, so that cost-effective risk control priorities may be established.

Risk treatment is sometimes referred to as risk response or risk control, and it includes the selection and implementation of actions to reduce risk likelihood and risk impact. The types of controls described in Chapter 16 should be considered in turn when deciding the nature and extent of risk control activities that should be implemented. When reasonably practicable, it is obvious that preventive controls should be introduced as the first option. If prevention is not possible, then corrective controls should be introduced to minimize the likelihood and impact of an adverse event.

When risks have been prevented and corrected to the greatest extent that is cost-effective, the organization should then consider directive controls that are designed to direct the actions of people involved in the management of that particular risk. Finally, and in addition to the three other types of controls, the implementation of detective controls may be appropriate. Detective controls are used in a wide range of applications, including health and safety.

The examples in the sections below cover the main hazard risks that are likely to be of concern to an organization, as outlined in Table 15.2. In each case, the section sets out to describe what can go wrong in relation to the hazard, and the considerations and the issues that need to be evaluated. The control options that are available in relation to that particular risk are considered, followed by consideration of the controls that are necessary and appropriate.

Table 16.2 provides examples of the four types of controls described in Chapter 16 as applied to two types of hazard risks. The examples of fraud and health and safety are selected, so that the application of different types of controls to these two hazards can be illustrated. For other hazard risks not listed below, a similar generic approach can be taken and the types of controls that are possible can be listed, using the format of preventive, corrective, directive and detective controls.

When selecting and implementing controls, it is important to ensure that cost-effective controls are selected. Figure 23.2 plots increasing the level of control (horizontal-axis) against both the increasing cost of controls and the reducing potential loss (vertical-axis). By adding the total cost of controls and the equivalent potential loss for each level of control, the figure illustrates that there is an optimum level of control that represents the lowest combined cost as a sum of the cost of control and the level of potential losses.

It can be seen in Figure 23.2 that a significant reduction in potential loss is achieved with the introduction of low-cost controls. This section of the diagram is labelled

Figure 23.2 Cost-effective controls

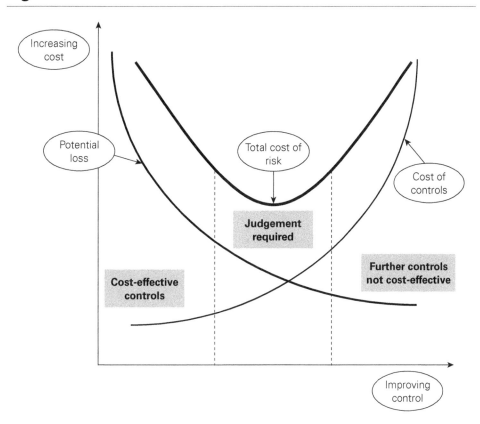

'Cost-effective controls'. The centre section of the diagram illustrates that spending more on controls achieves a reduction in the net cost of risk up to a certain point. In this segment, judgement is required on whether to spend the additional sum on controls. On the right-hand side of the diagram, spending more on controls achieves only a marginal reduction in potential loss. In this segment, further controls are not cost-effective.

Learning from controls

The various examples considered in this chapter give an oversight of the wide range of hazard risks that can be faced by an organization. There are many other examples of risks that have been discussed throughout this book. A constant feature of all types of hazard risks is that decisions have to be made on the most appropriate and cost-effective controls that should be introduced.

Uncertainty in terms of likelihood, impact and consequences is at the heart of risk management. Both Figures 23.2 and 23.4 illustrate that judgement is required when undertaking risk analysis and risk evaluation, as well as when consideration is being given to existing controls and the need for additional controls. In all cases, judgement based on the best available information is required.

Another important advantage of seeking to learn from controls is that unnecessary and inappropriately complex controls will be identified and steps can be taken to remove the control, modify it or replace it with a more cost-effective option. Risk assessment activities should take account of the continuing review of controls that is taking place, because the level of risk will be affected by the nature and quality of the controls. The role of monitoring controls is an area of expertise that is well established for internal audit.

Learning from controls may be mainly concerned with increasing their efficiency. However, it is also necessary to ensure that they are effective and they are

Figure 23.3   Learning from controls

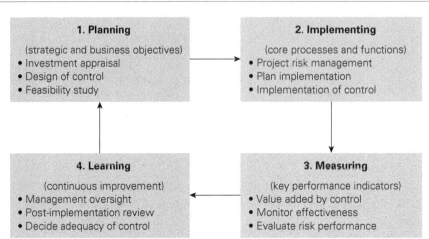

Figure 23.4   Risk and reward decisions

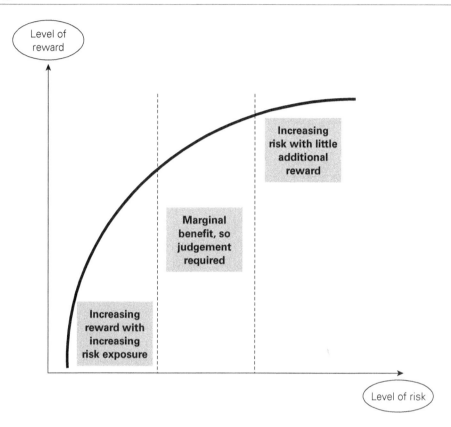

the correct controls. Internal audit will assist with the evaluation of the effectiveness and efficiency of existing controls and this will assist with learning from controls. The evaluation of controls should also pay regard to the level of reward that is being sought. Therefore, there is a need to evaluate strategy and tactics, as well as evaluating the effectiveness and efficiency of hazard and compliance controls.

Throughout this chapter, the emphasis has been on hazard controls, with details presented on some of the more common hazards that will be faced by many organizations. The ideas and principles explained in this chapter are also appropriate to opportunity management, and Figure 23.4 illustrates how the relationship between risk exposure and anticipated reward affects business decisions.

Initially, as risk exposure increases, a higher reward will be expected and the increase in reward is greater than the increase in risk exposure. Ultimately, there will be increasing exposure, but no increase in expected reward, so there is no benefit in taking that extra risk. In between these two situations, increasing risk exposure will produce a marginal increase in anticipated reward.

It is in this intermediate area that the judgement of management is required as to whether the increase in risk exposure is within the appetite of the organization.

Although it may not seem appropriate to increase risk exposure for a marginal increase in anticipated reward, this may be necessary to satisfy existing customer requirements or to help fulfil a longer-term business objective.

The analysis in Figure 23.4 relates to opportunity risks. There is a similar analysis that can be undertaken in relation to hazard risks, whereby the cost of further controls has to be evaluated against the reduced risk exposure that would result. When deciding whether to introduce further controls, the organization will need to also consider risk appetite and make a judgement concerning the risks that it is willing to take in pursuit of strategic objectives.

Control of financial risks

Fraud

One of the key areas of financial risk faced by all organizations is fraud, which can be committed by employees, customers or suppliers. Also, fraud may be committed by the organization itself by falsely reporting the results of operations. The Sarbanes–Oxley Act requirements are primarily aimed at the avoidance of fraudulent reporting by organizations.

Fraud occurs when there is the motive for undertaking it, the organization has assets that are worth stealing, there is an opportunity to undertake the theft or fraud and there is a lack of adequate control. Concerns about fraud should also extend to measures that are designed to reduce theft. These will include the provision of security fences and gates, as well as the provision of security guards, improved lighting and secure building access.

Organizations need to undertake an analysis of the effectiveness of their fraud controls. This is an area where internal audit is often involved. This analysis should check for losses in terms of money or goods, as well as evaluating areas where controls are insufficient. The analysis should be a proactive review that should include an analysis of vulnerable assets, who is responsible, how fraud might be undertaken and the effectiveness of the existing controls.

As well as undertaking an analysis of the effectiveness of existing controls, organizations should make an annual review of circumstances where fraud has been detected. These reports should be supplied to the audit committee.

In order to prevent fraud, the organization should introduce a corporate fraud policy that sets out the attitude of the organization towards fraud, the methods for controlling and investigating it, responsibilities for fraud control and details of the resources that are allocated to fraud detection. The arrangements for whistle-blowing and a policy for dealing with persons suspected of committing fraud should also be established.

Risk control actions related to fraud can be divided into the categories listed above as preventive, corrective, directive and detective. The following methods are available to organizations for minimizing fraud:

- improve recruitment procedures;
- reduce the motive for fraud;

- reduce the number of assets worth stealing;
- minimize the opportunity to steal;
- increase the level of supervision;
- improve financial controls and management systems;
- improve detection of fraud;
- improve record keeping.

Historical liabilities

One of the most difficult financial risk areas for organizations is related to their exposure to historical liabilities. These liabilities arise from previous activities of an organization, or acquired parts of the organization that were purchased together with their historical liabilities.

An area that is very difficult to quantify for industrial organizations is the previous exposure to agents that may give rise to delayed industrial diseases. The most obvious example is exposure to asbestos and the potential for the development of mesothelioma, a malignant cancer of the pleura or lining of the lungs. For many organizations, claims related to mesothelioma arise 30 or 40 years after the alleged exposure. Exposure will have occurred at a time when insurance arrangements may be difficult to confirm and the evidence of the exact working conditions will no longer be available.

Another area of exposure to historical liabilities relates to pension funds. Previously, many pension funds offered pension arrangements related to the final salary that the employee was earning. These are often referred to as defined benefit pension plans. Risks associated with the value of the pension fund and the level of pension that the available fund will purchase rest entirely with the employer in a defined benefits pension plan.

There has been a strong recent trend towards pension arrangements that build up a sum of money that is available to the employees to purchase a pension at the time of retirement. The member of staff is required to contribute money to his or her pension fund, and this arrangement is usually referred to as a defined contribution pension plan. In this arrangement, the risks attached to the value of the fund have been much reduced and the risk associated with the value of pension that the fund will purchase has been transferred to the employee.

The particular risk control issue of concern to employers is related to the defined benefit pension plan and the liability to persons who are no longer employed by the company but have pension entitlements within the defined benefit pension plan. These are often referred to as deferred benefits. The organization will need to look at the risk control options for dealing with these deferred benefits. Options available include encouraging former staff members with deferred benefits to opt out of the scheme by paying them a sum of money, transferring the deferred benefits arrangements to an insurance company on payment of an annuity premium or seeking to transfer the deferred benefits into a captive insurance company.

Historical liabilities of this type are, by definition, more of an issue for organizations that have been in existence for some time. This means that the organization will have a long history and third parties will be able to pursue liabilities that arose some considerable time ago. These historical liabilities may be more severe if the organization has changed in nature over time, especially if it is a much smaller organization than it had been previously. Also, organizations that have undergone a good deal of acquisition and merger activity will be more at risk.

Control of infrastructure risks

Health and safety at work

One of the major areas of concern in relation to infrastructure risks for organizations is health and safety at work. This is a highly regulated topic that should be a priority concern for all organizations. It is a well-established discipline within risk management, although it is often managed as an independent function.

The health and safety risks faced by an organization include prosecution by a regulatory authority, being sued by an injured employee and disruption caused by accidents and dangerous occurrences. Many health and safety tools and techniques are applied in broader risk management activities and there is no doubt that the full cooperation of health and safety specialists is vital to the success of any risk management initiative.

Undertaking risk assessments in relation to health and safety has been established for a long time. These risk assessments can be generic when the risks are relatively low. For high-risk activities, specific written detailed risk assessments will usually be required.

The features of a risk assessment include identification of the hazard, identification of who might be injured by the hazard and analysis of how serious it would be if an injury occurred. Details of the controls and precautions in place, together with the information on further actions that are required, should also be included as part of the risk assessment. The only purpose in undertaking a risk assessment is to ensure that controls are adequate and that people are not inappropriately at risk.

There is a hierarchy of controls that is well-established in relation to health and safety risks and this hierarchy is set out in Table 16.2. The overall generic control categories of preventive, corrective, directive and detective controls also apply to fraud risks, and Table 16.2 shows the equivalent categories of fraud control in comparison with the well-established terminology for the hierarchy of health and safety at work controls.

Having undertaken a risk assessment of the health and safety risks, organizations need to introduce controls that will include strategies for minimizing the risks (preventive controls), strategies for controlling the hazard (corrective controls), together with strategies for controlling staff and exposure (directive controls). Finally, health and safety controls that are intended to detect the early signs of ill-health may also be required in certain circumstances (detective controls). Management of stress at work is an example where detective controls may be appropriate to identify early warning signs that stress is affecting staff.

The range of workplace hazards that should be considered when undertaking risk assessments will depend on the exact nature of the organization. Detailed guidance is available on the management of specific health and safety risks, including:

- dangerous machinery;
- pressure systems;
- noise and vibration;
- electrical safety;
- hazardous substances;
- lifting and manual handling;
- slips, trips and falls;
- display screen equipment;
- human factors and repetitive strain injury;
- radiation;
- vehicles and driving risks;
- fire safety;
- stress at work.

Property fire protection

One of the most common causes of loss and disruption for manufacturing, warehousing and leisure and retail businesses is fire. More than half the organizations that suffer a major fire fail to fully recover from the event. Fire is a particularly serious event for manufacturing, transport/distribution and retail, and especially for residential, hospitality and leisure occupancies. There is also a strong link between the level of building security in place and the prevention of arson attacks.

When designing a fire risk strategy, it is important for the organization to evaluate the fire risks in relation to the common causes of fire at places of work. Most fires at work are caused by one or more of the following:

- electrical hazards;
- hot work;
- machinery;
- smoking materials;
- flammable liquids;
- bad housekeeping;
- arson.

The most important reason for having fire precautions in place is to protect the safety of people who may be affected by the fire. Careful attention should be paid to the adequacy of fire exits and the provision of emergency evacuation signs. Also, buildings should be of proper construction and fire escape routes should be adequately protected, possibly by the use of sprinklers if necessary.

Although the safety of people is the most important consideration in relation to fire safety, organizations should also evaluate the potential for the disruption that could result. The application of loss-control techniques to fire prevention is very well established. Adequate attention should be paid to loss prevention, damage limitation and cost containment.

Property loss prevention involves the application of preventive controls to the avoidance of a fire. These preventive controls will include maintenance of the electrical installations, the avoidance of sources of ignition and the correct storage of flammable and combustible materials. Corrective controls will include the installation of sprinkler systems and the provision of fire separation arrangements.

The use of directive controls will reduce the impact of a fire and the amount of damage that the fire causes. Directive controls include directions and information for employees on actions to be taken in the event of a fire. These will include early notification to the fire authorities, as well as the use of the portable fire extinguishers by employees if this can be done safely. Finally, detective controls include the provision of fire and heat detectors as well as routine patrols by fire and security officers to detect any fire at an early stage.

IT security

One of the key dependencies for most organizations is the information technology (IT) infrastructure. The failure of a computer system can be a very disruptive event for many organizations. One of the best-established examples of disaster recovery planning (DRP) is in relation to the IT infrastructure.

Loss of computer data can be very serious for an organization, and it is more likely to be associated with hardware problems than other issues such as software problems, electrical failure or human error. The consequences of IT failure can include:

- loss of business or customers;
- loss of credibility or goodwill;
- cash flow problems;
- reduced quality of service;
- inability to pay staff;
- backlog of work or loss of production;
- loss of data;
- financial loss;
- loss of customer account information;
- loss of financial controls.

With increasing dependency on computer systems, it is important for organizations to identify the losses that could occur and take actions to manage the associated risks. It is generally considered that the main causes of loss associated with IT systems are as follows:

- theft of computers and other hardware;
- unauthorized access into IT systems;

- introduction of viruses into the system;
- hardware or software faults and failures;
- user error, including loss or deletion of information;
- IT project failure.

Most organizations will need to set up an IT policy that is designed to ensure correct use of data as well as protecting the IT infrastructure of the organization. The policy should include information on responsibility for IT systems, details of back-up procedures, anti-virus and spyware procedures, use of personal data, personal use of the internet and restrictions on personal e-mails.

Most organizations will allow a certain amount of personal use of computer systems by employees. However, this should not be allowed to become excessive and specific restrictions should be placed on internet access to inappropriate websites. Another area of concern to organizations is data protection and the use or disclosure of personal information by the organization. Most countries have extensive legal requirements in place related to the protection of personal data held on computer.

Computer and IT failures will occur from time to time and the organization should ensure adequate back-up arrangements, so that only limited data is lost. Organizations with a very high dependency on their IT infrastructure should have detailed DRPs in place. In many circumstances, these will extend to arrangements for an emergency duplicate back-up computer facility, available either in a mobile trailer driven to the existing office location of the organization or at an alternative location.

The emergency back-up facilities can range from a complete duplicate facility with fully up-to-date information (often referred to as a hot-start facility) to an alternative computer system that has no data preloaded (referred to as a cold-start facility). There are a range of options for back-up systems that are a combination of these two approaches, and these are usually referred to as warm-start facilities.

HR risks

All organizations require a workforce of employed staff/contractors and/or volunteers. Therefore, there will always be human resources risks attached to the operation of every organization, regardless of its size, nature and the range of activities it undertakes.

There are a number of risk areas associated with the employment of staff and the utilization of the human resource within the organization:

- employee engagement and termination;
- legislative and regulatory compliance;
- recruitment, retention and skills availability;
- pension arrangements;
- performance and absence management;
- health and safety.

Large organizations usually have personnel and/or human resources expertise available in an HR department. There has been a general feeling that large organizations are more exposed to HR risks than smaller ones. This belief has been based on the thought that people know each other better in small organizations and there are fewer individuals involved, so closer working relationships exist across the whole organization. It has been assumed that these closer working relationships mean that the organization is less vulnerable to legal action or other disruption caused by personnel issues.

In recent times, however, it has become obvious that smaller organizations are also exposed to significant HR risks. In response to this realization, most small organizations now produce a staff handbook that sets out the terms and conditions of employment, including arrangements for sickness absence, maternity leave and annual leave, appraisals, behaviour at work, and roles and responsibilities.

Organizations need to set down arrangements that will ensure full compliance with the relevant employment legislation, including diversity arrangements, to ensure that there is no discrimination on the basis of ethnic origins or physical ability. When building on these basic legal requirements, organizations should look at the opportunities that will arise from having supportive, clear and beneficial recruitment, retention and employment practices.

Control of reputational risks

Brand protection

One of the most valuable assets of any organization is its brand name, and it is important to avoid damage to the organization or any of its brands. Damage to brand can occur for a number of reasons, including:

- changes in government policy;
- changes in the marketplace;
- new entrants into the marketplace;
- price and specification competition;
- counterfeiting and fake goods;
- inappropriate franchisee behaviour;
- failure of sponsor or joint-venture partner.

A trend in recent times has been the use of established brands to sell goods or services that have no obvious link to the brand itself. For example, supermarkets now sell insurance and other financial products, as well as selling petrol from forecourt garages. Extending or stretching the brand in this way represents a huge opportunity for many organizations, but the brand extensions have to be appropriate and credible as well as successful.

Most organizations recognize the value of their brands and have procedures in place to identify opportunities for brand extension. However, ownership of the brand within many large organizations is sometimes not well defined. Successful use of the brand to extend into new product areas and new business sectors should only be undertaken where there is clear responsibility within the organization for managing the brand.

As well as brand extensions, there has been a trend in recent times towards allowing branded concessions to be established within other organizations. It is now commonplace to see high-profile catering brands running the restaurant and cafe facilities in large department stores. This trend has developed at the same time as the increase in high-profile sponsorship deals. For example, many sports clubs have a new stadium that is actually called by the name of their main sponsor.

Many organizations operate on a franchise basis, whereby the brand is franchised to an individual or other business. These developments in branding enable maximum benefit to be gained from a high-profile brand. However, there are significant risks attached to these opportunities, and brand use and extension continues to be an issue that requires careful management.

Successful management of a franchise brand has many challenges. The expectations and requirements of the franchise or brand owner would be set out in a detailed contract in most cases, although some franchise organizations have been in existence for a long time and the early franchisees may not have the same rigid contract conditions. Most franchise owners provide extensive training for franchisees, including training on the quality of products. A significant issue for many franchise owners is arrangements for procurement of supplies. Often, the franchise owner will prohibit procurement of supplies locally, so that the product delivered by the franchisee is always consistent.

Environment

One of the most rapidly developing concerns in society is global warming and how the activities of individuals and organizations might have an impact. Environmental concerns can range from issues to do with historical land contamination and contamination of water supplies, to industrial emissions into the atmosphere and the desire of organizations to be seen as green.

Disposal of waste is an issue of concern to all organizations. For organizations producing industrial waste, the legislation is extremely detailed on how the waste must be treated and the arrangements for discarding it. For commercial organizations that do not produce industrial waste or by-products, there are still issues of concern. The disposal of commercial waste can be costly and most countries require or (at least) encourage a large degree of recycling.

The concerns for many organizations therefore relate to minimizing the amount of commercial waste that they produce, as well as adopting other green policies. For many organizations in the public sector, recycling arrangements are detailed and recycling targets are important because of the greater scrutiny of the performance of public bodies.

Arrangements that may be investigated will include the procurement of supplies or raw materials that have less impact on the environment and/or are easier to recycle. Organizations may also wish to introduce a recycling policy and make specific arrangements for the collection of recyclable waste materials. For some organizations, there is also scope to look at travel arrangements and encourage employees to use public transport where this is feasible, as well as reducing the amount of travel that employees undertake.

For industrial operations, there are detailed standards, rules and regulations in place, with the enforcement agencies having considerable powers. As well as paying regard to the legislative requirements, these regulators will also pay regard to broader public opinion and seek to evaluate the following issues:

- What impacts to the environment may occur?
- How harmful are these impacts to the environment?
- How likely is it that these impacts will occur?
- How frequently and where will these impacts occur?

Control of marketplace risks

Technology developments

One of the main challenges facing organizations is keeping up with customer expectations and demands. This challenge is made more difficult by continuing developments in technology. Organizations supplying consumer goods that are technology-based face a continuous challenge, which can be turned into a continuous set of opportunities.

Changes in the technology used to provide home and mobile communications and entertainment have been considerable in recent times. Until relatively recently, home entertainment and mobile entertainment were based on CDs. Organizations operating in this area were confronted with the introduction of MP3 technology and had to make decisions about which technology to pursue. The investment required to change technology was considerable and the marketplace risks very significant. For the organizations that correctly identified (and influenced) the developments, the rewards have proved to be enormous. In a rapidly changing marketplace, technology advantages can be significant but the challenge of correctly identifying the most likely successful technology is always present and the investment required is huge.

Consumer decisions regarding new technology are led by convenience, quality, price and fashion. Another factor affecting consumer decisions and the availability of new technology is that significant developments in technology of this type occur on a worldwide basis. Therefore, only a very limited number of organizations have the resources to undertake the research required to develop products based on the new technology. Also, these are the same organizations that design, manufacture and supply goods that utilize the new technology.

In order to take advantage of these new technologies, many organizations have to enter into joint-venture partnerships, share expertise and share the cost of developing the new technologies. Selection of joint-venture partners can be difficult and correct decisions are essential. When developing a new entertainment technology that will be introduced across the world, attempts are sometimes made by competitors to agree the technology that will be adopted. This strategic approach has the advantage that research costs are shared and technology battles are avoided. However, the disadvantage is that the scope for a huge future competitive advantage is reduced.

Regulatory risks

One of the most difficult risk issues for many organizations is regulatory risk. A key component of the COSO ERM cube is the achievement of compliance by the organization. Compliance may appear to be a relatively straightforward issue, but there are often complexities associated with the potential for changes to regulations, changes in the regulatory environment and different regulatory requirements in different territories.

Different societies have different and changing views of certain commercial sectors. For example, the sex industry has different standards and different regulatory frameworks in different parts of the world. Also, gambling faces different public attitudes, different regulatory frameworks and variable restrictions on activities in different countries. Ensuring regulatory compliance and maintaining good working relationships with regulators can be difficult, especially when public opinion is changing and/or regulatory frameworks are being developed or modified.

There has been a great deal of consideration recently of the difficulties associated with ensuring compliance in the purchase and delivery of multinational or global insurance programmes. Two major issues have received considerable attention. These are the payment of insurance premium tax in different territories and the acceptability of insurance provided in a country by an insurance company that has no presence in that territory. (Insurance written by an insurance company with no presence in a territory is referred to as non-admitted insurance.)

In relation to global insurance policies, the problems arise when a global policy is issued by a large company based in one specific country, but with the insurance coverage applying across all the operations of the organization and in several different countries. Each country will have its regulations regarding the payment of insurance premium tax on that part of the insurance premium that relates to the operations of the organization in that country. Also, many territories in the world do not allow non-admitted insurance policies.

The range of risk control options available to organizations seeking to achieve compliance is, of course, restricted. Compliance is a basic requirement of all business and commercial activities. Ensuring compliance may require cooperation with third parties and detailed advice from specialists with expertise in the discipline in that part of the world. In the example of insurance, it may be necessary for a local insurance company to be involved in the insurance programme in territories where non-admitted insurance is not allowed, and this will add cost to the insurance programmes. Also, arrangements for the payment of insurance premium tax may need to be made through third-party fiscal representatives within the territory where the taxes are due.

PART SIX
Risk culture

LEARNING OUTCOMES FOR PART SIX

- describe the key features of a risk-aware culture (LILAC) and how the key components are defined and can be measured;
- describe the components of risk maturity of an organization (4Ns) and the influence on risk management activities (FOIL);
- describe the importance of risk appetite and how this can be demonstrated on a risk matrix, together with the risk exposure and risk capacity;
- review the nature of risk appetite statements and how these can be used to influence decision making within organizations;
- explain the importance of risk training and risk communication and the influence on the risk culture of an organization;
- summarize the importance of risk training and risk communication, including the use of risk management information systems (RMIS);
- explain the features of a risk competency framework and the relationship to plan, implement, measure and learn (PIML);
- outline the people skills required by a risk practitioner summarized as communication (5Cs), relationship, analytical and management (CRAM).

PART SIX FURTHER READING

ASIS SPC.1-2009 *Organizational Resilience: Security, preparedness and continuity management systems*, **www.asisonline.org**

Canadian Institute of Chartered Accountants (1995) *Criteria of Control*, **www.cica.ca**

Hillson, D (2016) *The Risk Management Handbook: A practical guide to managing the multiple dimensions of risk*, **www.koganpage.com**

Seville, E (2016) *Resilient Organizations: How to survive, thrive and create opportunities through crisis and change*, **www.koganpage.com**

Sheffi, Y (2015) *The Power of Resilience: How the best companies manage the unexpected*, **https://mitpress.mit.edu**

Taylor, E (2014) *Practical Enterprise Risk Management*, **www.koganpage.com**

PART SIX CASE STUDIES

Network Rail: Our approach to risk management

The purpose of our enterprise risk management (ERM) approach is to mitigate risks to the delivery of a safe, reliable and cost-effective service to our customers. ERM supports the building of capability in all areas of the business to recognize both risk and opportunity early. Early recognition of risk allows us to work collaboratively and proactively with customers, stakeholders and suppliers to manage our extensive portfolio of works better.

Across the group our approach to risk management balances the need to manage risks with identifying opportunities to improve performance through careful acceptance of some risk. We recognize our status as a regulated rail network infrastructure provider and the importance of maintaining essential service provision.

We take an enterprise-wide approach to risk management and have in place an ERM framework for the identification, analysis, management and reporting of all risk to strategic objectives. The framework also takes account of operational risk and recognizes the need for specialist approaches in areas such as safety, project management and information security.

The ERM framework provides a standardized approach to the identification, assessment, recording and reporting of significant risks. We analyse the possible causes of a risk and assess what the impact could be if the risk were to occur. For each risk we identify current controls and their effectiveness to manage underlying causes and minimize consequences. The full risk assessment process is conducted using the Bow-Tie methodology which provides a structured approach. We identify risks from a strategic view (top-down) and from the operational environment (bottom-up) to give better visibility of risk exposure across the enterprise.

Edited extract from Network Rail Limited
Annual Report and Accounts 2015

Ekurhuleni Metropolitan Municipality (EMM): Risk management

The EMM regards enterprise risk management (ERM) as a critical cornerstone of good corporate governance and essential for the achievement of its business objectives. The starting point for the municipality's ERM policy implementation is an ERM framework that respects the needs and aspirations of all with whom the EMM has relationships. To this end, all risks that may prevent the EMM from achieving its business objectives are proactively identified on a continuous basis and formally assessed at least once per annum to ensure achievement of these objectives and for the purpose of reporting on the process of risk management in the annual report.

These risks are managed formally and proactively through a factual approach to decision making, based on the logical and intuitive analysis of data and information collected about those risks and the planning, arranging, and controlling of activities and resources to minimize the impact of all risks to levels that can be tolerated by the municipality and other stakeholders.

A centralized coordination of ERM processes includes regular awareness programmes, risk identification and assessment, risk monitoring, reporting and independent verification of the status of internal controls, incidents investigation and reporting, and counter-measures across the EMM's operations, programmes and projects in order to achieve an integrated ERM system as part of its corporate governance responsibility.

To ensure that the municipality's strategy and, consequently, its mandate as outlined in the constitution of the Republic of South Africa are fulfilled, the municipality's ERM programme arms its people with tools and capabilities to overcome the barriers that arise in striving to exceed customer and stakeholder expectations.

Ekurhuleni Metropolitan Municipality (EMM)
Annual Report 2013–14

Ericsson: Corporate governance report

Ericsson's risk management is integrated into the operational processes of the business to ensure accountability, effectiveness, efficiency, business continuity and compliance with corporate governance, legal and other requirements. The board of directors is also overseeing the company's risk management. Risks related to long-term objectives with reference to core business, targeted areas and new areas, are discussed and strategies are formally approved by the board as part of the annual strategy process. Risks related to annual targets for the company are also reviewed by the board and then monitored continuously during the year. Certain transactional risks require specific board approval in excess of pre-defined limits:

- Operational risks are owned and managed by operational units. Risk management is embedded in various process controls, such as decision tollgates and approvals. Certain cross-process risks are centrally co-ordinated, such as information security, IT security, corporate responsibility and business continuity and insurable risks.

- Financial risk management is governed by a group policy and carried out by the treasury and customer finance functions, both supervised by the finance committee. The policy governs risk exposures related to foreign exchange, liquidity/financing, interest rates, credit risk and market price risk in equity instruments.

- Ericsson has implemented group policies and directives in order to comply with applicable laws and regulations, as well as its code of business ethics and code of conduct. Risk management is integrated in the company's business processes. Policies and controls are implemented to comply with financial reporting standards and stock market regulations.

- Strategic risks constitute the highest risk to the company if not managed properly as they could have a long-term impact. Ericsson therefore reviews its long-term objectives, main strategies and business scope on an annual basis and continuously works on its tactics to reach these objectives and to mitigate any risks identified.

Edited extract from Ericsson
Annual Report 2015

Risk-aware culture

24

Styles of risk management

We have already seen that there are three (complementary) styles of risk management, related to the nature of the risk under consideration. Hazard management, control management and opportunity management define and describe the approach and, to some extent, the level of sophistication that is applied to risk management by an organization at a point in time.

Hazard risks will always have a negative outcome associated with the risk. The maximum exposure to the risk that is acceptable to the organization is the hazard tolerance. Control risks will have a cost associated with controlling the risks, and this cost can be described as the control acceptance. Opportunity risks have a range of possible outcomes from highly positive to highly negative. The intended and planned outcome is, of course, positive. The organization will be willing to put resources at risk in pursuit of opportunity risks, and this is the opportunity investment.

The type of risk under consideration helps determine the style of risk management that will be applied. However, some risks may need to be managed using all three styles of risk management, at different stages in the lifecycle of the risk. In summary, the four styles of risk management can be viewed as follows:

- *Compliance management*: based on fulfilling legal obligations, such as health and safety (1970s).
- *Hazard management*: 'total cost of risk' approach developed by the insurance world (1980s).
- *Control management*: based on the internal control approach of internal auditors (1990s).
- *Opportunity management*: interface between risk management and strategic planning (2000s).

The hazard tolerance, control acceptance and opportunity investment are the values that the organization is willing to put at risk. These three components added together are the risk appetite of the organization and represent the total acceptable risk exposure of the organization. The total risk exposure is the sum of the risk exposures for the individual risks and this actual risk exposure may differ from the risk appetite of the board and/or the risk capacity of the organization.

The insurance risk manager will normally manage motor vehicle risks as a loss minimization or 'total cost of risk' issue. The avoidance of internal fraud will normally be managed as an internal control issue and will be monitored and reviewed by the internal audit department. Risks associated with a merger or acquisition should be managed as an opportunity issue by the CEO or a nominated senior executive.

Steps to successful risk management

In order to improve the risk management performance of an organization, a risk management initiative will be required. The nature of this initiative will depend on the size, complexity and nature of the organization. There is no single correct approach to implementing risk management in an organization. The drivers for undertaking risk management and the expected outputs and impacts will vary between organizations.

Although there is no single correct approach, Table 24.1 sets out some of the key steps in achieving successful risk management. Appendix C provides an approach that is entirely compatible with the issues mentioned in Table 24.1. The appendix also draws together the acronyms used throughout this book and lists the various risk management tools and techniques associated with each stage in the implementation of a successful enterprise risk management initiative.

The initial, and perhaps most important, step is ensuring that the risk management initiative is sponsored by a member of the board or a senior member of the executive committee of the organization. Information on the successful introduction of a risk management initiative is also available in the various risk management standards and frameworks discussed throughout this book.

As risk management changes and develops, the steps that will be taken by different organizations will change. With the emergence of governance, risk and compliance (GRC), the risk management context has changed and developed. Risk management professionals need to be aware of these changes and developments and ensure that their activities are always fully aligned with the other activities within the organization. In other words, risk management activities should always be fully aligned with the internal context.

Although it is important to have an overall plan relating to the implementation of the risk management initiative, it is also vital that the risk manager identifies barriers

Table 24.1   Achieving successful enterprise risk management

1   Engage senior management and board of directors to provide organizational support and resources.

2   Establish an independent ERM function reporting directly to a board member.

3   Establish the risk architecture at executive and board levels, supported by internal audit.

4   Develop the ERM framework that incorporates an appropriate risk classification system.

5   Develop a risk aware culture fostered by a common language, training and education.

6   Provide written procedures with a clear statement of the risk appetite of the organization.

7   Agree monitoring and reporting against established objectives for risk management.

8   Undertake risk assessments to identify accumulations and interdependencies of risk.

9   Integrate ERM into strategic planning, business processes and operational success.

10   Contribute to the success of the organization by delivering measurable benefits.

to the implementation of the initiative in some detail. The potential barriers and enablers to the successful implementation of a risk management initiative are set out in Table 24.2. There are many factors that will influence the effectiveness of the approach, including:

- senior management influence within departments;
- external influences, including corporate governance;
- nature of the business, its products and culture;

Table 24.2   Implementation barriers and actions

Barrier	Action
Lack of understanding of risk management and belief that it will suppress entrepreneurship	Establish a shared understanding, common expectations and a consistent language of risk in the organization
Lack of support and commitment from senior management	Identify a sponsor on the main board of the organization and confirm shared and common priorities
Seen as just another initiative, so relevance and importance not accepted	Agree a strategy that sets out the anticipated outcomes and confirms the benchmarks for anticipated benefits
Benefits not perceived as being significant	Complete a realistic analysis of what can be achieved and the impact on the mission of the organization
Not seen as a core part of business activity and too time-consuming	Align effort with core processes and achievement of the mission of the organization
Approach too complicated and over-analytical (risk overkill)	Establish appropriate level of sophistication for risk management framework and undertaking risk assessments
Responsibilities unclear and need for external consultants unclear	Establish agreed risk architecture with clear roles and accepted risk responsibilities
Risks separated from where they arose and should be managed	Include risk management in job descriptions to ensure that risks are managed within the context that gave rise to them
Risk management seen as a static activity not appropriate for a dynamic organization	Align risk management effort with the mission of the organization and with the business decision-making activities
Risk management too expansive and seeking to take over all aspects of the company	Be realistic: do not claim that *all* the business activities within the organization are risk management by another name

- corporate attitudes, including previous RM experiences;
- origins of the risk management department.

Identification of barriers, as set out in Table 24.2, leads to the ability to put in place actions to overcome them. These include the fact that successful risk management requires the commitment of all parties and that implementation will only be as good as the least committed member of a department. Analysis of these barriers within the context of the specific organization will lead to the identification of the best options to ensure that risk management delivers the optimum benefits.

There is no single action that will ensure adequate implementation and no single timeframe by which implementation will be fully achieved. It is the experience of many organizations that full implementation of all stages of the approach may take between two and five years.

One of the important considerations regarding the timeframe for implementation will be the documentation methodology. If a comprehensive risk management information system (RMIS) is to be introduced, the timescale for successful and complete implementation may be extended.

Defining risk culture

The culture of an organization is difficult to define. However, it is generally accepted that it is a reflection of the overall attitude of every component of management within a company. The culture of an organization determines how individuals will behave in particular circumstances. It will define how an individual feels obliged to behave in all circumstances.

A good risk culture will be the product of individual and group values and of attitudes and patterns of behaviour. This will lead to a commitment to the risk management objectives of the organization. Organizations with a risk-aware culture are characterized by communication founded on mutual trust and a shared perception of the importance of risk management. There also needs to be a sharing of confidence in the selected control measures and a commitment to adhering to the established risk control procedures.

Table 24.3 sets out the suggested components of a risk-aware culture. These components are suggested by recent UK Health and Safety Executive (HSE) research as leadership, involvement, learning, accountability and communication. This makes the acronym LILAC. Creating a culture where effective risk management is an integral part of the way people work is a long-term aim for most organizations.

If an organization decides to raise awareness of security issues, it may decide to launch a campaign to focus on the risks and the relevant controls. The campaign should use more than one means of communication if it is to be successful. The awareness campaign could include all of the LILAC components and may extend to:

- risk awareness training;
- awareness poster campaigns;
- site inspections;
- arrangements for reporting defects;
- leaflets and brochures.

Table 24.3   Risk-aware culture

A risk-aware culture is achieved by LILAC:	
Leadership	Strong leadership within the organization in relation to strategy, projects and operations
Involvement	Involvement of all stakeholders in all stages of the risk management process
Learning	Emphasis on training in risk management procedures and learning from events
Accountability	Absence of an automatic blame culture, but appropriate accountability for actions
Communication	Communication and openness on all risk management issues and the lessons learnt

A risk management initiative cannot be successful unless the culture of the organization is receptive to it. In order to be receptive, a risk-aware culture is required in the organization. A high level of maturity in relation to leadership will require senior management to actively promote a risk-aware culture. This will include setting risk management performance targets and ensuring that the commitment of senior management to the risk-aware culture is clear. This will require verbal and written communications.

Involvement and participation of senior management is a necessary component of achieving a risk-aware culture. Involvement can be achieved by adequate training, so that ownership of risks is fully understood. Specialist risk functions should play an advisory or consultancy role. There should be feedback mechanisms in place to inform staff about any decisions that are likely to affect them.

The existence of a learning culture is vital to the success of a risk-aware culture. A learning culture enables organizations to learn, and to identify and change inappropriate risk behaviour. In-depth analysis of incidents and good communication of feedback enables a learning culture to develop. Workshops on risk issues are another key component of a learning culture.

Embedding risk management

Many institutions have set up committees to oversee the implementation of risk management practices and procedures. Often these are management committees, although they can sometimes be supported by members of the governing body.

One institution has established a group to advise on the development of risk management processes. Significantly, this group includes academics from the institution's business school, tapping into existing expertise. This practice is evident at another institution, where the group, a management sub-committee, includes an academic expert in risk management from the local business school.

As risk management processes become embedded within the daily routines and management of the institutions, these committees will evolve or be replaced. Institutions with more effective risk management processes have increasingly charged their senior management teams with this role, rather than establishing separate committees. In such cases, risk management processes have become more effectively embedded because the senior management team is in a better position to identify and manage risk, and to promote risk management. One institution visited was exploring a new role for its risk management committee as a facilitator in sharing good practice between departments.

Accountability is vitally important if the risk-aware culture is to be successful. However, it is not the same as a blame culture. The organization should ensure that it moves from a blame culture to a just culture based on accountability. When investigating incidents, management should demonstrate care and concern towards employees. Employees should feel that they are able to report issues and concerns without fear that they will be blamed or disciplined personally.

A risk-aware culture requires good communication of risk information from senior management. Good communication also requires that reports from all employees, as well as reports from outside the organization, are welcome and well received. Information on risk performance should be included in the communication activities.

Measuring risk culture

It can be difficult for an organization to measure risk culture. However, the risk culture of the organization is so important that measurements need to be taken. Audit committees will often ask how seriously a department or location takes risk management. In general, it will be easy to answer this question on a qualitative basis. However, quantitative measurements are required, so that areas of weakness can be identified and improvement actions planned.

The Canadian Criteria of Control (CoCo) framework represents a means for measuring the risk culture of the organization. Another measure of the risk culture is that the audit committee seeks to evaluate the level of risk assurance that is available from the particular unit or division under consideration.

Another means of measuring risk culture is to look at the level of risk maturity within the organization. A later section of this chapter considers risk maturity models in more detail. Quantitative measures that indicate the level of risk maturity can be taken and areas for improvement can then be identified. The box below provides an example of risk awareness and the embedding of risk management into the culture of an organization.

Risk awareness campaign

The embedding of risk management into the organization has been undertaken by following three routes: a risk awareness campaign, the implementation of new risk identification processes at directorate level, and the ongoing development of existing risk processes at a strategic level.

The primary aim of the awareness campaign was to make staff realize their responsibilities towards risk, whilst at directorate level the introduction of risk registers has been collaborative and inclusive. Strategically, further development of the corporate risk register aims to bring tighter control of risk and provides comprehensive evidence and assurance to the board that risks are managed.

The quality of a risk management policy and details of the requirements and procedures contained in the risk guidelines or protocols will give an indication of the risk culture of the organization. For many organizations, improvement in the risk culture is a valid strategic risk objective. This will be especially true when areas of weakness in the level of risk awareness have been identified.

When undertaking actions to improve the risk culture within an organization, it is important to acknowledge that improving the risk management processes must lead to improvements in risk management outputs. This, in turn, should have a positive impact that delivers greater benefits from risk management.

There is little point in improving the risk management processes as a means of improving the risk culture of the organization if the overall effectiveness of the risk management effort is not enhanced. There is a danger that enhancing and improving the risk management process in an organization is automatically assumed to have improved the risk culture.

It is possible for the risk management process to be enhanced without the risk culture of the organization being improved. For example, a more aggressive internal audit programme may improve compliance standards, but that does not guarantee that the risk culture of the organization has been enhanced. Improvements to the risk management process may not deliver any additional benefits, whereas improvements to the risk culture should be expected to provide an enhanced level of risk assurance.

ISO 31000 places considerable importance on context, and this is illustrated in Figure 6.4. Information is provided in the standard on the importance of the external context, internal context and risk management context for the organization. Context is closely related to risk management culture and the benefits that will be derived from enhanced risk management within the organization.

The Canadian Criteria of Control (CoCo) framework of internal control concentrates on the control environment in an organization. Additionally, the COSO ERM cube (2004) refers to the internal environment of the organization, rather than the control environment that is described in the COSO Internal Control cube (2013). The control environment and the internal environment are measures of the risk culture and the level of risk awareness within the organization.

An overall improvement in risk performance will be achieved through improvements in the internal context, risk management context, control environment or internal environment. The level of risk maturity, the achievement of a risk-aware culture and the fulfilment of the LILAC criteria set out in Table 24.3 are all means of improving the control or internal environment.

During the 1990s, a system called the balanced scorecard became a popular management tool. This is a management system that enables organizations to clarify their vision and strategy and translate them into action. Many large organizations use balanced scorecards as a means of establishing context for the various initiatives that are undertaken within the organization. The government agency used as the basis for Figure 28.2 is an example of an organization that uses the balanced scorecard.

If an organization uses the balanced scorecard, it is sensible to use the same framework for risk management activities. When risk management processes and procedures are compatible with existing activities, the risk management requirements are more likely to be accepted and fulfilled. This represents an alignment of risk management activities with existing protocols, in order to embed risk management in the organization and create a more risk-aware culture.

Alignment of activities

Risk management activities and the risk architecture, strategy and protocols should be aligned with the core business processes within the organization. Risk information flows around the risk management framework and (if successful) this will produce various outputs. These outputs have already been described as mandatory obligations fulfilled, assurance provided, decision making enhanced and effective and efficient core processes achieved (MADE2).

Most risk management standards make reference to the upside of risk or discuss the management of opportunity risks. Project risk management, or the management of control risks, has become a separate discipline within risk management, and project risk management has become well developed, with separate guidance material.

When considering the contribution that risk management can make to the organization, it is important to decide whether the contribution will relate to strategy, projects and/or operations. This decision will enable the risk management activities within the organization to be aligned with the other business operations, activities and imperatives.

It is important that risk management activities are aligned with other operations, so that the risk management procedures can be fully embedded into the existing management procedures and activities within the organization. This will also ensure that risk management activities are undertaken in an efficient and embedded manner and are not seen as a separate activity detached from management of the organization.

There should also be alignment of the activities of internal audit with the culture or context of the organization. The approach followed by internal audit when deciding to design a risk-based audit programme has two components. Firstly, internal audit will look at the high-risk activities and focus the audit programme on those activities. Secondly, the risk-based audit programme will take account of the level of risk management maturity across the organization. If part of the organization has a less risk-mature approach, then internal audit may decide to undertake an increased amount of audit activity in that part of the organization.

Another measure of how well-embedded enterprise risk management is within an organization can be represented by the fragmented–organized–influential–leading (FOIL) approach. Table 24.4 describes the four stages of risk maturity (as identified

Table 24.4   Four levels of risk maturity

Level	Status (4Ns)	Characteristics (FOIL)
1	**Naïve** Level 1 organizations are unaware of the need for enterprise risk management and/or do not understand the benefits that will arise.	**Fragmented** Risk management activities are fragmented and focused on legal compliance activities, such as health and safety.
2	**Novice** Level 2 organizations are aware of the benefits of enterprise risk management, but have only just started to implement an ERM initiative.	**Organized** Actions are planned to co-ordinate risk management activities across all types of risk, although plans may not have been fully implemented.
3	**Normalized** Level 3 organizations have embedded ERM into business processes, but management effort is still required to maintain adequate ERM activities.	**Influential** Embedded ERM processes are influencing processes and management behaviours, but this may not yet happen consistently or reliably.
4	**Natural** Level 4 organizations have a risk-aware culture with a proactive approach to ERM and risk is reliably considered at all stages to gain competitive advantage.	**Leading** Consideration of risk is a substantial factor in making business decisions and decisions about strategy are led by ERM considerations.

by the 4Ns) and the characteristics associated with the FOIL approach and it can be seen that the influence of enterprise risk management increases as the four levels are implemented.

A fragmented approach to enterprise risk management is present when different risks are managed in different departments by specialists who do not, necessarily, work together. For example, an organization can have excellent health and safety, security and business continuity standards, but the benefits of working together may not have been established. The next stage is for these activities to become co-ordinated, so that the approach to enterprise risk management becomes more organized. All risks are then considered together and the result is likely to be a comprehensive risk register.

However, there is more benefit to be gained from enterprise risk management. Organizations that establish ERM activities that are influential on decision making gain these additional benefits. Risk management (and the risk manager) influence decision making and ensure that risk-related issues are taken fully into account as strategy and tactics are developed. The final stage is for risk management to lead the development of strategy and tactics within the organization. This will require the risk manager to be part of a senior management team, so that the development of strategy and tactics is led by risk considerations, rather than the risk implications being considered after the strategy and tactics have been decided.

Risk maturity models

Increases in risk management effectiveness can also be measured by the use of risk maturity models. The level of risk management sophistication provides an indication of the benefits that can be achieved from risk management. The level of risk maturity in the organization is a measure of the quality of risk management activities and the extent to which they are embedded within the organization.

Risk maturity models can be used to measure the current level of risk culture within the organization. The greater the level of risk maturity, the more embedded risk management activities will become within the routine operations undertaken by the organization. The hallmarks of successfully embedded risk management are considered later in this chapter.

Risk maturity is not the same as considering the level of sophistication that an organization achieves in respect to risk management. An organization may have limited expectations of risk management, but nevertheless have a very mature approach to the way in which it seeks to obtain the available benefits. The level of risk maturity within an organization is an indication of the way in which risk processes and capabilities are developed and applied. In an immature organization, informal risk management practices will take place. However, there is likely to be a blame culture in existence when things go wrong and a potential lack of accountability for risk. Also, resources allocated to manage risks may be inappropriate for the level of risk involved.

When explicit risk management is in place, there will be attempts to keep the processes dynamic, relevant and useful. There is likely to be open dialogue and learning so that information is used to inform judgements and decisions about risks. There will be confidence that innovation and risk-taking can be managed, with support when things go wrong.

When an organization becomes obsessed with risk, there will be over-dependence on process, and this may limit the ability to manage risk effectively. There will be over-reliance on information at the expense of good judgement, and dependence on process to define the rationale behind decisions. Individuals may become risk-averse for fear of criticism and procedures are followed only to comply with requirements, not because benefits are sought.

Table 24.4 sets out a system for determining the level of risk maturity within an organization with regard to risk management processes. This table sets out four levels of risk maturity, described as naïve, novice, normalized and natural (4Ns). The characteristics of each of these levels are described in the table. Table 24.4 also aligns the 4Ns model with the FOIL methodology for describing the level of risk maturity in an organization. Clearly, it is better for an organization to seek a higher level of risk maturity. However, the approach to achieving risk maturity in the organization should be proportionate to the level of risk that the organization faces.

The level of risk maturity within an organization will help define the level of sophistication that the organization has in its risk management activities. Figure 4.2 discusses the level of sophistication of the contribution that risk management can make to company activities. The greater the level of risk management sophistication achieved by an organization, the greater the benefits. Achieving an improved level of maturity in relation to risk management processes does not necessarily guarantee that a greater level of sophistication will be achieved, or that a higher level of benefits will be obtained.

Nevertheless, achieving an improved level of risk maturity may be one of the strategic aims for risk management within the organization. If that is the case, an established framework for measuring risk maturity is required. It is important that the organization uses a risk maturity model that aligns with its own ambitions in relation to risk management maturity and provides a practical approach that can be embedded within the organization.

Figure 24.1 provides an interpretation of the level of risk maturity of an organization, based on the 4Ns model. The figure suggests that there is a relationship between whether behaviour is embedded or automatic on one hand against

Figure 24.1   Risk maturity demonstrated on a matrix

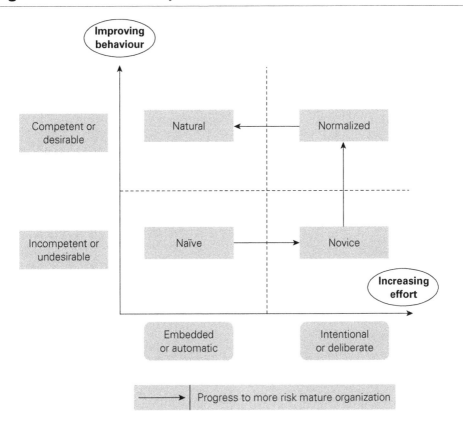

competent or desirable on the other. A naïve organization will automatically accept incompetent or undesirable behaviours. A novice organization will become aware that the behaviours are incompetent or undesirable and will have started to make an effort to improve behaviour, but it will not yet have achieved change. However, as change is achieved, it will move towards improved normalized behaviours.

The status achieved by an organization with the natural state of risk maturity is that competent or desirable behaviours will automatically occur, with little management effort or enforcement. The achievement at this point is to ensure that behaviours are also consistent. One of the primary reasons for producing risk management policies and procedures is to ensure that appropriate behaviours are consistently achieved. Ensuring consistent desirable behaviours is one of the primary objectives of a risk management initiative.

The normalized organization is successful in achieving competent or desirable behaviours, but these are not yet automatic. When the organization reaches the stage of being a natural in risk management, then the competent or desirable behaviours will become unconscious or automatic. This model provides a means of illustrating the four levels of risk maturity (4Ns) on a matrix and also indicates that the decline from natural behaviour back to naïve may be a short step for organizations that do not put sufficient effort into maintaining their level of risk maturity.

Several types of risk maturity approaches are in existence, including the Criteria of Control (CoCo) framework. The approach adopted by the CoCo framework focuses very heavily on the importance of risk maturity. The approach of this internal control framework is that if the risk culture and the risk architecture, strategy and protocols are correct then good levels of risk management and internal control will be achieved. Another risk maturity model that is frequently used is the European Foundation for Quality Management (EFQM) model.

Finally, the similarities between Figure 24.1 and 4.2 are worth considering. There is a need to *inform* a naïve organization and *reform* a novice organization. A normalized organization will *conform* with requirements and a natural organization will be successful and *perform*.

Importance of risk appetite

25

Nature of risk appetite

Risk appetite is a vitally important concept in the practice of risk management. However, it is a very difficult concept to precisely define and apply in practice. Risk appetite is sometimes considered to be defined by the risk criteria established by the organization. The risk appetite or risk criteria are important components in the risk ranking phase of the risk management process. This is the next phase of the risk management process after the risks have been rated in terms of likelihood and impact. Risk appetite is the immediate or short-term willingness of an organization to undertake an activity that involves risk. Risk attitude and the risk criteria represent a longer-term view of risk in the same way as a person will have an immediate appetite for food and a longer-term attitude towards food. Risk attitude is illustrated in Figure 10.1.

One of the fundamental difficulties with the concept of risk appetite is that, generally speaking, organizations will have an appetite to continue a particular operation, embark on a project or embrace a strategy, rather than a direct appetite for the risk itself. In other words, risk appetite and risk exposure should be considered as a consequence of business decisions rather than a driver of those decisions. The decision on risk appetite is normally taken within the context of other business decisions, rather than as a stand-alone decision. The typical advice in most risk management standards is that risk should not be managed out of context, so questions about the risk appetite can only be answered within the context of the strategy, tactics, operations and compliance activities being considered.

Many commercial organizations make adequate profits but take too much risk or make inappropriate use of the risk capacity of the organization. Risk capacity, or the capability of the organization to take risk, is not the same as the cumulative total of all of the individual values at risk associated with the risks facing the organization. This cumulative total is the risk exposure of the organization.

By contrast risk appetite is the total value of the corporate resources that the board of the organization is willing to put at risk. Most organizations have not determined the value they should risk (risk appetite), nor calculated how much value is actually at risk (risk exposure), nor the capability of the organization to take risk (risk capacity). A range of definitions of risk appetite is shown in Table 25.1 and it is obvious that different professional bodies have produced very similar definitions of risk appetite.

Table 25.1   Definitions of risk appetite

Organization	Definition of risk appetite
IRM (2011)	The amount of risk that an organization is willing to seek or accept in the pursuit of long-term objectives.
ISO Guide 73 (2009)	The amount and type of risk that an organization is willing to pursue or retain.
Orange Book (2004)	The amount of risk that an organization is prepared to accept, tolerate or be exposed to at any point in time.
CIIA (2005)	The level of risk that is acceptable to the board or management. This may be set in relation to the organization as a whole, for different groups of risks or at an individual risk level.

An organization should be able to decide how much it wishes to put at risk, based on the attitude of the organization to risk. Agreeing the risk appetite will ensure that the organization does not put too much (or too little) value at risk. The risk capacity of the organization needs to be fully utilized to ensure that risk taking is at the optimal level and delivers maximum benefit. Similarly, the organization should not put more value at risk than is appropriate, given the sector in which it operates and prevailing market conditions.

The portion of risk appetite that is associated with opportunities can be considered to be the opportunity investment that the organization is willing to embrace. Organizations will be willing to invest resources in opportunities that the organization believes will produce a positive gain. However, the organization should recognize that value put at risk in this way may not produce a positive gain. Implementation of strategic decisions may result in losses. In fact, more value can be destroyed by incorrect strategic decisions than by hazard, control or even compliance risks.

The organization may have an appetite for investing a sum of money in an opportunity, but it needs to be sure that it has the capacity to endure any loss that may result. It also needs to be sure that the total amount invested, or value at risk, is not beyond the capacity of the organization. Careful identification of the nature of the risks and calculation of the actual risk exposure associated with the opportunity should be undertaken.

Risk appetite and the risk matrix

Figure 25.1 illustrates the concepts of risk appetite, risk exposure and risk capacity. Risk appetite is illustrated by way of shaded squares on the risk matrix and the overall risk exposure of the organization is shown as a curved line. This illustration represents risk appetite, exposure and capacity for a risk-averse organization.

The medium-shaded area represents a situation where the organization is comfortable with taking the risk. The lighter areas represent the cautious and concerned

Figure 25.1   Risk appetite, exposure and capacity (optimal)

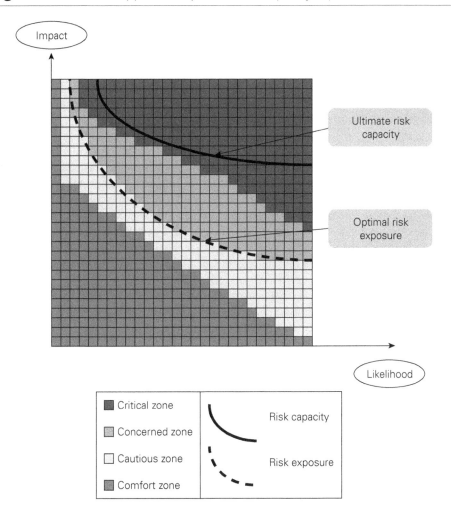

zones, where management judgement is required before the risk is accepted. The risks shown in the darkest area are critical risks and these risks will only be accepted when there is a business imperative.

The curved lines in Figure 25.1 represent the overall risk exposure of the organization and this is the optimal position, where the overall exposure cuts through the lighter section. The risk capacity of the organization is shown as higher than both the risk appetite and the risk exposure and is embedded well within the darker area. This represents an optimal state of affairs. This ensures that the organization is taking risks that are within the appetite of the board and not exceeding its ultimate risk capacity.

Total cost of risk calculations were commonplace in the 1980s and the intention was to calculate the total risk exposure. These calculations were usually undertaken by organizations or their insurance brokers. They enabled an organization to determine the total cost of hazard risks to the organization. The calculation had three main components: insurance premium, money spent on loss-control actions and cost of claims not covered by insurance.

Tables were published on the total cost of risk in various organizations and it was possible to benchmark the performance of an organization against other companies in the same sector. This sort of total cost of risk calculation was useful and was often used as a justification for setting up an in-house or captive insurance company, as discussed in Chapter 17.

The difficulty with this type of calculation was that it depended substantially on historical information. Historical loss data is not necessarily a good guide to future loss performance. This approach was intended to encourage organizations to seek the lowest overall cost for the management of hazard risks. Unfortunately, this lowest-cost approach often proved to be a mistake when a major incident occurred.

Organizations should be aware that the total cost of risk calculation could represent the lowest cost for the management of hazard risks, but that might be achieved at a high overall risk position. It is worth noting that the purchase of too much insurance could represent a position for the organization that is the lowest risk position but achieved at a high overall cost.

The type of total cost of risk calculation undertaken by organizations is now somewhat different. Organizations often use the concept of risk appetite to undertake calculations that identify the level of risk that the organization is willing to accept. The risk appetite of the board can then be compared with the actual risk exposure that the organization faces. The actual risk exposure in this calculation is an updated version of the total cost of risk calculation, but should include all types of risks – not just those that can be insured.

Generally speaking, as the marketplace becomes more volatile, the organization will be forced to increase its risk exposure. This requires a discussion in the boardroom leading to an agreement to increase the total value that the organization is willing to put at risk and/or to find mechanisms to reduce the total risk exposure. As a consequence, risk management becomes more important in times of rapid change and increased marketplace volatility.

Risk exposure will also increase when an organization decides whether to embark on a merger or acquisition. Organizations need to undertake an opportunity analysis of all acquisition opportunities and this analysis should include consideration of at least the following features of the acquisition opportunity:

- financial strength and reputation of the proposed acquisition;
- potential for developing further revenue/profit from the acquisition;
- risks associated with suggested purchase contract terms and conditions;
- anticipated profitability and sustainability of the proposed acquisition;
- investment required to deliver the anticipated future plans for the acquisition;
- impact on existing investment and business development plans.

Risk exposure is the actual cumulative total at risk, but it is often calculated on a risk-by-risk basis, without consideration of whether the risks are correlated. An organization will need to allow for correlation of risks and thereby take account of the likelihood of the risks materializing. When calculating the total actual risk exposure of the organization, it is important that the cumulative total of the values at risk is adjusted to take account of whether risks are correlated.

Risk and uncertainty

Figure 25.2 illustrates the range of outcomes for different risk exposures. In relation to opportunity investment, a range of outcomes are possible, from complete loss of the invested resources to a substantial gain. Sometimes, the losses may exceed the initial investment, if the total negative risk exposure associated with the investment is not correctly calculated.

Figure 25.2 represents the relationship between risk and uncertainty. It illustrates the typical range of outcomes for hazard risks, control risks and opportunity risks. By including all three types of risk in a single figure, it is possible to demonstrate that the three types of risk are related, interdependent and form a continuum. The sum of all of the hazard exposures, control acceptances and opportunity investments will represent the total risk appetite of the organization.

The curved lines in Figure 25.2 represent the range of possible outcomes for each risk position, to within a 95 per cent certainty or a 1 in 20 chance of being outside that range. An organization may decide that it has a risk appetite such that it is willing to tolerate a hazard risk shown at point A. Risk appetite point A represents the risk appetite for that type of hazard risk. In setting a risk appetite, the organization will realize that a range of outcomes for that risk appetite is possible. That range of outcomes is shown as the 95 per cent certainty lines.

Likewise, in pursuit of an opportunity, the organization will have an appetite represented by point B. Again, there will be a range of possible outcomes for this opportunity investment. The intended outcome is a positive return, but a loss may be suffered if the investment is not successful. The range of possible outcomes is demonstrated by the 95 per cent certainty lines. Figure 25.2 is used to demonstrate that a range of outcomes is possible when a value is put at risk.

Organizations face a number of risks that can cause disruption. These are the hazard risks that have been discussed throughout this book and give rise to the organization having a hazard exposure. In other words, the organization will be willing to accept exposure to certain hazard risks as part of its normal operations. Guide 73 defines risk appetite as the 'amount and type of risk that an organization is willing to pursue or retain'.

There will be a cost associated with hazard risks, both in terms of the cost of incidents that do occur and also in terms of the cost of loss-prevention, damage-limitation and cost-containment activities, including insurance costs. For each hazard risk, there will be a range of possible outcomes, all of them negative, and this is illustrated in Figure 25.2.

The organization will need to quantify the possible hazard risks and costs associated with those risks. It should be able to decide how much hazard risk it will tolerate, and this is part of the total risk appetite. Although the organization may

Figure 25.2   Risk and uncertainty

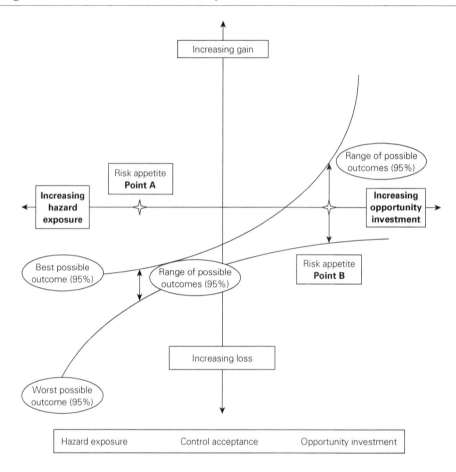

decide how much hazard risk it will tolerate, the actual exposure to hazard risks may be greater than anticipated. Many hazard risks are subject to legislation and organizations therefore face the compliance risks associated with that regulated hazard. Almost all organizations tend to have a zero-risk appetite for non-compliance with legislation.

Also, all organizations face uncertainties and the control risks that give rise to these uncertainties. These are risks linked to events that, if they materialize, will have uncertain outcomes. As an example of control risks, if all fraud controls in an organization were removed, there would be a net saving represented by the cost of the controls. However, fraudulent behaviour might result and substantial losses might be suffered, but there would be uncertainty about how much fraud would actually result from the removal of all controls.

There will be control risks embedded within the projects that the organization is currently undertaking. The cost of necessary controls may be part of the overall budget for a project. When planning a large project, it would be unwise not to include the cost of necessary controls in the budget for the project. The cost of the controls within the project budget represents the control acceptance of the organization.

Risk exposure and risk capacity

Figure 25.3 represents a risk-aggressive organization with a much larger comfort zone for accepting risk than the organization represented in Figure 25.1. The cautious and concerned zones are smaller and the darkest zone is an even smaller part of the overall matrix. This situation can be described as representing an approach that has a very limited universe of risk. The universe of risk for the organization is represented by the darkest squares and it is only in this area that the board of the organization will consider that the risks are significant.

The organization represented in Figure 25.3 has a greater risk appetite, simply because it has a more aggressive attitude to risk. By adopting a more aggressive attitude to risk, the organization will have fewer risks in the critical zone. In this case, the 'universe of risk' for the board of the organization will be very restricted. The 'universe of risk' shown in the diagram represents those risks that will be considered at board level. It can be seen in Figure 25.3 that a risk will have to be of very high likelihood and impact before it receives boardroom attention.

In Figure 25.3, the ultimate risk-bearing capacity of the organization is shown as within the lighter-shaded zones. This represents a situation where the organization may be taking risks that are beyond the ultimate risk capacity of the organization. To make circumstances worse, the actual risk exposure of the organization is shown as well within the darkest area. This makes the organization vulnerable to risk, because its actual risk exposure is shown to be well beyond its ultimate risk-bearing capacity.

The identification of the risk appetite for the organization requires judgement, and this judgement can be exercised at different levels within the organization. Consideration of risk appetite will be a strategic driver at board level. Risk appetite is likely to be an operational constraint at line-manager level because line managers will be expected to operate within the risk appetite policy that has been established by the board.

At the individual level, it is likely that consideration of risk appetite will be a behaviour regulator. This is because individual members of staff should only operate within the risk appetite framework that has been developed at board level and is implemented by line managers.

The definition and application of the concept of risk appetite remains a considerable difficulty for risk management practitioners. It is the case that many current risk management standards, as well as those that are under development, all state that organizations should recognize their risk appetite at an early stage. Although ISO 31000 does not explicitly use the phrase 'risk appetite', it suggests that an organization should establish the risk criteria at an early stage.

This appears to contradict a key tenet of risk management, which is to say that risks should not be managed out of context. Just as risks should not be managed out of context, so the identification of risk appetite out of context is illogical and probably impossible. Risk appetite has to be identified within the context of the organization, its strategy, tactics, routine operations and compliance core processes.

Figure 25.3   Risk appetite, exposure and capacity (vulnerable)

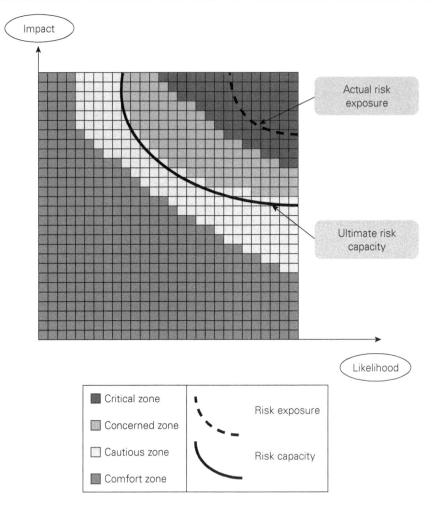

There can be no doubt that the topic of risk appetite will receive more attention in future, and risk management practitioners need to get a better understanding of what this concept means and how it can be applied. The riskiness index described in Chapter 14 takes a somewhat different approach.

Organizations, just like individuals, do not actively seek risk. An individual may be described as a risk taker, but the reality will be that such a person enjoys activities that have a high level of risk attached. It is the activity that appeals to the individual in the first instance, not the actual risk. People may be identified as risk takers because they have a high-risk hobby or pastime. That does not mean that the risk taking for this individual will extend to crossing a busy road without looking. In other words, risk taking has to be seen within the context of the activity and the intended rewards.

Organizations are similar in that it is the strategy, project or activity that appeals to the board, not the actual risk. An organization may embark on a risky strategy, approve a risky project or be operating risky activities or core processes. However, it is the business drivers and imperatives that are the primary concern for board members, not the level of risk involved. It is more often the case that the level of risk comes with the defined strategy, rather than the risk appetite defining the strategy.

Risk appetite statements

Other features associated with the risk appetite include the thought that an appetite will normally relate to a range of possible outcomes. Therefore, around the risk appetite there will be a certain zone of risk exposure or level of risk that is within appetite. This may be referred to as the risk tolerance range for exposure to that particular risk. COSO ERM (2004) defines risk tolerance as:

> The acceptable level of variation relative to achievement of a specific objective, and often is best measured in the same units as those used to measure the related objective. In setting risk tolerance, management considers the relative importance of the related objective and aligns risk tolerances with risk appetite. Operating within risk tolerances helps ensure that the entity remains within its risk appetite and, in turn, that the entity will achieve its objectives.

It should be noted that the nature of risk appetite relates to three different considerations. For some organizations, risk appetite may be a driver of strategy. This will be true for organizations such as banks and other financial institutions. For banks, risk is at the heart of the business and the appetite of an organization to, for example, lend money to particular companies or groups of people will be a reflection of its risk appetite and will be the main driver of the business. If risk appetite is a driver of the business, then the organization will wish to embrace risk in order to gain the benefits.

For many organizations, risk is not a driver of the business, but it is a consequence of the strategy, tactics, operations and compliance core processes that the business undertakes. In this case, risk appetite is unlikely to be a driver for the business but will be a planning mechanism for the organization to decide whether it wishes to adopt certain tactics, given the risks that would be embedded within those tactics, projects or changes. Where an organization is using risk appetite as a planning tool, the organization will wish to operate within certain tolerance levels and manage the uncertainty associated with risk.

In other circumstances, risk appetite may simply reflect the constraints that are placed on staff in the organization. Authorization levels, expenditure limits and other constraints are often established in a Delegation of Authority within an organization. Levels of authority are a clear indication of the risk appetite of the organization. In these circumstances, exposure to risk is a consequence of the size, nature and complexity of the organization, and the organization will wish to set limits that define risk appetite and thereafter mitigate or minimize the risk exposure and possible impact and consequences.

Table 25.2   Risk appetite statements

Assessment	Description
High risk appetite	The college accepts opportunities that have an inherently high risk that may result in reputation damage, financial loss or exposure, major breakdown in IT systems, significant incidents of regulatory non-compliance or high potential risk of injury to staff and students.
Moderate risk appetite	The college is willing to accept risks that may result in reputation damage, financial loss or exposure, major breakdown in IT systems, significant incidents of regulatory non-compliance, potential risk of injury to staff and students.
Modest risk appetite	The college is willing to accept some risks in certain circumstances that may result in reputation damage, financial loss or exposure, major breakdown in IT systems, significant incidents of regulatory non-compliance, potential risk of injury to staff and students.
Low risk appetite	The college is not willing to accept risks in circumstances that may result in reputation damage, financial loss or exposure, major breakdown in IT systems, significant incidents of regulatory non-compliance, potential risk of injury to staff and students.

In simple terms, if risk management is about achieving the most favourable outcome and reducing uncertainty, then risk appetite is about identifying the optimum level of risk that will achieve the most favourable outcome. Risk appetite is a reflection of the risk attitude and the risk criteria that have been established by the organization and the risks that it is willing to take. Risk appetite can be a driver of strategy, planning guide for tactics or a set of operating constraints.

Many organizations have attempted to produce risk appetite statements without clearly focusing on whether risk is a driver, planning guide or set of operating constraints. If all three approaches are applied, the risk appetite statement will reflect the complexity of that approach. Table 25.2 provides a set of risk appetite statements that could be in place for a college or educational establishment.

The stages that would be involved in developing this risk appetite statement are as follows:

1 Identify stakeholders and their expectations, making reference to the possible range of stakeholders, as defined by CSFSRS.

2 Define the company-wide risk exposure through an analysis of strategy, tactics, operations and compliance, as set out in the risk register.

3 Establish the desired level of risk exposure that will lead to a risk appetite statement that provides a set of qualitative and quantitative statements.

4 Define the range of acceptable volatility or uncertainty around each of the types of risks, leading to a statement of acceptable risk tolerances.

5 Reconcile the risk appetite and risk tolerances with the current level of risk exposure and plan actions to bring exposure in line with risk appetite.

6 Formalize and ratify a risk appetite statement, communicate the statement with stakeholders and implement accordingly.

Logically, risk appetite statements should be structured to align with the risk classification system used in the organization. Risk appetite statements may be structured on the basis of risk sources, components of the organization that may be impacted by the risk event and/or the impact or consequences categories, such as the FIRM risk scorecard, or the strategy, tactics, operations and compliance (STOC) of the organization. The Network Rail risk appetite statement summarized below uses a structure similar to the FIRM risk scorecard. Risk appetite statements can also be structured in a way that reflects the bow-tie approach to risk management shown in Figure 11.1. Table 25.3 shows an example of a risk appetite statement from a manufacturing organization.

Network Rail risk appetite statement

Network Rail has no appetite for safety risk exposure that could result in injury or loss of life to public, passengers and workforce. Safety drives all major decisions in the organization. All safety targets are met and improved year on year.

In the pursuit of its objectives, Network Rail is willing to accept, in some circumstances, risks that may result in some financial loss or exposure including a small chance of breach of the loan limit. It will not pursue additional income-generating or cost-saving initiatives unless returns are probable.

The company will only tolerate low to moderate gross exposure to delivery of operational performance targets including network reliability and capacity and asset condition, disaster recovery and succession planning, breakdown in information systems or information integrity.

The company wants to be seen as best in class and respected across industry. It will not accept any negative impact on reputation with any of its key stakeholders, and will only tolerate minimum exposure, that is minor negative media coverage, no impact on employees, and no political impacts.

Network Rail Limited
Annual Report and Accounts 2015

Risk appetite and lifestyle decisions

There is a relationship between personal risk appetite and lifestyle decisions. Decisions will be taken about, for example, long-term health issues, depending on family history and personal lifestyle. Decisions will also be taken on medium-term health issues, based on medical treatment, dieting and weight v. Short-term

Table 25.3   Risk appetite for a manufacturing organization

Business component	Risk appetite statement
Target credit rating	Maintain a credit rating of at least BBB+
Earnings per share	Maintain an earnings per share level within the upper quartile of the peer group
Target capital ratio	Maintain a debt-to-capital ratio in the range 45% to 50%
Self-sustaining growth	New business will not dilute target capital ratio and maintain a capital working ratio in the range 1.5% to 2%
Financial strength	Maintain an earnings-before-interest and taxes-to-interest ratio between 5% and 7.5%
Customer dependence	No single customer will exceed 15% of total sales
Regulatory compliance	Score in the upper quartile of the peer set in regulatory reviews
Social responsibility	Seek a position in the upper quartile of the peer group in a social responsibility index

decisions will also need to be taken on health issues, including those related to exercise, alcohol and recent illness or accident.

Individuals will need to take lifestyle decisions based on risk attitude, risk appetite, risk exposure and risk capacity. In relation to health issues, decisions will need to be taken on the level of exercise that the individual is willing to take in the short term to maintain weight within a healthy range.

There may be a certain appetite for risk issues associated with health and well-being, but the exposure that an individual actually suffers may be greater than the appetite for such risks. For example, people are willing to smoke cigarettes, but also wish to develop a healthier lifestyle. This is an example where the appetite for risk may be less than the actual risk exposure.

There is a tendency for people to take a course of action when the outcome is immediate, positive and certain. Therefore, a smoker will want a cigarette because the nicotine effect will be immediate, positive and certain. In contrast, giving up smoking will probably result in long-term benefit, but that benefit will be delayed and uncertain and there will also be negative feelings of being without nicotine.

The attitude of people to risk taking will vary considerably depending on the type of risk that is being considered. For example, individuals may be very risk-averse in the way they drive their cars, but accept significant risk factors in relation to their health. Risk appetite statements related to the risks that individuals are willing to take are, perhaps, just as difficult to construct as risk appetite statements for organizations. In both cases, a clearly defined risk attitude would help define the appetite for a range of risk factors.

Table 25.4   Controls for the risks of owning a car

Risk	Controls
Opportunities of owning a car (embrace the opportunities)	
1 You can travel more easily than depending on others	• Plan to make full use of the car • Inform friends and family of your mobility
2 Enhanced job opportunities because you will be more mobile	• Explore broader employment options • Pro-actively seek new employment
3 Save money on other forms of public transport	• Plan for optimum use of the car • Seek paying passengers (insurance required!)
Uncertainties of owning a car (manage the uncertainties)	
1 Cost of borrowing money to buy the car could change	• Borrow as little money as possible • If possible, obtain a fixed-rate loan
2 Price of fuel (petrol or diesel) could go up or down	• Buy the cheapest petrol available • Enter into a car-share pool
3 Maintenance, breakdown and repair costs will vary	• Arrange regular maintenance • Join vehicle breakdown service
Hazards of owning a car (mitigate the hazards)	
1 You pay too much for the car or it is in poor condition	• Benchmark relevant car prices • Arrange inspection to confirm condition
2 You are involved in a collision or road accident	• Drive carefully and defensively • Buy accidental damage insurance
3 The car gets stolen or vindictively damaged	• Fit appropriate security devices • Buy motor theft insurance
Compliance requirements of owning a car (minimize the compliance risks)	
1 Insufficient and/or inadequate third-party car insurance	• Buy insurance to cover all uses of the car • Read policy terms and conditions
2 Inattentive or aggressive driving results in traffic offence(s)	• Obey all road signs and instructions • Do not react to aggressive driving of others
3 Tyres in poor condition and other maintenance obligations	• Arrange routine safety checks • Check condition of tyres at start of journey

The willingness of individuals to take risks will also depend on the nature of the risk and the ability to put effective controls in place. Table 11.4 includes car ownership as one of the financial expenditure personal issues and Table 3.1 considers the specific compliance requirements, hazards, uncertainties and opportunities associated with owning a car. Table 25.4 outlines some of the cost-effective controls that can be put in place to mitigate hazards, manage uncertainties and embrace opportunities. Overall, the level of expenditure that an individual is willing to allocate to funding a control will be an indication of the risk attitude and risk appetite of that individual.

This practical example demonstrates part of the embrace, manage, mitigate and minimize (EM3) approach related to strategy, tactics, operations and compliance (STOC). The overall approach to personal and organizational issues should be to:

- embrace opportunity risks (strategy);
- manage uncertainty risks (tactics);
- mitigate hazard risks (operations); and
- minimize compliance risks (compliance).

Risk training and communication   26

Consistent response to risk

One of the main reasons for communicating risk information and providing risk training is to ensure that a consistent response to similar risk events is always achieved. This can only be ensured by sharing information and experience. A consistent response is required in relation to hazard, control and opportunity risks. When an organization has an intranet, this is an ideal way of achieving a consistent response to risk by ensuring that appropriate information is readily available.

As well as a consistent response to individual risks, consistent risk protocols also need to be defined and communicated. Part of ensuring a consistent response is to identify risks in advance and confirm the controls that will be in place for them. This approach is relevant to strategic, project and operational risks, and training and communication protocols should be introduced to increase the consistency of response to risk across the organization.

It should be a requirement of every organization that a risk assessment is attached to each capital expenditure request. This risk assessment should include both the risks that the project is seeking to manage and the risks within the project itself. The risks within the project may affect the ability to deliver the project on time, within budget and to specification.

Risk assessment attached to strategic analysis is also a vitally important issue and is part of ensuring a consistent response to risk. Production of an 'issues manual' as a means of communicating risk across the organization and ensuring a consistent response to risks may also be valuable. The issues manual will identify risks, circumstances and other events where a response is required. The provision of adequate information, supervision and training will ensure that consistent and appropriate risk management procedures are more likely to be followed.

An important consideration related to the need for consistent responses to risk is when a new risk appears or an existing risk changes substantially. In these circumstances, risk escalation may be required so that the changed circumstances are viewed by senior management. The design and introduction of robust risk escalation procedures is required, with appropriate training provided in these procedures.

The need for a consistent response to risk is vitally important in a crisis. When a disaster recovery plan has been produced by an organization, training for directors, managers and staff is essential. Also, the requirements of the business continuity plan will need to be communicated to all persons who may be affected if the plan is implemented. Again, the importance of training in order to ensure a consistent response to adverse circumstances is essential.

Risk training and risk culture

As set out in Table 24.3, the risk culture of the organization can be defined by leadership, involvement, learning, accountability and communication (LILAC). The LILAC headings also provide an indication of the components of a successful initiative to embed risk management in the organization. The involvement, learning, accountability and communication components of a risk-aware culture are all highly relevant to risk training and risk communication.

Appropriate risk management documentation will provide managers and staff with information on the involvement that is required and the level of accountability that the organization expects. A good level of learning and communication can be established by adequate risk training and this will enhance the risk-aware culture of the organization.

Consider the example of a publisher facing libel and slander risks. The company should prepare risk guidelines, protocols and procedures including reference to awareness training for all staff. Comprehensive procedures for managing libel and slander risks should reflect the level of risk exposure. The level of attention paid to such risks will depend on each magazine title and the following framework may be appropriate:

- all journalists to be given basic libel and slander training;
- specific review procedures introduced for political titles;
- legal evaluation of every issue of a satirical magazine.

Training needs to be provided for staff in the revised procedures, and information should be included on the company intranet site. Managers and staff need to be encouraged to comment on the new procedures, so that they may be improved further as part of the learning culture within the company.

Risk training is a key part of learning and communication and it is essential for manager, staff and other stakeholder engagement. It should cover a wide range of topics and achieve a greater understanding of all the risk-related issues, as well as providing information on the control measures that are in place and the vital role played by staff in the successful implementation of these controls. Risk management training is required on a continuing basis, but Table 26.1 provides some examples of when risk management training might be particularly relevant and/or necessary.

The following partial extract from the 2010 risk management handbook of the United Nations Educational, Scientific and Cultural Organization (UNESCO) is a good example of a well-structured training programme with clearly defined training objectives:

> The purpose of risk management training is to raise basic awareness of risk management concepts and mechanisms, to enable participants to identify and manage risks in their own units and to strengthen project management through adequate forward planning of potential risks.
>
> The half-day training module on risk management introduces the definition of risk and the purpose of risk management and discusses steps towards the effective management

of risks. The course goes beyond the provision of generic tools and extends to re-visiting elements of organizational culture, decision making and situational awareness.

By the end of the training session, participants should be able to:

- understand UNESCO's approach to risk management;
- understand how risk management affects decision-making;
- conduct a risk analysis by drawing up a risk profile and using a risk matrix;
- identify risks/uncertainties to achieving a set of objectives and expected results;
- prioritize these uncertainties; and
- decide how to act on the uncertainties.

Table 26.1   Risk management training

Examples of when to undertake risk training:

- When a manager is newly appointed or has been given new or additional responsibilities.
- When an individual member of staff has been given a new role and/or procedures have been updated.
- Following a recent incident or loss at the organization or at a competitor's premises or location.
- On a refresher basis – and this may be a legal requirement in certain circumstances.

When to provide safety training

When identifying the health and safety training needs within your organization, you should:

- take into account the capabilities, training, knowledge and experience of workers; and
- ensure that the demands of the job do not exceed their ability to carry out their work without risk to themselves and others.

Some employees may have particular training needs, for example:

- New recruits need basic induction training on how to work safely, including arrangements for first aid, fire and evacuation.
- People changing jobs or taking on extra responsibilities need to know about any new health and safety implications.
- Young employees are particularly vulnerable to accidents and you need to pay particular attention to their needs, so their training should be a priority. It is also important that new, inexperienced or young employees are adequately supervised.
- Some people's skills may need updating by refresher training.

Your risk assessment should identify any further specific training needs.

Risk information and communication

Component 7 of the COSO ERM cube considers the importance of risk information and communication. Risk communication starts with the identification of the stakeholders that have an interest in the particular risk under consideration. Once the stakeholders have been identified, the nature of the risk information that needs to be communicated must be decided. Finally, the purpose of communicating risk information to each group of stakeholders should be analysed.

Stakeholders will already have a perception of risks, so risk communication should be provided against the background of that existing perception. The guidelines relevant to risk communication set out in Table 26.2 should be followed. These guidelines seek to establish rules for communicating risk issues to a broad range of stakeholders.

Clearly, these rules become more important when the communication about risk is with external bodies. Nevertheless, they provide a useful set of guidelines for risk communication with internal as well as external stakeholders. Internal stakeholders have additional reasons for being provided with risk information. There will normally be an expectation by the organization that managers and staff will play a role in the future management of the risk, whereas this may not always be the case for external stakeholders.

The provision of risk training should be aligned with other training activities within the organization. As with all other types of training, the content of the training must be consistent with the requirements of the job. Training on risk matters will be required in a number of circumstances, including when new risks have appeared or existing

Table 26.2   Risk communication guidelines

Know the stakeholders, by identifying both external and internal stakeholders and finding out their interests and concerns

Simplify the language and presentation, although not the content if complex issues need to be communicated

Be objective in the information provided and differentiate between opinions and facts

Communicate clearly and honestly, taking account of the level of understanding of the audience

Deal with uncertainty and discuss situations where not all information is available and indicate what can be done to overcome these problems

Be cautious when putting risks in perspective, although comparing an unfamiliar risk with a familiar one can be helpful

Develop key messages that are clear, concise and to the point, with no more than three messages communicated at any one time

Be prepared to answer questions and agree to provide further information if it is not currently available

---

risks have changed significantly. Training will also be required when an individual takes a new job or assumes additional responsibilities. Also, risk training will be important after an incident has occurred and new or enhanced procedures are introduced.

An important part of risk information and communication is ensuring that there are adequate arrangements in place for 'whistleblowers'. Although members of staff and other individuals may collect confidential information about an organization that would not normally be disclosed, there need to be arrangements in place for staff and other stakeholders to raise concerns, if they have reasonable grounds for believing there has been serious malpractice. The text box below provides an extract from the University of Cambridge whistleblowing policy.

Whistleblowing investigation process

The person to whom the disclosure is made will normally consider the information and decide whether there is a prima facie case to answer. He or she will decide whether an investigation should be conducted and what form it should take. This will depend on the nature of the matter raised and may be:

- investigated internally;
- referred to the external auditors;
- the subject of independent enquiry.

Following investigation, some matters will need to be referred to the relevant outside body, including the police or funding council. If the person to whom the disclosure is made decides not to proceed with an investigation, the decision will be explained as fully as possible to the individual who raised the concern. It is then open to the individual to make the disclosure again either to another person or to the chair of the audit committee.

University of Cambridge

Shared risk vocabulary

Part of communicating successfully on risk matters is the development of a common language of risk. Appendix B provides the vocabulary that is used in this book, as well as making reference to the definitions used in ISO Guide 73, which provides internationally recognized terms related to risk management. However, it is sometimes necessary for an organization to develop its own risk vocabulary, for aspects that may be particular and unique to it. A common understanding of risk based on the use of terminology within the organization is more important than arguments about precisely what a term means to different risk management practitioners.

In fact, as part of aligning risk management effort and embedding risk considerations into routine operations, it may be appropriate for the risk manager to use the terminology already in place in an organization. Even if the vocabulary of the organization conflicts with strict risk management definitions, communication will be more successful if the established vocabulary is used.

In this book, a standard vocabulary has been used in order to assist with the introduction and explanation of concepts relevant to risk management. Sometimes, this vocabulary contradicts ISO Guide 73, but it has been used to aid communication and understanding. The subject of a risk vocabulary and agreeing definitions can take a great deal of time and effort, and compromise is usually required.

A common language and agreed definitions are important so that all parties to a discussion have the same understanding of the terminology being used. This is illustrated by the summary in the box below.

Common language of risk

The first reason an organization needs a risk language is to underpin its risk culture. Everyone in the organization has a role in an effective risk management process. Most organizations have many layers (eg executives, line managers and employees) and 'silos' (eg technology, treasury, operations, quality management and compliance). A common language is needed to cut through the layers and break down the silos. Conversely, without a common language, the risk management team will spend too much time resolving communication issues at the expense of their primary responsibilities.

Risk information on an intranet

Risk information can be made available to stakeholders by a variety of means. Many organizations produce brief guides and leaflets for stakeholders to communicate the current risk issues and concerns. The appropriate means of communication will vary according to the nature of the stakeholder and the nature and complexity of the message to be communicated.

Formal means of risk communication exist where the organization has to report to financial stakeholders. When risk communication is required, a range of communication techniques can be used. A formal report to the stock exchange or to other financial stakeholders may be backed up by an informal video, slide presentation and/or a telephone conference call, as appropriate.

There is often an additional means of risk communication available to organizations. Many organizations have developed an intranet for use by staff and this can be used to cover risk and risk management information. For many large organizations, it is common for the intranet to be used to communicate health and safety information and business continuity plans.

Information can be provided on the intranet about the generic risk assessments that have been undertaken and the control measures that have been identified. The intranet can also be used to communicate urgent risk information, as well as providing updates on risk assessments, control measures and the current level of any particular risk.

Table 26.3 Risk management information system (RMIS)

The following types of information may be handled, stored, managed, distributed and communicated using a risk management information system (RMIS):

Risk management policy and protocols

Risk profile data, values and information

Emergency contact arrangements and contact details

Insurance values and cost of risk data

Insurance claims handling and management protocols

Historical loss/claims experience/information

Insurance policy coverage and other information

Risk management action plans (risk register)

Risk improvement plans and implementation

Business continuity plans and responsibilities

Disaster recovery plans and responsibilities

Corporate governance arrangements and reports

An important consideration in the collection, retention and supply of risk information is that it should be aligned with other management information systems within the organization. Providing risk information as a separate management information stream is likely to result in risk management activities failing to be aligned or embedded within other activities. The danger that risk information will become irrelevant to managers in the organization is greater when the organization has a dedicated risk management information system (RMIS).

Risk management information systems (RMIS)

The distribution of risk management guidelines, protocols and procedures may be undertaken by way of a risk management information system (RMIS) software package. The RMIS could be placed on the intranet of the organization. The RMIS will also facilitate the collection and communication of risk information, including the reporting of events by local management as they occur. Typically, the RMIS could include a wide range of information, as summarized in Table 26.3.

RMIS have been used for some time to record details of insurance claims. In recent times, the use of a RMIS has become more sophisticated. It is now possible to record details of the risk exposure, risk control and risk action plans using such a software package. For RMIS that are used in connection with insurance, details of insurance policies, insurance claims procedures and insurance claims history can all be recorded and made available to authorized individuals. Such a system can also be used to pool risk exposure information and report accidents or other events that may lead to an insurance claim.

As well as information-recording RMIS systems, there are a number of software products that support risk management. These include software packages that can undertake various analytical activities and systems that can undertake risk analysis and dependency-modelling reviews.

It is generally accepted that the application of a RMIS software tool to an enterprise risk management (ERM) initiative can be very helpful. However, the disadvantage that is often encountered is that entering a substantial amount of risk data onto a computer database can be very time-consuming. Nevertheless, the benefits of having the data available for detailed analysis can make the effort worthwhile.

Risk information needs to be shared throughout an organization to enhance risk awareness and ensure improved risk performance. It is almost always the case that individuals within an organization will have the best understanding of the risks, as well as detailed practical knowledge of the actions that should be taken to mitigate risk events. Communication is also important to share information about incidents that have occurred, including lessons that were learnt and the actions that were taken to ensure that the event is not repeated.

An analysis of the advantages and disadvantages of RMIS is set out in the box below. In general, an RMIS becomes more valuable when the risks are complex or the amount of data that needs to be recorded is substantial.

Risk management information system (RMIS)

Without more advanced RMIS technology, risk managers are limited to recording the exposure data and loss experience of the company relevant to the ERM initiative, using techniques like modelling and scenario simulations.

It is possible that the cost of developing a robust, ERM-supportive RMIS will exceed the benefits. The costs are immediate and tangible; the benefit is difficult to estimate or demonstrate. Risk managers already struggle to explain the value of a loss that is prevented or financed. Even if the risk reduction is significant, it is a potential future benefit, not an assured, immediate expense reduction.

Whether the risk assessments from RMIS are likely to lead to enough marginal benefits to offset the cost of data tracking and analysis depends on the risk profile of the company. Large firms stand to gain the most from RMIS, but as the costs of the computing tools needed to collect data and perform the sophisticated modelling continue to decrease, the benefits grow for all organizations.

Ultimately, RMIS may pay for itself by enabling an organization to avoid or effectively finance that one catastrophic loss that would otherwise slash the financial results of the company.

Risk practitioner competencies   27

Competency frameworks

Risk management is increasingly seen as a profession, rather than a set of activities. For any profession, it is essential that a set of competencies is established that defines the activities that practitioners within the profession will need to display. There are several styles and formats for competency frameworks, but most are based on the stages that are involved in the practice of the profession. Having identified the stages that are involved in the profession, the levels of competency required at different stages of seniority are then described.

It is generally accepted that there are technical or hard skills that are required by individuals working in any profession, together with the range of people or soft skills that are required in order to become a successful practitioner in the profession. In short, the risk practitioner needs more than technical competence in order to successfully assist an organization with the design and implementation of a risk management framework.

Two areas of technical skills are required by a risk practitioner. Firstly, and most obviously, the practitioner needs to have competency across a range of risk management issues and activities. He or she will also need a range of business skills in order to understand the external context and internal context within which the organization operates. An understanding of business and the development of appropriate business skills is essential if the risk management practitioner is to successfully develop an appropriate risk management process and supporting risk management framework or internal context.

This textbook is not about the development of business skills, so the greater focus is placed on the risk management technical skills that will be required by the risk practitioner. These risk management technical skills will be closely aligned with the stages in the implementation of a risk management initiative, as set out in Appendix C. Table 27.1 provides an overview of the risk management technical skills that will be required by a successful risk management practitioner.

Range of skills

The range of skills required by a successful risk management practitioner includes technical or hard skills and people, interpersonal or soft skills. Technical skills can be divided into risk management technical skills and business technical skills. The risk

Table 27.1   Risk management technical skills

Skills associated with planning risk management strategy	
Evaluate status	Evaluate the organizational context and objectives and map the external and internal risk context
Develop strategy	Develop risk strategy and risk management policy and develop the common language of risk
Skills associated with implementing a risk management architecture	
Design architecture	Design and implement risk management architecture, roles and responsibilities
Develop processes	Develop and implement the risk management processes, procedures and protocols
Build awareness	Build a culture of risk awareness aligned with other management activities
Skills associated with measuring risk management performance	
Facilitate assessments	Facilitate the identification, analysis and evaluation of risks, and design record-keeping procedures
Evaluate controls	Evaluate existing performance and evaluate efficiency and effectiveness of existing controls
Improve controls	Facilitate the design and implementation of necessary and cost-effective control improvements
Skills associated with learning from risk management experience	
Evaluate framework	Evaluate risk management strategy, policies and processes, and introduce improvements
Design reports	Develop understanding of reporting requirements, design reporting formats and produce appropriate reports

management technical skills can be set out as a competency framework, in the way described in Table 27.1.

The range of business skills that will be required will vary according to the type of organization. In general, they will include skills related to accounting, finance, legal affairs, human resources, marketing, operations and information technology.

The importance of people skills has increased considerably as communication within and between organizations has changed. People skills are often referred to as soft skills. Technical skills are usually considered to be associated with intellectual intelligence, whereas soft or people skills are associated with emotional intelligence. To be successful, the risk practitioner needs a combination of both types of intelligence and both sets of skills.

Benefits of people or 'soft' skills

While labelling them 'soft' may make them sound less important than technical skills, in fact people skills are essential for all businesses, and can actually mean the difference between success and failure. Employing staff with good people skills will mean they are more effective when interacting with people. This is particularly important if your business is largely based on face-to-face contact with clients.

Just as technical skills can be learnt and developed, so too can people skills. In fact, people skills are continuously developed over the course of a lifetime, but there are ways that you can encourage this in your business. These include workshops, seminars and encouragement to staff to provide input, suggestions and advice in business discussions.

As well as technical and people skills, the successful risk manager will also require the skills associated with self-management and self-development. Typically, these will be the skills expected of all technical professionals and will often be underpinned by adherence to a code of ethics or code of conduct. Self-development covers activities that enhance talents and potential, as well as increasing job satisfaction and future employability. Self-development also includes developing other people, and this may include activities such as teacher, mentor, training provider and/or professional coach.

Table 27.2 describes the range of people skills that are required in the business environment. These skills can be classified as communication, relationship, analytical and management (CRAM) skills. Technical skills can be acquired through a combination of training and experience, but people skills are far more reliant on the personality of the individual. Therefore, it is a greater challenge for risk practitioners to master the range of people skills that are required in order to be successful.

Table 27.2 People skills for risk management practitioners

Key skill	Skill requirements
Communication	• Excellent written and oral skills • Presentation and public-speaking skills • Committee and meeting participation skills
Relationship	• Influencing skills to work with 'challenging' behaviour • Negotiating skills to defuse conflict and identify solutions • Networking skills across organizational silos
Analytical	• Strategic thinking skills and creativity skills • Data-handling skills to get to the heart of a problem • Research skills to present arguments based on facts
Management	• Time-management skills to manage teams and projects • Leadership skills to motivate and develop staff • Facilitation skills to assist with setting priorities

Communication skills

Accurate communication on risk issues is vitally important. Internal communication within the organization will be undertaken through the risk architecture. This is the formal risk communication structure related to risk control activities and the collecting of information for external risk reporting purposes. For example, a road haulage company may wish to bring focus to the efficient operation of the organization and ensure that risk management receives appropriate attention.

In these circumstances, the company might decide to introduce a number of measurable loss-control programmes. The board of the company has requested a report at every board meeting on the number of road accidents, frequency of vehicle breakdowns, level of fuel consumption and reported incidents during deliveries. These reports will enable the board to benchmark the performance of the company, in comparison both with competitors and with historical data for the company itself. In this case, the board is monitoring performance, whereas the management of the improved risk performance remains an executive responsibility to be delivered by line management.

Within some organizations, risk communication may also be more informal. Communication will take place during risk assessment workshops and at risk training courses. Communication arrangements are part of the risk culture. External risk communications will need to take place with external stakeholders, including the media, the general public and pressure groups.

For example, if a road haulage company wishes to extend its vehicle storage depot, there will be a need to communicate with stakeholders, as well as local authority planning departments. The company will need to prepare arguments that provide an evaluation of any risks to the community that may increase when the depot is extended. The public perception of what is proposed and the impact on the vicinity may not be fully accurate. Accordingly, the company will need to prepare honest, open and detailed arguments that assure all interested parties that adequate risk control arrangements are in place.

The box below provides an example of risk communication in relation to nuclear and chemical industries in the United States. The lesson here is that the public perception of risk may not be aligned with the scientific evidence. The information presented by an organization needs to do more than present intellectual information. The communication should also address emotional concerns.

Development of risk communication

The formal development of risk communication as a subject began in the late 1970s with efforts by the nuclear and chemical industries in the United States to counteract widespread public concern about those technologies. It was believed that clear, understandable information was all that was needed to make people see that the risks were lower than many feared.

For decades this approach has failed, and most risk communication experts say it is inadequate. Perceptions of risk, and the behaviours that result, are a matter not only of the facts but also of our feelings, instincts and personal life circumstances. Communication that offers the facts but fails to account for the affective side of our risk perceptions is simply incomplete.

Risk communication is also commonly thought of as what to say under crisis circumstances, but this is inadequate. While it is certainly true that communication in times of crisis is important in managing the public response, countless examples have taught that a great deal of the effectiveness of risk communication during a crisis is based on what was done beforehand.

An important consideration in relation to communication skills is the ability to run a training course. In particular, risk practitioners will need to facilitate risk assessment workshops. There are a number of basic skills that are required in running a successful workshop, but the starting point is to establish its structure and format. In general, the key will be to ensure that the discussion is well structured and that all attendees have an opportunity to contribute on an equal basis.

Techniques that are used during workshops include the use of sticky notes to capture ideas from delegates. These notes are then collated according to the way they relate to the specific questions that have been asked. Consolidation of the many ideas into a small number of agreed issues requires skill on the part of the facilitator, who will need to identify similarities in the ideas and consolidate compatible ideas into a smaller number of issues or, more specifically, identified risks.

Running training courses requires a different set of skills, although the overriding requirement to engage all attendees remains a top priority. It is often said that training courses should be based on the three-stage approach of: tell the delegates what you are going to tell them, tell them it and, finally, tell them what you have told them. Although this approach seems laboured and unsophisticated, it is usually the most successful way of ensuring that the messages are transmitted and received. Perhaps it is more structured to consider that a training course should be in three parts, as shown in Table 27.3.

Table 27.3   Structure of training courses

Stage		Intention
1	Set up	This stage will describe what the course will provide. It is often achieved by delegate introductions and expectations, a group exercise or a simple quiz to get everybody thinking about the topic of the day.
2	Set out	This stage provides the detailed information that the training course is intended to impart. It can be a combination of structured inputs, group tasks, discussion exercises, feedback sessions and training films.
3	Set down	This stage summarizes what the course has covered and confirms general understanding. It will often ask delegates to confirm what they have learnt and/or indicate what actions they will take following the course.

Other communication skills relate to verbal and written presentation skills. These will include the ability to write reports, both for internal and external distribution. Depending on the organization, the style of written reports will vary greatly. Most organizations require short summary reports for the board with substantial back-up papers available if required. It is important that the risk practitioner adopts the style of communication that fits within the culture of the organization.

If graphics are normally contained in reports, then the presentation of risk information can be used in this style. However, if all reports within the organization are narrative only, then it becomes a challenge to the risk practitioner to present risk reports in an engaging way only with the use of words. Likewise, if the risk practitioner is invited to make a presentation to the board, then the style of presentation must be in keeping with other board presentations. Detailed preparation and knowledge of relevant background information is essential.

When making a presentation to the board, it is important for the risk practitioner to decide what should be gained from the presentation. If the risk practitioner is only providing a report for information, that is a different style of presentation from a report to the board that is requiring a decision and/or authorization to take a specific course of action. The expression 'know your audience and their expectations' is vitally important when the audience is the board of the organization.

When communicating a message, it is useful to think about the '5Cs' of communication. The message should be clear, concise, coherent, credible and complete:

- clear message will ensure that the recipient understands your purpose in communicating with them;
- concise message is more likely to be received because you have stuck to the point and kept it brief;
- coherent message is logical with all the points being connected and relevant to the main topic;
- credible message will convince the audience that you understand their concerns and priorities;
- complete message provides the audience with everything they need in order to take necessary action.

Relationship skills

There is a range of relationship skills that are required, as indicated in Table 27.2. Perhaps the most important are influencing and negotiating skills. Relationship skills are important, including motivation and political skills. As with other people skills, relationship skills need to be exercised within the culture of the organization and in a way that pays full regard to its internal context.

Relationship skills also include listening skills. It is vitally important to listen to the point of view of an individual you are negotiating with or are seeking to influence. Generally speaking, influence is achieved by using positive energy and enthusiasm about the issues that need to be changed.

Successful influencing is best achieved by individuals who have the ability to gain support, inspire others, create relationships and engage the imaginations of other people. Achieving improvements in risk management standards often requires continuous negotiation. The means of achieving successful negotiations are well established, and risk practitioners need to be aware of and embrace negotiating techniques.

Political skills can often be difficult and the subject sounds quite sinister. Nevertheless, in being a good influence, the successful risk practitioner needs to understand the importance of political skills. All organizations have challenging individuals who display inappropriate behaviours. The risk practitioner will need to understand group dynamics and be able to defuse conflict and negotiate solutions in a flexible way. Political skills include awareness of cultural influences and differing stakeholder requirements.

In many ways, political skills are at their most important when the risk practitioner is chairing a meeting. All persons attending the meeting are entitled to voice their opinion in full, for as long as their message is clear, concise, coherent and credible. The role of a chairman, especially when present in a non-executive role is to stay neutral and remain unbiased whilst guiding the meeting to an appropriate consensus.

The essence of relationship skills is to build relationships with various stakeholders. A risk practitioner must engage with stakeholders who will be many and varied, as discussed in Chapter 29. The range of stakeholders in an organization will include customers, staff, financiers, suppliers, regulators and society (CSFSRS). With such a wide range of stakeholders, not all of whom will be interested in risk and risk management, it is obvious that the risk practitioner needs excellent communication and relationship skills.

Confronting the opinions of some stakeholders will require risk practitioners to have very well-developed people skills. An example of the challenges faced by risk practitioners in general, and health and safety specialists in particular, is offered by Jeremy Clarkson, when he worked at the BBC, and who wrote in the *Sunday Times* on 4 April 2004:

> Health and Safety is now so out of control that I find it nearly impossible to do my job. On *Top Gear*, we refer to the BBC health and safety people as Prohibition Officers from the PPD or the Programme Prevention Department.

Analytical skills

Analytical skills range widely and require strategic and logical thinking. On occasions, when problem solving is involved then creative lateral thinking is also a key requirement of the risk practitioner. Many risk practitioners are involved in quantification of risks, either as part of a Basel II capital requirement calculation or as part of an analysis to determine the appropriate level of insurance that is required.

However, analytical skills are not always mathematically based and well-developed problem-solving skills will be of considerable benefit to a typical risk practitioner. In addition to analytical skills, research skills are often a requirement of many risk practitioners. The ability to locate and analyse information quickly and efficiently will be of considerable benefit to a risk practitioner.

Risk practitioners are often required to evaluate a great deal of information about a specific topic, find the common thread within that information and present the findings in a concise and logical manner. This will almost invariably be a requirement when the risk practitioner is drafting a written report or preparing a training course or presentation. The benefit of being skilled in analytical activities is at its greatest when the risk practitioner is seeking to facilitate a risk assessment workshop.

It is often the case in risk assessment workshops that the delegates will have different views of the level of risk presented by a specific situation. A skilful facilitator is able to listen to these conflicting views and identify the underlying presumptions that have resulted in the different conclusions. Having identified the presumptions and assumptions, the skilled facilitator will then be able to challenge the different parties with the reasons for their differing opinions. This will be the most successful way of coming to a common view.

Analytical skill involves the ability to understand, challenge and articulate problems and concepts and thereby make decisions based on the available information. These skills include the ability to demonstrate and apply logical thinking to the gathering and analysis of information, as well as the designing and testing of solutions to problems. The output from analytical skills is the ability to formulate appropriate alternative solutions and challenge the alternatives so as to develop the most logical plan of action.

Problem solving and decision making are important skills for business life. Problem solving often involves decision making and decision making is especially important for risk management. There are activities and techniques to improve decision making and the quality of decisions. Decision making is more natural to certain personalities, so these people should focus more on improving the quality of their decisions. People who are less natural decision makers are often able to make quality assessments, but may need to be more decisive in acting upon the decisions made.

Problem solving and decision making are closely linked and each requires creativity in identifying and developing options. Brainstorming techniques are particularly useful and these will include SWOT and PESTLE analysis structures. Good decision making requires a mixture of skills, including creative development and identification of options, clarity of judgement, firmness of decision and effectiveness of implementation.

Management skills

Although it is typical for risk management departments to be quite small, this is not always the case. In any event, even if the risk practitioner does not have direct management responsibilities, there is a need to understand management skills. Such skills may be relevant in relation to persuading other managers to take a different course of action. This awareness of management skills should extend to team management and delegation of authority.

Many of the people skills described in this section are also relevant as management skills. Perhaps the most important of these people skills as a manager is that of motivation. Motivational skills are important for risk practitioners, especially where a change in behaviour or a development of risk-aware culture is required. The risk practitioner will need to motivate individuals, managers and directors to behave differently.

Also of considerable importance are self-management skills. These will include the ability to set appropriate priorities, meet necessary deadlines and maintain self-motivation. Time management, organizational and self-motivation skills remain important for the risk practitioner throughout his or her working life.

Perhaps it is worth reflecting on the fact that there is a difference between management and leadership. An individual may be able to manage a department by exercising tight control over the activities of individuals. This is not the same as the leader who has established a set of priorities and empowers members of the team to manage their own activities towards fulfilment of those priorities. Ideally, the leader will have ensured that the priorities have been developed in full consultation with the individuals responsible for delivering those priorities.

Leadership versus management

The biggest difference between managers and leaders is the way they motivate the people who work for them and this sets the tone for most other aspects of what they do.

Managers have subordinates and have a position of authority and their subordinates work for them and largely do as they are told. Managers are paid to get things done and pass on this work-focus to their subordinates. Managers seek control and this indicates that they are relatively risk-averse and they will seek to avoid conflict where possible.

Leaders have followers, rather than subordinates. Many organizational leaders do have subordinates, but only because they are also managers. When they want to lead, they give up formal authoritarian control. Leaders consider it natural to encounter problems that must be overcome. They are comfortable with risk and will see routes that others avoid as potential opportunities, but may break rules in order to get things done.

PART SEVEN
Risk governance

PART SEVEN FURTHER READING

APM Publishing (2010) *Project Risk Analysis and Management Guide* **https:// www.apm.org.uk**

British Standard BS 13500:2013 *Code of practice for delivering effective governance of organizations*, **www.standardsuk.com**

London Stock Exchange (2004) *Corporate Governance: A practical guide*, **www. londonstockexchange.com**

Office of Government Commerce (2007) *Management of Risk: Guidance for practitioners*, **www.tsoshop.co.uk**

Taleb, NN (2008) *The Black Swan: The impact of the highly improbable*, **www.penguin.co.uk**

Woods, M (2011) *Risk Management in Organizations: An integrated case study approach*, **www.routledge.com**

PART SEVEN CASE STUDIES

Severn Trent Water: Our approach to risk

We have set ourselves some very challenging targets and continually strive to improve our standards of service delivery to customers and our overall performance. The group's risk management and internal control systems are vital to the delivery of these targets and enable the identification, assessment and mitigation of risks inherent in our business activities.

Accountability for the effectiveness of the group's enterprise risk management (ERM) policies sits with the board, with oversight from the executive team, supported by operational risk owners and the central ERM team who are responsible for carrying out the ERM process.

Within Severn Trent Water, our approach reflects our status as a regulated utility providing essential services and operating as part of the critical national infrastructure for the UK. We aim to have a strong control framework in place to enable us to understand our risks and manage these risks both effectively and efficiently.

In our non-regulated businesses we take a more commercial approach to our decisions around which risks are acceptable. However, we recognize that we provide products and services for clients who operate in regulated environments. As a result, for risks that could impact on our clients' services, we take a similar approach to risk as in our own regulated business.

The ERM process covers all types of risk including operational, financial, legal and regulatory. Our assessment of risk includes explicit consideration of the possible impact of the risk on the reputation of the group as a whole. Resilience of our services is vital and we regularly carry out exercises jointly with other agencies such as local authorities, police and fire services to test this resilience.

Edited extract from Severn Trent Plc
Annual Report and Accounts 2015

Tim Hortons: Sustainability and responsibility

Sustainability and responsibility at Tim Hortons is integrated through a framework that is divided into three core pillars: individuals, communities and the planet. Within each pillar are a number of key issues determined to be of importance to our stakeholders such as nutrition, food safety, employees, children, animal welfare, community giving, environmental stewardship, climate change and sustainable supply-chain practices. We have developed a number of commitments and goals with respect to each of these areas of focus, and have reported our performance against these goals in our annual sustainability and responsibility report.

Our sustainability and responsibility policy includes a structure and supporting processes for effective sustainability and responsibility governance and accountability, and is reviewed regularly. The board governs sustainability and responsibility through the nominating and corporate governance committee of the board. Oversight activities include: review of policy development; sustainability and responsibility strategies, including mitigation of risks; and organizational sustainability and responsibility commitments, goals and external reporting. Management accountability for sustainability and responsibility resides within the Tim Hortons executive group.

The assessment and management of sustainability-related risks and opportunities is embedded as part of our governance framework, as is our sustainability and responsibility strategy and its supporting implementation plan. Key aspects of our approach include the assessment of sustainability and responsibility impacts of major business decisions; the integration of sustainability and responsibility into the enterprise risk management programme, as applicable; the development of internal performance scorecards; monitoring our relations with our stakeholders; the assessment of sustainability and responsibility trends; and consideration of public policy, consumer, corporate, and general public trends, issues, and developments that may impact the company.

Edited extract from 2013 Tim Hortons
Annual Report on Form 10-K

DCMS: Capacity to handle risk

Within the core department, risk is managed actively and risk management is embedded into all departmental processes. The department's risk framework identifies risk management as a key role of the board, the executive board and its sub-committees. Policy and guidance are available to staff on the intranet, and risk management masterclasses have been provided. The corporate committee has overall responsibility for the risk management framework.

The risk management framework consists of three management levels at which risks are managed:

- At the local level, risk is managed and risk registers maintained by policy and operational teams and by project and programme teams across the department.

- At the committee level, risk is managed by the corporate committee. The committee maintains its own risk register and manages red-rated operational risks within the corporate area.

- Risks escalated by the corporate committee, investment committee, governance board and department-wide operational, delivery and strategic risks are managed by the executive board.

An internal audit review of the department's risk management systems found that they provided reasonable assurance. It concluded that the department understood and was managing key business risks for business as usual and programme activities. However, differing approaches to risk management methodology showed there is not universal compliance with the agreed risk management framework or single-risk severity scoring method, and that it needed to develop a more structured and consistent approach to monitoring and comparing risks in these areas.

Edited extract from Department of Culture, Media and Sports
Annual Report and Accounts for the year ended 31 March 2014

Corporate governance model

28

Corporate governance

Corporate governance covers a very wide range of topics, and risk management is an integral part of the successful corporate governance of every organization. Most countries in the world place corporate governance requirements on organizations. These requirements are particularly strong in relation to companies quoted on stock exchanges, organizations that are registered charities and government departments, agencies and authorities. For instance, companies listed on the London Stock Exchange have to be guided by the UK Corporate Governance Code (2016) published by the Financial Reporting Council.

The purpose of corporate governance is to facilitate accountability and responsibility for effective and efficient performance and ethical behaviour. It should protect executives and employees in undertaking the work they are required to do. Finally, it should ensure stakeholder confidence in the ability of the organization to identify and achieve outcomes that its stakeholders value.

There are two main approaches to the enforcement of corporate governance standards. Some countries treat corporate governance requirements as 'comply or explain'. In other words, the organization should comply with the requirements or explain why it was not appropriate, necessary or feasible to comply. If appropriate, an organization could explain that an alternative approach was taken to achieve the same result. In these countries, the requirements may be regarded as one means of achieving good practice, but equally effective alternative arrangements are also acceptable.

Other countries require full compliance with detailed requirements, although limited alternatives for achieving compliance are sometimes included within these requirements. In these countries detailed compliance is expected and exceptions would not be acceptable.

Corporate governance requirements should be viewed as obligations placed on the board of an organization. These requirements are placed on board members by legislation and by various codes of practice. Often, these corporate governance requirements are presented as detailed codes of practice. To start the task of enhancing corporate governance standards, an organization may develop a code of ethics for company directors, together with appropriate 'delegation of authority' documents. An annual statement of any potential 'conflicts of interest' should be required from directors and training should be provided for the board on corporate governance.

Also, the organization should set up appropriate committees (as listed below) with established terms of reference and membership of each of these committees, which may be established as sub-committees of the board. Reports on corporate governance standards, concerns and activities should be received at every board meeting, and these papers will often be presented by the company secretary. Such committees may include:

- risk management committee;
- audit committee;
- disclosures committee;
- nominations committee;
- remuneration committee.

Purpose of corporate governance

The purpose of corporate governance is to facilitate accountability and responsibility for efficient and effective performance, and ethical behaviour. It should protect executives and employees in undertaking the work they are required to do. Finally, it should ensure stakeholder confidence in the ability of an organization to identify and achieve outcomes that its stakeholders value.

OECD principles of corporate governance

A basic definition of corporate governance is 'the system by which organizations are directed and controlled'. Corporate governance is therefore concerned with systems, procedures, controls, accountabilities and decision making at the highest level and throughout an organization.

Because corporate governance is concerned with the way that senior management fulfil their responsibilities and authority, there is a large component of risk management contained in the overall corporate governance structure for every organization. Corporate governance is concerned with the need for openness, integrity and accountability in decision making, and this is relevant to all organizations regardless of size or whether in the public or private sector.

The Organization for Economic Cooperation and Development (OECD) is an international organization helping governments tackle the economic, social and governance challenges of a globalized economy. The OECD updated (in 2015) the set of principles for corporate governance and these are set out in Table 28.1. These principles focus on the development of an effective corporate governance framework that pays due regard to the rights of stakeholders.

The principles require the equitable treatment of all stakeholders and an influential role for stakeholders in corporate governance. Finally, the principles require disclosure and transparency. All of these principles are delivered by the board of the organization and the principles, therefore, make detailed reference to the responsibilities of the board.

Table 28.1   OECD principles of corporate governance

I. Effective corporate governance framework	Promote transparent and fair markets, efficient allocation of resources and be consistent with the rule of law and support effective supervision and enforcement.
II. Rights and equitable treatment of shareholders	Protect and facilitate the exercise of shareholder rights and ensure equitable treatment of all shareholders, including minority and foreign shareholders.
III. Institutional investors, stock markets and other intermediaries	Sound incentives throughout the investment chain and provide for stock markets to function in a way that contributes to good corporate governance.
IV. Role of stakeholders in corporate governance	Recognize the rights of stakeholders established by law or through mutual agreements and encourage active co-operation between corporations and stakeholders.
V. Disclosure and transparency	Timely and accurate disclosure is made on all material matters, including the financial situation, performance, ownership and governance of the company.
VI. Responsibilities of the board	Strategic guidance of the company, the effective monitoring of management by the board and the board accountability to the company and the shareholders.

There have been a number of standards published recently on corporate governance and British Standards has recently published BS 13500:2013 'Code of practice for delivering effective governance of organizations'. When it published the standard, British Standards commented that: 'It is increasingly obvious that society's expectations of organizational behaviours and performance, and thus: "governance", are rising. This rise in expectations is partly in response to a steady flow of major incidents and perceived abuses of authority.'

The approach in BS 13500 is based on the evidence that good governance promotes success of organizations and society. Therefore, the scope of the code goes beyond the avoidance or mitigation of problems. It defines different accountabilities to different stakeholders and is intended to be used as a basic checklist to ensure that all the elements of a good governance system are in place. The point is also made that having a corporate governance system in place does not guarantee effective governance, but it does encourage and support positive organizational values and behaviours.

LSE corporate governance framework

The London Stock Exchange (LSE) has produced guidance on corporate governance, and the focus of that guidance is on the effectiveness of the board. In the view of LSE,

Figure 28.1   LSE corporate governance framework

corporate governance is about the effective management of the organization and the appropriate responsibilities and the role of the senior managers and board members within the organization.

Figure 28.1 provides a summary representation of the London Stock Exchange governance framework. Governance activities are centred on the board of the organization and the LSE guidance refers to these boards as supervisory and managerial boards. The corporate governance framework has two main components: 1) the responsibilities, obligations and rewards of board members; and 2) the fulfilment of stakeholder expectations, rights, participation and dialogue.

The importance of board member responsibilities, obligations and rewards are emphasized and include arrangements for:

- determining membership of the board;
- accountability of board members;
- delegation of authority from the board;
- remuneration of board members.

The responsibilities of board members must be fulfilled in five important areas, in respect of the fulfilment of stakeholder expectations, rights, participation and dialogue. In summary, these five areas are:

- strategic thinking, planning and implementation;
- corporate social responsibility;

- effective management of risks;
- audit and risk assurance;
- full and accurate disclosure.

The OECD principles and the LSE corporate governance framework provide the overall requirements and framework within which corporate governance must be delivered. However, the activities that are employed to deliver each of the five areas of stakeholder expectation will vary.

Risk management activities should be viewed within the wider framework of corporate governance. Although risk management is presented as a separate component of corporate governance in the LSE framework, risk issues also underpin strategy, corporate social responsibility, audit and disclosure.

Non-executive directors play an important role in corporate governance. Generally speaking, the audit committee will be a non-executive group and represents the third line of defence, as described in Chapter 35. It is generally accepted that an effective non-executive director will:

- uphold the highest ethical standards of integrity and probity;
- support executives in their leadership of the business;
- monitor the conduct of executives;
- question, debate, challenge and make decisions objectively;
- listen to the views of others inside and outside the board;
- gain the trust and respect of other board members;
- promote the higher standards of corporate governance;
- seek compliance with the provisions of applicable governance codes.

Corporate governance for a bank

Corporate governance and risk management activities within a financial organization are strictly governed and regulated. Most financial organizations, including banks, produce their own internal corporate governance guidelines. Typically, these guidelines will cover director qualifications, director responsibilities and the responsibilities and delegated authority of board committees. The guidelines should also consider arrangements for the annual performance evaluation of the board and the arrangements for senior management succession.

The corporate governance structure will normally be a set of governing principles for the conduct of the board of directors. These governing principles will include information for board members on dealing with conflicts of interest, confidentiality and compliance with laws, rules and regulations.

A major part of ensuring adequate corporate governance for a financial institution will be adequate training and induction for board members. Typically, the orientation programme for new members of the board will include details of:

- the legal and regulatory framework;
- risk management;

- capital management and group accounting;
- human resources and compensation;
- audit committee, internal audit and external audit;
- communication, including branding.

The global financial crisis has resulted in banks and other financial institutions reviewing their own corporate governance standards. The review in the box below provides an overview of a large national bank and sets out criticisms of that bank in relation to failures of corporate governance.

Operational risk

The bank is the largest financial services institution listed on the national stock exchange and is among the 30 most profitable financial services organizations in the world. In January 2004, the bank disclosed to the public that it had identified substantial losses relating to unauthorized trading in foreign currency options. These losses were classified as operational risk.

Concurrent issues of further substantial losses on home loans called into question the strength of the risk management practices and lack of auditor independence, reinforcing the view that corporate governance had not been given the priority it deserved over a number of years.

Corporate governance for a government agency

For government agencies, robust corporate governance arrangements are usually mandatory. Also, for many government agencies, the main reason for paying attention to risk management is to ensure that adequate corporate governance arrangements are in place. In other words, the main motivation for ensuring good standards of risk management in a typical government agency will be the desire to support the corporate governance arrangements in the agency. Figure 28.2 shows the corporate governance components for a typical government agency.

For commercial organizations, corporate governance and risk management are designed to assist the organization to achieve its objectives, including commercial or marketplace objectives. The motivation for government departments to ensure good standards of corporate governance is narrower and is often focused on accountability.

In government agencies, the driving principles include value for money and avoidance of inappropriate behaviour. Corporate governance is often seen by government agencies as establishing a framework of control that supports innovation, integrity and accountability and encourages good management throughout the organization.

Figure 28.2   Corporate governance in a government agency

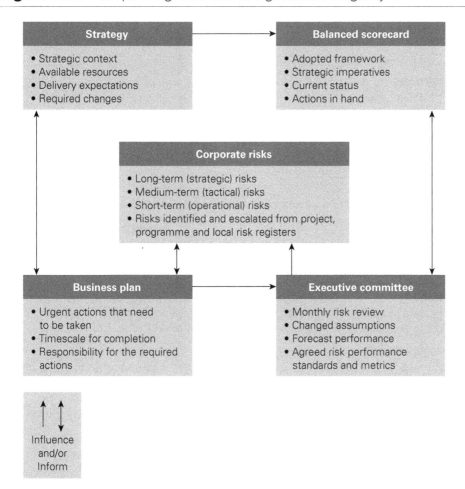

Within the corporate governance framework, responsibilities of individual members of staff are frequently specified. The reporting structure for risk issues is also outlined. Linking risk management efforts to corporate governance can also enable specific areas of risk to be identified for particular attention. Typically, these will include value for money, business continuity, fraud prevention and IT security assurance. Underpinning corporate governance activities within a government department, agency or authority will be the principles of public life, often referred to as the Nolan principles. These principles are set out in Table 28.2.

The box below provides an example of the importance of corporate governance arrangements within a government agency. The important contribution of risk management and corporate governance arrangements and management practices is highlighted in this example.

Table 28.2   Nolan principles of public life

1 **Selflessness**
Holders of public office should act solely in terms of the public interest and should not seek benefits for themselves, their family or friends.

2 **Integrity**
Holders of public office should not place themselves under any financial or other obligation to outside individuals or organizations.

3 **Objectivity**
In carrying out public business, the holders of public office should make choices on merit.

4 **Accountability**
Holders of public office are accountable for their decisions and actions to the public and must submit themselves to appropriate scrutiny.

5 **Openness**
Holders of public office should be as open as possible about all the decisions and actions that they take and give reasons for their decisions.

6 **Honesty**
Holders of public office have a duty to declare any private interests relating to their public duties and to take steps to resolve any conflicts.

7 **Leadership**
Holders of public office should promote and support these principles by leadership and example.

Welsh Assembly Government: Risk management policy

The risk policy of the Welsh Assembly Government (WAG) sets out policy on the identification and management of risks that it faces in the delivery of its objectives. Its aims are to ensure that risk is taken into account at all stages in the development and delivery of WAG activities, including risk analysis and the development of actions to manage risks, and to monitor, review and evaluate such activity.

The Accounting Officer and Strategic Delivery & Performance Board of the Welsh Assembly Government have adopted the following risk management policy to create the environment and structures for the implementation of the WAG plans, to:

- ensure that the objectives of the Welsh Assembly Government are not adversely affected by significant risks that have not been anticipated;

- ensure achievement of outputs and outcomes and having reliable contingency arrangements to deal with the unexpected that might put service delivery at risk;

- promote a more innovative, less risk-averse culture in which the taking of appropriate risks in pursuit of opportunities to benefit the WAG is encouraged;

- provide a sound basis for integrating risk management into decision making;
- form a component of excellent corporate governance and management practices.

Risk Improvement Manager

Corporate Governance and Assurance

Welsh Assembly Government

February 2008

Evaluation of board performance

The board has overall responsibility for the organization in terms of setting strategy and ensuring satisfactory governance. Management of the organization is the responsibility of the executive management, and top management, by way of the executive directors of the organization, will often be members of the board. When executive and non-executive directors are members of the same board, this is referred to as a unitary board. In many organizations, the board comprises non-executive directors only, and is referred to as the supervisory board. Where the supervisory board is in place, the executive directors will meet as the executive committee. The structure of separating non-executive and executive directors into separate committees is sometimes referred to as a two-tier board structure.

In some countries, the two-tier board structure is more common. Also, it is usual for a two-tier board structure to be in place in charities and public-sector organizations. Regardless of whether the structure is unitary or two tier, the board will have a range of responsibilities. It is standard practice for the board to identify those issues where it will retain ultimate authority and responsibility. These issues are usually referred to as matters reserved for the board. A key area of responsibility for the board that is usually not delegated is setting the risk appetite of the organization.

Having decided the matters that are reserved for the board, it will then be necessary to decide how authority and responsibility will be delegated in respect of other issues. It is common for large organizations to produce a statement of the delegation of authority, which will be an important document related to the governance structure in the organization.

Executive directors, managers and staff represent the three levels of management within an organization, and together these are the first line of defence in ensuring satisfactory standards of governance, including risk management and internal control. The board should be aware of specialist risk management functions within the organization and should be made aware of the activities of these functions and their role as the second line of defence. Non-executive members of the board would be the members of the audit committee and they should be aware of their functions as the third line of defence in ensuring adequate risk governance.

Evaluation of board performance is a critically important part of the corporate governance arrangements for any organization. Table 28.3 provides a checklist of

Table 28.3   Evaluating the effectiveness of the board

Membership and structure

Does the board have the necessary range of knowledge, skills and experience?
Is there appropriate turnover of board membership to ensure new ideas?
Are the sub-committees of the board effective, with appropriate delegated authority?
Are board decision-making processes satisfactory, with adequate information available?
Do communication processes exist between board members outside board meetings?

Purpose and intent

Do all board members understand and share the vision and mission?
Do members of the board understand the objectives and position statements?
Is there sufficient knowledge and understanding of the significant risks?
Are board members sufficiently involved with the development of strategy?
Have measurable budget and performance targets been put in place?

Involvement and accountability

Does the board have shared ethical values, including openness and honesty?
Are the established policies unambiguous and consistent with the ethics?
Do board members understand their duties, responsibilities and obligations?
Is there a feeling of mutual trust and respect at board meetings?
Are adequate delegation and authorization procedures in place?

Monitoring and review

Is there sufficient monitoring of performance using appropriate measurements?
Does the board challenge planning assumptions when and where appropriate?
Does the board demonstrate the ability to respond rapidly to changes?
Is there a mentality that demands continuous improvement in performance?
Does the board assess financial and other controls and seek assurance on compliance?

Performance and impact

Is there a satisfactory level of attendance at board, committee and other meetings?
Are board decisions and actions fully recorded and actions tracked and confirmed?
Are the agreed targets and performance indicators evaluated and assessed?
Is the impact of board decisions and actions evaluated in a timely manner?
Is there an emphasis on accuracy, honesty and open reporting to external agencies?

---

issues that should be included in the evaluation of the effectiveness of a board. The areas for evaluation are as follows:

- membership and structure;
- purpose and intent;
- involvement and accountability;
- monitoring and review;
- performance and impact.

The checklist set out in Table 28.3 focuses on corporate governance effort and on the level of performance of the board. When deciding issues related to strategy, tactics, operations and compliance, the board will need to ensure that adequate procedures are in place for reaching decisions. These decisions will result in a course of action and the implementation of that course of action needs to be monitored.

The course of action will result in some outputs, and these need to be evaluated in terms of the impact that is achieved. When evaluating the effectiveness of the board, the impact of its decisions is the ultimate test. The level of impact can then be evaluated against the vision, mission and objectives of the organization. This needs to be supported by an effective organizational structure, as outlined in the text box below.

Governance structure

A good organizational structure supports the effective management of risk. The structure should be appropriate to the organization but typically would provide for three levels of governance with respect to risk:

- direct responsibility for the management and control of risk (that is, staff and management working within or managing operational business units and the board);
- co-ordination, facilitation and oversight of the effectiveness and integrity of the risk management framework (for example, the risk committee and risk management function);
- provision of independent assurance and challenge across all business functions in respect of the integrity and effectiveness of the risk management framework (that is, internal and external audit).

Stakeholder expectations

29

Range of stakeholders

Organizations will have a wide range of stakeholders, some of whom may indeed be unwanted as far as the organization is concerned. For example, if a distribution company wishes to build an extension to its depot, local residents may want to object to it. The local residents are stakeholders in the operation of the company, even though the owner of the company may not wish to acknowledge that fact. ISO Guide 83 suggests that the term 'interested party' is preferred, but stakeholder is an acceptable alternative. ISO Guide 73 defines a stakeholder as a 'person or group concerned with, affected by, or perceiving themselves to be affected by an organization'.

There will be a wide range of stakeholders in a typical organization that can be summarized as CSFSRS, as follows:

- customers;
- staff;
- financiers;
- suppliers;
- regulators;
- society.

Stakeholders may have contradictory expectations of the organization. For example, staff at a sports club will seek pay that is as high as possible. This would be in opposition to the requirements of financiers, who want the club to be as profitable as possible. It is part of the role of management to balance the conflicting interests of different stakeholders and implement actions that provide the best balance between conflicting stakeholder expectations.

For organizations in different sectors, the range of stakeholders will be different. For government agencies, the general public will be a major stakeholder. Specific groups within the general public will be stakeholders in different agencies, depending on the purpose of each particular agency. For organizations that have significant environmental interests or exposures, a different range of stakeholders would need to be considered. For some energy companies, environmental pressure groups are often unwelcome stakeholders. There may be a substantial conflict between a mining company that wishes to extract minerals and the local population who do not want heavy industrial activities taking place in the area.

Business process re-engineering (BPR) is a technique to ensure that an organization has the most effective and efficient processes and operations. A starting point for many BPR exercises is to identify stakeholders and their expectations. The delivery of shared stakeholder expectations is then undertaken by the core processes of the organization. Core processes are the high-level collections of activities that are fundamentally important to the organization.

For a sports club, the 'delivering success on the pitch' core process will be fundamental. This process will be important to many stakeholders, including supporters (or customers), players (or staff) and sponsors (or financiers). The benefit of this approach is that the organization can be defined by a small number of core processes that should cover strategy, tactics, operations and compliance. An enterprise evaluation of these core processes and the risks that could impact the core processes can then be undertaken. By taking this approach, risk management activities will be fully embedded in the organization.

Depending on the nature of the stakeholder, questions should be asked about the risk awareness of the organization, the activities that are designed to achieve risk improvement, and risk governance arrangements within the organization. Relevant stakeholders are entitled to receive information on the risk profile of the organization. They are also entitled to information on the arrangements for risk improvement and the metrics that are in place to monitor risk performance. Finally, stakeholders are entitled to information on the risk appetite of the organization and the arrangements for incorporating risk into the development of strategy.

The box below provides an example of how stakeholders will have different expectations of an organization. Sometimes, these expectations will be contradictory. Even if they are not contradictory, it is helpful for one group of stakeholders to have an understanding of the expectations of the other groups.

Stakeholders in a theatre

Assume that a theatre is seeking to involve all stakeholders in its activities. This will extend to consideration of the objectives of performers at the theatre, including artistes and actors. There needs to be a distinction between the objectives of the performer and the requirements of the audience. For example, an established musician may wish to promote a new album, but the audience will want to hear the well-known favourites from previous ones.

The performer will have the best chance of presenting a successful show if the starting point is an evaluation of audience expectations, followed by an evaluation of the expectations of the theatre. The performer can then plan the specific content of the show to be consistent with those expectations as well as taking account of his or her professional and personal objectives. The theatre may encourage this approach and recognize the performer as a stakeholder, but encourage the performer to consider other stakeholders and their expectations.

Stakeholder dialogue

Dialogue with stakeholders should be based on a mutual understanding of the objectives of the organization. The board is responsible for ensuring that the dialogue is satisfactory. Although specific members of the organization may have the day-to-day responsibility for communications with particular groups of stakeholders, the board will retain overall responsibility. Table 29.1 provides a summary of the information that should be provided to shareholders of a company. This information will focus on the provision of accurate financial data.

The level and nature of dialogue with stakeholders will depend on the particular interests of the stakeholder in the operations of the organization. The supporters of a sports club will require different information from the banks that are providing the necessary financial support for the club.

To obtain the fullest picture of the risks facing an organization, analysis of stakeholders and their expectations is necessary. The identification of stakeholder expectations is one output from the external evaluation stage of the business cycle. Different stakeholders may have expectations that are contradictory or even mutually exclusive in terms of the demands placed on the organization. The importance of communication with stakeholders also extends to whistleblowing and the text box below gives an illustration of how whistleblowing can be valuable to the organization and should be encouraged.

Table 29.1   Data for shareholders

General
A clear statement of strategy and vision
Corporate profile and principal markets
Financial data
Annual report and financial statements
Archived financial information for the past three years
Corporate governance and CSR
Information related to compliance with Combined Code
Information on the company CSR policies
Shareholder information
Shareholder analysis by size and constituent
Information on directors' share dealings
Relevant news
Access to all news releases and presentations
Developments that might affect the share value

Whistleblowing policy

Rank aims to maintain a culture of openness, honesty and opposition to fraud, corruption and unethical business conduct. It is Rank policy to implement and maintain procedures that promote ethical business conduct and reduce the risk of fraud and other irregularities, enabling early detection, investigation and reporting. Rank has a fraud and unethical business conduct whistleblowing policy which sets out the ways in which employees can voice their concerns about suspected fraud, corruption or unethical business conduct.

During the period under review two frauds came to light within the Grosvenor retail casino business in circumstances where it would appear that others not directly involved must potentially have had suspicions that they never raised. This has led management and the committee to question whether the whistleblowing policy is sufficiently effective.

Although reports are made under the group whistleblowing policy, the matters which are the subject of the reports are rarely related to fraud or unethical business conduct, and are more often than not related to human resource issues. Managers in the businesses are being consulted as to how best to address the cultural resistance to using the whistleblowing policy for matters for which the policy is intended.

The Rank Group Plc
Annual Report and Financial Statements 2015

Stakeholders and core processes

Core processes deliver stakeholder expectations and are related to the internal and external context of the organization. Therefore, a risk can be defined as an event with the potential to impact the fulfilment of a stakeholder expectation. This approach has the advantage that both internal and external stakeholders can be identified, together with their short-term, medium-term and long-term expectations. Figure 29.1 provides a graphical illustration of the relationship between stakeholder expectations and the core processes of the organization. The figure illustrates that the core processes of an organization can be strategic, tactical, operational or compliance (STOC). Figure 29.1 shows compliance core processes as separate processes, although compliance core processes should also underpin and support the other types of core processes.

This classification of core processes as strategic, tactical and operational is acknowledged in British Standard BS 31100 when it discusses risk management perspectives. Strategic perspectives set the future direction of the business; tactical perspectives are concerned with turning strategy into action by achieving change; and operational perspectives are related to the day-to-day operations of the organization, including people, information security, health and safety, and business continuity. Again, compliance processes are assumed to underpin the other types of core processes.

An approach based on stakeholder expectations has many advantages. It facilitates a full and thorough validation of the core processes of the organization in

Figure 29.1 Importance of core processes

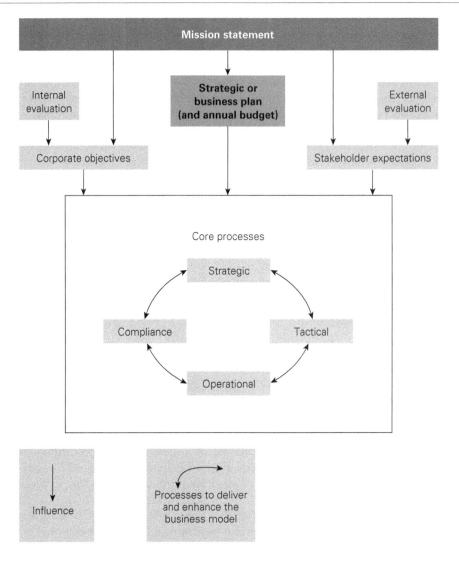

relation to the expectations that each stakeholder places on each core process. An important aspect of managing an organization is balancing the various stakeholder expectations. There are dangers inherent in achieving this balance, and a risk identification procedure based on analysis of stakeholder expectations is the most robust way of ensuring that these dangers are recognized, analysed and minimized.

The analysis of stakeholder expectations is also one of the fundamental requirements of the business process re-engineering (BPR) approach. The stakeholders in the current and future activities of the organization can be identified. The expectations of each stakeholder in relation to each stated objective and the corporate mission can then be evaluated. Shared expectations will emerge and the core processes of the organization can then be defined (or refined) specifically in terms of the delivery of these shared expectations.

Although the analysis of stakeholder expectations can be one of the most robust ways of identifying risks, there are implications in terms of the time and effort required for this approach to be successful. BPR can be a very time-consuming exercise when undertaken thoroughly. The benefits of taking a BPR or core processes approach include the ability to identify the core processes that are most vulnerable to risk events. This will enable the identification of stakeholders whose expectations are most likely to be dissatisfied because their expectations have not been delivered.

Stakeholders and strategy

It has been clearly established and demonstrated by research that incorrect risk management decisions related to strategy can destroy more value for an organization than incorrect risk management decisions associated with the operations or projects undertaken by the organization.

Stakeholder expectations are delivered by the core processes of an organization. Table 29.2 sets out the range of stakeholder expectations for a typical sports club. The core processes that deliver stakeholder expectations can be strategic, tactical, operational or compliance (STOC), shown in the bow-tie representation of the risk management process in Figure 11.1. Strategic core processes need to be the most robust processes in the organization, and indeed this will be required by major stakeholder groups. Such stakeholders include financiers and other shareholders who are interested in the long-term success of the organization.

The expectations of supporters include good stadium facilities, and a strategic core process may need to be established to manage the building of a new stadium. This would be a significant investment that will require substantial support from financiers. In order to secure support, the club will need to be aware of the expectations of the financiers and ensure that the plans for the new stadium and the financial arrangements that will be put in place fulfil the necessary stakeholder expectations. The construction phase of acquiring a new stadium will be a significant project for the club, with a different range of stakeholders to consider.

Stakeholders and tactics

Tactical stakeholders of an organization may be very different from those who are concerned with the organization's operations. If the tactics of an organization involve improvements to products, investment in new production techniques, response to technological changes or other developments that require a project, then finance is likely to be required. This means that financial bodies are likely to be key stakeholders in projects and similar tactical changes. Other stakeholders in projects may

Table 29.2   Sports club: typical stakeholder expectations

	Stakeholder	Expectations
1	Customers (and supporters)	Sustained success on the pitch Good facilities available in the ground Affordable range of merchandise
2	Staff (including players)	World-class coaching standards Excellent pay and conditions Fair team selection procedures
3	Financiers (including sponsors)	Appropriate income and profit Good financial security and internal controls High-profile brand publicity and exposure
4	Suppliers	Fair and ethical treatment by the club Safe, clean and adequate facilities for franchisees Adequate marketing and visitor numbers
5	Regulators	Compliance with rules and regulations Co-operative approach with regulators Willingness to share good practice with others
6	Society	Enhancing the reputation of sporting activities Fair and ethical behaviour by the club No hooliganism in the neighbourhood

include building contractors and providers of other specialist professional support, such as architects.

The importance of employees in the implementation of tactics should not be underestimated. Staff will also have an interest in operational issues and be major stakeholders in the organization's operations. If changes to work practices or product features are to be successfully incorporated into the operations of the organization, then the support of staff is vitally important and good communication with them is essential.

It is important to consider the effect that changes, developments, projects and tactics will have on the full range of stakeholders. By considering the interests of stakeholders in detail, many unexpected surprises can be avoided. The impact of the project, both in execution and after delivery of the project, should be considered in detail. This consideration should extend both to internal and external stakeholders for whom the changes that the project will bring may be significant. These changes could relate to environmental factors during the construction project and after the work has been completed, as well as changes to the working arrangements for staff.

It may be a good idea to bring some people who are not directly involved in the activities of the organization into the project planning. This will enable the organization to fully understand the impact of the work that will be undertaken. When considering stakeholder management, the level of detail will often dictate whether engagement with stakeholders is successful. Even with successful projects, being able to minimize negative impacts by early attention to key stakeholders and their expectations may prove invaluable.

Stakeholders and operations

There may be many stakeholder groups involved in the operational activities of an organization. To continue with the example of a sports club, fans will be major stakeholders in a large number of different aspects of the club's activities. One of the primary concerns of fans will be good results on the pitch. They will also be interested in other operational aspects, including the arrangements for buying tickets, transport and access arrangements, as well as the facilities provided within the stadium.

Pharmaceutical companies are generally large organizations with a very diverse range of stakeholders. In particular, a pharmaceutical company producing a critical medication has an obligation to ensure a constant availability of that medication for all its patients. Patients should be viewed by the pharmaceutical company as important stakeholders who have expectations regarding the availability and effectiveness of the medication that has been prescribed.

The stakeholder groups that have an interest in the operational activities of an organization are likely to be customers, suppliers and others that may be affected by disruption to the normal efficient operation of the organization. For example, customers are likely to be affected if a hazard risk were to materialize. Likewise, suppliers are stakeholders in the organization and they will suffer if the organization is disrupted to the extent that their supplies/produce/components/services are no longer required.

Other stakeholder groups that are likely to be affected by hazard risks will also have an interest in the continuity of the activities of the organization. For financial organizations such as banks, customers would be immediately affected if critical IT systems fail.

Corporate governance models require the involvement of stakeholders and adequate stakeholder dialogue. In several countries, employees are recognized as stakeholders in the organization to the extent that employee representation on the board may be mandatory. The box below considers the position in some European countries.

Employee representation on the board

Board-level employee representation involves employee representatives who sit on the supervisory board, board of directors or similar structures in companies. These employee representatives are directly elected by the workforce, or appointed in some other way, and may be employees of the company, officials of organizations representing those employees, or individuals considered to represent the employees' interests in some way.

Board-level representation also differs from other types of indirect participation such as works councils in that it attempts to provide employee input into overall company strategic decision making rather than focusing on information and consultation on day-to-day operational matters at the workplace.

In most cases in western Europe, employee representatives are in the minority, and board-level participation is associated with the obtaining of information and understanding followed by the expression and exchange of opinions, views and arguments about an enterprise's strategy and direction. In a few cases, however, when employee representatives are equal in number to those of shareholders or other parties, issues of control, veto and real influence over company strategy – sometimes known as 'co-determination' – come into play.

Operational risk management   30

Operational risk

The importance of managing operational risk has been well established for some time. Operational risk may be considered to be the type of risk that will disrupt normal everyday activities. In many ways, operational risk is closely related to infrastructure risks described in the FIRM risk scorecard classification system.

Operational risks are usually hazard risks, and historically this has been an area of strong application of risk transfer by way of insurance. However, operational risk now has a more extensive application and a more specific definition, especially in financial institutions. Whilst addressing the same types of risks, operational risk in financial institutions is differentiated by the fact that there is a need to quantify these risks in terms of potential financial loss.

Financial institutions are required to have sufficient capital reserves available to meet the actual and potential financial losses and obligations faced by the organization. This is a key requirement of the regulatory framework set out for banks in the Basel II Accord and under emerging regulation for European insurance companies through the Solvency II European Directive. Therefore, financial institutions need to measure the level of operational risk that they face. A major contributing factor to the global financial crisis was that banks adopted high-risk strategies that resulted in the banks having insufficient capital when the risks materialized.

The capital adequacy regulations that are based on Basel II require that banks take their operational risk exposure into account in determining their capital requirements. This operational risk management framework should include identification, measurement and monitoring, reporting, control and mitigation frameworks for operational risk. This assessment of capital requirements is often called economic capital.

In addition, the regulations require that banks must follow one of three specific quantitative methods to provide another measure of capital requirement. This is the so-called regulatory capital. Two of the methods are based on the incomes of the financial institution. The third method requires assessment of all material operational risk exposures to a high degree of statistical quality. Under the Solvency II European Directive, insurance companies in the EU will have to adopt a similar approach.

Basel II is the second of the Basel Accords that set out recommendations on banking laws and regulations, as issued by the Basel Committee on Banking Supervision. The purpose of Basel II (2004) is to create an international standard that banking regulators can use when creating regulations about how much capital banks need to put aside to guard against the types of financial and operational risks they face. Basel III requirements have been developed, although it is not anticipated that Basel III will come fully into force until 2019.

Definition of operational risk

Operational risks faced by banks and other financial institutions represent essentially the same types of disruptive hazard risks that are faced by other organizations, although the definition may be broader and the terminology slightly different. The specific point in the case of operational risk for financial institutions is that the level of operational risk needs to be quantified, because the level of risk has to be covered by available capital within the institution. This leads to an imperative for the bank to reduce the level of operational risk to the lowest level that is cost-effective.

Banks have long been concerned with market risk and credit risk (and insurance companies with underwriting risk as well), but the advent of Basel II and Solvency II requires financial institutions to consider broader operational risk exposures. Operational risk was initially defined as being any form of risk that was not market risk or credit risk. This imprecise definition was replaced by Basel II with a definition of operational risk as: 'the risk of loss resulting from inadequate or failed internal processes, people and systems or from external events'.

The Basel II definition includes legal risk, but excludes strategic and reputational risk. The types of risks associated with the Basel II definition include the following:

- internal fraud, including misappropriation of assets, tax evasion and bribery;
- external fraud including theft, hacking and forgery;
- employment practices and workplace safety;
- clients, projects and business practices;
- damage to physical assets;
- business interruption and systems failures;
- execution, delivery and process management.

However, there is also recognition that operational risk is a term that has a variety of meanings and that certain financial institutions use a different term or a broader definition. The Basel II definition identifies four types of risk categories: people, process, system and external risks. People risks include failure to comply with procedures and lack of segregation of duties. Process risks include process failures and inadequate controls. System risks include failure of applications systems to meet user requirements and the absence of built-in control measures. Finally, external risks include action by regulators (change of regulation, but excluding enforcement or disciplinary action), unsatisfactory performance by service providers and fraud, both internal and external. External risks also include legal action by customers of financial institutions in relation to negligence or fraud committed by staff.

The definitions of market risk and credit risk are also worth considering in relation to financial institutions. Market risk is the risk that the value of investments may decline over a period, simply because of economic changes or other events that impact large portions of the market. Credit risk is the risk that there will be a failure by a customer/client to repay the principal and/or interest on a loan or other outstanding debt in a timely manner, or at all. Underwriting risk is also important for insurance companies; it is the exposure to the risks of the client through insurance policies.

Failure of operational risk management

Operational risk management is at a crucial point in its development. Numerous approaches have been developed across different industries, but many institutions are struggling to make these fully effective by really embedding them into the day-to-day management of their business. In order to overcome this challenge, it is essential to define clearly the relationship between operational risk processes and the overall control environment.

Indeed, the effectiveness of operational risk management has been impeded by a common failure to truly embed operational risk into the overall management of risk and control. Group risk functions must demonstrate to business-unit staff the full potential of using operational risk processes, developed under the group framework to manage the actual risks in the business.

As a consequence, the governance of operational risks involves more than just calculating the yearly operational risk capital. As economies and financial conditions change over time, so does the operational risk exposure. This implies that a number of specific operational risk events may become even more likely, which in times of crises require the attention of top management.

The losses associated with the failure to manage operational risk can be very substantial. Losses suffered by so-called rogue traders are sometimes attributed to market risk. The argument is that the losses occurred because market conditions changed in an unexpected way and significant losses materialized. From an operational risk perspective, this analysis is incorrect.

It is more correct to say that the losses occurred because of a failure to control the activities of traders. If the operations had been controlled by adequate operational risk controls, the traders would not have been in a position to have put substantial assets of the bank at risk. Blaming the losses on the market risk when such substantial assets of the bank should not have been in the market at all is incorrect.

Basel II and Basel III

Basel II has been in existence for some time and, at the time of writing this book (April 2018), Basel III requirements have been developed, but may not be introduced until 2019. The revised requirements contained in Basel III are likely to be consistent with what has gone before. Likewise, the development of Solvency II that will define capital requirements for insurance companies has been completed

Table 30.1　ORM principles (Basel II)

The 10 principles on 'Sound Practices' of the Basel II committee are as follows:

1　The board is responsible for establishing the operational risk strategy.
2　Senior management is responsible for implementing the operational risk strategy.
3　Information, communication and escalation flows must be established.
4　Operational risks inherent in activities, processes, systems and products should be identified.
5　Processes necessary for assessing operational risk should be established.
6　Systems should be implemented to monitor operational risk exposures and loss events.
7　Policies, processes and procedures to control or mitigate operational risks should be in place.
8　Supervisors should require banks to have an effective system to identify, measure, monitor and control operational risk.
9　Supervisors should conduct regular independent evaluations of these principles.
10　Sufficient public disclosure should be made to allow stakeholders to assess the operational risk exposure and the quality of operational risk management.

and the date for full implementation is currently anticipated to be as late as 2019. The approach taken in Solvency II is consistent with the approach in Basel II and Basel III.

The 10 principles of 'Sound Practices' on operational risk put forward by the Basel II committee are set out in Table 30.1. One of the key requirements, as set out in Principle 5, is that processes necessary for assessing operational risk should be established. The intention of Basel II is to help protect the international financial system from the types of problems that might arise should a major bank or a series of banks collapse.

Basel II attempts to protect the international financial system by setting up rigorous risk and capital management requirements designed to ensure that a bank holds capital reserves appropriate to the risk the bank exposes itself to through its lending and investment practices. These rules mean that the greater risk to which the bank is exposed, the greater the amount of capital it needs to hold to safeguard its solvency and overall economic stability. Basel II aims to ensure that capital allocation is more risk sensitive, that operational risk is separated from credit risk (both of which should be quantified) and that a global regulatory regime is in place.

The Basel II Accord describes a comprehensive minimum standard for capital adequacy that national supervisory authorities are working to implement. In addition, Basel II is intended to promote a more forward-looking approach to capital supervision that encourages banks to identify the risks they face and improve their ability to manage those risks. As a result, it is intended to be more flexible and better able to evolve with advances in markets and risk management practices.

There has been considerable debate about the effectiveness of the Basel II Accord (2004) in achieving its stated objectives. The effectiveness of the accord should be assessed against the failure of the banking system in 2008. The role of that failure in the global financial crisis has been the topic of much detailed evaluation.

Measurement of operational risk

Operational risk has become a specific issue in financial institutions, because of the requirement to measure/quantify the level of operational risk that they face. The measurement of operational risk can involve a number of methods and these are normally based on historical information, simulated information or a combination of these. Table 30.2 sets out examples of operational risks faced by a bank or financial institution.

Basel II offers three alternative approaches to measuring operational risk for regulatory capital purposes, as set out below. The first two methods are a proxy for operational risk management exposure; whilst research work was undertaken to validate these methods, individual firms could vary substantially from the assessments these two methods would provide:

- *Basic indicator approach*: calculates the value of operational risk capital using a single indicator for the overall risk exposure.

- *Standardized approach*: calculates the value for operational risk, using a broad financial indicator, multiplied by operational loss experience.

- *Advanced approach*: uses the internal loss data and a combination of qualitative and quantitative methods to calculate the operational risk capital.

Table 30.2 Operational risk for a bank

Event category	Definition	Description	Examples
Internal fraud	Losses due to fraud, misappropriation or circumvention of regulations by internal party	Unauthorized activity, theft and fraud	Unreported transactions Unauthorized transactions Theft and fraud Tax non-compliance Insider trading
External fraud	Losses due to fraud, misappropriation or circumvention of the regulations by third party	Systems security, theft and fraud	Theft/robbery Forgery Hacking/theft of information

(continued)

Table 30.2 (*Continued*)

Event category	Definition	Description	Examples
Employees	Losses arising from injury or non-compliance with the employment legislation	In a safe environment, damaged employee relations and discrimination	Compensation claim Discrimination allegation
Clients	Losses arising from failure to meet professional obligations to clients	Disclosure and fiduciary	Fiduciary breaches Disclosure violations Misuse of confidential information
Physical assets	Losses arising from loss or damage to physical assets	Disasters and other events	Natural disaster losses Terrorism/vandalism
Systems	Losses arising from disruption of business or system failures	Systems	Hardware or software failure Telecommunications Utility disruption
Processes	Losses from failed transaction processing or process management	Transaction capture, execution, documentation and maintenance	Data entry, or loading error Missed deadline or responsibility Failed reporting obligation Incorrect records

In order to measure operational risk, the financial institution needs to adopt a structured approach. Even after the identification of the risks, quantification is only possible if the amount of damage and risk probabilities are determined. Operational risks are hard to quantify since loss histories are usually not available and some risks cannot easily be quantified.

Many banks have undertaken detailed evaluation and quantification of their operational risks. In general, it has been discovered that the size of the bank (measured in terms of number of employees) influences the size of losses that will be suffered. This appears to indicate that larger banks tend to have larger clients. The other general trend being identified is that the number of losses is strongly correlated to the number of customers that use the bank.

Difficulties of measurement

The development of interest in operational risk has been based on the need to quantify operational risk in financial institutions. The challenges of quantifying operational risk have been considerable. Expected levels of loss can only be estimated, even if the probability of loss is fairly accurately known. Although statistical approaches have been adopted and developed, a universally accepted approach is still not available.

The expected losses can have a direct and indirect cost. Indirect costs are often larger, and include the loss of a customer. This loss can be represented by the present value of that customer and all future gains from that relationship. Actions that should be taken will include internal control measures as well as evaluation by internal audit. Internal audit within a financial institution has the familiar, but vitally important, responsibility of checking whether procedures are followed in practice and whether the procedures themselves are likely to be effective in reducing the level of operational risk.

Table 30.3 illustrates the different natures of operational risk faced by financial and industrial companies. The table provides a comparison of the nature and impact of human error in a financial institution, compared with an industrial undertaking. It is clear that the control of staff behaviour and actions is much more difficult in financial institutions than in manufacturing facilities.

It is worth noting that operational risk quantification is possible for non-financial institutions, and a transport company (for example) could investigate the operational risks associated with its activities. The risks associated with the operations include the price of fuel, tax obligations and the financial impact of delivery mistakes. Operational risks can arise from road traffic accidents or other delivery delays and changes by customers that have not been correctly incorporated into the delivery schedule.

Table 30.3 Operational risk in financial and industrial companies

Financial	Industrial
Errors mostly arise when people reach their mental limits.	Errors are mostly due to people reaching their physical limits.
Systems are highly complex and widely distributed and the environment is only partly manageable.	People are working in relatively simple relationships and the environment is highly manageable.
Loss prevention is concerned with security of value and assets.	Loss prevention is mainly concerned with physical safety, equipment protection and avoiding accidents.
Loss prevention is aimed at avoiding financial loss.	Loss prevention is aimed at avoiding physical harm to people or equipment and/or the manufacture of faulty goods (scrap).
The main incentive for committing mistakes is personal financial gain or self-interest.	The main incentive for making deliberate mistakes is reducing effort or (possibly) sabotage.
Risk management is a key skill in financial services and has central importance to the organization.	Risk management is not central to operations, although the aim is to avoid disruption to manufacturing processes.

It is likely that the most important operational risks faced by a transport company would be incorrect customer deliveries and road traffic accidents. The quantification of risk exposures associated with the various categories of operational risk will help a transport company focus on those risks with the greatest potential to cause disruption to normal efficient routine operations, and then take the appropriate control actions to reduce these operational risk exposures.

Developments in operational risk

Before considering developments in operational risk, it is worth noting that concerns about operational risks are universal in all organizations. Although the banks and other financial institutions may have a specific approach to operational risk, the issues that are being considered are the same issues that affect all other types of organizations in the public, private and third sectors. (The third sector refers to not-for-profit organizations, including charities, membership and voluntary bodies.)

Although the issues are the same, the approach in banks and other financial institutions can be different. In a non-financial institution, the questions related to operational risk may well be: 'What is the value of my assets, how do I protect them and to what extent and value (or limit of indemnity) do I need to purchase insurance?' In the financial sector, the questions are more likely to be: 'What are the capital requirements attached to my assets?' and 'Can I afford to keep that amount of (non-productive) capital in reserve, or do I need to purchase insurance and to what value or limit of indemnity?'

It is generally accepted that operational risk concerns need to be integral to the management of a financial institution. It is often the case that management trainees within financial institutions spend some time in the risk management function, as they progress with their career in the general management side of the business. It is the intention that this involvement with risk management will create greater awareness before the individual progresses into other roles.

The measurement of operational risk in financial institutions is still proving to be a challenge, especially during the global financial crisis, which has showed that the extent of operational risk exposure was greater than most banks believed. Certain financial institutions are seeking to adopt risk management standards, such as ISO 31000, the IRM standard and the COSO ERM cube. Basel II does not prescribe or require any particular framework for use with operational risk management, except that the adopted framework is conceptually sound and pays high regard to integrity issues.

There are other tensions that exist with the development of operational risk within financial institutions. In many cases, the quantification of operational risk is seen as a compliance requirement rather than a business opportunity. Given that the quantification of operational risk can be quite technical, there may be a tendency for management within an organization to feel that it is the role of the operational risk manager to take responsibility for this work.

The responsibility for the management of risk and the implementation of controls usually rests with the line managers. If this responsibility is not accepted, there is a danger that operational risk management will not be fully integrated into management of the financial institution, with disastrous consequences.

Calculation of operational risk exposure is a requirement of Basel II, and financial institutions therefore have to undertake this work. Financial institutions are driven by increasing regulatory demands and other corporate governance pressures. Raising the level of operational risk awareness by quantifying the level of risk and explaining the full significance of risk management to relevant members of staff should be to the benefit of the organization. This increased awareness will enable the organization to identify the sources of operational risk and take appropriate cost-effective actions to optimize the level of operational risk exposure.

The US-based Risk and Insurance Managers Society (RIMS) has undertaken an evaluation of the causes of the global financial crisis. This evaluation considered the contribution that could have been made by enterprise risk management (ERM) and the reasons for the failure in the application of ERM tools and techniques. RIMS concluded that the global financial crisis was not a failure of ERM, but was caused by the following failures:

- There was an over-reliance on the use of financial models, with the mistaken assumption that the 'risk quantifications' (used as predictions) based solely on financial modelling were both reliable and sufficient tools to justify decisions to take risk in the pursuit of profit.

- There was an over-reliance on compliance and controls to protect assets, with the mistaken assumption that historic controls and monitoring a few key metrics are enough to change human behaviour.

- There was a failure to properly understand, define, articulate, communicate and monitor risk tolerances, with the mistaken assumption that everyone understands how much risk the organization is willing to take.

- There was a failure to embed enterprise risk management best practices from the top all the way down to the trading floor, with the mistaken assumption that there is only one way to view a particular risk.

The text box below provides an example of how financial institutions report on their operational risks. This edited extract demonstrates the scope of operational risk, but also illustrates that financial institutions (FIs) face exactly the same range of operational risks as non-FIs. The key difference is that FIs are required to quantify their operational risk, so that capital can be allocated to fund these risks.

Scope of operational risk

The group risk department defines and prescribes the insurance, market and operational risk assessment processes for the business. It performs second-line reviews, including the reserving and capital modelling processes, and undertakes regular reviews of all risks in conjunction with management, with the results of these reviews recorded in risk registers.

Listed below are the principal operational risks that Admiral has identified through its ERM framework:

- People risk:
  - Failure to recruit, develop and retain suitable talent.

- Process risk:
  - A failure in processes or failure of their associated controls.

- Technology risk:
  - Failure to invest and successfully implement, appropriate technology.

- Cyber risk:
  - Financial loss, data loss, business disruption or damage to reputation from failure of IT systems.

- Customer outcome risk
  - Failure of products, processes or services to meet customer and regulator expectations.

Admiral Group plc
Annual Report and Accounts 2015

Project risk management

Introduction to project risk management

Projects will be undertaken by organizations for a number of reasons. When alterations to strategy are being planned, a project (programme of work) or series of projects will often be necessary in order to implement the revised strategy. Also, improvements to operational core processes will require changes that will be implemented by undertaking a project. Selection of projects and programmes of work define the tactics of the organization for the implementation of strategy.

It is important to draw a distinction between project risk management, which is about delivering the project on time, within budget and to quality, and the reason why the project was undertaken. Project risk management is concerned about the risks embedded within delivery of the project. There are also the risks of the project and whether the project is the correct allocation of funds. The risks of the project can be identified by asking whether: 1) the full benefits of the project will actually be delivered; and 2) this particular project represents the best tactics for delivering strategy.

The London Olympics 2012 are an example of a major project that was delivered on time, within budget and quality. Whether staging the Olympic Games in London in 2012 was a correct decision and whether the legacy of the Olympic buildings and other infrastructure will be delivered is a much broader issue. This question can only be answered by reference to the overall strategic plan for the City of London and the UK economy, and answering the question whether staging the Olympic Games in London in 2012 was the correct tactic for delivering the overall strategy for the City of London.

Project risk management should be seen as an extension of conventional project planning. The main requirements for any project are that it is delivered on time, within budget and to specification or performance. Risk is often defined in terms of uncertainty or deviation from the expected/required outcomes. It is in relation to project risk management that the definition of risk being represented by uncertainty is most relevant. Within project management, variability of outcomes is very undesirable. Therefore, the focus of risk management in projects is often on the reduction in the variability of outcomes and the management of control risks.

There will be uncertainties within any project related to events, conditions and circumstances. The requirements of project risk management are to identify the events that could give rise to uncertainty and respond to the event appropriately. The style of risk management most relevant to project risk management is control management.

As well as managing the risks and uncertainties in a project, the project manager should also be looking for opportunities that may arise when certain developments within the project are more favourable than expected. Project risk management should take account of these positive developments and ensure that the structure for managing risks in projects is sufficiently flexible for the opportunities to be recognized and benefits obtained.

For example, consider a project of building a new road where one of the bridges can be completed well ahead of schedule because of favourable ground conditions. There may be an opportunity to build the benefit of this early completion into the future project plan, so that this gain is not lost in the overall timescale for delivery of the final completed project. For a project as large as building Olympic venues, the ground conditions and the level of ground contamination represent significant variables that can have a huge impact on time and cost.

Development of project risk management

Project risk management is a type of control management. Projects may relate to the delivery of a finite, specific or tactical development or process enhancement, such as new:

- construction;
- products;
- IT systems;
- technology;
- markets.

Projects and enhancements are fundamentally important to organizations. Most projects are undertaken either to keep ahead of competitors or to catch up with them. In the context of risk management, the project itself may be considered to be a risk reduction exercise that is designed to achieve specific management objectives. The only purpose in spending money on business enhancement projects is to achieve a business or value-for-money advantage.

Project risk management is a well-developed discipline, with risk control and (especially) event management as the risk management activities that are most important. Project risk management is one of the more sophisticated and successful areas for the application of risk management tools and techniques.

The requirement for all projects is that they are delivered within the defined cost, time and quality parameters. Quality is the relationship between specification and performance. Some projects require that the outcomes comply with a certain specification, such as a new floor in a restaurant that has to be constructed from specified materials. Other projects may require a desired level of performance, such as specifying the level of slip resistance of the floor. Sometimes, both a specification and a performance will be required.

Because of the nature of projects, historical loss data will not usually be available. Accordingly, project risk management needs to be forward-looking in order to anticipate problems before they arise.

Compliance hazard, control and opportunity risks need to be considered as part of the successful management of any project. There are risks associated with failure to obtain necessary permissions and approvals (compliance risks). There are risks to the project that can prevent it being delivered on time and within budget (hazard risks). There are risks to the project concerning the specification, performance and quality of the final outcome (control risks). Finally, there are risks that can enhance the delivery of the project, such as earlier than expected availability of materials (opportunity risks).

Uncertainty in projects

In order to manage uncertainty in projects, organizations have a range of possible actions they can take. An organization can decide to respond in one of the following ways:

- accept the risk or uncertainty;
- adapt activities and procedures;
- adopt contingency plans and responses;
- avoid the risk or uncertainty.

For low-exposure/low-uncertainty risks, the organization (or project) will usually accept uncertainty attached to each risk. For high-exposure/low-uncertainty risks, the organization will adapt activities and procedures and introduce controls, including (when appropriate) insurance. For low-risk/high-uncertainty risks, the organization will adopt appropriate contingency plans and for high-exposure/high-uncertainty risks, the organization will wish to avoid the uncertainty attached to the risk.

Figure 31.1 illustrates the use of the risk matrix to plot the possible range of risks on the project. The matrix plots the possible time delay that could result against the potential for cost increases associated with that event. This diagram will help the project manager identify whether the risks fit into the comfort, cautious, concerned or critical zones. The other variable shown in the diagram equates to the likelihood of each event occurring, and this is indicated by the size of the bubble used to represent that risk.

The delivery of the Olympic Games in London in 2012 required the biggest construction project undertaken in London during the second half of the first decade of the 2000s. During the course of construction, the global financial crisis arose and the financial structure for delivering the project had to be renegotiated. Although this was a major concern, it was successfully completed. Figure 31.1 identifies adverse ground conditions as a possible cause for concern in any construction project. In the case of the Olympic Games 2012, the construction of the Olympic village received a boost in terms of time and cost because the ground was found to be less contaminated than expected.

Figure 31.2 represents the risk management process in project management as a bow-tie. In this use of the bow-tie, the sources of risk are shown as inception, planning, execution and closure. At the centre of the bow-tie are the uncertainties

Figure 31.1   Risk matrix to represent project risks

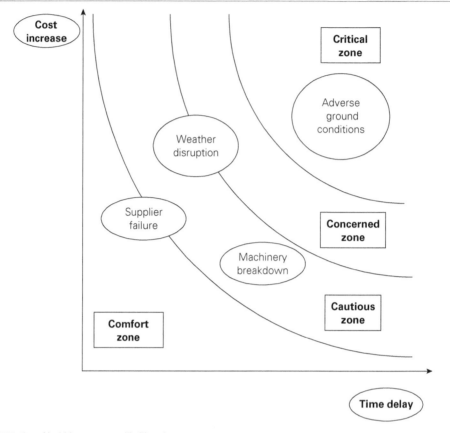

NOTE Size of bubble represents likelihood.

Figure 31.2   Bow-tie to represent project risks

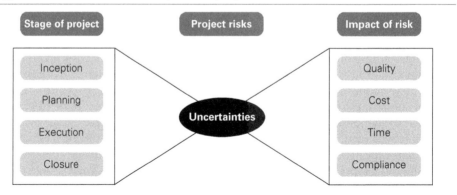

associated with the project, because the management of uncertainties is the essence of project risk management. The purpose of this bow-tie representation is to illustrate that controls can be introduced to reduce the uncertainties in the centre of the bow-tie, manage the uncertainties as they arise, and introduce further controls to limit the impact of those uncertainties on quality, cost, time and compliance.

Project risk register

A risk register or risk matrix should be populated and updated regularly throughout the duration of the project. A risk management software tool can often be a cost-effective way of maintaining your risk register as it can reduce the manual workload and help prioritize risk management activity.

Once risks have been identified and plans to reduce them put in place, it is imperative that they are reviewed regularly. The internal and external project environment is continually changing. Some risks will fall away, others will arise that could never have been envisaged at the outset.

The risk register must therefore be continually updated and reports generated at regular and frequent intervals. Management reports should provide clear visibility on the risks faced, enable prioritization of the activity and facilitate decision making.

Project lifecycle

Project risk management has become one of the best-developed and respected branches of risk management. This is not surprising given the dynamic and pressured environment in which many projects are undertaken. Projects can range from the implementation of a new software package on a computer system through to the building and commissioning of a substantial new sports stadium or delivering the Olympic Games in London (2012).

Whatever the size of the project, a number of specific stages will always be present. Figure 31.3 illustrates the key stages in the project lifecycle. An important additional feature of project risk assessment is that the requirements of the client should always be of the utmost importance. The client may be external to the organization, but is sometimes part of the same organization.

Figure 31.3 sets out the project lifecycle as having four stages. These are project inception, project planning, project execution and project closure. The activities within each of these four stages are listed in the figure. It is important to understand the stages in the project lifecycle, so that the risk management inputs into each stage can be planned and executed, and the required benefits obtained.

The risk management process as applied to project management is similar to the standard risk management process discussed in Chapter 6. However, the framework that supports the risk management process in each case may be quite different, because of the dynamic nature of the projects.

Figure 31.3 Project lifecycle

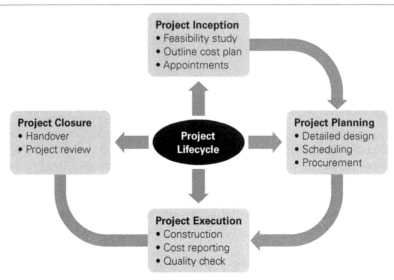

SOURCE Reproduced with permission from Feasible.

Each stage of the project lifecycle will have significant risk and uncertainty issues embedded within it. The uncertainty embedded in each stage of the project will include such issues as defining the project precisely, agreeing the timescale and budget, and confirming the performance/specification. There will also need to be arrangements for changes and developments within the project specification, as well as arrangements for any deviation from expected circumstances.

Figure 31.4 illustrates how uncertainty decreases during the various stages of a project. Uncertainty can be associated with cost, time and quality. The issue that is identified by Figure 31.4 is that as the project develops, the cost of making any alteration increases. It is easier and cheaper to amend the specification before any work has commenced than in the latter stages of a project. The fact that amendments and alterations are more costly as the project progresses reinforces the need for risk management throughout the project, to increase the likelihood of the project being delivered to time, within budget and to quality.

Many organizations include a fourth variable in what is otherwise known as the project triangle. This uncertainty may relate to the scope of the project, the effectiveness of the tactics that gave rise to the project or the ability of the project to comply with stakeholder expectations. The stakeholders will almost certainly include regulators and so compliance is often added as the fourth output from a project that has to be successfully delivered. Sustainability is also used by some organizations as an alternative fourth output from a project. The simple approach is to include compliance and sustainability as part of the third output of quality, specification or performance.

Take the example of refurbishing a block of flats. There will be a large number of interested parties, including architects and the principal contractor. External agencies

Figure 31.4   Decreasing uncertainty during the project

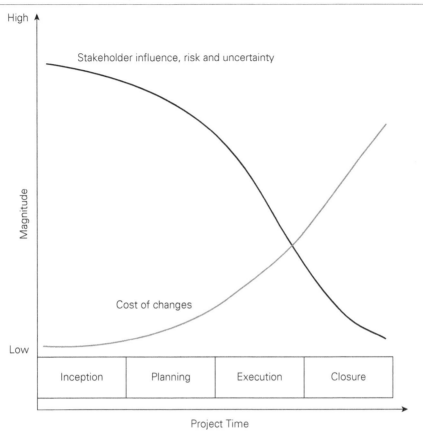

will also need to be involved, including planning, building regulations requirements, health and safety, environmental protection and the utilities. Successful management of a project of this type will require the following:

- making risk management part of the project;
- identifying risks early in the project;
- communicating about risks;
- considering both threats and opportunities;
- clarifying ownership issues;
- prioritizing risks;
- analysing risks;
- planning and implementing risk responses;
- registering project risks;
- tracking risks and associated tasks.

Opportunity in projects

Projects are undertaken because they represent an opportunity to be embraced or a challenge that needs to be overcome. Often a number of projects will need to be undertaken at the same time. A collection of projects of this sort is referred to as a programme.

Good project planning requires arrangements to overcome unexpected events or circumstances. This is often referred to as contingency in the budget or timescale. Contingency may be for additional time to complete a task, or additional costs that may arise to ensure that the final project deliverable operates to the required specification. As the project develops, any perceived difficulties will need to be addressed and opportunities to reduce the impact of these difficulties explored.

Very frequently, the specification of a project will change during the course of the work. A well risk-managed project will take the opportunity of change to specifications to provide a greater level of customer satisfaction, as well as a greater level of income for the organization delivering the project.

The main opportunity offered by undertaking a project is that the project will prove to be the correct tactic for delivering the strategic objectives. In some organizations, projects are only authorized if they reduce the risks faced by the organization. This is particularly true in energy companies, where the justification for undertaking projects will be to improve output, efficiency or quality of operations. This in turn reduces the risk associated with reduced output, wasted resources and poor quality.

As well as achieving the opportunities offered by undertaking the project, organizations will also wish to take advantage of opportunities that are offered within the project. These opportunities may reduce costs, reduce time and/or increase quality. For example, if a construction project assumes a certain level of ground contamination but this proves to be less than expected, there would be an opportunity for the project to be delivered ahead of schedule and at reduced cost. Some construction project contracts will include clauses to share the benefits should the circumstances arise.

Within many established cities, there are archaeological remains that may be of considerable historical interest, if uncovered during the excavation phase of the project. When undertaking construction work to replace buildings in the old cities around the world, there is a chance that the construction company will come across such archaeological remains. Cautious construction companies will plan for this eventuality and build the consequences into the project plan. The possible time delays introduced by finding archaeological remains can be built into the project timeline, and the increased costs associated with these delays may be covered by archaeological insurance, if it is available at a cost-effective price.

Project risk analysis and management

The Association for Project Management (APM) developed the Project Risk Analysis and Management (PRAM) Guide in the mid-1990s. The key considerations that underpin the PRAM approach are set out in Table 31.1. Perhaps one of the most

Table 31.1 PRAM model for project RM

Project risk analysis and management is a process that enables the analysis and management of the risks associated with a project
Properly undertaken, it will increase the likelihood of successful completion of a project to cost, time and performance objectives.
Risks for which there is ample data can be assessed statistically.
However, no two projects are the same.
Often things go wrong for reasons unique to a particular project, industry or working environment.
Dealing with risks in projects is therefore different from situations where there is sufficient data to adopt an actuarial approach.
Because projects involve a technical, engineering, innovative or strategic content, a systematic process is preferable to an intuitive approach.
Project risk analysis and management (PRAM) has been developed to meet this requirement.

important points made is that there is often no historical experience specific to the project that will enable accurate prediction of the impact of risk-based events. The PRAM Guide provides steps to project risk management that are broadly consistent with the steps outlined above.

The PRAM approach represents a continuous set of activities that can be started at almost any stage in the lifecycle of a project. There are five points in a project where particular benefit can be achieved from using the PRAM model:

- *Feasibility*: at this stage the project is most flexible, enabling changes to be made that can reduce the risks at a relatively low cost.
- *Sanction*: the client can view the risk exposure associated with the project and check that all steps to reduce/manage the risks have been taken.
- *Tendering*: the contractor can ensure that all risks have been identified and that risk contingency or risk exposure limits have been set.
- *Post-tender*: the client can ensure that all risks have been identified by the contractor and assess the likelihood of programmes being achieved.
- *During implementation*: the likelihood of completing the project to cost and timescale will increase if all risks are identified and correctly managed.

The text box below provides further commentary and advice on the importance of risk management in projects. Some important characteristics of risk management in projects, as well as some of the means of achieving success are discussed.

Risk management embedded in projects

Embedding risk management within project management leads some to consider that it is just another project management technique or that its use is optional and appropriate only for large, complex or innovative projects. These attitudes often result in risk management being applied without full commitment or attention, and are often responsible for the failure of risk management to deliver the benefits.

To be fully effective, risk management must be closely integrated into the overall project management process. It must not be seen as optional, or applied sporadically only on particular projects. Risk management must be built into project management and not seen as a bolt-on.

Built-in risk management has two key characteristics:

- First, project management decisions are made with an understanding of the risks involved. This understanding includes the full range of project management activities, including scope definition, pricing/budgeting, value management, scheduling, resourcing, cost estimating, quality management, change control and post-project review.

- Second, the risk management process must be integrated with other project management processes. Not only must these processes use risk data, but there should also be a seamless interface across process boundaries. This has implications for the project approach and infrastructure, as well as for project procedures.

Supply chain management 32

Importance of the supply chain

ISO 28000:2007 'Specification for Security Management Systems for the Supply Chain' provides the following definition of supply chain:

> A supply chain is a set of interconnected processes and resources that starts with the sourcing of raw materials and ends with the delivery of products and services to end users. Supply chains may include producers, suppliers, manufacturers, distributors, wholesalers, vendors, and logistics providers. They include facilities, plants, offices, warehouses, and branches and can be both internal or external to an organization.

Many organizations outsource major parts of their operations and support services. This can range from the use of contract cleaners through to transport, communications and manufacturing outsourcing. Many leading suppliers of fashion goods design the products and supply the finished items through franchised retail stores. All manufacturing and distribution activities are frequently outsourced to third-party providers in different parts of the world.

Because of these developments, supply chain management has become vitally important. Managing the supply chain in an increasingly globalized and competitive world can be very challenging. Uncertainties in supply and demand, globalization of marketplaces, shorter product lifecycles and rapid changes in technology have led to a higher exposure to risks in the supply chain. The Japanese earthquake in March 2011 caused considerable disruption to the supply of components for Toyota cars constructed in Japan.

Toyota is reported to have reviewed supply chain management to ensure that it is prepared for future incidents. A Toyota executive vice president commented:

> We are making checks to see what needs to be done to enable a recovery within two weeks of when the next earthquake comes.

All kinds of uncertainties can cause problems in the supply chain and this has increased the importance of risk management. It is impossible to eliminate risk entirely, but adequate attention to risk management matters can reduce the likelihood and magnitude of any disruption to supply. As the trend towards obtaining components and finished goods continues to lead to greater use of manufacturing facilities overseas, the corporate social responsibility issues also tend to increase.

Take the example of a sports club that has decided to outsource the procurement of merchandise sold to fans of the club. The expectation of fans is that merchandise will be desirable, available, distinctive and of appropriate quality, and will represent value for money. The club itself will require that merchandise is of an appropriate quality and high availability, desirable, profitable and ethically sourced. The risks associated with the supply chain and the risks of managing conflicting stakeholder expectations need to be assessed.

The conflicting stakeholder requirements of value for money and profitability have led the club to take the decision that merchandise will have to be procured from a low-cost manufacturer, probably based in a country with lower employment costs. However, the club may have also decided that it will not procure directly from a manufacturer, but will use a third-party procurement agency. The requirements then placed on the procurement agency will include the goods being of appropriate quality and obtained at the lowest cost available from an ethical supplier.

There are many risks associated with the course of action that the club has decided to take. There may be quality and availability issues that could cause dissatisfaction amongst fans and result in reduced sales. There are also questions of corporate social responsibility that need to be addressed. It is likely that the decision to use a third-party importer will reduce these problems, because the importer should be in a better position to establish and monitor corporate social responsibility standards.

The essence of the supply chains for many organizations is that they have gone from 'lowest risk at any cost' to a situation of 'lowest cost at any risk'. In reality, both hazards and opportunities need to be managed. In other words, the potential downside of outsourcing needs to be identified and mitigated with the same level of diligence as the upside or assumed benefit of outsourcing is embraced.

Scope of the supply chain

Because of the increased use of outsourcing, there is an increasing interest in the risks associated with reliance on third parties. Outsourcing of operations is normally undertaken because it is assumed that costs can be reduced and risks transferred. A careful evaluation of the balance between risk and reward should be undertaken before any supply chain outsourcing decisions are taken.

The organization should be aware of the fact that outsourcing means that the organization will not only have to focus on its own risks but should also look at the risks associated with other links in the supply chain. Supply chain management and risk management are interrelated. Supply chain considerations are becoming more common, as well as much more complex.

Outsourcing of the various components of the infrastructure of an organization is only part of supply chain management. Successful management of the supply chain will rely on strategic partnerships and may also extend to joint-venture arrangements. Supply chain issues also extend to simple outsourcing decisions, such as the appointment of cleaners and caterers. There was a strong trend in the 1980s towards the outsourcing of many types of facilities management within buildings.

In summary, the scope of the supply chain can extend to strategic partnerships, joint ventures, support services and outsourcing of facilities management activities. Many organizations also choose to outsource the transportation component of their business. It is not unusual for chains of retail stores to outsource warehousing arrangements and the delivery of goods to their individual shops. The operation of the shops themselves may also be outsourced by way of a franchise agreement.

The box below is a summary of the supply chain considerations that affected Nike in the mid-2000s. The company took actions to address the ethical sourcing issues that had been raised. In order to protect its reputation, Nike took rapid and decisive action in response to critical reports.

Nike supply chain

Nike has said that it has been facing a lot of problems with manufacturing in China, with suppliers giving falsified documents, under-age workers and unpaid wages topping the list. The sneakers and sportswear manufacturer, in what is believed to be its first country-specific supply chain report, has said that the company has been trying to get the Chinese suppliers to follow its code of conduct and Chinese law.

It is reported that the company's difficulties are a reflection of the depth of some of the problems faced by manufacturing businesses in China, which reportedly is Nike's largest single sourcing country, with around 180 manufacturers and about 210,000 employees, at a time when prices are rising and the legal environment is stiffening.

The report, which was posted on Nike's website, said: 'As China continues to develop we see progress and best practices emerging. But like our partners in any other country, the factories we contract with in China continue to face challenges as well.' According to the report, the company faced several labour-related problems, which included falsification of payroll records (details of age in particular), hiring practices and the absence of a proper grievance system for workers.

There is frequent reference to upstream supply chain and downstream supply chain. Generally speaking, upstream supplies are those items that are delivered to you and downstream supply chain refers to the goods that you deliver onwards. This can be explained as a timber grading company situated on the side of a river waiting for timber to be delivered from upstream. The company grades the timber and then delivers the graded timber downstream to customers. However, this terminology is not universally used and can give rise to confusion.

Perhaps it would be better to think of goods delivered to you by your suppliers as the supply chain and goods that are provided or delivered by you to your customers as the delivery chain. Whatever terminology is used, it is the case that most organizations receive goods and services from component suppliers or outsourced services providers. Organizations will need to assess the risks associated with their various suppliers, as well as considering the risks arising from their position as suppliers of products and services that are delivered to their own customers and clients.

Strategic partnerships

When setting up arrangements to outsource part of its operations, an organization will need to consider very carefully the selection of each strategic partner. For example, the production of an in-house magazine will be outsourced by many organizations. Depending on the importance placed on this magazine, an organization may wish to set up a strategic partnership with the publisher.

Supply chain risk management becomes even more important when production activities are involved. When a supermarket sets up an arrangement for the supply of manufactured goods, there are many considerations. The ability of the supply chain partner to deliver the required goods on time and within the agreed cost on a sustainable basis will be a key consideration.

In order to secure exclusive supply, a supermarket may wish to enter into strategic partnerships with its suppliers. These strategic partnerships will result in the supermarket receiving priority treatment in the event of potential disruption to supply. The benefit to the supermarket of this arrangement is that continuity of supply is guaranteed and costs will be reduced. For the supplier, the benefits will be a secure market for its goods and a long-term contract. The disadvantage for the supplier is that the price may be fixed, even though the supplier could obtain a better price on the open market from time to time. There is a further disadvantage that the supplier may be dependent on orders from only one customer.

With increased focus on cost and use of 'just-in-time' delivery, single supplier arrangements may increase the risk of business interruption. Although organizations will wish to limit potential losses by purchasing insurance, it is unlikely that traditional insurance will adequately protect the reputation and market share of the organization in these circumstances. Therefore, organizations will need to look at business continuity strategies and developing strategic partnerships. These issues explain why greater emphasis is being place on organizational 'resilience' and this emerging topic is discussed further in Chapter 9.

Strategic partnerships are very useful alliances formed for the benefit of stakeholders. They can sometimes involve two competitors working together. A good example of this type of partnership is described in the text box below.

Importance of strategic alliances

When International SOS and Control Risks joined forces in 2008 to tackle some of the biggest emergencies on the planet, they proved a centuries-old adage: 'two heads are, indeed, better than one'. The partnership resulted in joint mitigation risk services that provide travel security and medical assistance for clients around the world. Specialist execution units offer advanced security training, risk forecasting and emergency support worldwide; assistance centres and regional aviation units provide evacuation services in 150 countries.

Control Risks had a vision for medical security as well as security for ex-patriots, and we viewed SOS as competition in our new turf. We had clients who were seeking emergency medical support and security planning from the same association, so we looked at partnering options and approached SOS, which had clients looking for a similar combination of services. We decided not to give it its own separate name and identity: it is International SOS/Control Risks.

www.strategic-alliances.org

Joint ventures

Securing priority status from suppliers may be part of the arrangements for an organization to secure its supply chain. However, for very critical components or support operations, priority status may be insufficient. Many organizations, therefore, explore the possibility of setting up joint ventures with their suppliers in order to ensure priority supply status.

Setting up joint ventures also allows the organization to have some management control over the operation of a supplier and eliminate the possibility that the supplier will deliver goods to a competitor in difficult market conditions. Joint-venture arrangements may also be an appropriate way of responding to competitor activities by denying the competitor access to the products produced by the joint-venture partner. Joint ventures may also be a successful way of responding to technology changes in the marketplace, because the organization will not need to find all of the funding required to embrace the new technology.

These sorts of competition and technology changes in the supply chain may be very significant. In fact, it may be beyond the resources of existing organizations operating in the marketplace to respond to these changes. Joint-venture operations can ensure continuity of supply chains and also, if correctly executed, deliver competitive advantage. All of this can be achieved while putting less capital at risk.

An organization may have a strategic objective of reducing its dependency on suppliers. Tactical options will be available, including taking over the supplier or setting up a new organization jointly with your supplier as a separate joint-venture organization. Setting up a joint-venture organization will put the organization into a situation where more of the risks are under their direct control. Setting up such a joint venture may be the appropriate tactical option, because it will require less capital and/or less resources to be allocated than would be the case if the supplier was purchased outright.

The advantage of joint ventures is that the risks are shared. These are usually shared by contractual agreements or by the establishment of a separate company with an agreed allocation of capital to fund that company. Because the capital is shared, the risks involved with the venture will be shared and, accordingly, the benefits and rewards will be shared. Joint ventures are a mechanism whereby an organization can exploit benefits but with a lower risk exposure. This will be a suitable way forward for organizations that do not have the appetite to fully fund the venture.

Outsourcing of operations

There are many benefits associated with outsourcing the manufacture of components to specialist sub-contractors. However, organizations that decide to outsource the manufacture of components need to be aware of the risks and introduce appropriate controls. Outsourcing (or transferring) the manufacture of components does not completely transfer the risks associated with the activity. As with any transfer of

Table 32.1   Risks associated with outsourcing

Risks for car manufacturer outsourcing supply of components:

- Late or delayed delivery from supplier as a result of loss of control and increased dependency on third-party supply.
- Risk that the components may be outside technical specification or otherwise of poor/unacceptable quality.
- Unethical or other inappropriate behaviour by the component supplier may damage reputation of the car manufacturer.
- Cost reduction may not be maintained after the car manufacturer has lost the ability to manufacture the components.

risk, a suitable contract needs to be developed and implemented and this contract should provide clarity on where risk is allocated within the contract. The contract is likely to include penalty clauses for failure to perform, but contracts that also include provisions for rewarding exceptional performance provide a greater sense of co-operation. Table 32.1 identifies examples of the risks associated with outsourcing for a car manufacturer.

Outsourcing of non-core operations can also give rise to supply chain exposures. Table 32.2 sets out a list of considerations when setting up a contract for the supply of outsourced support. It is important that organizations consider the scope of the outsource arrangements and the range of services to be supplied. Various other features of the outsourced agreement will need to be addressed.

In many countries, there is legislation covering the protection of employees when an operation is outsourced. For example, if an organization decides to transfer the catering or the cleaning services to an outsourced company, the employment rights

Table 32.2   Scope of outsourcing contracts

As a minimum, the agreement between the organization and the outsourced service provider must address the following issues:

- scope and duration of the arrangement
- services to be supplied and restrictions on sub-contracting
- pricing, fee structure, service levels and performance requirements
- audit and monitoring procedures
- confidentiality, privacy and security of information
- default arrangements and termination provisions
- dispute resolution arrangements
- insurance requirements, liability and indemnity

of staff previously employed by the organization may be protected. This can be a significant obstacle to the outsourcing of certain facilities management and other activities and thereby obtaining the cost reduction that would result.

Outsourcing of operations is usually considered to be a mechanism for having non-core activities undertaken by a contractor. For example, an office-based business may decide to outsource cleaning and catering, as well as other facilities management operations. The benefits will normally focus on reduced cost while, at the same time, receiving a greater level of expertise from the outsourced contract.

The box below considers some of the benefits of outsourcing. Outsourcing is often undertaken to save costs, but it may also be undertaken so that the work is fulfilled by a specialist company. For example, a mortgage lender may outsource property surveys to a company with greater resources and more expertise.

Benefits of outsourcing

Most businesses outsource certain functions, but this is a major decision and the benefits can be difficult to define. Outsourcing can cut costs by reducing overheads and having a professional perform the operation. Although this benefit is attainable, it should not be the only reason a company decides to outsource.

The benefits of outsourcing can be divided into two types. First, there are the direct benefits of having a specialist company undertaking the outsourced activities. Then, there are the indirect benefits of giving greater focus to the core activities that remain in-house. The direct benefits of outsourcing are reduced costs, decreased cycle times and improved customer perception and satisfaction, including:

- focus on core competency;
- reduction in the cost of manufacturing and logistics services;
- reduction in head count of hourly workers and management;
- improved accuracy;
- flexibility and wider range of services;
- access to global networks and superior technology;
- improved service and quality;
- reduced capital investment and increased cash flow.

Risk and contracts

Risk management is clearly an important component when setting up supply chain contracts or deciding to outsource certain activities. The need for a detailed contract between the organization and the suppliers of the outsourced service is clear from the factors considered in Table 32.2. The nature and complexity of the contract will depend on at least the following factors:

- level of the risk associated with the contracted service;
- value of the contract for supply of goods or services;
- duration and scope of the contract;
- level of skill required in the delivery of the contracted services;
- critical nature of the goods or services that are being contracted.

The desire to achieve greater value for money and reduce costs has resulted in complex supply chains that are far more fragmented than was previously the case. Many organizations will contract out key parts of their activities, so that money can be saved and a greater level of specialist expertise is available from the outsourced company. Outsourcing also enables organizations to focus on their own core operations and competencies.

However, this has resulted in complex global supply chains that are more vulnerable to potential disruption through external sources such as terrorism, pandemics and natural disasters. Organizations need to undertake a thorough risk assessment of their supply chain and outsourcing arrangements to ensure that the risks associated with these contracted services are adequately managed. Remember that contracting out the supply of goods or services does not transfer all of the risks. The scope of factors that need to be considered are discussed in the text box on the next page.

Outsourcing arrangements should be introduced only when they offer a cost-effective and efficient way of running the business. Outsourcing decisions based on a belief that risks are being completely transferred to a third party may prove to be incorrect. Damage to reputation may still be suffered if the outsourced manufacturing activity produces sub-standard goods or is exposed as operating unethical business practices.

For example, an organization that decides to have manufacturing undertaken in a lower-cost territory may discover that the goods produced do not comply fully with safety requirements. There have been examples of toys manufactured in one part of the world that were illegal in the country where the toys were to be sold because of the use of lead-based paint.

It is possible that the cost of supply will be reduced, but the risks may actually be increased. When contracting out services and supply, the organization needs to be satisfied that the risks associated with this transfer are within the risk appetite and consistent with the risk attitude of the organization, as well as being within its risk capacity. Finally, evaluation should be undertaken to determine the actual risk exposures that are associated with increasingly complex supply chain arrangements.

Insurance may be available for incidents that occur at the supplier premises. However, the arrangement is normally such that physical damage such as a fire, flood or earthquake is required to have happened at the supplier premises. In these circumstances, a policy extension may be available to the property damage insurance bought by the organization. Events such as poor quality of components, late delivery or the bankruptcy of the supplier are generally not insurable.

Motor industry supply chain

The automotive supply chain is as complex as it gets. There are approximately 20,000 parts in a car, and if only one of those parts is unavailable the finished product cannot be shipped. Automotive manufacturers need to re-evaluate risk mitigation strategies to deal with large-scale disruptions of their supply chains. There are a number of avenues open to them, including:

- challenging suppliers to develop disaster plans so that they can make provisions to move to alternative sites for production, in the event that they are unable to produce product at their main plant;

- eliminating sole-source suppliers and developing the capabilities of additional companies; having one supplier is probably too few, but having five suppliers is too many in terms of achieving economies of scale;

- analysing where suppliers are located and limiting the number of critical component suppliers that are geographically situated in a risky area;

- reviewing insurance policies and considering whether to take out contingent business interruption insurance that protects against losses relating to the inability of suppliers to deliver.

PART EIGHT
Risk assurance

PART EIGHT FURTHER READING

Cabinet Office (2009) *National Risk Assessment*, **www.cabinetoffice.gov.uk**
Canadian Institute of Chartered Accountants (1995) *Criteria of Control*, **www.cica.ca**
COSO (2013) *Internal Control: Integrated framework*, **www.coso.org**
Hillson, D (2016) *The Risk Management Handbook: A practical guide to managing the multiple dimensions of Risk*, **www.koganpage.com**
Institute of Internal Auditors (2004) *The Role of Internal Auditing in Enterprise-wide Risk Management*, **www.theiia.org**
Woods, M (2011) *Risk Management in Organizations: An integrated case study approach*, **www.routledge.com**

PART EIGHT CASE STUDIES

Unilever: Our risk appetite and approach to risk management

Unilever adopts a risk profile that is aligned to our vision to accelerate growth in the business while reducing our environmental footprint and increasing our positive social impact. Our available capital and other resources are applied to underpin our priorities. We aim to maintain a strong single A credit-rating on a long-term basis.

The Unilever boards assume overall accountability for the management of risk and for reviewing the effectiveness of Unilever's risk management and internal control systems. The boards have established a clear organizational structure with well-defined accountabilities for the principal risks that Unilever faces in the short, medium and long term. This organizational structure and distribution of accountabilities and responsibilities ensures that every country in which we operate has specific resources and processes for risk review and risk mitigation.

Unilever's approach to doing business is framed by our purpose. Our code of business principles sets out the standards of behaviour that we expect all employees to adhere to. Day-to-day responsibility for ensuring these principles are applied throughout Unilever rests with senior management across categories, geographies and functions.

Assurance on compliance with the code of business principles and all of our code policies is obtained annually from Unilever management via a formal code declaration. The boards regularly review the significant risks and decisions that could have a material impact on Unilever. These reviews consider the level of risk that Unilever is prepared to take in pursuit of the business strategy and the effectiveness of the management controls in place to mitigate the risk exposure.

Edited extract from Unilever PLC
Annual Report and Accounts 2015 – Strategic Report

Colgate Palmolive: Damage to reputation

Damage to our reputation could have an adverse effect on our business. Maintaining our strong reputation with consumers and our trade partners globally is critical to selling our branded products. Accordingly, we devote significant time and resources to programmes designed to protect and preserve our reputation.

Third parties sell counterfeit versions of our products, which are inferior or may pose safety risks. As a result, consumers of our brands could confuse our products with these counterfeit products, which could cause them to refrain from purchasing our brands in the future.

Adverse publicity about us or our brands regarding health concerns, legal or regulatory proceedings, environmental impacts, including packaging, energy and water use and waste management, or other sustainability issues, whether or not deserved, could jeopardize our reputation. In addition, negative posts or comments about us on any social media website could harm our reputation. Damage to our reputation or loss of consumer confidence in our products for any of these reasons could adversely affect our business, results of operations, cash flows and financial condition, as well as require resources to rebuild our reputation.

If one of our products, or a raw material contained in our products, is perceived or found to be defective or unsafe, we may need to recall some of our products. Whether or not a product liability or false marketing claim is successful, or a recall is required, such assertions could have an adverse effect, and the negative publicity surrounding them could harm our reputation and brand image.

Furthermore, if we suffer a loss or disclosure of confidential business or stakeholder information as a result of a breach of our information technology systems or failure of third-party service providers, we may suffer reputational, competitive, and/or business harm.

Edited extract from Colgate Palmolive Company
Form 10-K (Annual Report) 2013

Sainsbury's and Tesco: Principal risks and uncertainties

The table below provides an edited version of the descriptions of three of the principal risks faced by two major UK-based retailers. They agree that all three of these risks have increased since the previous report and accounts.

Sainsbury's: Our principal risks and uncertainties	Tesco: Principal risks and uncertainties
The risk management process is closely aligned to our strategy. Risk is an inherent part of doing business.	We have an established risk management process to identify the principal risks that we face as a business.
Colleague engagement, retention and capability Attracting and maintaining good relations with talented colleagues and investing in their training and development is essential to the efficiency and sustainability of the group's operations. Delivery of the strategic objectives, including development of new businesses and progress on multi-channel, increases the risk of ability to attract, motivate and retain talent, specific skill sets and capability. In addition, the challenging trading environment requires a focus on efficient operations which may include change initiatives impacting colleagues and presenting a risk of loss of colleague trust or engagement.	**People** Failure to attract, retain, develop and motivate the best people with the right capabilities across all levels, geographies and through the business transformation process could limit our ability to succeed. There is a risk that our leaders may not play their critical role in shaping the organization that we want to be and that they do not inspire great performance from our teams.

(continued)

(*Continued*)

Sainsbury's: Our principal risks and uncertainties	Tesco: Principal risks and uncertainties
Data security It is essential that the security of customer, colleague and company confidential data is maintained. A major breach of information security could have a major negative financial and reputational impact on the business. The risk landscape is increasingly challenging with deliberate acts of cyber-crime on the rise targeting all markets and heightening the risk exposure.	**Data security and privacy** Increasing risks of cyber-attack threaten the security of customer, colleague and supplier data. We must ensure that we understand the types of data that we hold and secure it adequately to manage the risk of data breaches.
Trading environment and competitive landscape Effective management of the trading account is key to the achievement of performance targets. The sector outlook has been and is set to remain challenging. The challenging trading environment, food price deflation and the price reduction and price matching activity across the sector may adversely impact performance.	**Competition and markets** If we fail to address the differing challenges of the budget retailers, the premium retailers and online entrants, it may adversely impact our market share and profitability.

Edited extracts from J Sainsbury plc
Annual Report and Financial Statements 2015

Edited extracts from Tesco plc
Annual Report and Financial Statements 2015

The control environment

Nature of internal control

The system of internal control within an organization is an important component in the successful management of its risks. Internal control is concerned with the methods, procedures and checks that are in place to ensure that a business or organization meets its objectives. There are alternative definitions of internal control and some of the key definitions are set out in Table 33.1. Internal controls can be considered to be the actions taken by management to plan, organize and direct the performance of sufficient actions to provide reasonable assurance that objectives will be achieved.

The phrase 'control environment' is preferred by internal auditors. ISO 31000 refers to the 'risk management context'. The COSO ERM cube refers to the 'internal environment'. In all cases, the intention is to refer to the level of maturity of the organization with regard to internal control activities. When referring to internal control activities, it is important to have a single definition within the organization. Table 33.1 sets out some of the best known definitions of internal control.

ISO Guide 73 defines control as a measure that is modifying risk. It also states that controls include any procedure, policy, device, practice or other action that modifies risk. Guide 73 also makes the important point that controls may not always exert the intended or assumed modifying effect. Internal control incorporates the organizational and hierarchical structure, as well as planning and objective setting. The scope of internal control extends to evaluation of controls designed to support the organization in achieving objectives and executing strategy, but it also applies to the control of actions to ensure that the organization does not miss business opportunities.

When designing effective internal controls, the organization should look at the arrangements in place to achieve the following:

- maintenance of reliable systems;
- timely preparation of reliable information;
- safeguarding of assets;
- optimum use of resources;
- preventing and detecting fraud and error.

Effective financial controls, including maintenance of proper accounting records, are an important and well-established element of internal control. These financial controls help ensure that the company is not unnecessarily exposed to financial risks and that financial information used within the business and for public reporting is reliable.

Table 33.1   Definitions of internal control

Organization	Definition of internal control
CoCo (Criteria of Control)	Internal control is all the elements of an organization that, taken together, support people in the achievement of the organization's objectives. The elements include resources, systems, processes, culture, structure and tasks.
COSO	A process, effected by an entity's board of directors, management and other personnel, designed to provide reasonable assurance regarding the achievement of objectives in the following categories: • effectiveness and efficiency of operations; • reliability of financial reporting; • compliance with applicable laws and regulations.
IIA (Institute of Internal Auditors)	A set of processes, functions, activities, sub-systems, and people who are grouped together or consciously segregated to ensure the effective achievement of objectives and goals.

Purpose of internal control

The primary purpose of internal control activities is to help the organization achieve its objectives. Typically, internal controls have the following purposes:

- safeguard and protect the assets of the organization;
- ensure the keeping of accurate records;
- promote operational effectiveness and efficiency;
- adhere to policies and procedures, including control procedures;
- enhance reliability of internal and external reporting;
- ensure compliance with laws and regulations;
- safeguard the interests of shareholders/stakeholders.

The internal control system includes internal control activities and the structure and responsibilities that relate to them. The purpose of this internal control system is to enable directors to drive the organization forward with confidence, in both good and bad times. A further purpose of the internal control system and internal control activities is to safeguard resources and ensure the adequacy of records and systems of accountability.

The purpose of the control environment is to ensure consistent responses to risks that materialize. A well-developed control environment will also ensure that pre-planned responses to a crisis situation are efficiently and effectively implemented.

There are a number of approaches to the evaluation of the control environment, including LILAC, CoCo and risk maturity models such as FOIL and the 4Ns, as described in Chapter 24.

In many ways, the use of a maturity model will help evaluate the status of the control environment in terms of the implementation of the selected structure that will be used to drive improvements in the control environment and achieve a greater level of risk awareness in the organization. In summary, the LILAC or CoCo model will be selected as the means of driving and measuring improvements in the control environment. The level of success in implementing the selected framework will be reflected in the level of risk maturity, as measured by FOIL and the 4Ns, that has been achieved. An enhanced level of maturity will enable the organization to achieve more sophisticated outcomes from its risk management efforts, as illustrated in Figure 4.2. Risk maturity models can be used as a means of benchmarking the risk management status of an organization and targets can be set to increase risk maturity.

Control environment

The Criteria of Control framework, otherwise known as CoCo, produced by the Canadian Institute of Chartered Accountants (CICA) is a structured means of measuring the quality of the control environment within an organization. The control environment, which the COSO ERM cube labels as the 'internal environment', is a measure of the risk culture within the organization. The view taken by the CoCo framework is that if the control environment is satisfactory, risk management and internal control activities will be successfully and appropriately undertaken.

The structure of the CoCo framework is set out in Figure 33.1. The framework has four components, which are represented as a continuous cycle. The components are based on a sense of direction of the organization, a sense of identity and values, a sense of competence and a sense of evolution.

A number of organizations use the CoCo framework as a means of benchmarking compliance with the internal control component of the COSO ERM cube. This approach will, therefore, be based on a framework that is a combination of CoCo and the remaining seven components of the COSO ERM cube. Table 33.2 gives more information on the specific requirements of each of the four components of the CoCo framework, as set out below:

- purpose;
- commitment;
- capability;
- monitoring and learning.

The rationale behind CoCo is explained in the framework as follows:

> A person performs a task guided by an understanding of its purpose and supported by capability. The person needs a sense of commitment to perform the task well. The person monitors his or her performance and the external environment to learn how to do the task better and any required changes. In any organization of people, the essence of control is the four components set out above.

Figure 33.1   Criteria of Control (CoCo) framework

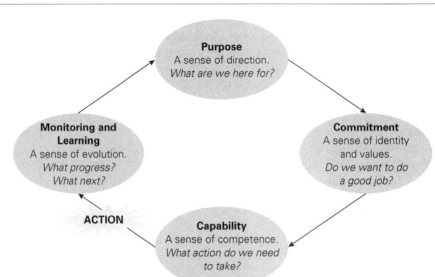

SOURCE Reproduced with permission from *Guidance on Control*, Canadian Institute of Chartered Accountants (1995, Toronto).

There are similarities between the CoCo approach and the LILAC measure of risk awareness or risk culture that has been mentioned previously. The LILAC approach suggests that risk management activities will be embedded when the risk culture displays leadership, involvement, learning, accountability and communication. Individual organizations should decide how they wish to measure the control environment/risk-aware culture within the organization. Whatever method is used to measure the risk culture, there is no doubt that it is critical to the successful implementation of risk management.

CoCo is an internal control framework, but it is described in this chapter because it is an established framework. There is a strong interface between risk management activities and internal control, and the CoCo framework therefore provides a useful means of evaluating the risk culture of an organization. CoCo defines three major objectives of controls:

- effectiveness and efficiency of operations;
- reliability of internal and external reporting;
- compliance with applicable laws and regulations and internal policies.

Features of the control environment

There are significant differences between COSO Internal Control and CoCo, as well as several key similarities. CoCo has a broader approach to the control environment than is set out in COSO. To give two examples of the broader approach in CoCo, it

Table 33.2   Components of the CoCo framework

Purpose
Objectives should be established and communicated.
Significant internal and external risks should be identified and assessed.
Policies should be established, communicated and practised.
Plans should be established and communicated.
Plans should include measurable performance targets and indicators.

Commitment
Shared ethical values should be established, communicated and practised.
HR policies should be consistent with ethical values.
Authority, responsibility and accountability should be clearly defined.
Mutual trust should be fostered to support the flow of information.

Capability
People should have the necessary knowledge, skills and tools.
Communication processes should support the values of the organization.
Sufficient and relevant information should be identified and communicated.
Decisions and actions within the organization should be co-ordinated.
Control activities should be designed as an integral part of the organization.

Monitoring and learning
Environment should be monitored to re-evaluate controls.
Performance should be monitored against the targets.
Assumptions behind objectives should be periodically challenged.
Information needs and related information systems should be reassessed.
Procedures should be established to ensure appropriate actions occur.
Management should periodically assess the effectiveness of control.

---

recognizes that controls are required in the setting of objectives, strategic planning and corrective actions; it also recognizes that the control environment of an organization is important when making decisions.

When undertaking an evaluation of the control environment using the structure of CoCo, a company may discover that good scores were obtained for the purpose, commitment and capability of the organization. However, the score for the monitoring and learning component may not be good enough. This information will enable the company to identify that it needs to pay more attention to the areas of challenging objectives and the assumptions that lie behind them. Better auditing of controls and a structured senior management review of risk management and internal control activities can then be introduced.

The main differences in approach between COSO Internal Control and CoCo are that CoCo is more explicit about the following issues:

- identification of a need to exploit opportunities;
- mitigation of weaknesses in business resilience;

- the importance of individual trust to the quality of the control environment;
- the need to periodically challenge assumptions.

There are two versions of the COSO cube, and it is the COSO ERM cube (2004) that is considered in detail in this book. COSO Internal Control was originally published in 1992, but was updated in 2013 and the first component of the COSO Internal Control cube is called the control environment. The features of the control environment that are considered to be important by COSO Internal Control can be summarized as:

- organization is committed to integrity and ethical values;
- board has oversight of development and performance of internal control;
- management sets structures, reporting lines, authorities and responsibilities;
- organization seeks to attract, develop, and retain competent individuals; and
- organization holds individuals accountable for internal control responsibilities.

Components of a good risk culture

A good risk culture consistently supports appropriate risk-awareness, behaviours and judgements about risk taking within a strong risk governance framework. A good risk culture bolsters effective risk management, promotes appropriate risk taking, and ensures that emerging risks or risk-taking activities beyond risk appetite are recognized, assessed, escalated and addressed.

A good risk culture should emphasize the importance of ensuring that: 1) an appropriate risk–reward balance consistent with risk appetite is achieved when taking on risks; 2) an effective system of controls commensurate with the scale and complexity of the organization is in place; 3) the quality of risk models, data accuracy, capability of available tools to accurately measure risks, and justifications for risk taking can be challenged; and 4) all limit breaches, deviations from established policies, and operational incidents are investigated with proportionate disciplinary actions when necessary.

Based on Financial Stability Board (2014)

CoCo framework of internal control

The first component of the CoCo framework is concerned with the establishment and communication of objectives, the significant internal and external risks faced by the organization and the policies designed to support achievement of the organization's objectives. Plans to assist with the achievement of objectives and the inclusion of measurable performance targets and indicators are also important aspects of the purpose component of CoCo.

When establishing and analysing the purpose of the organization, CoCo makes it clear that the risks and opportunities facing the organization should be analysed in detail. The importance of risk assessment and organizational resilience is emphasized, together with the importance of recognizing the sources and origins of risk.

The commitment component of CoCo is concerned with shared ethical values, including integrity. It is also concerned with human resource policies and practices and communication throughout the organization. Authority, responsibility and accountability are also included, together with the requirement to achieve an atmosphere of mutual trust.

The capabilities component of CoCo is concerned with the fact that people should have the necessary knowledge and skills to support the organization's objectives, as well as its values. Sufficient relevant information should be identified and communicated, together with decisions and actions of different parts of the organization. Activity should be co-ordinated and designed as an integral part of the organization.

The monitoring and learning component of the CoCo framework is concerned with external and internal environments and the fact that they should be monitored to obtain information. Performance should be monitored against targets and indicators and assumptions behind the objectives of the organization should be periodically challenged.

The information needs and related information systems should be assessed when objectives change, and a procedure should be established and performed to ensure that appropriate change actions occur in these circumstances. Finally, management should periodically assess the effectiveness of control in the organization and communicate results to appropriate stakeholders. An example of an organization evaluating its control environment is set out in the box on the next page.

Evaluating the control environment

Many organizations have created their own formulas for educating employees about why controls are important and what adopting such measures means to them. The common element among these organizations is a commitment by senior management that embraces the internal control model.

Canada Post Corporation uses eight major groupings to evaluate the control environment, as follows:

- leadership;
- planning;
- customer focus;
- people focus;
- process management;
- partnership;
- business performance;
- continuous improvement.

During self-assessment workshops, executives receive the final results of all audit work performed throughout the year. The group then discusses business objectives for the coming year and the risks that could interfere with achieving them. The participants rate themselves on a scale of 1 to 10 for each of the criteria. Internal audit then compares the information it received directly from a business process to the information the group acquired about that process during other workshops.

Using the workshop results, internal audit develops an audit opinion on the effectiveness of controls and an audit plan for the coming year. Additionally, internal auditing provides a summary of the results to the board of directors to consider in its strategic planning session. The report includes a commentary on the company's five highest risks and five weakest controls.

Good safety culture

Ensuring a risk-aware culture in the organization is vitally important. A risk-aware culture will be achieved when all members of staff and management understand and accept the importance of adequate risk management. In addition, management and staff need to understand the role they will play in the successful management of risks and have a desire to fulfil that role enthusiastically.

There are many ways in which a risk-aware culture can be demonstrated. Clearly, one of the ways of demonstrating such a culture is to achieve high scores in a CoCo analysis. The COSO ERM cube also has an internal environment component, although this component is not as comprehensive as the CoCo framework. Nevertheless, evaluation of the internal environment and the level of risk awareness within the organization can be undertaken using the COSO ERM cube.

Many organizations regard the combination of COSO ERM and CoCo as an ideal way of combining the detailed approach to measuring culture within CoCo with the more exhaustive approach of COSO ERM. ISO 31000 refers to the context of risk management. Context has three components in ISO 31000, described as the internal context, the external context and the risk management context. Together, analysis of these three contexts will provide information on the status of the risk-aware culture in the organization.

A subset of a good risk-aware culture is a strong safety culture. Following a major rail crash at Ladbroke Grove near London Paddington railway station in 1999, the Ladbroke Grove Inquiry heard various definitions of the word 'culture'. Counsel to the Inquiry submitted that:

> A good safety culture is the product of individual and group values, of attitudes and patterns of behaviour that lead to a commitment to an organization's health and safety management. Organizations with a positive safety culture are characterized by communication founded on mutual trust, by shared perception of the importance of safety and by confidence in the efficiency of preventative measures.

Research by the Health and Safety Executive into the components of a safety culture produced a detailed report and the key components of the safety culture were identified as leadership, involvement, learning, accountability and communication. This gives rise to the acronym LILAC, which is described in more detail in Chapter 24. This represents an alternative approach to the purpose, commitment, capability, monitoring and learning components of the CoCo framework.

Risk assurance techniques   34

Audit committees

An increasing number of organizations have decided that it is appropriate to have an audit committee. Almost invariably, the audit committee consists of non-executive directors, with senior executive directors in attendance at audit committee meetings. It is chaired by a non-executive director, often referred to as the lead non-executive director, but usually not the non-executive chairman of the organization. The audit committee is generally not considered to be a sub-committee of the board, but has a status and a seniority that enables the audit committee to evaluate all activities in the organization, including the activities of the board itself.

Although the audit committee may be considered to be the guardian of compliance within the organization, the terms of reference are usually much broader than just compliance. The board of an organization will be responsible for governance throughout the organization, including co-ordinating the activities of specialist risk management functions. In this way, the board is responsible for the first and the second lines of defence. In other words, the board is responsible for the governance and risk components of governance, risk and compliance.

The audit committee is in a position to evaluate the governance standards within the organization, ensure that risk management receives appropriate attention, and seek assurance on the levels of compliance achieved within the organization. The role of the audit committee may be much broader than this, and includes evaluation of the arrangements for governance of the board itself. Many large organizations establish separate committees for making senior appointments, including appointments to the board. This committee will normally be referred to as the nominations committee. Likewise, many large organizations will have a committee responsible for establishing remuneration and benefits structures that will apply throughout the whole organization.

The existence of a separate nominations or remuneration committee does not diminish the role and responsibilities of the audit committee. Nominations and remuneration, as well as some other committees, will be sub-committees of the board and are likely to have joint executive and non-executive membership. In reviewing the effectiveness of the board, the audit committee will also evaluate the effectiveness of the sub-committees. Given this role, the audit committee will retain its position as the ultimate monitor of governance, risk and compliance throughout the whole operation. The audit committee will seek assurance relating to all aspects of the strategy, tactics, operations and compliance of the organization.

The outcomes and impact of risk management activities are often reported to an audit committee in a large organization. Audit committees have a range of responsibilities, including the obligation to obtain adequate risk assurance in the organization. Table 34.1 provides a list of typical responsibilities of the audit committee. Audit committees should be non-executive bodies that do not have executive responsibility for risk management. Similarly, they should not have responsibility for the identification of significant risks or the identification and implementation of critical controls.

The function of the audit committee is to seek risk assurance and check that the procedure for the identification of significant risks is appropriate. The audit committee should validate that the significant risks have been correctly identified, as well as seeking assurance that critical controls have been correctly implemented.

Table 34.1   Responsibilities of the audit committee

External audit

- recommend the appointment and re-appointment of external auditors
- review the performance and cost-effectiveness of the external auditors
- review the qualification, expertise and independence of external auditors
- review and discuss any reports from the external auditors

Internal audit

- review internal audit and its relationship with external auditors
- review and assess the annual internal audit plan
- review promptly all reports from the internal auditors
- review management response to the findings of the internal auditors
- review activities, resources and effectiveness of internal audit

Financial reporting

- review the annual and half-year financial results
- evaluate annual report against requirements of the governance code
- review disclosure by CEO and CFO during certification of annual report

Regulatory reports

- review arrangements for producing the audited accounts
- monitor and review standards of risk management and internal control
- develop a code of ethics for CEO and other senior management roles
- annually review the adequacy of the risk management processes
- receive reports on litigation, financial commitments and other liabilities
- receive reports of any issues raised by whistleblowing activities

The audit committee is concerned with internal control in the organization. Internal control is described in guidance to the UK Corporate Governance Code as the whole system of controls, financial and otherwise, established in order to provide reasonable assurance of effective and efficient internal control and compliance with laws and regulations.

It is worth considering the role of the audit committee in relation to the requirements of the UK Corporate Governance Code. The code only applies to companies that are listed on the London Stock Exchange, although the principles set out in the code appear to be gaining wider acceptance and application. One of the requirements is that companies without an internal audit function should review the need for such a department on a routine basis.

Even if these requirements do not apply to an organization, it is still appropriate for the audit committee to ensure that it can fully respond to these questions, by ensuring that necessary information is collected. An important component of governance requirements is the acknowledgement of the limitations of internal control.

Role of risk management

The risk management policy should set out the roles and responsibilities for risk management and internal control. The purpose of risk management is to fulfil mandatory obligations, provide assurance, support decision making and help ensure the effectiveness and efficiency of core processes (MADE2).

When allocating risk management responsibilities, consideration should be given in respect of each of the significant risks faced by the organization to the separate allocation of responsibilities for:

- determining strategy;
- designing controls;
- auditing compliance.

For example, a head office department may decide on the appropriate level of security for an organization. The design of the appropriate controls may be the responsibility of the production department. This is appropriate because security risk may be an integral part of production that needs to be under the ownership of the production department. In other organizations, it may be appropriate for the security arrangements to be designed by a specialist security adviser or the head of security within the company. Auditing of compliance with the security arrangements is likely to be the responsibility of the internal audit department.

Even in a small organization, it may be important for responsibilities for the management of fraud risk to be separated between different employees or departments. In a small charity, for example, it may be appropriate for a non-executive board member to undertake the internal control audit and thereby provide an objective view of the efficiency and effectiveness of the internal financial controls in place in the organization.

The role of the risk manager in the allocation of these responsibilities should be a facilitation role. The risk manager may facilitate a workshop designed to identify the fraud risks within the organization and allocate responsibilities for controlling them.

However, the risk manager cannot be responsible for implementing controls or auditing compliance. Risk management and internal audit should restrict their roles to the evaluation of the effectiveness of the controls and assist with the identification of whether additional and/or different control measures should be introduced. Risk managers should be aware of the added value of internal audit, as outlined in the text box below.

Added value of internal audit

Although what constitutes value-added activity will vary based on many factors, there are some general rules that apply across the board. Four factors that can help auditors determine what will add the most value to their organization are:

- knowledge of the organization, including its culture, key players, and competitive environment;
- courage to innovate in ways stakeholders don't expect and may not think they want;
- ability to adapt to the organization in ways that exceed stakeholder expectations;
- knowledge of those practices that the profession, in general, considers value-added.

Three of these factors (organizational knowledge, courage and ability to adapt) are competencies and personal qualities that, for the most part, are self-explanatory. However, knowledge of the practices that the profession considers value-added is a continuing professional challenge for internal auditors.

Risk assurance

Risk assurance is an important component of the overall risk management process. The audit committee will seek assurance that all of the significant risks are being adequately managed and that all of the critical controls are effective and that they have been efficiently implemented.

There are often discussions at audit committees about 'how seriously a particular department takes risk management and internal control'. The risk manager and the internal auditor will undoubtedly be able to offer an opinion. However, what the audit committee will require is an objective evaluation of the performance of that department. This objective evaluation of the risk culture within the department will form the main basis of assurance for the audit committee. There are other sources of assurance available to the audit committee and these are set out in Table 34.2. Subject to the nature of the organization, the audit committee may depend on some or all of these sources of assurance. Risk assurance is also available from the external auditors, although this may be limited to validation of the accounting processes and financial performance.

Assurance will also be required in relation to the risk management activities themselves. The review and monitoring stage of the risk management process is usually represented as an information and experience loop that provides feedback to the beginning of the process. When considering the review and monitoring activities that need to be undertaken, the following stages should be borne in mind:

- review of the process as it operates in the organization;
- review of the standards of risk control in force;
- review of the level of success in reducing risk exposures;
- review of the level of success in achieving business objectives;
- review of why a high-risk strategy, project or operation was successful;
- delivery of risk assurance across this whole range of activities.

When a company plans to borrow more money from the bank, it may be asked to demonstrate how the board obtains assurance that the management of significant risks is satisfactory. The sources of assurance available might include:

- evaluation of the risk culture of the organization;
- quality of audit reports produced by internal audit;
- quality of reports produced by the various departments;
- overall business success of individual departments.

The company may decide that the reports from internal audit and the quality of reports from departments will be the basis of risk assurance. The company can also introduce a control risk self-assessment (CRSA) procedure that will be based on the components as set out in the 2014 risk guidance published by the Financial Reporting Council. Areas of weakness identified in the CRSA returns will be reported to the executive committee and remedial action will be required. All of these actions will provide the board with greater assurance and place the company in a better position to secure the additional funding from the bank.

When considering risk assurance, the organization will need to evaluate different issues, depending on whether the evaluation is related to strategy, tactics, operations or compliance. Assurance on adequate management of hazard risks can be achieved by evaluation of the hazard risk performance of the department.

Depending on the risk priorities of the organization, the board or audit committee may require annual reports on certain hazard risks. Because of the importance of health and safety at work, boards usually receive annual reports on safety performance.

Table 34.2   Sources of risk assurance

Culture measurement – by use of a recognized framework such as CoCo or COSO in order to gain a quantitative evaluation of the control environment.

Audit reports – produced by internal audit and external auditors on a range of issues including risk assessment, implementation, compliance and training.

Unit reports – on such issues as risk performance indicators, CRSA, response to audit recommendations and reports on incidents that have occurred.

Performance of the unit – on risk-related issues, losses, significant weaknesses in control measures and details of any material losses suffered by the unit.

Unit documentation – on topics such as the risk management policy, health and safety policy, business continuity plans and disaster recovery plans.

Likewise, the audit committee will wish to receive an annual report on the incidents of fraud that have been detected within the organization. This will be especially true of organizations that handle large amounts of cash.

Risks that are concerned with uncertainty, and in particular with the successful completion of projects, are often the subject of a review by the board or audit committee. Within large organizations, it is typical to have a post-implementation review of a project. For example, if the board of a retail company has authorized the opening of a new store, the audit committee will require a review of the completion of the project for opening the store. This post-implementation review will evaluate whether the project was delivered on time, within budget and to specification. It is also common for the audit committee to require a further post-implementation review of the first 12 months trading of the new store.

Risk assurance related to strategy/opportunities is more difficult and somewhat less well developed. Nevertheless, there is an increasing number of examples of organizations that undertake opportunity evaluations. This has become increasingly common in the professional consultancy firms. When a new business prospect arises, many professional consultancy firms have an opportunity review committee that decides on whether the organization wishes to offer its services to the client prospect. This type of opportunity evaluation may initially be achieved by attaching a risk assessment to a new business proposal.

Risk management outputs

When working together, risk management and internal audit should always concentrate on the outputs from the risk management process and the impact that is sought. The contribution of risk management is to ensure a greater chance of achieving the objectives of the organization, and this is also a stated intention of internal audit activities.

Overall, risk management/internal audit outputs are intended to achieve enhanced performance of the organization in the four important areas of effective and efficient strategy, tactics, operations and compliance (STOC). These outputs will be achieved by ensuring minimum disruption to routine operations from hazard risks, together with selection of effective processes that are appropriate for the organization. Selection of effective processes requires informed decision making and the successful design and delivery of projects. Risk management and internal audit should work together to achieve these outputs.

The most important decisions taken by an organization relate to strategy. Risk management and internal audit both have roles to play in helping the organization reach strategic decisions that result in the development of effective and efficient strategy. For example, risk management should ensure that risk assessment workshops address strategic decisions and internal audit should evaluate the quality of the strategic decision-making procedures.

The required outputs from risk management/internal audit can be summarized as fulfilling mandatory obligations, providing assurance, supporting decision making and ensuring the existence of effective and efficient core processes (MADE2). Risk management and internal audit should work together to achieve these outputs. Due regard should always be paid to the desire of internal audit to remain independent of executive management as they fulfil their activities. The need to retain this independence is another reason why internal audit should not become too closely involved in the executive role and responsibilities related to the management of risk.

Control risk self-assessment

As well as undertaking physical audits, internal audit departments will often facilitate a procedure of self-certification of controls. Self-certification of controls is an arrangement whereby local senior management complete a regular (often annual) return confirming details of the level of risk assurance that has been achieved in the department.

This type of self-certification is generally known as control risk self-assessment (CRSA) and it is frequently undertaken as an electronic return or recorded on the intranet of the organization. The questionnaire for the control risk self-assessment can be based on the criteria set out in COSO Internal Control, CoCo or any other relevant internal control framework, such as the 2014 risk guidance from the UK Financial Reporting Council (FRC).

As well as providing confirmation of adequate levels of internal control and risk assurance, the CRSA return can also provide details of situations where significant weaknesses in controls have been identified. This information will enable the internal auditors to identify areas where additional controls may be required. Also, in addition to identifying significant weaknesses, the CRSA return can require information on any material failures that have occurred.

A benchmark test for identifying a material failure should be supplied and will be much lower than the test for materiality applied by external auditors. For example, an organization that had set a test of materiality at £1 million might require reports on the CRSA return of any failure in controls that resulted in an incident/loss in excess of £100,000 at departmental level.

Approaches to CRSA

The executive has recommended the use of an annual 'control risk self-assessment' (CRSA) exercise, to be conducted by internal audit, as part of the annual review of corporate governance. Each year a sample of the governance policies will be chosen by the governance panel for inclusion in the CRSA exercise. Policy custodians will be required to help formulate questionnaires and report back on the feedback received from services to internal audit.

The findings from the CRSA exercise, together with the assessment of compliance against each of the supporting principles and work carried out by internal audit in accordance with the annual audit plan will be drawn together into the annual governance statement, for review by the governance panel, the audit committee and the executive committee.

Benefits of risk assurance

Corporate governance is a major concern for all organizations and their stakeholders. Therefore, risk assurance should not be an administrative or box-ticking exercise. Organizations need to demonstrate that corporate governance is a priority for management. Many organizations recognize the need for openness of risk reporting. This requires effective communication activities to be in place at all times.

Having established good communication activities, the organization needs to ensure that there are positive messages to be communicated to stakeholders. Undertaking risk assurance activities will provide assurance to all stakeholders, including employees, suppliers, customers, government departments, external audit and internal audit, as described in the text box overleaf.

Obtaining risk assurance is an important part of the corporate governance arrangements for all organizations, as well as being of benefit to the strategic, tactical, operational and compliance (STOC) core processes, activities and decisions of the organization. The benefits of adequate risk assurance are that it:

- builds confidence with stakeholders;
- provides reassurance to sponsors and financiers;
- demonstrates good practice to regulators;
- prevents financial and other surprises;
- reduces the chances of damage to reputation;
- encourages the risk culture within the organization;
- allows more secure delegation of authority.

Level of risk assurance

Whilst the work of the external auditor is not primarily conducted for the benefit of the organization, the audit and risk assurance committee should nevertheless engage with this activity. As well as considering the results of external audit work and resolution of identified weaknesses, they should enquire about and consider the planned audit approach of the external auditor.

They should also consider the way in which the external auditor is co-operating with internal audit to maximize overall audit efficiency, capture opportunities to derive a greater level of assurance and minimize unnecessary duplication of work. In addition, they should review and consider the potential implications for the organization of the wider work carried out by the external auditor, for example, value for money reports and good practice findings.

HM Treasury (2016)

Internal audit activities

Scope of internal audit

There needs to be a close working relationship between risk management and internal audit. The responsibilities allocated to each of these functions will vary according to the nature, type and size of the organization. This is an important working relationship, because successful management of risk depends on four important risk-based outputs, which can be summarized as MADE2:

- mandatory as required by laws, customers/clients and standards;
- assurance for the management team and other stakeholders;
- decision making based on the best information available;
- effective and efficient core processes throughout the organization.

It is clear that if these outputs are to be successfully delivered, all stakeholders need to work together, and that includes co-operation between risk management and internal audit. The range of activities that are related to risk assurance are explored in Chapter 34. The important contribution made by internal audit and the range of activities that the internal audit department undertake are considered in more detail in this chapter.

Internal control is concerned with the methods, procedures and checks that are in place to ensure that a business organization meets its objectives. Because internal control is concerned with the fulfilment of objectives, there is a clear link with risk management activities. Internal control activities within a large organization are likely to be evaluated by the internal audit department. In some cases, the internal audit function may be outsourced to an external accountancy firm.

Although there is a distinction between the approach and activities of internal audit and of risk management, there are areas of common interest. It is generally accepted that risk management is an executive function that should be undertaken by the executive members of the organization. This leads to the conclusion that the risk management committee should be chaired by an executive board-level director.

Internal audit is primarily concerned with risk assurance, and this will be the concern of the non-executive audit committee in a large organization. Given that internal audit is validating the controls and procedures in place to manage risk, it is inappropriate for internal auditors to fulfil an executive function by assisting management with the identification, design and implementation of those risk control measures.

Expectations of internal control

A sound system of internal control reduces, but cannot eliminate, the possibility of poor judgement in decision making, human error, control processes being deliberately circumvented by employees and others, management overriding controls, and the occurrence of unforeseeable circumstances.

A sound system of internal control therefore provides reasonable, but not absolute, assurance that a company will not be hindered in achieving its business objectives, or in the orderly and legitimate conduct of its business, by circumstances that may reasonably be foreseen. A system of internal control cannot, however, provide protection with certainty against a company failing to meet its business objectives or all material errors, losses, fraud, or breaches of laws or regulations.

Internal financial control in a charity

Internal financial controls are just one part of a charity's overall control framework. The wider framework should cover all the charity's systems and activities.

Executive management, staff and volunteers are responsible for ensuring that the controls put in place by the trustees are implemented. There should be a culture of control embedded in the operations of the organization; this culture is created by the trustees and senior management, who should lead by example in adhering to internal financial controls and good practice.

The trustees should, at least annually, ensure a review is conducted of the effectiveness of the internal financial controls. This should include an assessment of whether the controls are relevant to, and appropriate for, the charity and not too onerous or disproportionate.

A key feature of internal financial controls is to ensure that no single individual has sole responsibility for any single transaction from authorization to completion and review. It is important where the trustees administer the charity personally, more likely in smaller charities, that there is sufficient segregation of duties amongst them, so that no one trustee is overburdened or exercises sole responsibility.

Role of internal audit

Figure 35.1 illustrates the range of activities that need to be undertaken in order to fulfil a successful ERM initiative. The diagram identifies those activities that are core to the work of the internal audit department. These activities include reviewing the management of key risks, evaluating the reporting of those risks and evaluating risk management processes.

The diagram also identifies activities that should not involve internal audit. These activities include setting the risk appetite, imposing risk management processes and taking decisions on risk responses. In between these two sets of activities there are

Figure 35.1   Role of internal audit in ERM

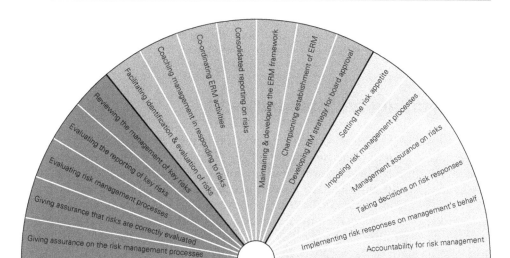

Core internal audit roles in regard to ERM
Reviewing the management of key risks
Evaluating the reporting of key risks
Evaluating risk management processes
Giving assurance that risks are correctly evaluated
Giving assurance on the risk management processes

Legitimate internal audit roles with safeguards
Facilitating identification & evaluation of risks
Coaching management in responding to risks
Co-ordinating ERM activities
Consolidated reporting on risks
Maintaining & developing the ERM framework
Championing establishment of ERM
Developing RM strategy for board approval

Roles internal audit should not undertake
Setting the risk appetite
Imposing risk management processes
Management assurance on risks
Taking decisions on risk responses
Implementing risk responses on management's behalf
Accountability for risk management

SOURCE This diagram is taken from *Position Statement: The role of internal audit in enterprise-wide risk management*, reproduced with the permission of the Institute of Internal Auditors – UK and Ireland. For the full statement visit www.iia.org.uk.

activities where it is legitimate for internal audit to become involved, provided that suitable safeguards are in place. These activities include facilitating the identification of risks, co-ordinating ERM activities, developing the ERM framework and championing the establishment of ERM. The division of responsibilities set out in Figure 35.1 is not just compatible with the three lines of defence approach; it reinforces that approach and provides considerable detail on the allocation of responsibilities. Use of the information shown in Figure 35.1 will help an organization allocate responsibilities to management as the first line of defence, specialist risk management functions as the second line of defence, and internal audit as the third line of defence.

Establishing audit priorities is an important function of the audit department. In relation to risk management activities, internal auditors will need to establish their priorities for the testing of controls. There is an important interface between risk management and internal control. Risk management professionals are very good at assessing risks and identifying the appropriate type of control that should be in place. The risk register will often record current controls and make recommendations for the implementation of additional controls.

The core work of the internal auditor starts at this point. Having identified the critically important controls, the auditor will need to check that they are implemented in practice and that they are correct and effective. The outcome of testing of controls is to ensure that the intended level of risk is actually achieved in practice. In other words, the control actually moves the level of risk from the inherent level to the intended current level in the way that was planned and often assumed.

If the control is not effective and efficient, it will need to be modified. This is another area where risk management and internal audit share expertise. Although these discussions on controls can be facilitated by risk management and internal audit, the ultimate decisions on the controls and their anticipated effectiveness have to be made by the members of line management who are responsible for the controls.

Undertaking an internal audit

Undertaking an internal audit exercise involves a number of steps, as set out in Table 35.1. Essentially, the steps involved are planning the internal audit exercise, undertaking the fieldwork during which controls are tested, producing the audit report and, finally, ensuring that there is adequate follow-up. As part of the audit exercise, the auditor should collect information relevant to the audit that is to be undertaken. Analysis of the information that has been collected will enable the auditor to determine and agree the priorities and objectives of the review. For example, an audit of the supply chain will require the auditor to collect information on the contracts that are in place with suppliers.

Table 35.1   Undertaking an internal audit

Planning

1   Initial contact: to inform the client (audit target) or involved association about the auditing and its objectives.

2   Initial meeting: conference meeting, so that the client can describe the areas for review and state the available resources and processes.

3   Preliminary survey: the auditors will gather all the needed data so they can have a good overview of the auditing.

4   Review internal control structure: the auditor will determine the priority areas for the audit to review.

5   Audit programme preparation: the audit programmes will outline the required fieldwork related to the audit topic/area.

Fieldwork

1   Testing for the critical internal controls: this process tests if randomly selected records are accurate.

2   Regular updates: the auditor will carry out financial reporting, mostly in oral communication and the client may help in resolving any issues raised.

3   Drafting the audit summary: when fieldwork is done, the auditor will summarize findings, conclusions and recommendations.

(continued)

Table 35.1   *(Continued)*

Audit report

1   Audit report: the report will be reviewed by the audit team before presenting it to the client for further review.

2   Creating the report: comments and suggestions on the first draft are taken into account in producing the final report.

3   Distribution of the final audit reports to people involved, senior management, audit committee, as agreed.

Follow-up

1   Audit follow-up: response from the client will be reviewed, so that the findings may be tested and resolved.

2   Reporting the audit follow-up: the effects of resolved and unresolved findings will be included in the follow-up.

In many ways, the fieldwork is the most important part of the audit exercise. The auditor may need to visit locations, including supplier locations if the audit is concerned with the supply chain. The purpose of the fieldwork is to understand the risks and the controls that are in place to manage those risks. Testing of the controls will then be undertaken to ensure the efficiency and effectiveness of the controls that are in place. Testing of these controls will be based on discussions with the managers and staff, as well as observation of the activities as they are carried out.

Based on the fieldwork that has been undertaken, the auditor will produce the audit report. The audit report will contain comments on the efficiency and effectiveness of the controls that are in place and recommendations for further improvement, if considered necessary. The internal auditor will need to form an independent opinion of the level of control that has been achieved so that assurance can be provided to the audit committee, to the extent that this is justified. Also, if the audit report sets out recommendations, these should be agreed with the local/departmental management. The reason for agreeing the recommendations is that they are more likely to be implemented, if they have been agreed. However, if the internal auditor feels that controls are inadequate but local management does not accept this conclusion, escalation of the issue will be required.

Risk management and internal audit

In many large organizations, the working relationship between risk management and internal audit can be difficult. Internal audit will be working to an agenda that concentrates on the effective implementation of efficient controls. In general, the head of internal audit will have a senior reporting line to the most senior non-executive member of the board, perhaps even the chairman.

The risk manager will often have a less senior reporting line, typically to an executive member of the board. This is likely to be the company secretary or finance director. The difference in reporting lines can be a frustration for the risk manager, but the complementary roles of risk management and internal audit should be seen as an opportunity to ensure more effective implementation of the risk management protocols and procedures.

Both parties should look for areas where they can co-operate without compromising the overall aims of their individual contributions. For example, both risk management and internal audit should attend risk assessment workshops. Risk managers may facilitate the risk assessment workshop, but the responsibility for managing risk will always rest with the manager of each operational department. Also, the presence of an internal auditor at the risk assessment workshop should not be seen as a threat by line management.

Internal audit professionals require that control measures are identified in very precise terms that can be audited. The focus of internal audit activities is on the impact that the control measures actually have in practice. During an audit, internal auditors will request and be provided with information and data. The approach of the internal auditor is to test that information, so that the facts of the situation may be established. In summary, internal auditors take the somewhat challenging view that information plus testing equals facts.

An approach that has become increasingly popular in recent times is usually referred to as the three lines of defence. This approach is entirely consistent with the role of internal audit in enterprise risk management, as identified in Figure 35.1. The three lines of defence model is based on the ideas that: 1) management has primary responsibility for the management of risk; 2) specialist risk management functions can assist management in developing an approach to fulfilling their responsibilities; and 3) the internal audit function checks that the risk management process and the risk management framework are effective and efficient.

The primary role of management can be divided into the three layers of top management (directors), middle management (managers) and staff or employees. This division is compatible with the roles and responsibilities allocated to the three levels of management in Table 22.1. Specialist risk management functions may operate at corporate or group level as an overall facilitator of the development, implementation, monitoring and improvement of the risk management framework. Risk management functions will also include business continuity, as well as health and safety. These specialist risk management functions fulfil the same role as the group risk management function, but in a more specific area of risk. Typical roles and responsibilities allocated to risk management functions are also shown in Table 22.1.

The three lines of defence approach is also compatible with the concept of governance, risk and compliance (GRC), which is illustrated in Figure 35.2. The GRC approach is based on the overall view that the board is responsible for governance issues across the whole organization. In this role, the board will look to all three lines of defence to ensure adequate attention is paid to risk. The non-executive directors, in particular, will look to internal audit to provide assurance on the broad range of compliance issues within the organization.

The requirement for keeping accurate financial records applies to all organizations, and these will often be produced by an external accountancy firm, which will also

Figure 35.2   Governance, risk and compliance

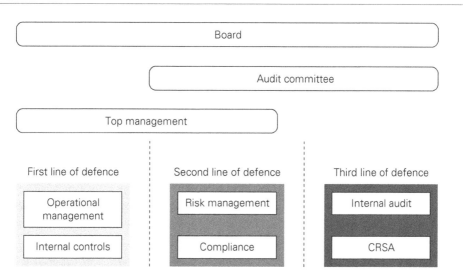

act as external auditors. External auditors will be required to confirm, and in some cases attest to, the accuracy of the financial records. These external auditors may be considered to be the fourth line of defence. Additionally, for highly regulated organizations, there will be regulators requiring compliance with the rules and regulations within their scope. In the circumstances, the regulator may be considered to be the fifth line of defence.

As with so many areas of risk management and internal control, the terminology used will vary from organization to organization. The box on page 410 describes the three lines of defence approach applied to tax and how it varies from the approach defined above. Nevertheless, the organization in this example is recognizing that responsibilities need to be divided and three lines of responsibilities is an appropriate and robust way of ensuring adequate governance and compliance and, in the case of the example, efficient and effective management of tax risks.

An area where risk management and internal control can work together is in establishing the risk management/internal control priorities for the coming year. When an organization sets up a risk-based audit programme, it will be seeking to ensure that internal audit activities are focused on the priority significant risks facing the organization. The board may well be looking for a joint risk management/internal audit contribution that will achieve better strategic decisions, more successful delivery of projects and more efficient core processes.

The introduction of a risk-based audit programme will be facilitated by ensuring that internal audit participates in risk assessment workshops and that risk management and internal audit produce a joint annual programme of work. The overall intention is to ensure that control measures discussed at risk assessment workshops are described in the risk register as fully auditable controls, and to ensure that managers have greater awareness of their control responsibilities and fulfil those responsibilities in practice.

Three lines of defence applied to tax

Three lines of defence is a concept that seems quietly to be taking over the whole field of risk management. It now seems ubiquitous in financial services and is finding its way, often through public-sector procurement requirements, into a vast range of new areas.

But while it may be in use elsewhere in an organization, so far it hasn't been widely applied to the management of risk in tax. Tax risk management is about having clearly defined and understood roles and responsibilities covering data management, transaction processing, information gathering, verification and escalation. Applied to tax, the three lines concept could broadly look like this:

- *First line*: this means having a strategic understanding and the right people responsible for the basic business processes as they affect tax – the complete and accurate recording of transactions, for example the purchase-to-pay, record-to-report and fixed asset processes, and the gathering and processing of the related tax information.

- *Second line*: this is the regular monitoring process. It requires frameworks and guidelines, developed by the tax and finance functions together, which are designed to facilitate effective monitoring of tax risks, pick up problems early and identify weaknesses in the process. People are human and they do make mistakes.

- *Third line*: this is independent assurance that the tax function is running properly, through both internal and external auditing. It requires both that internal auditors bring themselves up to speed on tax risk matters, and that tax functions welcome the additional assurance that a successful audit can bring. After all, it's better to have your internal auditor spot a mistake than to have to explain it to a tax authority.

There are advantages and disadvantages in having a close working relationship between risk management and internal audit. In many ways, there is a complementary fit between the two disciplines and there are benefits in having a common focus and co-ordinated planning related to the management of risk. Also, there is an opportunity for sharing best practice regarding risk management tools and techniques.

However, there are also disadvantages in a common approach. It is desirable that line management realize that responsibility for deciding the level of control of a particular risk, the responsibility for implementing enhanced controls and the responsibility for auditing compliance are separate issues. Also, there will often be different reporting relationships in an organization between risk management and internal audit. Finally, internal audit are proud of their independent status, and closer involvement in the risk management decision making could compromise that independence.

Management responsibilities

An alternative way of allocating the responsibilities set out in Figure 35.1 is that internal audit is responsible for the activities that are identified as core internal audit roles. Risk management should facilitate and support the activities in the centre of the fan identified as legitimate roles for internal audit (with safeguards), and line management at the appropriate level should have responsibility for the roles identified as activities that internal audit should not undertake. This alternative means of allocating the responsibilities illustrated in Figure 35.1 is shown in Table 35.2.

The working relationship between risk management and internal audit will vary between organizations. The roles and responsibilities that are defined will be a reflection of the structure that seems most suitable for an organization. The allocation of roles and responsibilities should take account of the guidance produced by the Institute of Internal Auditors referenced under Figure 35.1.

A clear definition of the responsibilities of risk management, internal audit and line management is essential so that ownership of risk becomes clear. In summary, risk management can assist with the risk assessment activities and the design of the controls. Internal audit can provide support by auditing the controls to ensure that they are effective and efficient and that they have been fully implemented.

Table 35.2   Allocation of responsibilities

Internal audit activities

- giving assurance on risk management processes
- giving assurance that risks are correctly evaluated
- evaluating risk management processes
- evaluating the reporting of key risks
- reviewing the management of key risks

Risk management support

- facilitating identification and evaluation of risks
- coaching management in responding to risks
- co-ordinating ERM activities
- consolidated reporting on risks
- maintaining and developing the ERM framework
- championing establishment of ERM
- developing RM strategy for board approval

Management responsibilities

- setting the risk appetite
- imposing risk management processes
- management assurance on risks
- taking decisions on risk responses
- implementing risk responses on behalf of management
- accountability for risk management

However, the primary responsibility for the management of risk remains with the executive management of the organization. It is important that the activities of risk management and internal audit do not in any way diminish or undermine the owner-ship of risk by the management of the organization. This approach is also consistent with the statement in most of the risk management standards that risks should not be managed outside the contexts that give rise to the risk.

Five lines of assurance

There has been considerable discussion about the operation of the three lines of defence model. For example, an organization that has adopted this approach will need to consider where head office functions operate within the three lines, as they will often undertake activities that are first- and/or second-line activities and, poten-tially, operate as third-line as well.

Specifically, the treasury function within the head office of a large company will manage the treasury requirements of the organization as first-line managers. Addition-ally, the treasury function will be an area of expertise that decides the strategy and tactics to be adopted by the organization. In some cases, audit of the treasury function is specifically outside the scope of an internal audit department in a large company. It will, therefore, be the external auditors that review and audit the treasury function.

Another weakness of the three lines of defence model is that it is more relevant to hazard (or operational) risks, including internal financial control. The three lines of defence model is also well suited to the governance of compliance risks. However, the audit committee generally does not audit the upside of risk, or seek to identify circumstances where opportunities have been missed. Therefore, it is possible that there will be a disconnect between the scope of work of the risk management and internal audit departments compared with the full range and scope of enterprise risk management activities.

Another aspect of the three lines of defence relates to the particular role and status of the board of directors. The board provides assurance, but the board is not usually identified as a line of defence. In fact, the board both receives assurance as a stakeholder group and provides assurance to other stakeholders, including external stakeholders. The board will receive assurance from departments inside the organization, as well as receiving assurance from outside, including external auditors.

The three lines of defence model is well established, but sometimes, it is extended to five lines of defence by showing external audit as the fourth line and regulators as the fifth line. However, this does not represent the five lines of assurance approach, as it is currently being developed. In order to enhance the effectiveness of the three (or five) lines of defence model, the alternative approach of the five lines of assurance has been put forward.

The five lines of assurance model suggests the following sources of assurance:

1 The board of directors with overall responsibility for ensuring that effective risk management processes are in place and the other lines are managing risk to within appetite.

2 Senior executives and senior managers with overall responsibility for building and maintaining a robust risk management process and delivering reliable information on the principal risks.

3 Business unit leaders with assigned ownership or responsibility for reporting on specific risks, and ensuring resources are protected and objectives are being achieved.

4 Specialist units providing expertise on specific types of risk, such as treasury, safety, environment, legal and insurance with responsibility for related risk management processes.

5 Internal audit activities, providing independent and timely information to the board on reliability of the risk management processes in the organization and producing consolidated reports.

Inevitably, there are variations on the format described above and different organizations will develop a structure for the five lines of assurance that suits their specific needs. The main enhancement to the three lines of defence model, as provided by the five lines of assurance model, is that the first line of defence is divided into the board, senior executives and business unit leaders, each of these identified groups being responsible for providing assurance in relation to their allocated responsibilities.

One of the benefits of the five lines of assurance model is that improved communication is required between the board of directors, members of the executive and the business unit leaders. Also, close liaison is required between the specialist expert risk units and the internal audit activities. The focus is on providing consolidated assurance across the organization, to enhance a risk-aware culture, rather than concentrating on the design and implementation of controls.

Therefore, the five lines of assurance model is more relevant to the management of strategic and tactical risks (including opportunities) than the three lines of defence model. This fact arises directly from the increased focus on assurance in the five lines of assurance model, rather than control in the three lines of defence model. It should be noted that, in both models, external auditors and regulators will continue to fulfil their specific responsibilities.

Reporting on risk management 36

Risk reporting

There is a wide range of risk management documentation that is relevant to risk management activities. Table 21.2 lists the types of risk management documentation that may be required as follows:

- risk management administration;
- risk response and improvement plans;
- event reports and recommendations;
- risk performance and certification reports.

The risk management manual should describe the control environment or risk culture. Typically, it will include a range of information, as set out in Table 21.3. The four categories of reports mentioned above can be characterized as established procedures, action plans, incident reports and performance reports. Chapter 21 discussed the established procedures in some detail, when describing the contents of the risk management manual. Action plans, especially those embedded within the risk register, together with the recommendations that come from incident reports, will help maintain risk management as a dynamic set of activities within the organization.

Chapter 21 describes risk management documentation in detail but the subject is mentioned again here because of the importance of risk performance and certification reports. In fact, the importance of these documents has increased considerably in recent times, because of the introduction of the Sarbanes–Oxley Act of 2002. Enhanced reporting requirements have been applied to all types of organizations in most parts of the world. It is important for an organization to ensure that the reports it submits achieve the highest standards that apply, whilst being compatible with other requirements.

For example, there may be specific requirements that apply, such as the Sarbanes–Oxley Act when an organization is listed on the New York Stock Exchange. However, that organization may also be listed on another stock exchange with different requirements. Additionally, the organization may have subsidiaries that are registered as a charity, or operate as (for example) an insurance company, perhaps a captive insurance company.

Risk performance and certification reports include operational management reports as well as more formal declarations and certified reports to stakeholders. In certain cases, certification of the financial results of operations of the organization will be undertaken as a formal attestation by a third party. Typically, this third-party attestation will be undertaken by an external auditor. Such a written attestation will also include an evaluation of the effectiveness of the control activities related to financial reporting.

The risk guidance from the Financial Reporting Council (FRC), published in 2014, provides a comprehensive set of responsibilities for the board of an organization. Table 36.1 provides a summary of the risk management obligations allocated to the board and it is Item 6 on Risk Communication and Reporting that is the most relevant to this chapter. It is important to note that the risk management reporting and communication obligations refer to both internal and external communications and the obligations also refer to the importance of risk management information being communicated both to and from the board.

Reporting requirements have become increasingly detailed and it is sometimes necessary for organizations to produce separate reports for different regulatory authorities. Also, some organizations may decide to issue specific reports to achieve a high profile for certain aspects of their organization. In particular, several organizations issue separate corporate social responsibility reports to highlight their

Table 36.1　Risk management (RM) responsibilities of the board

The FRC risk guidance identifies the risk management responsibilities of the board and these can be summarized, as follows:

1	Risk management processes	• Ensure that RM is incorporated within normal processes. • Identify the principal risks facing the company.
2	Principal risks and risk appetite	• Assessment of risks to the business model and strategy. • Risks the organization is willing to take or 'risk appetite'.
3	Risk culture and risk assurance	• Risk culture is embedded throughout the organization. • Adequate RM and assurance discussions take place at the board.
4	Risk profile and risk mitigation	• Risk profile of the company is kept under review. • Measures to manage or mitigate the principal risks are taken.
5	Monitoring and review activities	• Monitoring and review of risk management is undertaken. • Monitoring and review is ongoing and not just annual.
6	Risk communication and reporting	• Internal and external risk management communication takes place. • Necessary risk information is communicated to and from the board.

In summary, the FRC risk guidance requires that board attention should be paid to the risk management process, profile, principal risks and mitigation; the business model, strategy, risk appetite, risk culture and risk reporting; as well as the longer-term viability of the organization.

achievements in this important area. The case studies presented at the beginning of each part of this book are all extracts from reports of companies listed on the London Stock Exchange. These case studies indicate the wide range of topics that are reported by listed companies in relation to the broad range of risk management and internal control issues that are covered in this book.

Sarbanes–Oxley Act of 2002

The Sarbanes–Oxley Act (SOX) was passed in response to a range of corporate scandals in the United States. These scandals involved misrepresentation of the financial status of various organizations, leading to misleading financial statements. The primary purpose of SOX is to ensure that information disclosed by companies listed on the stock exchanges in the United States is accurate.

SOX requires that controls are in place to ensure the accuracy of all information reported by the organization. Section 302 of the SOX requires that all data produced by the organization must be validated. In relation to financial statements, detailed analysis of risks that could result in misrepresentation of the financial results of the organization has to be undertaken. The procedures for compiling financial information and attestation of the financial disclosures by external auditors (as required by section 404) are very detailed and are considered by many to be extremely onerous and costly to undertake.

When complying with section 404 of SOX, the risk assessment is designed to identify weaknesses in the financial reporting structure. This is a very detailed procedure that requires considerable work by the internal audit department. The financial results of the organization and the evaluation of the financial reporting structure have to be reviewed by external auditors, who have to provide an attestation that they consider the results to be accurate.

SOX requirements state that an approved risk management framework should be used to evaluate risks to accurate financial reporting. The framework recommended for ensuring the accuracy of financial disclosures is the COSO Internal Control cube (2013). Note that the COSO ERM cube (2004) includes all of the requirements of the earlier internal control version of the COSO cube. The SOX requirements apply to subsidiaries of US companies operating in other countries. They will also apply to organizations based in other countries if the company has a listing on a US stock exchange. Therefore, the internal control version of COSO is used by companies in many countries in the world.

In order to comply with the requirements of Sarbanes–Oxley, many organizations have decided to set up a disclosures committee to validate all information disclosed by the organization. Because of the extensive application of SOX, many companies based in countries other than the United States have also been obliged to set up disclosures committees. The risk architecture shown in Figure 22.1 for a large corporation includes a disclosures committee.

Compliance with the requirements of the Sarbanes–Oxley Act of 2002 is a costly and time-consuming exercise. Questions have been asked about whether the Act has been effective in improving the accuracy of reports from companies that are listed on US stock exchanges. These criticisms are relevant, given that the SOX requirements relate primarily to accuracy of reporting, rather than the achievement of enhanced risk management standards. A summary of some of the views of the CEOs of some US companies is presented in the box below.

Sarbanes–Oxley ineffective

Chief executives across the United States view the Sarbanes–Oxley law as reactionary and over-burdensome. Yet they still cite 'improper accounting practices' as the number one ethical issue facing business today. A survey of CEOs on business ethics by Georgia State University polled nearly 300 chief executives at both private and public companies.

   Among its findings, most executives agreed that the Sarbanes–Oxley Act strengthened public and investor trust in corporate America, although it had done nothing to improve ethical standards at their businesses. Many agreed that the act was an over-reaction to the ethical failures of a handful of executives and has proven burdensome and unnecessary.

Risk reports by US companies

Companies that are listed on a US stock exchange are required to make extensive disclosures about risk factors. These risk management reports are intended to be forward-looking, rather than a commentary on the risks that have materialized in the past. The reports are contained in the periodic Form 10-K or Form 20-F filings. It is not unusual to find several pages dedicated to risk factors. Typically, this section of the filing will be between 3 and 10 pages long.

   Table 36.2 provides a partial list of the industry, economic and environmental risks reported in Form 20-F for the company identified. Extracts from another example of the risk factors that are reported by a US-listed company are set out in Table 36.2. It is normal for the list to be introduced by a comment, such as 'important factors that may cause future financial difficulties include, but are not limited to', and then followed by a long list with detailed explanations. Items listed typically include:

- regulatory developments and changes;
- competition in our businesses;
- decisions of competition authorities regarding proposed joint ventures;
- compliance with governmental regulations;
- general economic conditions;
- loss of a strategic customer;
- higher costs of insurance for terrorism, sabotage or hijacking;
- our ability to achieve cost savings;
- fluctuations in fuel costs;
- changes in currency and interest rates;
- disruptions at key sites and facilities;
- incidents resulting from the transport of hazardous materials;

- strikes, work stoppages and work slowdowns;
- disruptions due to employee illness as a result of an influenza pandemic;
- market acceptance of our new service and growth initiatives;
- changes in customer demand patterns;
- the impact of technology developments on our operations;
- disruptions to our technology infrastructure;
- adverse weather conditions;
- if our sub-contractors' employees were considered our employees;
- changes in tax laws or their interpretation by authorities;
- higher costs related to implementation of the Sarbanes–Oxley Act;
- changes in environmental laws.

Table 36.2 is an example of a list of risk factors, but it does not include all of the items contained in the full list filed as part of Form 20-F. Each of the listed risks would usually be described in more detail, by way of a detailed explanation of up to half a page. Additionally, the Securities and Exchange Commission (SEC) is considering whether to require more detailed reports on the risk committee reporting structure in companies listed on US stock exchanges. The SEC is the federal regulator of US stock exchanges and has the mission to protect investors, maintain fair, orderly and efficient markets, and facilitate capital formation.

Table 36.2 Risk report in a Form 20-F

In relation to industry, economic and environment risks, the following have been identified for further detailed comment:

- risk of expiration of patents or marketing exclusivity
- risk of patent litigation and early loss of patents, marketing exclusivity or trademark
- risk of expiration or earlier loss of patents covering competing products
- failure to obtain patent protection
- impact of fluctuations in exchange rates
- debt-funding arrangements
- the risks of owning and operating a biologics and vaccines business
- competition, price controls and price reductions
- taxation
- risk of substantial product liability claims
- performance of new products
- environmental/occupational health and safety liabilities
- developing our business in emerging markets
- product counterfeiting

Charities' risk reporting

Risk reporting by charities is compulsory in most countries in the world. In general, there is an expectation that charities should have detailed risk management procedures broadly equivalent to those required of government departments or of companies listed on a stock exchange. A shortened version of the advice on risk reporting set out in the UK Charity Commission guidance is as follows:

> The form and content of risk reporting should reflect the size and complexity of an individual charity. The Charity Commission is not seeking to standardise risk reporting. A narrative style report that addresses the key aspects will be an acceptable approach to reporting, provided that the report provides:
>
> - an acknowledgement of trustees' responsibility;
> - an overview of the risk identification process;
> - an indication that major risks have been reviewed or assessed;
> - confirmation that control systems have been established.

It is recognized that some charities, particularly larger charities or those with more complex operations, will wish as a matter of best practice to expand on this basic approach in their reporting. Where this more detailed approach to reporting is adopted it will be desirable to address the following broad principles, describing how they have been incorporated into the risk management procedures of the charity:

- linkage between the identification of major risk and the operational and strategic objectives of the charity;
- procedures that extend beyond financial risk to encompass operational, compliance and other categories of identifiable risk;
- linkage of risk assessment and evaluation to the likelihood of its occurrence and impact should the event occur;
- ensuring risk assessment activities and monitoring are ongoing and embedded in management and operational procedures;
- trustees' review and consideration of the principal results of risk identification, evaluation and monitoring.

Most charities are already likely to consider risk in their day-to-day activities. In fact, it has been reported that many charities now see risk management and other governance requirements as the most significant challenges facing the organization. This appears to imply that charities are becoming more risk-averse and spend more effort on compliance issues than on fundraising.

Even where a formal risk management process has not been completed, it will often be possible for aspects of the approach to risk to be drawn out for comment. A typical report on risk management for a small charity may be as follows:

- Risk assessment processes are in place to identify priority significant risks facing the charity.
- Risk management policies, protocols and procedures are embedded into routine operations.

- Analysis of strategy is undertaken to identify significant risks that could impact the delivery of the strategy.
- Procedures are in place to ensure legal compliance, including routine reports on legal matters to the board of trustees.
- Trustees receive training on those risk management and corporate governance issues relevant to the charity.
- Trustees receive an annual report of risk management activities and evaluation of the control environment.
- Trustees also receive additional reports about any significant weaknesses in controls and details of any material failures of controls.

Public-sector risk reporting

Attention to risk management in government departments and other areas of the public sector is mandatory in most countries. Much of the information on risk management in government bodies is freely available on websites and this information forms very useful reference material. However, because the information is publicly available, there is often no specific mention of the risk reporting to external stakeholders. The government in the UK has produced a set of principles on risk reporting. Table 36.3 sets out those risk reporting principles as openness and transparency, involvement, proportionality, evidence and responsibility.

There is usually extensive information on how the risk-reporting structure will work within a government body. The information set out below is typical of a report by a UK local government authority:

Table 36.3   Government risk-reporting principles

Openness and transparency Government will be open and transparent about its understanding of the nature of risks to the public and about the process it is following in handling them.
Involvement Government will seek wide involvement of those concerned in the decision process.
Proportionality Government will act proportionately and consistently in dealing with risks to the public.
Evidence Government will seek to base decisions on all relevant evidence.
Responsibility Government will seek to allocate responsibility for managing risks to those best placed to control them.

All risks on the strategic risk register are monitored via quarterly clinics. Reports from these clinics are forwarded to the executive committee twice per year. The strategic risk register is reported to full council through its inclusion in the annual strategic plan reporting. Service-specific business risks are included within service group plans and monitored through the directorates' performance management arrangements. This includes reporting, twice per year, to relevant council members.

Government report on national security

One of the biggest steps forward in risk communication in recent times has been the willingness of governments to be more open about security threats. Many governments undertake a national security threat analysis and publish the results. For example, the UK government published in 2011 a document entitled the *National Security Strategy of the United Kingdom*. This publication gives details of the threats to national security faced by the UK. More recently, the UK Cabinet Office published the National Risk Register.

Within this analysis, there is no mention of the objectives or key dependencies of the UK or the UK government. However, the threat analysis is robust and detailed. The main threat categories identified in the document are as follows:

- natural events, including weather, coastal and river flooding and human or animal disease;
- major accidents, including industrial and transport;
- malicious attacks on crowded places, infrastructure, transport and electronic infrastructure (including nuclear or non-conventional attack).

The document provides detailed analysis of the various threats and the measures that are in place to minimize these threats. The report also discusses the drivers that are changing the risk profile of nations. These drivers include:

- political;
- climate;
- competition for energy;
- poverty/inequality/poor governance;
- globalization – economic, technological and demographic.

This analysis by the UK government is an interesting example of the detailed risk assessment being undertaken at national level. It demonstrates that risk management is now embedded into the heart of national government. The fact that risk management has been embraced by national governments indicates that the importance of risk management is recognized at the highest level. Figure 36.1 shows some of the significant risks to UK national security identified by the government, at the time of the assessment in 2011.

The UK government has not classified risks in this way, but if the risk attitude structure described in Figure 10.1 is used, then it is possible to identify the major threats where a government is comfortable that it can respond, such as transport

Figure 36.1 Selected UK security threats

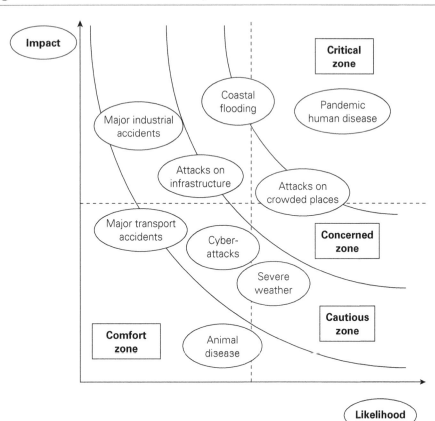

accident, cyber-attack and animal disease. If the government were to use this structure, it would appear that the government is cautious about major industrial accidents,
attacks on infrastructure and severe weather. The government is concerned about
coastal flooding and attacks on crowded places. Finally, the risk attitude analysis
appears to suggest that the government is identifying the critical issue facing national
security as pandemic human disease.

Looking back 100 years and more, the protection of national security was
fairly straightforward. Government would focus its attention on national defence
using armed forces, with the particular expertise in land and sea defence.
Nowadays, however, protection of national security is much more complicated.
The box below questions the ability of traditional government structures to tackle
this complexity.

Government structures

Some governments are beginning to realize the complexity of national security and have invented new language, like 'the comprehensive approach', in the hope that this will solve the problem. But mostly, in so far as the 'comprehensive approach' exists at all, it does so in theory but is pretty well absent in practice on the ground where it matters.

Meanwhile, government structures and cultures remain resolutely stuck in the past. Ministers are judged on how well they defend the territorial integrity of their department, preserve its budget and defend its payroll. Senior civil servants have a similar attitude. Networking with other departments is regarded as a threat, not an opportunity. Vertical hierarchies and stove-piped minds know that they ought to be networking, but find it impossible to do so. What is needed is a wholesale restructuring of government along more modern lines.

APPENDIX A
Abbreviations and acronyms

The table below sets out the main abbreviations and acronyms and is provided as a reference list for the 50 most important abbreviations and/or acronyms that are used in the book. This appendix should also be cross-referenced with the definitions set out in Appendix B. However, not all of the abbreviations and acronyms have corresponding entries in Appendix B, because some of the entries in this appendix relate to concepts and ideas, rather than a topic that can be summarized by way of a short definition.

The reference provided in the right-hand column refers to a specific figure or table, where one is provided. If there is no specific figure or table, a general reference to the chapter that discusses the abbreviation or acronym is provided.

Abbreviation	Term in full	Reference
4Cs	Comfort, cautious, concerned and critical	Figure 10.1
4Es	Explore, exit, exploit and exist	Figure 15.2
4Ns	Naïve, novice, normalized and natural	Figure 24.1
4Ps	People, premises, processes and products	Table 3.2
4Ts	Tolerate, treat, transfer and terminate	Chapter 15
5Cs	Clear, concise, coherent, credible and complete	Chapter 26
5Es	Explore, exit or expand, exploit and exist	Figure 15.3
6Cs	Cost, coverage, capacity, capabilities, claims and compliance	Chapter 17
8Rs	Recognition, rating, ranking, responding, resourcing controls, reaction planning, reporting and reviewing	Figure 4.1
BCP	Business continuity plan	Chapter 18
BIA	Business impact analysis	Chapter 18
BPR	Business process re-engineering	Chapter 19
CASE	Capabilities, activities, standards and ethics	Chapter 20
CEO	Chief executive officer	Chapter 22

(continued)

(Continued)

Abbreviation	Term in full	Reference
CoCo	Criteria of control	Figure 33.1
CORR	Customer, offering, resources and resilience	Chapter 20
COSO	Committee of sponsoring organizations of the Treadway committee	Figure 6.3
CRAM	Communication, relationship, analytical and management	Table 27.2
CRO	Chief risk officer	Chapter 22
CRSA	Control risk self-assessment	Chapter 34
CSFSRS	Customers, staff, financiers, suppliers, regulators and society	Chapter 29
CSR	Corporate social responsibility	Table 20.1
DRP	Disaster recovery plan	Chapter 18
EM3	Embrace, manage, mitigate, minimize	Chapter 3
ERM	Enterprise risk management	Chapter 8
FIRM	Financial, infrastructure, reputational and marketplace	Table 11.2
FOIL	Fragmented, organized, influential and leading	Table 24.3
FMEA	Failure modes effects analysis	Chapter 10
GRC	Governance, risk and compliance	Figure 35.2
HAZOP	Hazard and operability	Chapter 10
IIA	Institute of Internal Auditors	Chapter 35
IRM	Institute of Risk Management	Table 1.1
LILAC	Leadership, involvement, learning, accountability and communication	Table 24.3
LSE	London Stock Exchange	Chapter 28
MADE2	Mandatory, assurance, decision-making, effective and efficient core processes	Table 5.2
OECD	Organization for Economic Cooperation and Development	Table 28.1
ORM	Operational risk management	Chapter 30

(continued)

(Continued)

Abbreviation	Term in full	Reference
PACED	Proportionate, aligned, comprehensive, embedded and dynamic	Table 5.1
PCDD	Preventive, corrective, directive and detective	Table 16.1
PDCA	Plan–do–check–act	Chapter 9
PESTLE	Political, economic, social, technological, legal and ethical	Table 11.3
PIML	Plan, implement, measure and learn	Appendix C
PRAM	Project risk assessment and management	Table 31.1
RASP	Risk architecture, strategy and protocols	Chapter 21
RMIS	Risk management information system	Table 26.3
SEC	Securities and Exchange Commission	Chapter 36
SEE	Social, ethical and environmental	Chapter 20
SOX	Sarbanes–Oxley Act of 2002	Chapter 36
STOC	Strategy, tactics, operations and compliance	Chapter 3
SWOT	Strengths, weaknesses, opportunities and threats	Chapter 10

APPENDIX B
Glossary of terms

The table below sets definitions and (as necessary) cross references for a total of 101 risk management terms used in this book. Appendix A provides a list of the abbreviations and acronyms that are used in the book. It should be checked against the list below, as necessary. The reference column provides information on the location within the book where further information is provided, including reference to a relevant figure or table when appropriate. The relationship between many of the acronyms is shown in the implementation guide set out in Appendix C.

There is an international standard related to risk management vocabulary and definitions. This is ISO Guide 73 (2009) 'Risk Management – Vocabulary'. Where appropriate and to the extent that is possible, the definitions used in Guide 73 are referenced in this book.

However, it is not possible to use a unified terminology because risk managers in different disciplines and business sectors use their own words and definitions. Indeed, the various risk management standards produced around the world use different terminology and definitions. ISO Guide 73 attempts to provide a unified language of risk, but it may take some time for these definitions to be universally adopted.

Term	Definition	Reference
Accept	See 'Tolerate'	Chapter 15
Avoid	See 'Terminate'	Chapter 15
Benchmark test	Established criteria to determine whether a risk is significant to the organization	Table 12.1
Business continuity plan (BCP)	Plan to ensure continuity of business operations in the event of a serious incident that impacts the organization	Chapter 18
Business impact analysis (BIA)	Analysis to assess the potential damage, loss or disruption that would be caused by the failure of critical business processes	Chapter 18
Business model	Customer offering that utilizes resources, underpinned by resilience (CORR)	Chapter 20

(continued)

(*Continued*)

Term	Definition	Reference
Captive insurance company	Subsidiary, owned by an organization, that provides insurance for the organization and sometimes for customers of the organization	Figure 17.1
Chief risk officer (CRO)	Job title for senior risk manager appointed to board or executive of an organization	Chapter 22
Communication, relationship, analytical and management (CRAM)	Set of people skills that are required by risk management professionals, in addition to their risk management and business technical skills	Chapter 27
Compliance risk	Category of risk that is associated with the management of mandatory obligations	Chapter 3
Consequences	Effect on the strategic, tactical, operational and compliance (STOC) core processes resulting from a risk materializing	Chapter 19
Control	Actions to reduce the likelihood and/or magnitude of a risk. Hazard controls can be preventive, corrective, directive or detective (PCDD)	Chapter 16
Control environment	Attitude, awareness and culture of the organization regarding risk management and/or internal control, referred to in COSO ERM as the 'internal environment'	Chapter 33
Control risk	Category of risk that is associated with the management of uncertainty	Chapter 3
Control risk self-assessment (CRSA)	Self-audit exercise completed by a manager or director to report on current status of controls and control activities	Chapter 34
Core process	Set of co-ordinated business activities to deliver a stakeholder expectation that may be strategic, tactical, operational or compliance (STOC)	Figure 29.1
Corporate governance	Set of activities and policies that control the way in which an organization is directed, administered and/or controlled	Figure 28.1
Corporate social responsibility (CSR)	Actions to take account of the impact of activities on stakeholders (CSFSRS), as well as the environment	Table 20.1

(*continued*)

(*Continued*)

Term	Definition	Reference
Corrective control	Type of control designed to limit the scope for loss and reduce any undesirable outcomes that have been realized	Table 16.1
Cost containment	See 'Loss control'	Chapter 13
Current risk	Existing level of risk taking into account the controls in place, sometimes referred to as 'net risk' or 'managed risk', but most frequently as 'residual risk'	Figure 23.1
Customer offering that utilizes resources underpinned by resilience (CORR)	Description of the business model defined by operational and compliance core processes that can be modified by strategic and tactical core processes	Chapter 20
Damage limitation	See 'Loss control'	Chapter 13
Detective control	Type of control designed to identify that a hazard risk has materialized, so that actions can be taken to avoid further or greater losses	Table 16.1
Directive control	Type of control based on giving directions to people to behave in a certain way and/or follow established procedures	Table 16.1
Disaster recovery plan (DRP)	Plan for use in the event of a serious loss, such as IT failure, fire or earthquake to assist the recovery of the organization and support crisis management	Chapter 18
Eliminate	See 'Terminate'	Chapter 15
Embedded risk management	See 'Leadership, involvement, learning, accountability and communication' (LILAC)	Table 24.3
Enterprise risk management (ERM)	Integrated and co-ordinated approach to all the risks faced by the organization – see range of definitions in Table 8.2	Table 8.2
Frequency	See 'Likelihood'	Chapter 1
Governance, risk and compliance (GRC)	Integrated approach to risk management and risk assurance based on the three lines of defence	Chapter 35
Gross risk	See 'Magnitude'	Figure 1.1

(*continued*)

(*Continued*)

Term	Definition	Reference
Hazard risk	Category of risk that is associated with the management of pure risks or perils – the effects of hazard risks need to be mitigated	Chapter 3
Impact	Effect on the finances, infrastructure, reputation and marketplace (FIRM) when a risk materializes	Chapter 12
Inherent risk	Level of a risk before any control activities are applied, sometimes referred to as the 'gross level' or 'absolute level' of the risk	Figure 23.1
Insurance	See 'Transfer'	Chapter 17
Internal audit	Internal or outsourced, yet independent group of people, or set of activities, monitoring the effectiveness and efficiency of control activities	Chapter 35
Internal control	See Table 33.1 for a range of definitions of 'Internal control'	Table 33.1
Leadership, involvement, learning, accountability and communication (LILAC)	Set of attributes that should be present in order to achieve successful embedding of (enterprise) risk management in the organization	Table 24.3
Level of risk	Combination of the likelihood and impact of the risk, as established during the risk rating stage of risk assessment and can be determined at either gross (inherent) or net (residual) level	Chapter 10
Likelihood	Evaluation or judgement regarding the chances of a risk materializing, sometimes established as a 'probability' or 'frequency'	Chapter 12
Loss control	Range of activities to reduce the potential impact of hazard risks on the organization, including loss prevention, damage limitation and cost containment	Chapter 13
Loss prevention	See 'Loss control'	Chapter 13
Magnitude	Size of the event when a risk materializes, sometimes referred to as 'severity' of the event and representing the gross (or inherent) level of the risk	Figure 1.1

(*continued*)

(Continued)

Term	Definition	Reference
Mandatory, assurance, decision making, effective and efficient core processes (MADE2)	Summary of the main reasons for undertaking a risk management initiative	Chapter 5
Material failure	Failure of controls in an organization, resulting in loss of a magnitude that is considered important by auditors	Chapter 34
Net risk	See 'Impact'	Chapter 12
Operational risk	Defined in Basel II as 'risk of loss or gain, resulting from inadequate or failed internal processes, people and systems or from external events' and capable of impacting the operations of the organization	Chapter 30
Operational risk management (ORM)	Approach to risk management associated, in particular, with banks, insurance companies and other financial institutions, where the measurement of the level of 'operational risk' is required by Basel II, Solvency II or similar requirement	Chapter 30
Operations	Activities of the organization designed to deliver products and services to customers or clients	Chapter 19
Opportunity risk	Category of risk that is associated with the benefits of speculative opportunities	Chapter 3
Preventive control	Type of control that is designed to eliminate the possibility of an undesirable risk materializing	Table 16.1
Principles of risk management	Set of attributes defining the features of successful (enterprise) risk management, summarized as proportionate, aligned, comprehensive, embedded and dynamic (PACED)	Table 5.1
Project risk	Risk that could cause doubt about the ability to deliver a project on time, within budget and to quality	Chapter 31

(continued)

(Continued)

Term	Definition	Reference
Project risk assessment and management	Process developed by the Association for Project Management that enables the successful analysis and management of the risks associated with a project	Table 31.1
Proportionate, aligned, comprehensive, embedded and dynamic (PACED)	See 'Principles of risk management'	Table 5.1
Reduce	See 'Treat'	Table 15.1
Residual risk	See 'Current risk'	Figure 23.1
Retain	See 'Tolerate'	Table 15.1
Risk	Defined in Guide 73 as 'effect of uncertainty on objectives' – see Table 1.1 for a range of definitions	Table 1.1
Risk appetite	Defined in Guide 73 as 'amount and type of risk that an organization is willing to pursue or retain' but definitions of risk appetite can vary considerably	Table 25.1
Risk architecture, strategy and protocols (RASP)	See 'Risk management framework'	Chapter 21
Risk assessment	Means by which significant risks are evaluated and prioritized by undertaking the three stages of 'Risk recognition', 'Risk rating' and 'Risk ranking'	Chapter 10
Risk assurance	Means by which an organization receives reasonable assurance that the significant risks are being adequately controlled	Table 34.2
Risk attitude	Long-term view of the organization to risk defined by the 4Cs of comfort, concerned, cautious and critical	Chapter 10
Risk capacity	Maximum level of risk to which the organization should be exposed, having regard to financial and other resources	Figure 25.1
Risk criteria	Basis for ranking or evaluation of the significance of a risk – will define the risk appetite of an organization	Chapter 25

(continued)

(*Continued*)

Term	Definition	Reference
Risk exposure	Level of risk to which the organization is actually exposed, either with regard to an individual risk or the cumulative exposure to the risks faced by the organization	Figure 25.1
Risk management	Management activities to deliver the most favourable outcome and reduce the volatility or variability of that outcome – see Table 4.1 for range of definitions	Table 4.1
Risk management framework	Set of activities that support the risk management process, referred to as the risk architecture, strategy and protocols (RASP) and defined in Guide 73 as arrangements for designing, implementing, monitoring, reviewing and continually improving risk management	Table 21.1
Risk management information system (RMIS)	Computer software system or part of the intranet of the organization that records and communicates risk information	Table 26.3
Risk management manual	Documentation that includes all risk management policies, procedures, protocols and guidelines	Chapter 21
Risk management policy	Statement of the overall intentions and direction of the organization related to risk management – often a one-page document	Chapter 21
Risk management process	Activities that deliver management and control of risks – defined in this book as recognition, rating, ranking, responding, resourcing controls, reaction planning, reporting and review (8Rs)	Table 4.3
Risk management standard	Guidance that provides a description of the risk management process, together with advice on establishing a suitable risk management framework	Chapter 6
Risk map	See 'Risk matrix'	Figure 1.1
Risk matrix	Presentation of risk information on a grid or graph, also referred to as a risk map or heat map and often used to illustrate information from the risk register	Figure 1.1

(*continued*)

(Continued)

Term	Definition	Reference
Risk maturity model	Structure for determining the level to which risk management is embedded within an organization (4Ns)	Table 24.4
Risk profile	See 'Risk register'	Chapter 7
Risk ranking	Stage in the risk assessment process that analyses the likelihood and impact of a risk – referred to in Guide 73 as the level of risk	Chapter 10
Risk rating	Stage in the risk assessment process that evaluates the risk with reference to the risk appetite or the established risk criteria, to help select the appropriate risk response	Chapter 10
Risk recognition	Early stage in the risk management process, which involves the identification of all of the risks faced by the organization	Chapter 10
Risk register	Record of the significant risks faced by an organization, the controls currently in place, additional controls that are required and responsibility for control activities	Chapter 7
Risk response	Implementation of actions to respond to risks, including (for hazard risks) decisions whether to tolerate, treat, transfer or terminate (4Ts)	Table 15.1
Risk tolerance	Deviation from the expected level of risk leading to implementation of risk escalation procedures – definitions of risk tolerance can vary considerably	Chapter 25
Sarbanes–Oxley Act of 2002	US legislation that encourages use of the COSO Internal Control cube (2013) to ensure that the information disclosed by companies listed by the SEC is accurate	Chapter 36
Severity	See 'Magnitude'	Chapter 12
Significant risk	Risk with the ability to impact above the established benchmark for that type of risk	Table 12.1
Significant weakness	Weakness in controls in an organization with the potential to cause a significant or material loss	Chapter 34

(continued)

(*Continued*)

Term	Definition	Reference
Stakeholder	Persons or groups of persons with an interest in the activities of the organization, summarized by CSFSRS	Chapter 29
Strategic risk	Long-term or opportunity risk concerned with where the organization wants to go, how it plans to get there and how it can ensure survival	Chapter 19
Strategic, tactical, operational and compliance (STOC)	Types of core processes that define the mission of the organization and its business model	Chapter 19
Strategy	Statement of where the organization wants to be in three or five years time, often defined by strategic objectives	Chapter 19
Tactical risk	Medium-term, control or uncertainty risk associated with change and projects designed to ensure that the organization delivers the planned strategy	Chapter 19
Tactics	Developments, projects and programmes of work to implement strategy and move the organization from where it is now to where it wants to be in three or five years time	Chapter 19
Target risk	The ultimate level of risk that is desired by the organization when planned additional controls have been implemented	Figure 12.2
Terminate	Risk response that is appropriate when the level of risk is not acceptable to the organization or outside risk appetite, also referred to as 'avoid' or 'eliminate'	Table 15.1
Tolerate	Risk response that is appropriate when the level of risk is within risk appetite, also referred to as 'accept' or 'retain'	Table 15.1
Transfer	Risk response for risks outside risk appetite that the organization wishes to transfer or share, by means of insurance, contract or (perhaps) joint venture	Table 15.1

(*continued*)

(*Continued*)

Term	Definition	Reference
Treat	Risk response for risks that can be (further) treated by introduction of cost-effective (corrective) controls, also referred to as 'control' or 'reduce'	Table 15.1
Upside of risk	Additional benefits available to the organization by taking risk – see Table 14.1 for a range of interpretations of the 'Upside of risk'	Table 14.1

APPENDIX C
Implementation guide

The following table provides a detailed overview of the steps involved in the implementation of a successful enterprise risk management (ERM) initiative. It uses the structure described in Figure 23.3 to indicate the steps involved in learning from controls.

Successful implementation of an ERM initiative is an ongoing process that involves working through the 10 steps set out below on a continuous basis. Also, because it is sometimes difficult to recognize the distinction between planning, implementing, measuring and learning, the 10 steps in implementing an ERM initiative are presented under the headings:

- planning/implementing;
- implementing/measuring;
- measuring/learning;
- learning/planning.

The information in the table below is an extended version of the steps involved in achieving successful risk management, as set out in Table 24.1. In addition to identifying the 10 steps involved in the successful implementation of an ERM initiative, the table also describes the concepts or tools and techniques that are required to deliver each step.

The plan, implement, measure and learn (PIML) structure used in this appendix is sometimes referred to as plan–do–check–act (PDCA). PIML is preferred because it implies a more structured and proactive approach that places specific emphasis on measuring and learning to improve risk management performance. The American National Standards Institute *Organizational Resilience Standard ASIS SPC.1-2009* specifically mentions PDCA, whereas the **www.ready.gov** website uses the words planning, implementation, testing & exercises and program improvement, but describes the same methodology. Whatever the precise words used to describe the four steps, the approach described in this appendix has widespread acceptance.

Many acronyms are used in this book and these are referenced in the table below to show where they fit into the overall implementation of risk management in general, and ERM in particular. In addition to identifying the acronyms relevant to each step, the table also provides reference to the relevant chapters of the book where further information can be found.

The steps set out below relate to the implementation of an overall enterprise risk management initiative. Much of this book is concerned with the implementation of risk management in relation to specific individual risks. ERM is the overall philosophy that consolidates the management of individual risks into a unified and consistent approach to risk across the whole enterprise.

(*Continued*)

Activity	Concepts/tools and techniques	Acronym	References
Planning/implementing			
1 Identify intended benefits of the ERM initiative and gain board support	Business model Risk appetite Corporate governance	CORR ERM MADE2	Chapter 5 Chapter 6 Chapter 7 Chapter 8
2 Plan the scope of the ERM initiative and develop common language of risk	RM context Upside of risk Stakeholder expectations	PACED 8Rs	Chapter 5 Chapter 7 Chapter 14 Chapter 29
3 Establish the RM strategy, framework and the roles and responsibilities	Risk management manual Risk architecture Level of risk maturity	RASP 4Ns FOIL	Chapter 6 Chapter 21 Chapter 22 Chapter 24
Implementing/measuring			
4 Adopt suitable risk assessment tools and an agreed risk classification system	Risk protocols Risk management guidelines Risk classification systems Risk description	FIRM PESTLE SWOT	Chapter 6 Chapter 10 Chapter 11 Chapter 12
5 Establish risk benchmarks and undertake risk assessments	Benchmark tests of significance Risk register	EM3 RMIS	Chapter 11 Chapter 19 Chapter 20 Chapter 35
6 Determine risk appetite and risk tolerance levels and evaluate the existing controls	Risk appetite Risk matrix Loss control	4Ts PCDD	Chapter 10 Chapter 13 Chapter 14 Chapter 25

(*continued*)

(Continued)

Activity	Concepts/tools and techniques	Acronym	References
Measuring/learning			
7 Evaluate effectiveness of existing controls and introduce improvements	Risk improvement plans Reaction planning	BIA BCP/DRP	Chapter 13 Chapter 17 Chapter 18 Chapter 23
8 Embed risk-aware culture and align RM with other activities in the organization	Control environment Resource allocation Risk communications Business model	LILAC CRAM	Chapter 21 Chapter 22 Chapter 24 Chapter 33
Learning/planning			
9 Monitor and review risk performance indicators to measure ERM contribution	Audit plan Sources of risk assurance	STOC CRSA	Chapter 24 Chapter 27 Chapter 29 Chapter 34
10 Report risk performance in line with obligations and monitor improvement	Risk reporting Corporate governance FRC/Sarbanes–Oxley	CoCo GRC	Chapter 26 Chapter 33 Chapter 34 Chapter 36

INDEX

Note: bold page numbers indicate figures; italic numbers indicate tables.